ISSUES IN GLOBAL POLITICS

ISSUES IN GLOBAL POLITICS

Edited by
Gavin Boyd and Charles Pentland

THE FREE PRESS
A Division of Macmillan Publishing Co., Inc.
NEW YORK

Collier Macmillan Publishers
LONDON

The Free Press
A Division of Macmillan Publishing Co., Inc.
866 Third Avenue, New York, N.Y. 10022

Collier Macmillan Canada, Ltd.

Library of Congress Catalog Card Number: 80–69282

Printed in the United States of America

printing number

1 2 3 4 5 6 7 8 9 10

Library of Congress Cataloging in Publication Data

Main entry under title:

Issues in global politics.

Includes index.
1. International relations—Addresses, essays,
lectures. I. Boyd, Gavin. II. Pentland, Charles.
JX1395.I88 1981 327.1'1 80-69282
ISBN 0-02-904470-7

Contents

List of Contributors

Gavin Boyd is professor of political science at Saint Mary's University, Halifax, Nova Scotia, Canada. He edited, with Werner Feld, *Comparative Regional Systems* (1979); with James N. Rosenau and Kenneth W. Thompson, *World Politics* (1976), and, with the late Wayne Wilcox and Leo Rose, *Asia and the International System* (1972). He is the author of *Communist China's Foreign Policy* (1962) and has contributed articles to *International Journal, Asian Thought and Society, Asian Forum, Canadian Slavonic Papers,* and *The Australian Outlook.*

James E. Dougherty is professor of political science at Saint Joseph's University, Philadelphia, and senior staff member, Institute for Foreign Policy Analysis, Cambridge, Mass. His publications include *The Policy Maker, Area Studies, and International Relations* (1974), *How to Think about Arms Control and Disarmament* (1973), and *Security through World Law and World Government: Myth or Reality?* (1973). He authored, with Robert L. Pfaltzgraff, Jr., *Contending Theories of International Relations* (1971).

Harold K. Jacobson is professor of political science and a program director in the Center for Political Studies of the Institute for Social Research at the University of Michigan. His most recent book is *Networks of Interdependence: International Organizations and the Global Political System* (1979). He is a member of the board of editors of *International Organization.*

Andrzej Korbonski is professor and chairman of the department of political science, University of California, Los Angeles. He authored *The*

Politics of Socialist Agriculture in Poland (1965) and, with Thad Paul Alton and others, *Polish National Income and Product* (1965), and has contributed chapters to numerous works on Eastern Europe. His articles have appeared in *World Politics, Studies in Comparative Communism, Problems of Communism, Journal of International Affairs, Current History, Slavic Review,* and *International Conciliation.*

Donald E. Lampert is assistant professor of political science at Arizona State University, Tempe, Arizona. He authored, with R. W. Mansbach and Y. H. Ferguson, *The Web of World Politics: Nonstate Actors in the Global System* (1976) and *Beyond the National Interest* (1979), and has contributed to *International Studies Quarterly.*

Charles Lockhart is assistant professor of political science at Texas Christian University, Fort Worth, Texas. He is the author of *Bargaining in International Conflicts* (1979) and has published articles in *World Politics, The Journal of Conflict Resolution,* and *International Studies Quarterly.*

Charles Pentland is associate professor of political studies at Queen's University, Kingston, Ontario. He authored *International Theory and European Integration* (1973) and co-authored, with Peter Christian Ludz, H. Peter Dreyer, and Lothar Ruhl, *Dilemmas of the Atlantic Alliance* (1975). He contributed the chapter on "International Organization" to James N. Rosenau, Kenneth W. Thompson, and Gavin Boyd (eds.), *World Politics* (1976) and has published articles on international regionalism, Canadian foreign policy, and European integration.

John Pinder is director of the Policy Studies Institute in London. His publications include *Britain and the Common Market* (1961), *Europe after de Gaulle* (with Roy Pryce, 1969), *The Economics of Europe* (editor, 1971), and *The European Community's Policy towards Eastern Europe* (with Pauline Pinder, 1975). He has published numerous articles on problems of European integration, East–West economic relations, and the external relations of the European Community.

Timothy M. Shaw is visiting associate professor in the department of political science and the Norman Paterson School of International Affairs at Carleton University, Ottawa, on leave from Dalhousie University, Halifax, where he is associated with the Centers for Foreign Policy and African Studies. He authored, with Douglas G. Anglin, *Zambia's Foreign Policy* (1978) and edited, with Kenneth A. Heard, *Cooperation and Conflict in Southern Africa* (1976) and *The Politics of Africa* (1979). He also edited, with Douglas G. Anglin and Carl Widstrand, *Conflict and Change in Southern Africa* (1978) and *Canada, Scandinavia and Southern Africa* (1978).

Preface

THIS WORK has been designed as an introduction to the systematic and comparative study of foreign policy issues, of the ways in which such issues are contested between states, and of problems affecting the development of international institutions for common management of those issues. As the volume was being prepared, we felt that the extensive policy-oriented literature on choices in American foreign policy should be complemented by some comparative studies of issues in the policies of other global actors, and that this would help participants in the American policy process to function more effectively as contributors to the potentially most significant forms of statecraft in global politics. We also felt that questions of international political development should be examined on the basis of some of the analytical approaches that had evolved in the study of political development at the national level. To the extent that this could be done, the prescriptive literature on world order, we believed, would be made more relevant for scholars, opinion leaders, and policy makers.

The volume begins with a survey of the configuration of the global system. This prepares the way for examinations of foreign policy issues posed for the major actors. Matters contested between these actors are then studied in chapters dealing with interaction on economic, security, and political issues. Problems of institutionalizing the interactive processes are thus brought into view, and in the treatment of these there are references to questions of *participation, equity,* and *growth*.

Each contributing author has written with insight, sensitivity, and dedication. Each has lived through some of the dramas of international politics and has experienced the strains of theorizing. Each has sought understanding through exhausting analytical work and has attempted to help the work of foreign policy makers in the industrialized democracies. Our gratitude to our colleagues, we believe, will be shared widely in the transnational world of scholars, concerned citizens, and holistically inclined policy makers.

Both of us wish to acknowledge support from our universities on this project, and we thank numerous colleagues for their comments on our drafts. Gavin Boyd is grateful to the Center for Asian Studies and the Political Science Department at Arizona State University for generous assistance received as a Visiting Professor in 1980–81.

1

The Configuration of the Global System

James E. Dougherty

ONLY IN THE TWENTIETH CENTURY—and especially since World War II
—have the emergence and confluence of many political, economic, technological, strategic, and military factors of world-wide magnitude produced a genuine system which, despite undeniable discontinuities and
ambiguities, shows signs of becoming increasingly "conscious" of itself.[1]
A hundred years ago, there was no global system in the sense in which
we employ that term today. The states of the world then numbered fewer
than fifty. Only a dozen or so of these were considered important enough
to be mentioned regularly in the press of those countries that could boast
a press.[2] Most of the leading state actors were Western. One cannot really
speak of "global issues" in those days. From time to time there did arise
international issues of a diplomatic, military, or economic character involving, for example, questions of territorial control (including boundary
and colonial disputes), maintenance of the balance of power, legitimate
succession of rulers, intervention for the support or suppression of revolutions, and the collection of debts or the enforcement of claims to mari-

time passage rights. All of these were matters that could affect international peace and stability by the threat of war. As such these issues were primarily of interest to foreign offices, until they arrived at a sufficiently critical stage to command the attention of the press. There were no universal actors comparable to the League of Nations or the United Nations, capable of institutionalizing an international interest in these issues by giving them a priority or an agenda of items presumed to be of "global concern." Nor were there, within the nation-states, many organized groups working to promote interest in or to influence outcomes related to specific foreign policy issues. The linkages between domestic and international politics were relatively weak compared to the situation that prevails today in many Western democratic states.[3]

In the last quarter of the twentieth century, the international system is considerably more complex and "layered," as we shall see presently. The number of types and units of international actors has increased markedly (see the section on "Components of the Global System" below). Moreover, several factors have operated to strengthen the connection between domestic and foreign politics within both older and newer states. Only a few examples need be mentioned: (1) In many countries the development of democratic attitudes has eroded the traditional willingness of "the people," "the public," and "the masses" to leave foreign policy in the hands of "the rulers," "the government," and "the experts." (2) The experience of two world wars and the emergence of advanced weapons technology in the era of nuclear-tipped missiles has led to heightened popular interest in issues of war and peace. (3) The diffusion of communications and transport technology has produced a more intensive awareness of global happenings and has stimulated the organization of specialized outcome-influencing groups. (4) Whereas in the nineteenth century the international economic system and national political systems were somewhat insulated from each other in the sense that the former did not depend so much upon the political decisions of governments as upon the automatic, self-regulating mechanism of the gold standard, the contemporary international system is characterized by the intensive interpenetration of economic and political decision-making, especially at the level of national governments. (5) Special-interest groups the world over—ideological, political, religious, economic, military, ethnic, linguistic, and cultural—have begun to learn how to "globalize" the issues and conflicts in which they are interested parties.

Before we can adequately analyze the global political system from the standpoint of the way in which it processes global issues, we must first ask a prior, crucial question: What do we mean by "political"? The question is important, because historically the term was defined by reference to organized communities of less than global dimensions—especially city-states and nation-states. Traditional Western political theory—with some notable exceptions in the writings of Thucydides, Dante, Machiavelli, and the peace theorists of the Enlightenment period—did not focus systematically upon the problems of international politics. Most modern writers in the field of international politics have drawn a fundamental distinction between the national political system as we know it in the older established nation-states and the existing international system in that the former involves a legitimate and effective monopoly of coercive power (force) to back up its decisions and the latter does not.[4]

David Easton, in an effort to separate "political system" from "state," delineated the subject matter of politics as the "authoritative allocation of values for a society," where the term "authoritative" refers to policies that are accepted as binding, and that apply to the whole society.[5] Although Easton recognized the fear of force as one basis for complying with authoritative decisions—along with belief in legitimacy, expectation of reward, habit or custom, and expediency—he did not single out coercive sanctions as an essential ingredient of a political system.[6] Easton admitted that the sense of legitimacy does not play an important part within the international system, in which the proportion of measures taken through authoritative actions is extremely low, and that for the most part "decisions and actions performed by international systems rely for their acceptance upon accord with the perceived self-interest of the participating members."[7] While trying to "save the appearances" of the "authoritative allocation of values" within the international political system, he acknowledged that the process of authoritative allocation is much less centralized and less continuous than in modern national systems. Easton and others, picking up on suggestions made long ago by such social contract theorists as Hobbes, Locke, and Rousseau, have drawn an analogy between the international system and "primitive" or "stateless" societies.[8] Romano Romani, elaborating upon Easton, has called attention to the fact that decisions in the international system are made through bilateral or multilateral agreements, and thus values in that system can be called "authoritatively allocated" only in the sense that an economic contract between buyer and seller in the free market system might be.[9] Even that comparison is not completely valid, for a national court will enforce a contract entered into between two domestic parties, whereas most international agreements are not enforceable judicially.

The difference between the international system and national systems may be bridged, at least partially, if we advert to the distinction commonly drawn by political scientists between polyarchic and hierarchic systems. The distinction can best be illustrated by a description of nearly perfect types. The United States and—to a lesser extent—all Western democracies fall into the first category. They are marked by a great deal of political, economic and socio-cultural, religious and philosophical diversity, heterogeneity, and pluralism. No single, official ideology rules.

Power and influence are diffused by federalism, a constitutional separation of powers among branches of government, and the polycentralization of power among political parties, wings of parties, economic interest groups (business, labor, agriculture, consumer, etcetera), religious and ethnic communities, geographic areas, professional groups, specialized lobbies, the media, and various segments of the "public" or the electorate, classified by age, income, sex, education, and location on the urban–rural scale). In contrast, the U.S.S.R. and the People's Republic of China are much more rigidly and hierarchically structured, much more monistic and homogeneous in ideology. Only one party is recognized by an interlocking party–state mechanism, which holds a monopoly of communications media. There do exist different groups and group perspectives (party officials, governmental administrators, military leaders, industrial managers, scientists and engineers, artists and intellectuals, etcetera), but all are subject to a high degree of central direction and control. Whatever bargaining takes place in this system is very different from that which goes on in polyarchic systems, because it receives no publicity and is unrelated to electoral outcomes. There is no doubt that the international system behaves much more like the polyarchic than the hierarchic model. But this analogy cannot be carried too far, for even though the bargaining process in the international system may bear some resemblance to that in the polyarchic state, such that we can perhaps speak of a "negotiated allocation of values" in the international system, the authoritative seal which the polyarchic state sets upon the net outcome of the bargaining process is much more legitimate and more firmly effective than that of the international system.

Advocates of the "world order" approach, whether associated with world federalism, regionalism, or libertarian anarchism, criticize the adherence of the great majority of international relations specialists to a global system based upon sovereign states and such concepts as "balance of power" and "deterrence." They object strenuously to what they regard as a false dichotomy between "prudent realism" and "utopian idealism." They stress instead the relevance of religious, cultural, and value-change potentialities of human society for alternative world political futures.[10] To the contrary, Hedley Bull, after examining the anarchical setting of international society—anarchical in the sense that it lacks a single government—concludes that the state system, despite its many defects, is remarkably durable. Bull also argues that the present pluralistic system manages to achieve, through the institutions of international law, diplomacy, and the balancing of power, a certain order of its own which may not be inferior to, nor necessarily more conflict-ridden than, that of a universal state in which the stakes of political conflict would be raised to a higher level.[11]

There is a considerable difference between the international system and the typical modern, highly developed national system, and this difference should not be denigrated. The world of political action at all levels is, of course, a world in which cooperation and conflict are intermingled. There may be at times a good deal of conflict and widespread flouting of certain rules within a national society and a good deal of cooperation and adherence to the rules within the global system. But within the national system there is a readily identifiable central rule-making authority; its rule-making power extends to all members within the system and it has at its disposal the means of enforcing the rules it makes, if it is determined to do so. This is simply not the case with the global system. The latter has no central rule-making and rule-enforcing authority in any real sense. The United Nations is by no means unimportant; it can wield influence within the system, but its power is quite different from that possessed by well-developed national actors, since it depends more on the ability to focus attention upon specific problems and to facilitate the negotiations process than upon the ability to coerce or to issue authoritative commands with the expectation of obedience.

The content of international behavior rules is often vague because actors regard themselves as bound only by those "rules of the game" to which they have given their assent, and even these may be set aside when vital national interests are thought to be at stake. Most important of all, the normal tendency of modern national systems is to bring not only the superior coercive power of government but also its political conflict-solving intelligence to bear in support of peaceful adjudication of disputes. In the global system, by contrast, even those national members who seek to pursue foreign policy objectives without actually becoming involved in war nevertheless maintain an abiding readiness to resort to the use of force, or at least to threaten its use when basic national interests are at stake. There exists within the global system neither the political-ideological basis for a legitimate monopoly of coercive power nor the political-military foundation for an effective application of force in support of agreed principles of international right. Up to the present time, modern technology seems to have strengthened national systems more than it has the global system, inasmuch as military-technological power is still decentralized and national systems are still free to institutionalize the expectation of war by maintaining massive power either to deter or to retaliate against aggression.

Global Issues

What are global issues? How internationalized must an issue become before we are justified in calling it global? Global issues are those questions, problems, dilemmas, and challenges that pertain significantly to the basic requirements of international peace, security, order, justice, freedom, and progressive development. These issues are political-diplomatic, military-strategic and socioeconomic in the broadest sense, and they are characterized more by disagreement and conflict than by agreement and cooperation. Global issues, however, cannot be authoritatively formulated and given priority because their management is decentralized within nation-states and even more so within the international system. One can cite certain indicators that make issues "global": (1) They occupy the attention of the policy-making elites of a large number of governments, including some principal ones, and governments engage in public argument about them. (2) They receive persisting coverage in the world press —in newspapers and magazines, in radio and television broadcasting. (3) They are subjects of continuing serious study, inquiry, and debate by professional scholars, scientists, and technical experts throughout the international community. (4) They appear in the agenda or arguments about the agenda of international organizations (of both a universal-political and specialized functional nature).

Intellectuals, scientists, journalists, and radical social critics may berate political leaders in this country or that for ignoring the "real" issues while being excessively preoccupied with questions that are "traditional," "obsolete," or "irrelevant." Such criticism, which is often normative (that is, value-based) rather than scientific (or empirically grounded) reflects the fact that in politics there is never a consensus over what the important issues are or what should be done about them. (Once consensus is achieved, the issue ceases to be political.) Within a single nation-state, competing individual personalities, factions, political parties, governmental bureaucratic units, and organized interest groups will often be found to differ substantially over which international issues should be placed higher and which ones lower on the national policy-making agenda. The global system presents an even more diffuse picture. The two superpowers, with divergent ideological outlooks and geopolitical interests, are not likely to see eye to eye when it comes to setting priorities for most global issues, but there may be a surprising number of instances in which they formally or tacitly align to protect common or coincidental interests. On proliferation, the perspectives of "nuclear haves" and of "nuclear have-nots" will not be the same, nor will the perspectives of industrialized and nonindustrialized countries on tariffs and trade, nor of hard- and soft-currency countries on monetary matters, nor of coastal and inland states at the Law of the Sea Conference.

But it should be remembered that constant change and development are essential features of a rational political process. Permanent rigidity and immutability in political positions are incompatible with the operation of a rational political system. As new knowledge is acquired (the result of investigation and communication), the perception of interests is modified, bargaining and negotiation take place, tradeoffs are made and compromises reached, and polarized opposition can give way to mutually satisfactory (or mutually unsatisfactory) accommodation. The process of rational issue-resolution between states, however, is much more uncertain and imperfect. Nevertheless one hopes that despite the absence of an authoritative international allocator of values the global system—through a precarious groping by decentralized decision-making centers—will manage to survive and develop in ways conducive to progressive systemic rationalization.

Dimensions of the Global System

In the global system, structures and process are closely interrelated. Each of the actors (that is, states and other units) behaves in a way that is fundamentally related not only to its internal political, social, and economic structures and processes but also to its perception of its place and role within the total system. The global system is a hierarchical one in which the various actors are acutely conscious of their rank or status, for this to a very large extent determines what they can prudently dare to undertake. In individual cases, of course—and this is no less true of macrocosmic or intersocietal than of microcosmic or interpersonal relations—an actor may behave "imprudently" or "outlandishly" in terms of role or status. At certain times, bizarre, uncharacteristic behavior may become fashionable and those who engage in it may "get away with it." But such behavior only rarely in history becomes socially normative. Sooner or later social systems react, to re-establish what they regard as acceptable modes of action, either by punishing the deviant behavior or by bringing about a synthesis of values between the older and the newer, thereby sufficiently satisfying the demands of the erstwhile "deviants" to keep them incorporated within the system and basically loyal to its regulative norms.

According to virtually all leading theorists in the field of international relations, older and younger, and whether they ethically approve the fact or not, rank and status within the global system are commonly measured in terms of "power."[12] Or, to be more accurate, they would say that *perceptions* of relative power determine the stratified structure of the system and create the assumptions on which observers base their predictions of unit behavior. Power implies much more than the mere ability to coerce with physical superiority. Political power involves the capability of persuading, leading, influencing, threatening, promising, attracting, rewarding, or inspiring—as well as coercing. The power of a political community encompasses whatever will enable it to organize itself efficiently, maintain cohesiveness, create conditions of security and order, solve problems, and attain internal and external goals.[13]

Power has been defined most broadly and simply by Modelski as "the capacity to act."[14] Puchala has distinguished between Gross National Power (the absolute total of resources available in a given state or society) and Externally Projectable Power (the total of resources available to the government for the pursuit of foreign policy objectives).[15] After the Nazi invasion of 1941, the Soviet Union mobilized for its war effort the great bulk of its human and material resources, but this was most unusual. Since World War II, only during the Korean and Vietnam wars has the United States been able to allocate more than 10 percent of its Gross National Product to defense. At other times the military budget has on the average amounted to only 6 to 8 percent of the GNP,[16] with less than an additional 1 percent going to the costs of nonmilitary foreign policy (such as the maintenance of the diplomatic establishment, foreign economic assistance, and so forth). The proportion of the Soviet GNP devoted to military expenditures is much more difficult to estimate, but it is generally assumed to be larger than that of the United States both because the Soviets place a higher premium upon military power in the conduct of foreign affairs[17] and because the Soviet economic-technological base is smaller than that of the United States. Most European states aligned with one of the superpowers spend 3 to 5 percent of their GNP on defense, while most of the nonaligned states (with the exception of Sweden and Yugoslavia) spend 2 percent or less.[18] The majority of Asian and African states show comparable percentages, but several Middle East states in the 1970s have often been in excess of 10, 15, 20, and even 30 percent.[19] It must be remembered that defense-emphasis is not necessarily a precise measure of influence in the international system. Some states (for example, Germany and Japan) which allocate a relatively small percentage of GNP to military purposes may nevertheless exercise considerable political leverage because of their importance in international trade, monetary, and other economic affairs.

Power is unevenly distributed throughout the global system, and the importance of any actor is determined by its position along the scale of power distribution. As in the case of wealth, only a few enjoy substantial amounts of it; most actors are power-poor. The concept of power, which has often been criticized for its vagueness, is a complex sum of many variables, several of them constantly changing, and thus cannot be precisely measured by any single standard. Moreover, power theory seldom makes clear exactly what behavior the concept is supposed to explain.[20] In spite of these deficiencies and in spite of the fact that the notion is regarded as tautological since its certainty is demonstrated only when power has been successfully applied, most practitioners of international affairs—political leaders, their advisers, diplomats—appear to engage much of the time in a calculus of power, of relative advantages and disadvantages. In an era in which "interdependence" has become a byword, we are becoming increasingly aware that power in its many modes is just as relevant a consideration in decision-making about cooperative international behavior as it is in decision-making about conflict.

Traditional writers have analyzed power by inventorying elements such as population, geography, natural resources, the educational system, economic-industrial-scientific-technological factors, national character and morale, national ideology, values and sense of purpose, quality of the political system, leadership and diplomacy, and quantity as well as quality of military forces. They have recognized that ethnic, linguistic, and religious homogeneity normally contribute to unity, whereas diversity along these axes often provides a basis for the generation of internal political conflicts that weaken the community. The traditional writers have also called attention to such obvious probabilities or facts as the following: the degree of self-sufficiency in natural resources is likely to be proportionate to the size of the territory; the mere possession of raw material wealth is of little avail for economic development if the population lacks technical and organizational skills; a skillful, energetic, and enterprising population is able to compensate for a relative paucity of raw material resources (as the history of Britain showed); the power of individual states alters with changes in population, technology, and political, economic, and sociocultural factors. Finally, the traditional writers have described, usually with profuse historical illustrations, what the possession of power enables some states to do (to form alliances, go to war, deter war, intervene in the affairs of other states, acquire colonial empires, control maritime routes, and so forth) or what the absence of power compels some states to do (cede territory or otherwise submit to stronger states, accept outside intervention, accommodate to the political and economic interests of the more powerful, try to stay out of the way of great powers by pursuing policies of neutrality or nonalignment, etcetera).

More recent theorists, while extremely dissatisfied with the concept of power, have attempted to clarify it and express it in sophisticated behavioral terminology. They have viewed power as a means, a relationship, a process of influencing, a quantity and a distance between two actors. Whereas the traditional writers were inclined to stress military power as the culmination of all the elements of national power, the newer theorists are generally more interested in the wide variety of power/influence modalities and applications. Stanley Hoffmann has noted that "the postwar era has witnessed radical transformations in the elements, the uses, and the achievements of power."[21] It is now more readily recognized that economic and military power, no matter how formidable, is not always available for effective use, and that while "the strong can more easily punish or help the weak, they are not invulnerable to the other's actions."[22] But regardless of how subtle or euphemistic the terminology becomes, power still represents a potential for affecting outcomes, for speeding up or resisting rates of change, for influencing the actions of others and obtaining advantages. No matter how interdependent the system may become, there will always be asymmetries, and these will provide bargaining leverage for actors in their dealings with each other.[23]

According to Keohane and Nye, interdependence refers not to all transactions and interactions between states but rather to those which have significant costly effects. It need not, therefore, imply mutual benefit in the sense of equity. Since interdependence restricts autonomy, it always involves costs, and the benefits do not always necessarily exceed the costs. It is naïve to consider interdependence as evenly balanced mutual benefit, because the parties may not be at all equally free in their choices. The calculus of benefits depends not only on the different values of the parties, but also on the nature of the power relationship between them. This relationship—regardless of whether we are talking about political, economic, or military power—invariably contains asymmetric *sensitivities* (responsiveness to the impact of changes imposed from the outside before policy changes are made) and *vulnerabilities* (liability to suffer costs imposed by external events after policy changes have been made).[24]

Let us look at a few examples. The sensitivity of an industrialized nation to an Arab oil boycott depends upon the proportion of domestic oil needs normally met by imports from that region. Vulnerability, on the other hand, is a function of the ability of the importing nation to make adjustments to the situation of shortage by pursuing other alternatives available within cost and time constraints (for instance, inducing other foreign exporters to increase production, using domestic above-ground oil reserves, rationing gasoline for automobiles, shifting from oil to coal in some power plants and industries, and speeding up R & D designed to exploit new energy technologies).

We must not think that only the oil-importing country experiences sensitivity and vulnerability. When an oil-producing country cuts off exports, it stops earning foreign exchange, and this may sooner or later affect its ability to pay for the import of technology. If it has amassed large financial reserves from previous oil sales abroad, its sensitivity initially may be low, but this will rise if the boycott lasts long enough to compel the reduction of imports. The exporting country may hope to overcompensate for the cutoff by raising the price at which oil will be sold after the boycott comes to an end. But there are limits to price rises. An oil exporter with virtually unlimited reserves (such as Saudi Arabia) may be reluctant to raise the price so high as to cause ruinous inflation in industrial countries whose currencies it holds in surplus and from which it buys technology, and it will be very reluctant to push importing countries too rapidly into the development of alternative energy technologies.

Even in the purely military realm, power cannot be measured merely in terms of sheer physical capability to coerce. During the Vietnam war, the United States had at its disposal a vastly greater amount of military destructive potential than did its Southeast Asia foe. But for a variety of reasons, including fear of arousing adverse allied reactions and of possibly widening the war to include the Soviet Union or China, the United States did not bring its full military potential to bear against North Vietnam. Moreover, the North Vietnamese possessed a potent doctrine for warfare, in its total political-strategic context. The morale of the North Vietnamese political system held up much better than did that of the U.S. In the political bargaining that went on throughout the war, the "weaker" state proved more committed to its goals and more willing to suffer for them than did the "stronger" state.[25]

The fact that the world is becoming more interdependent does not mean that international cooperation will replace international conflict. Asymmetries of power and influence will probably continue to be manipulated with advantage by stronger states. The development of more complex international interdependencies inevitably increases opportunities for mutually satisfactory cooperation but also for disagreement and conflict.[26]

Even the two most autarkic powers—the United States and the Soviet Union—cannot be considered completely independent or self-sufficient, as we shall see presently. Members of the European Economic Community (EEC) have deliberately renounced the quest for autarky in many (but not all) economic dimensions. Western Europe depends upon the United States for its security, as does Japan. Eastern Europe, with less freedom of choice, is linked to the U.S.S.R. for purposes of military security. A number of less developed countries in Asia, Africa, and Latin America depend upon foreign assistance from one or more of the great powers and are heavily dependent upon the export of one or two raw material products—a fact which makes them vulnerable to fluctuations in world prices. Maritime nations are sensitive to factors that may affect the freedom of shipping—such as the seizure or closure of an important international waterway or the unilateral extension by one state of its territorial waters. Highly industrialized oil-importing states can be made to feel the pressure of price increases by the oil exporters, who are less industrially developed, while the latter are limited in their quasi-monopoly power by the knowledge that the requirements of their own development prevent them from causing substantial disturbances within those economies on which their buying power depends.

It is undeniable that if power is equated with military force, it is not an adequate concept for understanding contemporary international relations. Several new theoretical approaches must be added: those relating to dynamic processes, theories of communications and social integration, decision-making, images, bargaining, and games. But the newer approaches are neither useful nor valid if they completely ignore the basic political reality, namely, the tendency of all states to pursue their interests by engaging in some form of power manipulation and balancing, singly or in combination with others.

The world hierarchical structure is usually conceptualized with two triangular relationships linking countries at or near the top of the pyramid. These two are: (1) the political-military triangle (the United States, the Soviet Union, and China) and (2) the economic triangle (the United States, the European Economic Community, and Japan).[27] There are only two military superpowers, but China is a formidable political-military power because of its vast population, its social organization and morale, the size and discipline of its armed forces, and its geographical position and expanse. The Soviet Union is apprehensive over the possibility that the United States and allies will contribute to the development of Chinese economic, technological, and military power. In the early 1970s there was speculation in policy-making and academic circles to the effect that Western Europe and Japan might try to convert their great economic-technological potential into military power, thereby taking their places as the fourth and fifth centers of a "pentapolar world." Nevertheless both areas still remain primarily dependent for their defense upon the United States. China can become a formidable modern power only with substantial U.S., Western European, and Japanese aid. Whether the world will eventually become multipolar will probably depend heavily upon the policy of the United States, since it can influence both West European and Japanese decisions. The one historic development that, more than any other, put the United States in such a pivotal position was the Sino-Soviet dispute. This motivated China to shift toward closer relations with the West in order to strengthen its defenses against the U.S.S.R. It also led to some loosening within the Soviet and American alliance systems.

The Global Actors

Only the United States and the Soviet Union approach autarky in the political, economic, and military dimensions. They can act with the greatest degree of independence, without seeking approval or permission from others. But even they cannot afford to offend others with impunity. Nevertheless these two powers alone enjoy global strategic mobility and wield a military capability to intervene in virtually any region of the world. Of the two, the Soviet Union is the more autarkic in the political and military dimensions. The U.S.S.R. is favored by geography: its territory is twice as large as that of the United States, and size normally brings benefits in regard to self-sufficiency in raw materials and also in regard to the factor of "invulnerability," which figures importantly in the calculus of nuclear deterrence; moreover, the U.S.S.R. is geographically close to the economically and technologically significant "prizeland" of Western Europe—a fact which makes it more difficult for the United States to defend western interests in that region than for the U.S.S.R. to threaten them. The Soviet alliance system (Warsaw Pact) is considerably less complex than NATO, and it is less dependent upon the procedures of open consultation which invariably hamper planning. Moreover, Soviet military defense programs and security decision-making processes are much less influenced by inflation, public opinion, and debates between rival political groups.

Yet though the basic facts of geography appear to favor the Soviets, political and economic factors can provide some comfort to the West. The Atlantic Alliance, for example, is the result of decisions taken by freely elected governments, whereas the Warsaw Pact (regardless of what may have been originally defensive intentions) was imposed upon administrations largely dependent on the presence of the Soviet army. The negotiations which led to the Helsinki Pact of 1975, as well as the exchanges which took place prior to and during the Belgrade Conference of 1977, showed that the Soviet leaders are sensitive to Western political criticism of Soviet policies in Eastern Europe. Forced onto the defensive by President Carter's human rights campaign, their reactions at times became angry.

In the economic order, the self-sufficiency of the U.S.S.R. is far from absolute. Up to now, it has not been dependent on foreign sources of oil, but as its energy needs grow it will require either the exploitation of the Tyumen oilfields (for which it has sought Japanese cooperation) or the importation of larger quantities of oil. During the last decade the Soviet Union has had to turn to the United States to purchase grain in order to compensate for its own crop shortages, and it may have to do so again in bad-weather years. Finally, whereas the U.S.S.R. is highly efficient in the realm of military technology, it will probably remain dependent on the outside world (Western Europe, the United States, and Japan) for sophisticated technology in a number of nonmilitary areas for many years. Since the Soviet Union possesses only a limited ability to contribute toward the solution of other countries' economic problems (for example, food, energy, balance of payments deficits, industrial development), it can be expected to continue to rely on military power, and the image of such power, to extend its influence in such regions as Western Europe, Africa, and Southeast Asia.[28] In this connection, it may be noted that the nonaligned nations, which for decades had objected strenuously to Western imperialism, began in the late 1970s to express concern over Soviet imperialism in the Third World.

Since World War II, the United States has aimed at international stability, consistent with its security needs, political values, and economic interests. This has meant the construction of an intricate network of alliances and trade relationships from which it has derived both gains and losses. Having decided to help rebuild Europe economically after World War II, the United States had little choice but to provide for its defense through the Atlantic Alliance. Japan, which experienced a rapid economic recovery, came to be looked upon by U.S. policy makers as being of comparable importance. The United States, therefore, not wishing to see the Japanese rearm, undertook to defend them through a mutual security treaty. The task of ensuring that West Germany and Japan would remain satisfied powers, confident of their continued independence, devolved principally upon the United States. The remarkable economic-technological growth of those two countries, combined with the cost of providing strategic deterrence and regional defense capabilities for Western Europe and Japan, however, has produced some problems for the United States in recent decades, such as loss of foreign markets, difficulties in tariff and trade negotiations, balance of payments deficits, inflation, and a steady decline in the value of the dollar.

In many respects, the European Economic Community and Japan have been able to "hold their own" quite well in economic negotiations with the United States. But in regard to energy supplies—especially oil —they are considerably more dependent than the United States upon Middle East sources. Naturally, Western Europe and Japan try to insulate conflicts of economic interest with the United States from strains on security matters, and they occasionally display resentment when the United States links the two dimensions. In the final analysis, all of these allied parties have recognized—especially at their various "summit" gatherings—that they cannot afford to "go it alone," that there are limits to their ability to pursue policies of national interest and protectionism, and that they cannot allow recurring arguments over strategy, energy, trade, and monetary policies to weaken the fabric of their security alliances. The United States, to combat domestic inflation, cannot cut military spending if this reduces the credibility of its commitment to European allies, nor can it withdraw forces from South Korea without carefully weighing the implications of such a move for Japanese foreign policy. In sum, even the principal powers cannot forget that autarky is always tempered by interdependence.

Up to this point, we have referred to five "power centers," one of which (Western Europe) is characterized by tension between a centripetal tendency toward integrated planning and decision-making in the EEC and a centrifugal tendency toward decentralized decision-making in ten national capitals. There is still a great deal of uncertainty as to whether the EEC can properly be considered as a single actor within the global system. No doubt it is capable of acting as such on some international trade issues and in negotiations with potential new members. EEC members have also at times had some success in the formulation of a common foreign policy—notably for the Conference on Security and Cooperation in Europe (CSCE). But it has proved more difficult to achieve common policies on energy, the North–South dialogue (in which Britain demanded a separate voice), the election and powers of a European Parliament, and a European monetary union.

Almost in parallel with the European Community, Britain, France, and Germany continue to qualify as global actors. Britain and France continue to exert influence in many parts of their former imperial domains. Along with the two superpowers and China, they have nuclear weapons and the veto privilege in the United Nations Security Council. France ranks fifth in the world in Gross Domestic Product (GDP) and Britain sixth. Germany and Japan must be counted among the global actors for at least three reasons: (1) They are important in the global political balance, and the dominant actors are keenly interested in their future. (2) Japan and West Germany rank third and fourth, respectively, in GDP. (3) Each possesses the economic-technological capability to become a significant nuclear military power. Neither has manifested the slightest official interest in acquiring nuclear weapons. Both, however, are anxious to avoid being discriminated against in world politics, and both have exhibited misgivings over U.S. antiproliferation policies which affect the development of their peaceful reactor programs.

It can be seen, then, that even among the principal nations within the global system there are significant gradations of power, influence, capability, autarky, vulnerability, weakness, and dependence. These asymmetries make it extremely difficult to draw any valid generalizations that apply to more than one or two of them. Obviously, some of these actors are more global than others. But any one of them is capable of acting in such a way as to precipitate an international crisis, that is, a situation which intensely engrosses the attention of rival Great Powers and threatens abrupt change in a basic global system variable.[29]

Once we introduce as a criterion of global actor status the ability to precipitate a global crisis, several other states might qualify, simply by being able to do something irresponsible or desperate that would bring Great Powers into tense confrontation, for example, in the Middle East. But aside from that criterion, are there any other states that come close to being "global actors" besides those mentioned previously? It has often been suggested that since the early 1970s the Organization of Petroleum Exporting Countries (OPEC) should be included in this category because of its power to curb the vital flow of oil to the industrialized countries of the West. But the divisions of political ideology and economic interest among the members of OPEC are more profound than those in the European Economic Community. It would be just as plausible, therefore, to consider such major exporting countries as Iran and Saudi Arabia to be global actors as to put OPEC into that category. The attention which the world paid to governmental changes in Iran in 1979 attested to the pivotal role of that country in the global system; comparable changes in Saudi Arabia would create an even graver crisis in world politics.

Among the global actors, mention must be made of the main international organization: the United Nations. The development of international organizations cannot be discussed in any detail here; it will be treated amply elsewhere in this volume. At the moment, the following generalizations will suffice:

1. Since the admission of the People's Republic of China in 1971, the United Nations has become a genuine universal membership organization.

2. The United Nations has made a significant contribution to international functional integration and socioeconomic improvement in several fields (for example, non-self-governing territories; protection of children, minorities and refugees; health education; control of international narcotics traffic; international assistance for economic development; planning to meet the problems of population growth and environmental management; and facilitating efforts to refine international law in specific areas, such as outer space, treaty-making, diplomatic practice, and law of the seas). It has also provided training and experience for a large body of international civil servants.

3. In international conflicts, the United Nations has achieved some success in crisis management through mediation, reporting, the interposition of police forces, and a variety of supervisory activities which have contributed toward the localization, containment, or termination of conflicts under conditions conducive to "preventive diplomacy," but it has been much less successful in removing the underlying causes of international conflict. The organization's record in handling conflicts involving the vital interests of Great Powers has not been at all impressive.[30]

4. The United Nations serves as a central exchange in the communications process of the global system and facilitates contacts among governments that cannot afford to maintain missions in too many capitals. Through the construction of its agenda the United Nations has the opportunity to focus the political attention of the system upon specific problems and issues, although its ability to make headway toward the resolution of enduring and fundamental systemic problems is extremely limited,[31] as the meager results of the 1978 Special Session on Disarmament demonstrated. The United Nations cannot be faulted for shirking difficult, even intractable, problems. By stimulating efforts to develop an international legal regime for the oceans (involving numerous conflicts of interest over security, sovereign jurisdiction, freedom of passage, access to maritime routes, fishing rights, conservation, and exploitation of seabed resources), the United Nations through the Law of the Sea Conference has compelled governments to undertake intensive studies and negotiation in an area crucial to future international cooperation.[32]

5. The structure and operation of the United Nations reflect the essential characteristics of a decentralized global system in which the nation-state remains the principal decision-making unit. At present the emergence of an effective international government is not to be predicted. But in a multipolar system, the United Nations gradually gains utility as a mechanism for modulating an increasingly complex process of equilibration through communication and negotiation.

Other Actors

Up to now, we have spoken only of superpowers, major powers, critical states (such as Iran and Saudi Arabia), and the universal actor (the United Nations). Most of the actors in the global system do not qualify as "global actors," and they can be classified into several different categories. We should treat first the remainder of the 150 state actors within the system, and then look at other types of actors (such as international functional organizations; regional functional organizations; alliances, blocs, and other political associations or groupings; multinational enterprises and other transnational organizations; nonstate political entities; and individuals who assume such an importance as to qualify as international actors).

MIDDLE POWERS

The term "middle power" does not lend itself to precise definition. States might qualify for the designation by virtue of population, geographical position or size, possession of raw materials, role in international trade, technological potential (for example, a capability for the development of nuclear weapons), military forces in being, political-diplomatic skills, or some combination of these. Normally, a middle power is important because of its ability to contribute to stability or instability (political, economic, or military) within a region. Analysts could not be expected to agree unanimously on a membership list, but most would probably be willing to include the following states:

Argentina	Greece
Australia	Indonesia
Belgium	Iran
Brazil	Italy
Canada	Mexico
Cuba	Netherlands
Czechoslovakia	North Korea
East Germany	Pakistan
Egypt	Poland

Saudi Arabia	Turkey
South Africa	Venezuela
South Korea	Vietnam
Spain	Yugoslavia
Sweden	

Some might wish to exclude a few states listed and substitute Hungary, Rumania, Denmark, Finland, Norway, Chile, Colombia, Algeria, Nigeria, or Libya. The location of any actor along the world scale of power distribution, of course, fluctuates. The international role of middle powers may be amplified by their pivotal role in regional groupings, their capabilities for trade and development assistance, their availability to play a part in international peace-keeping operations, their ability to undertake initiatives in regard to specific issues, and their ability at times to exacerbate international instability or crises. Changes in economic and technological levels can enhance or undermine the international status of a state. The sudden discovery of oil or other significant natural resources or the acquisition of a new piece of military equipment as well as many other developments, may raise the prestige of an actor within the global system.

SMALL POWERS AND MINI-STATES

In 1946, the United Nations had only four members with populations under 5 million and only one member that could be called a "microstate" (Iceland). By the beginning of the decade of the 1980s, at least half of the 150 members had populations under 5 million, a third had fewer than 3 million and a fifth had fewer than 1 million. There are now fifteen members with populations smaller than 300,000, and the process toward fragmentation seems likely to continue. There could eventually be fifty members in this latter category unless recent trends are reversed. If all the smallest members combine, it would be possible for a bloc of states that contribute less than 2 percent of the total U.S. budget to control 56 percent of the votes in the General Assembly.[33] This discrepancy between voting power and political-economic responsibility has evoked several proposals for reform, so that voting might reflect not only the number of states but also total population and total economic potential.

Small states are often able to exercise negative rather than positive influence within the international system by threatening, obstructing, or supporting one of two rivals. A small country might deny the flow of a commodity on which others are dependent; it might interfere with international communications by closing off a waterway; it might decide to nationalize a foreign enterprise, or expel foreign nationals, or give to a major power the right to establish a military base on its territory, or provide a haven for guerrilla forces waging an insurgency against a neighboring government. Small states and mini-states usually try to maximize their leverage by aggregating it with that of similar states—for example, by pooling their voting power in a bloc against the West or against the superpowers in the United Nations. Most small states generally prefer to avoid being caught in conflicts between external major powers. Although a few might be tempted at times to play one rival off against another, they normally do not wish to see their territories converted into actual battlegrounds. Occasionally, however, a small state (or a weaker middle power) might do something in clear defiance of a great power. In such a case, a glaring discrepancy of power capabilities between the offender and the offended can produce sympathy and support for the "underdog" actor.

INTERNATIONAL AND REGIONAL FUNCTIONAL ORGANIZATIONS

By "international functional organizations" here we mean those that aspire to universal or transregional membership. Since World War II, analysts of international relations have not hesitated to assign the role of actor to a number of entities that would not have been accorded such a title in earlier times, when only nation-states qualified. Not all of them are important in the traditional power sense, but they are important as processors of global issues—processors not so much of decisions on a global scale as of international communications which can produce significant effects in the decision-making centers (the capitals) of member states. Indeed, these organizations often serve as the storm centers of debate over issues of global concern. The International Bank for Reconstruction and Development (IBRD or the "World Bank") has played this role in international development assistance; the Food and Agriculture Organization (FAO) and the World Food Council have served in the effort to coordinate policies for the alleviation of food shortage emergencies, the creation of international grain reserves, and the development of policies to improve agricultural production. Organizations established at the intergovernmental level may develop such a reputation for professional and technical competence as to enable national governments to rely upon them in the implementation of common purposes agreed to by treaty or convention. A prime example is the International Atomic Energy Agency, with headquarters in Vienna, which under the Non-Proliferation Treaty (signed by about a hundred countries) plays a significant part, through its safeguards system, in ensuring that treaty signatories comply with those provisions prohibiting the diversion of nuclear materials from authorized peaceful purposes to unauthorized military weapons programs. Even though a particular government, such as the United States, may not be entirely satisfied with the verification standards, it must acknowledge that in a world in which the standards of most governments are less demanding than its own, a verification system that may be only 90 percent effective is better than none. Other important international functional organizations include the International Labor Organization (ILO), the World Court, the World Health Organization (WHO), and the International Civil Aviation Organization (ICAO).

Mention should be made of two international organizations which lie somewhere between the universal membership and the regional categories. The first is the Commonwealth, successor to the old British Empire and to the former British Commonwealth of Nations. This entity, which was for a few decades an association of states based on traditional political, legal, and administrative arrangements, symbolic and sentimental ties, and mutual economic interests, has declined in importance as a pluralistic actor. The decline has been due to a number of factors: Britain's own waning role in world affairs, differences between the Conservative and Labour Parties over Commonwealth policy emphases (the former looking principally to the old English-speaking dominions and the latter to the newer Third World members), tensions in Britain over immigration from Commonwealth countries, racial antagonisms between white and nonwhite populations, the desire of formerly subordinate peoples to chart a course of their own, and the reorientation of the United Kingdom toward Europe as the Continent replaced the Commonwealth in the pattern of foreign trade.

The second is the continuing machinery which grew out of the 1964 United Nations Conference on Trade and Development (UNCTAD). At the 1964 Geneva meeting, attended by 2,000 representatives of 119 states and convened to discuss the economic relations of the richer and the poorer nations, the less developed countries of Asia, Africa, and Latin America joined forces to pursue a common strategy in demanding a fundamental reshaping of the world trading system.[34] This original "Group of 77" retained its name, although eventually it came to count in its ranks more than a hundred LDCs. The Group called for a reversal of trends that were making increasingly unfavorable the terms of trade between the primary goods exports of the poorest countries and the manufactured goods exports of the most industrially advanced. Pressure was applied to obtain special tariff preferences for the exports of poor countries, international stabilization of prices, stepped-up economic development aid from the wealthy states, and greater representation by LDCs in such financial institutions as the International Monetary Fund (IMF) and such negotiating arenas as the General Agreement on Tariffs and Trade (GATT). In defensive reaction against the criticisms of the Group of 77, separate groupings were formed within UNCTAD by the Western industrialized states and by the Marxist economies of the Soviet bloc. (The latter were generally viewed by the 77 as richer than themselves, not as exploitative as the West, but as not able to be very helpful to them, either). UNCTAD and the Group of 77 produced a series of U.N. Special Sessions, the seventh of which led to the convoking of the Conference on International Economic Cooperation (CIEC) in Paris in late 1975 to institute a North–South dialogue on energy, raw materials, development, and finance. It is important to realize that in the North–South dialogue there are significant differences of interests and perspectives within each general grouping: among the LDCs between the oil-exporting countries and the oil-importing countries and among the highly developed states over the questions of setting a specific percentage of GNP as a target level for foreign aid and of accepting the concept of "indexation" (that is, linking the future levels of pricing for oil and raw materials to the level of inflation in the industrialized countries from which the LDCs buy the products of advanced technology needed for development).[35]

Regional organizations are actors within the global system, although with few exceptions their impact may be more regional than global. A regional organization arises out of a regional subsystem, defined by Romano Romani as "a group of actors that have proportionately more interactions among themselves than with others."[36] This is generally valid in the long run for political interactions within regions, but significant exceptions to the rule must be cited in the case of economic interactions. The members of the European Economic Community have attained a high degree of economic interaction and integration as well as a high degree of political interaction (but not integration). But other regions—some characterized by considerably greater cultural and linguistic homogeneity than Western Europe—have not yet achieved much economic interaction. This is particularly true of Latin America, the Arab states, and Black Africa. Although all three of these regions have at times achieved a general ideological-political unity of feeling and rhetoric with respect to a single overriding issue (Yanqui imperialism, Zionism, or white rule in Southern Africa), their efforts at economic integration have met with very limited success, if any, simply because the economies of most states in those regions are oriented not to each other but externally to the industrialized world.[37] Virtually all regions, even the most industrially advanced, experience within themselves a variety of centrifugal forces in the form of disagreements, disputes, or conflicts over boundaries; aspirations to leadership; traditional, conservative regimes versus modernizing or revolutionary governments; the interests of "haves" and "have-nots" (for example, oil and raw materials); the interests of coastal and landlocked states; religious, cultural, ethnic, and linguistic differences; socialist and market economies; differing patterns of relations with extra-regional actors; and different approaches to regional organization as well as to the means of pursuing what may be agreed upon as the region's major objectives (security, development, anti-imperialism, antiracism, etcetera). Thus it is a mistake to attribute monolithic unity to any regional functional organization, such as the Organization of American States (OAS), the Central American Common Market (CACM), the Latin American Free Trade Association (LAFTA), the Council of Europe, the European Economic Community (EEC), the Organization for Economic Cooperation and Development (OECD), the Arab League, the Organization of African Unity (OAU), and the Association of Southeast Asian Nations (ASEAN).[38] Even the North Atlantic Treaty Organization (NATO), the most highly integrated military alliance of independent states known in history, has at times experienced serious disagreements over the optimal political and military strategies for coping with the security threat which NATO was designed to meet.

TRANSNATIONALS AND MULTINATIONALS

Some writers in international relations would categorize all the international and regional organizations discussed above (which are intergovernmental in character) as "transnational" actors within the global system. Whatever action these organizations are capable of taking depends strictly upon decisions in the capitals of member states. Others prefer to limit the term "transnational" to nongovernmental organizations—those with subsidiaries, members, or operations in several states but in which governments do not directly participate. For these writers, even though transnationals interact constantly with governments and the two entities are subject to influence and pressure from each other, their formal decision-making processes are separate and distinct. The definitional controversy is really not important so long as we distinguish between intergovernmental and nongovernmental actors on the global scene. Examples of the latter include such humanitarian, business, labor, professional, and sports organizations as the International Red Cross, Lions and Rotary International, the International Chamber of Commerce, the International Confederation of Christian Trade Unions, the International Political Science Association, and the International Olympic Committee. More significant for the global political system are such religious groupings as the Roman Catholic Church, the World Council of Churches, and various bodies of Judaism and Islam—all of which are constantly compelled to take positions on issues of global concern.[39]

Among the transnationals, it is the far-flung multinational corporations (MNCs) such as the oil companies (Exxon, Gulf, British Petroleum, Royal Dutch Shell), the global airlines (Pan-Am, TWA, BOAC, KLM), and the huge international mining, communications, and manufacturing enterprises (Anaconda, International Telephone and Telegraph, Dow Chemical, General Motors, Renault, Volkswagen, and many others) that have emerged as politically the most controversial class now operative within the global system. MNCs have been praised and defended for facilitating the transfer of technology from the industrially more advanced to the less developed nations, for providing jobs and training in technical and managerial skills, for raising the standards of production and living in the Third World, for increasing the export capabilities of LDCs and otherwise easing their balance of payments problems, for strengthening modernizing elites and thus contributing to international peace, trade, development, and cooperation. MNCs have also been criticized and condemned for serving as instruments of neo-imperialist oppression in the Third World, for introducing technology that is often not relevant, for raising local capital and exporting the earnings to the home-base country, for failing to place local nationals in top management positions, for creating new privileged classes oriented to Western capitalist consumerism, and for interfering in the policy-making processes of the host countries. The apologists for MNCs have probably claimed too much, just as their detractors have granted too little. Regardless of whether one admires or despises MNCs, it must be conceded that they have become a significant class of actors on the world scene. Moreover, despite the frequent references to the power of MNCs host countries have learned that they can impose conditions upon the MNCs with respect to the employment of nationals, the domestic sale or export of products, taxation and the expatriation of earnings, and other policies. If MNCs can be used by home-base governments to put pressure upon LDCs, host countries can also use the MNCs as intermediaries to influence the policies of home-base governments.[40]

Dependencies, Illegal Groups, and Individuals

Lastly, the student's attention should be called to three other classes of "actors" in the global system—all of them more controversial among academic theorists of international relations than the actors described previously. The first includes the few score territories throughout the world that are still dependent. Most of them we scarcely hear about from one end of the year to the other (for example, Christmas Island, Saint Pierre and Miquelon, Guernsey, Faroe Islands, and Pitcairn Island). But some are important in their own right (such as Bermuda and Hong Kong). Others have been important because they became areas of international conflict during the period of transition to independence (for instance, Affars and Issas, now known as Djibouti, and Southwest Africa, now known as Namibia). Still others, like Spanish Sahara and the U. S. Trust Territory of the Pacific Islands, have given rise to international political issues in recent years and are likely to continue to do so in the future.

The second category encompasses parties, groups, and movements which especially in the earlier phases of their existence are more outside the global system than within it because they promote revolution or other violent opposition to the established order. The Communist International (Comintern) belonged to this category throughout its entire history, since it was not officially recognized by any government, not even the Soviet Union. Other entities in this class, denied diplomatic recognition by nearly all pre-World War II states, include the Viet Cong, the Algerian FLN, and the Malayan Races Liberation Army (MLRA), all of which have ceased to exist since the conflicts to which they were parties have been terminated, as well as revolutionary guerrilla organizations carrying on violent conflict, continuous or sporadic, against incumbent governments. The Palestine Liberation Organization and several of the liberation armies fighting in Africa may be acknowledged by a majority of the members of the U.N. General Assembly or by the Organization of African Unity, but they remain illegitimate in the eyes of older states within the international community. Hardest of all to classify, because they often cannot even be identified, are those highly organized and well-trained and -financed groups (such as the Red Brigade and Black September) which conduct terrorist activities.

The third group are prominent individual personalities: politicians, diplomats, revolutionary leaders, and others. Many purists in the field of international relations contend that individual persons are not actors in the strict sense but only derivatively through the states and organizations in whose name they act. Such purists may be quite right. But it cannot be denied that such figures as Woodrow Wilson, Lenin, Churchill, Stalin, de Gaulle, Hitler, Gandhi, Khrushchev, Mao, and Kissinger have put their imprint upon the system and imparted to the international politics of their age a quality or tone it would not have had without them.[41]

Actors and Issues

The global system emerges as an extremely complex one, one which does not lend itself to neat, logical analysis. It is characterized much more by pluralism and asymmetries than by any unity and symmetry. If we look across the entire world, we cannot but be struck by the diversity of geographical conditions, cultural and religious values, social structures, political systems, levels of economic development, and national perspectives born of historical experience, ideological indoctrination and psycho-social temperament. We have treated the "states of the world" as actors within the global system, distinguishing them primarily according to power ranking. But obviously the structure and behavior of actors within this single category will vary widely according to differences not only in power (a factor of particular interest to social scientists) but also in the other factors just mentioned. The typical behavior of the states of Western Europe is quite different from the typical behavior of the communist states, or the states of Latin America, or the states of Africa. Regional organizations will differ commensurately in their approaches to international problems and issues. Just as most states' decision makers are necessarily more concerned over internal problems than they are about regional issues, so most regional organizations are more interested in regional issues than in global ones. Although the global system has developed its technical communications network to a remarkably high degree, growth in the system's ability to carry on communication for the purpose of arriving at political consensus has lagged far behind.

The states of the world still find themselves in serious disagreement over the priorities to be assigned to various international issues, and these disagreements are reflected within regional organizations and universal membership organizations, and in the communications net of the global system as a whole, substantially fragmented as it is along the lines of ideological-political groupings or blocs. Neither states nor regional-functional groups that are in a relationship of rivals or adversaries can easily draw up an agenda for a discussion-negotiation of their concerns that will readily enable them to convert international relations from a zero-sum game into a non–zero-sum encounter. Globalists are wont to speak glibly of a growing awareness of "global issues" throughout the capitals of the world. At various times within the last decade it has been suggested that the world as a whole is gradually being forced to pay attention to and come to grips with the "real global issues"—the threat of nuclear annihilation; population expansion; the limits of growth to an industrializing process that consumes increasing amounts of raw materials, squanders energy resources, and poisons the human environment; the need to replace an obsolescent East–West conflict with a genuine North–South dialogue, and the urgent requirement to build an international organization fully adequate to cope with the global challenges of the present and future.

We must avoid being swept along by the compelling eloquence of the rhetoric to Pollyannish conclusions about the nature of the contemporary global system and naïve hopes as to what mere verbal exhortation can accomplish. The hard fact is that very few global issues have been recognized as such on a universal scale, and even then the recognition has scarcely penetrated very deeply into the inner decision-making processes below the level of public speech-making. This is the case despite the ostentatious creation of specialized bureaucratic structures in Western countries (and nowhere else in the world) to plead special altruistic causes. Take, for example, the question of disarmament. Every government in the world publicly professes itself in favor. Yet no nuclear-weapon state acts as if it considers international nuclear disarmament a serious possibility for the foreseeable future, and when most of the non–nuclear-weapon governments deliver speeches at the United Nations about disarmament, they do so not with the ultimate intention of disarming themselves, but only to put pressure on the Great Powers to spend less on armaments and more on foreign development aid. Indeed, the discussion of many international issues is carried on in a similar atmosphere of hypocrisy and fraud on the part of all involved in the debate. It is important for students of international politics to acquire an appropriate skepticism of contemporary world political rhetoric (which is necessarily exaggerated to suit the demands of the mass media) and to study carefully the factors that limit change and the real possibilities for progress in resolving international issues.

It is essential for the student of international relations to study global issues in all their specific complexity, in particular reference to the pluralistic configuration of the global system. One should realize, as Robert L. Paarlberg has noted, that the "old issues of sovereignty and security continue to receive far more attention than any new agenda of global welfare management," principally because in the eyes of foreign policy leaders "such issues do not yield readily to interstate management."[42] The United States and the Soviet Union give high priority to the requirements for the maintenance of security through strategic deterrence in the nuclear age. The West Europeans, if they take strategic deterrence for granted, are somewhat more concerned than their American protector about preventing the theater balance in their region from tilting so sharply against them they they might become vulnerable to the process of "Finlandization." All the Western allies and Japan have been deeply worried about oil and energy since 1973, and again since the 1978–1979 political upheaval in Iran, but the allies berate the United States for its energy-guzzling proclivities and resent the fact that the alliance leader, which makes its Middle East policy without consulting them, may pursue a course that will disrupt their oil supply while the United States itself can fall back on coal reserves or effect substantial savings by cutting nonessential energy consumption.

For many years to come, the United States, the Soviet Union, and China are likely to focus greater attention on their triangular relationship, on the Sino–Soviet conflict in Asia, and upon their quadrilateral relationships with Japan and Western Europe than on issues of global welfare (population, energy, the development of LDCs, and pollution of the environment). The superpowers will have little choice but to continue striving toward arrangements for détente and the control of military competition—primarily in SALT, to a lesser degree in negotiations for mutual, balanced force reductions in Europe (MBFR), and still less in efforts to ban all nuclear tests and chemical weapons—or to regulate foreign arms sales and the levels of their forces in the Indian Ocean. The states of Black Africa will continue to assign top priority to the issue of white rule in Southern Africa, and they will join the LDCs of Latin America and Asia in calling for the creation of a new international order.

What is perhaps most fascinating for the student to ponder is the way in which the different issue priorities of various actors penetrate each other. During the first decade of the nuclear era, the United States, by promoting "atoms for peace," helped to lay the foundation for the "plutonium economy" and the potentiality for nuclear weapons proliferation which became an increasing cause for worry among U.S. policy makers. Since the 1960s, U.S. efforts to reduce the risks of proliferation by imposing international controls on the production of nuclear reactors and the export of nuclear supplies have led to controversy between the United States and allies such as West Germany and Japan, which see American nuclear policy interfering with their foreign trade. Several less developed countries, including India and Brazil, view the U.S. antiproliferation policy as a form of discrimination by the industrialized states.

The configuration of the global system is not a fixed thing. The system changes constantly. So do the numbers, the structures, and the policies of the actors. But the system does not undergo such rapid and fundamental change that the actors are unable to understand and adjust to the change. The change occurs in a continuum. There is a certain persistency in the goals and typical behavioral patterns of the actors that arises out of linkages between domestic realities and foreign policies.

Global Relationships

One of the central problems with which all analysts of international relations must deal is the degree to which the global system can be called an integrated entity. To what extent is there a sense of community that binds the international system together—a force capable of countering tendencies toward disintegration and fragmentation? These latter forces are always operative at every level of social-political organization. We can see them in the existence of rival guerrilla organizations in several African states where liberation movements are struggling against incumbent regimes; in the separatist or secessionist efforts of such subnational groups as the Walloons and Flemings in Belgium, the Basques in Spain, Scottish and Welsh nationalists in the United Kingdom, the Kurds in Iran and Iraq, the Pushtus in Afghanistan and Pakistan, the Nagas in India, the Eritreans in the Horn of Africa, and many others; and in the natural tendency of states or vested-interest groups to resist efforts aimed at increasing integration at any level. Religion enjoins humble obedience to the will of another, but it is a fundamental law of politics that "the will of another is always to be resisted." Perhaps, then, it is not too much to say that the overarching issue within the global system is that of rational order versus irrational chaos.

International theorists have come to speak of "social distance," employing transactions and communications as measures of this concept. Communication theorists observe the aggregate flow of goods, persons, and messages across territorial borders.[43] Michael Haas writes:

> One of the major hypotheses of communication theory, which is in part based on cybernetics and information theory, is that units interacting with each other at a very high level over a long period of time tend to develop positive affect for each other if mutual rewards for continuing to communicate exceed costs and loads. Positive affect leads to a harmonization of foreign policy goals and to the development of permanent institutions for the handling of interstate problems.[44]

It is generally assumed that when communication between parties is increasing, distance between them is decreasing and that the total amount of communication is directly related to the likelihood of cooperation or conflict de-escalation.[45]

There can be no doubt that modern communications and transport technology (movies, radio, TV, communications satellites, jet aircraft and supertankers), by reducing the costs of international distance, has rendered it theoretically possible for all parts of the globe to be united in an international community of interdependent societies characterized by a virtually unlimited expansion of exchanges in persons, goods, and ideas that would lead ultimately toward a universal homogenization of values, which is a necessary precondition for the creation of a genuine political community comprising the entire world. At the present time, that remains a very distant dream—not much less distant than it was when Dante first gave expression to it in the thirteenth century.

We know that the process of global integration has been extremely uneven. Virtually all countries carry on world trade, even though many do so on unfavorable terms, a fact that makes trade itself a factor for conflict as well as for cooperation. Many countries send and receive tourists, teachers, scientists, engineers, students, and businessmen. In all parts of the world, universities provide programs for studying the politics, economies, and culture of foreign countries. Nevertheless the process of decreasing international social distances has been carried much farther forward among certain segments of the global system than among others. Integration is not merely a matter of transaction in bills of sale, mail flows, and telephone calls. The sheer volume of transactions is important, of course, but in the final analysis qualitative factors are more significant than quantitative ones. Indeed, in many cases the qualitative relationships probably go far toward determining the direction of change in the quantity of communications and transactions by which two areas of the globe are judged to be "close" or "distant."

To a great extent integration or cohesiveness depends upon such noneconomic factors as culture, language, religion, political and ideological values, and security apprehensions. A common civilizational heritage helps to draw together the states of the Atlantic Community, of Latin America, and of the Arab World, and it is reinforced in the last two cases by a common language. Religion has long provided a bond of unity in the far-flung Islamic World. Even though Moslems have been internally divided by differences between Sunni and Shi'ite branches, Moslem leaders from many countries in recent decades have come together in international conferences in an effort to coordinate political positions on issues of common concern to them. The unifying influence of Christianity in the West, once dominant in medieval Europe, was attenuated for centuries as a result of the internecine wars of the Reformation and Counter-Reformation between Protestants and Catholics, but after World War II the ecumenical movement contributed to the success of Christian Democracy in Europe and to the growth of awareness that all heirs of the Judeo-Christian tradition have a common spiritual patrimony to defend against the forces of modern secularism, materialism, and militant atheism.

Europe was the home of modern virulent nationalism, but that force has exhausted itself. In the twentieth century nationalism has been on the rise in Asia, the Middle East, Africa, and Latin America, partly in reaction to colonial and imperial relationships, partly as a result of the fact that the elites of the colonial territories imbibed Western liberal ideas of freedom, sovereignty, and national self-determination, and partly because of the pervasive influence of the Leninist theory of imperialism, combined with Soviet support for wars of national liberation. Asian nationalism has often built upon pride in ancient civilizations, even where modern development ideologies would seem to contradict all traditional values. In view of the Sino–Soviet conflict, the conflict between India and Pakistan, the rivalry between Russia and China in Southeast Asia, and Japan's resentment over Soviet retention of former Japanese islands, it would appear that the quadrilateral relationship of the United States, the U.S.S.R., China, and Japan in Asia is potentially much less stable than the trilateral relationship of the United States, the U.S.S.R., and Germany in Europe.

In the Middle East and North Africa, a modern Arab nationalist upsurge has been powered by a spirit of political resentment against Western imperialism and Zionism. The latter is more a political than a religious phenomenon, but Zionism is inescapably related to Judaism, and thus the Arab–Israeli conflict has inevitably complicated the relations of Judaism with both Islam and Christianity. Moslems and Christians have had their own difficulties with each other in Lebanon and in states of Africa such as Chad and Eritrea, where religious communities have found themselves in political conflict or rivalry. Many observers have perceived in the Iranian revolution of 1979 a resurgence of Islamic nationalism which may be fraught with significance for future developments not only in the Persian Gulf region but far beyond. But within the more restricted Arab world itself, the conclusion of a peace treaty between Israel and Egypt after thirty years of war appeared to signal the ascendancy of Egyptian nationalism, in quest of Egypt's own national interest, over the brand of Arab nationalism formerly espoused by Nasser.

So far as conflict potential is concerned, Africa lies somewhere between relatively pacific Latin America and the high potential for conflict in Asia. With few exceptions, the states of Black Africa achieved independence without prolonged military struggles against the European colonial powers. Although Western observers had hoped for a while that those states might develop along democratic lines, armies, coups, and boundary disputes have become quite common in African political history. Africa abounds in ethnic-linguistic differences, and these contain considerable conflict potential, but the relative weaknesses of the African states have compelled them to accept boundaries inherited from the colonial era, however unsatisfactory they may be. What unites the Africans ideologically is the concept of *negritude* and opposition to white rule in Southern Africa. Nevertheless cooperation on this front is tempered by a variety of ethnic, political, religious, and personality differences which manifest themselves in the existence of rival revolutionary organizations. However opposed they may be ideologically to Western imperialism and "white solidarity," and however willing they may be to accept Soviet arms and Soviet and Chinese military training, many African leaders have learned how to operate within the global system by playing off one outside power against another. Moreover, they will not allow their ideological predilections to interfere with the pursuit of their countries' fundamental economic interests as they see them—witness the ties by which they have linked themselves to the Common Market in the Yaoundé and Lomé Conventions.

At this point we come back to the overarching U.S.–Soviet relationship within the global system. The two superpowers find themselves in a power rivalry in several areas of the globe now that the Soviets have achieved a naval mobility they did not previously possess. The U.S. government has become concerned in recent years over Soviet and Cuban activity in Africa and the Middle East. But the center stage of the superpower competition remains Europe, *simply because Europe is more vital to both than any other region of the world.* No matter how important Middle East oil may be for the convenience of American car drivers, the United States is much more likely to go to war with the Soviet Union over Europe than it is over the Middle East.

Europe emerged from World War II as a power vacuum into which the Soviet Union and the United States intruded and moved toward confrontation. Politically, economically, and militarily, Europe and Germany were divided to their depths: Western Europe has been characterized by political freedom and pluralism, parliamentary institutions, and a mixture of a market economy with moderate governmental regulation; Eastern Europe is ruled by authoritarian one-party systems. The two parts of Europe each have sought more integration within themselves than they have with each other, and at all levels the communications patterns are indicative of this condition. For security reasons, the Atlantic Community has managed to preserve cohesiveness despite growing differences between the United States and the Common Market over such economic issues as trade and monetary policies. The situation has undergone considerable change, of course. The dichotomy between East and West which had given rise to the international tensions known as the Cold War in the late 1940s and 1950s had given way to an ambiguous détente in the 1970s, reflected in U.S.–Soviet strategic arms limitations talks (SALT), the Berlin Quadripartite Accord, the German–Eastern Treaties and the Conference on Security and Cooperation in Europe (CSCE) which recognized the postwar territorial changes, and the effort to negotiate mutual and balanced force reductions (MBFR) between the two military alliances. There were recurring indications that the Soviet Union was interested in acquiring Western technology, although its willingness to make the kind of concessions demanded by the West, especially in respect to the rights of emigrés and dissidents, seemed limited. Meanwhile, as the superpowers sought to arrive at an agreement concerning the distribution of their strategic military power in SALT II, the West Europeans became more apprehensive over the theater balance between the two alliances in Europe, and over the "grey area" nuclear weapons which threatened Western Europe but which were not subjects of negotiation in SALT II. Not a few West European observers feared that their region might become neutralized or "Finlandized" in the shadow of Soviet power.

Everywhere throughout the global system, actors feel contrary tugs toward cooperation and conflict, toward accommodation and rivalry, toward inclusive and exclusive behavior. As the global communications net becomes more complex, the various actors within the system undoubtedly become increasingly aware of patterns of interdependence. But—to reiterate a point made earlier—interdependence furnishes no guarantee that actors will always prefer cooperation to conflict. Whether we are talking about trade, military preparedness, alliances, cultural exchanges, arbitration, or intervention, there are no phenomena in international relations that can be said to lead with inexorable certainty either to cooperation or to conflict. Military programs may serve to deter war or they may heighten tensions in such a way as to make war more probable. Trade and cultural exchange programs may contribute to international understanding, or they may add new irritants to existing hostility. Thus an increased awareness of global interdependence contains no promise of greater harmony among nations. Conceivably, it may do no more than furnish additional flashpoints at which human tempers might flare up in the direction of conflict. One can only hope that an increased sense of interdependence will help to strengthen the motivations of rational decision makers throughout the global system to manage inevitable conflict according to a sensible gain-versus-cost calculus that will enable the global system to remain in control of its destiny.

Notes

1. See the author's chapter, "The Study of the Global System," in James N. Rosenau, Kenneth W. Thompson, and Gavin Boyd, eds., *World Politics* (New York: Free Press, 1975), especially pp. 599–600. Donald E. Lampert, Lawrence S. Falkowski, and Richard W. Mansbach have recently made a useful suggestion concerning a multiple-system model based on a variety of actors and issues in world politics. "Is There an International System?" *International Studies Quarterly,* 22 (March 1978), 143–66. More will be said about this below.
2. In the closing quarter of the nineteenth century the leading Western actors were Great Britain, France, Germany, Russia, Austria-Hungary, the United States, Italy, and Spain. The Western press would also regularly report developments related to such nonwestern countries as Japan, China, Turkey, and Egypt.
3. The author is aware that the distinction between foreign policy and domestic politics has been criticized as unsatisfactory by some, for example, Eugene J. Meehan, "The Concept 'Foreign Policy' " in Wolfram F. Hanreider, ed., *Comparative Foreign Policy* (New York: David McKay, 1971), p. 284. Yet, however vague it may often be, the distinction appears inescapable and will probably remain common in the field of political science for a long time to come.
4. Modern political scientists and political sociologists who have drawn this sharp contrast between national systems and the international system include Max Weber, Hans J. Morgenthau, Raymond Aron, Stanley Hoffmann, A. F. K. Organski, Gabriel A. Almond, Inis L. Claude, Jr., and Richard Rosecrance.
5. David Easton, *The Political System* (New York: Knopf, 1953), pp. 129–141.
6. David Easton, *A Systems Analysis of Political Life* (New York: Wiley, 1965), p. 284.
7. Ibid.
8. Ibid., p. 487. See also Roger D. Masters, "World Politics as a Primitive Political System," *World Politics,* 16 (July 1964), 595–619.
9. See the editor's introduction in Romano Romani, ed., *The International Political System: Introduction and Readings* (Wiley, 1972), pp. 12–13.
10. Richard A. Falk, "Contending Approaches to World Order," *Journal of International Affairs,* 31 (Fall/Winter 1977), 171–75.
11. Hedley Bull, *The Anarchical Society: A Study of Order in World Politics* (New York: Columbia University Press, 1977), pp. 233–56. Lincoln P.

Bloomfield had earlier noted that the question of the feasibility of world government at present seems "totally academic," and he added: "Perhaps the most sobering consideration about world government is the nightmare prospect of world order at the price of world tyranny—a kind of global Holy Alliance to preserve the *status quo.*" "Arms Control and World Government," *World Politics,* 14 (July 1962), pp. 634, 643.

12. The following is but a partial list of writers in this century who have taken it for granted that power is a central organizing concept in foreign policy and international relations, even though some of them would have preferred to find an alternative approach: Raymond Aron, Hedley Bull, E. H. Carr, Inis L. Claude, Jr., Karl W. Deutsch, William T. R. Fox, Joseph Frankel, Ernst B. Haas, F. H. Hinsley, Stanley Hoffmann, K. J. Holsti, Stephen B. Jones, Bertrand de Jouvenel, Morton A. Kaplan, George F. Kennan, Robert O. Keohane, Henry Kissinger, Klaus Knorr, Harold Lasswell, George Liska, George Modelski, Hans J. Morgenthau, Reinhold Niebuhr, A. F. K. Organski, Norman D. Palmer, Donald J. Puchala, Richard Rosecrance, Thomas C. Schelling, Frederick L. Schuman, George Schwarzenberger, J. David Singer, Glenn H. Snyder, Nicholas Spykmann, Robert Strausz-Hupé, Kenneth R. Thompson, Vernon Van Dyke, Kenneth N. Waltz, Alan S. Whiting, Martin Wight, and Arnold Wolfers.

13. Dougherty, "The Study of the Global System," p. 603.

18. *World Armaments and Disarmament/SIPRI Yearbook 1978,* Stockholm International Peace Research Institute (London: Taylor and Francis, 1978), pp. 144–47.

19. Ibid., pp. 150–51, 154–55, and 160–61.

20. Michael P. Sullivan, *International Relations: Theories and Evidence* (Englewood Cliffs, N. J.: Prentice-Hall, 1976), pp. 161–64.

21. Stanley Hoffmann, "Notes on the Elusiveness of Modern Power," *International Journal,* 30 (Spring 1975), p. 183.

22. William D. Coplin, *Introduction to International Politics: A Theoretical Overview* (Chicago: Markham, 1971), p. 120.

23. See Chapter 1, "Interdependence in World Politics," in Robert O. Keohane and Joseph S. Nye, *Power and Interdependence: World Politics in Transition* (Boston: Little, Brown, 1977), pp. 3–22.

24. Ibid., pp. 12–13.

25. Ibid., p. 18.

26. Ibid., pp. 8 and 10.

27. William E. Griffith, ed., *The World and the Great Power Triangles* (Cambridge: M.I.T. Press, 1975).

28. *Strategic Survey 1976* (London: International Institute for Strategic Studies, n. d.), p. 2.

29. See Charles A. McClelland, "The Acute International Crisis," in Klaus Knorr and Sidney Verba, eds., *The International System* (Princeton, N.J.: Princeton University Press, 1961), pp. 182–204; Oran Young, *The Intermediaries: Third Parties in International Crisis* (Princeton, N.J.: Princeton University Press, 1967); Charles F. Hermann, "International Crisis as a Situation Variable," in James N. Rosenau, ed., *International Politics and Foreign Policy: A Reader in Research and Theory,* rev. ed. (New York: Free Press,

1969), pp. 409–21; Ole R. Holsti, *Crisis, Escalation, War* (Montreal: McGill-Queens University Press, 1972); Charles F. Hermann, ed., *International Crises: Insights from Behavioral Research* (New York: Free Press, 1972); and *International Crisis: Progress and Prospects for Applied Forecasting and Management,* edited by Robert A. Young, Special Issue of *International Studies Quarterly,* 21 (March 1977).

30. Ibid. (all citations).
31. See Joel Larus, ed., *From Collective Security to Collective Diplomacy* (New York: Wiley, 1965); James Barros, *The United Nations: Past, Present and Future* (New York: Free Press, 1972); K. J. Holsti, *International Politics: A Framework for Analysis* (Englewood Cliffs, N. J.: Prentice-Hall, 1977), pp. 488–507.
32. See John Temple Swing, "Who Will Own the Oceans?" *Foreign Affairs,* 54 (April 1976), pp. 526–46; Barry Buzan, "A Sea of Troubles? Sources of Dispute in the New Ocean Regime," Adelphi Papers No. 143 (London: International Institute for Strategic Studies, Spring 1978).
33. Elmer Plischke, "Microstates: Lilliputs in World Affairs," *The Futurist,* 12 (February 1978), 19–25.
34. For accounts of the origins of UNCTAD, see Richard N. Gardner, "The United Nations Conference on Trade and Development," *International Organization,* 22 (Winter 1968), 99–130, and Branislov Gosovic, "UNCTAD: North–South Encounter," *International Conciliation,* No. 568 (May 1968).
35. Michael Hudson, *Global Fracture: The New International Economic Order* (New York: Harper, 1977); Joan Edelman Spero, *The Politics of International Economic Relations* (New York: St. Martin's Press, 1977); Jagdish N. Bhagwati, ed., *The New International Economic Order: The North–South Debate* (Cambridge, Mass.: M.I.T. Press, 1977); William G. Tyler, ed., *Issues and Prospects for the New International Economic Order* (Lexington, Mass.: Lexington Books, 1977); W. Arthur Lewis, *The Evolution of the International Economic Order* (Princeton, N.J.: Princeton University Press, 1978).
36. Romano Romani, ed., *The International Political System* (New York: Wiley, 1972), Introduction, p. 27.
37. See Joseph S. Nye, "Patterns and Catalysts in Regional Integration" and "Central American Regional Integration," in Joseph S. Nye, ed., *International Regionalism: Readings* (Boston: Little, Brown, 1968); and E. Kanovsky, "Arab Economic Unity," in ibid.; Joseph S. Nye, "Comparing Common Markets," in L. N. Lindberg and S. A. Scheingold, eds., *Regional Integration: Theory and Research* (Cambridge: Harvard University Press, 1971), pp. 192–231.
38. See Louis J. Cantori and Steven L. Spiegel, *The International Politics of Regions: A Comparative Approach* (Englewood Cliffs, N.J.: Prentice-Hall, 1970); Joseph S. Nye, *Peace in Parts: Integration and Conflict in Regional Organization* (Boston: Little, Brown, 1971); Richard A. Falk and Saul H. Mendlovitz, eds., *Regional Politics and World Order* (San Francisco: W. H. Freeman and Co., 1973).
39. During the past decade, the Catholic Church has spoken out on such issues as liberation theology, military regimes and revolutionary movements in Latin America, conscientious objection to war, racism in Southern Africa, Ger-

many's postwar boundaries, world population growth, the arms race, development, and religious liberty and persecution in East Europe. The World Council, besides taking stands on many issues pertaining to international peace, human rights, and economic development, has experienced internal disagreements over the question of granting financial support to revolutionary liberation forces in Africa. Judaic groups have condemned *apartheid* in South Africa and worked to improve the status of Jews in the Arab world and also to facilitate Jewish emigration from the U.S.S.R. The Conferences of Islamic States have focused on the rights of Palestinians, the status of Jerusalem, and the conditions of Muslim minorities in the Philippines, India, Zanzibar, and elsewhere.

40. See Samuel P. Huntington, "Transnational Organizations in World Politics," *World Politics,* XXV (April 1973); George W. Ball, ed., *Global Companies: The Political Economy of World Business* (Englewood Cliffs, N.J.: Prentice-Hall, 1975); David E. Apter and Louis Wolf Goodman, eds., *The Multinational Corporation and Social Change* (New York: Praeger, 1976); Raymond Vernon, *Storm Over the Multinationals: The Real Issues* (Cambridge, Mass.: Harvard University Press, 1977); Louis Turner, *Oil Companies in the International System* (London: Allen & Unwin, 1978).

41. See Robert A. Isaak, *Individuals and World Politics* (Belmont, Calif.: Wadsworth Publishing, 1975).

42. Robert L. Paarlberg, "Domesticating Global Management," *Foreign Affairs,* 54 (April 1976), pp. 564–65.

43. Karl W. Deutsch, "Shifts in the Balance of Communication Flows: A Problem of Measurement in International Relations," *Public Opinion Quarterly,* 20 (Spring 1965), 143–160.

44. Michael Haas, *International Conflict* (New York: Bobbs-Merrill, 1974), p. 28.

45. Michael P. Sullivan, *International Relations: Theories and Evidence* (Englewood Cliffs, N.J.: Prentice-Hall, 1976), pp. 222–26.

2

Issues for Global Actors: The U.S.A.

Donald E. Lampert

AMERICAN FOREIGN POLICY following the twin national traumas of Vietnam and Watergate sometimes seems like an attempt by the United States government merely to catch up with the changing nature of global politics and the issues it presents. Not that the United States is necessarily unique in this regard. At the close of World War II Americans appeared able to define almost singlehandedly the issues on the global political agenda. Today such preeminence is a thing of the past with the American situation best summarized by phrases like "leadership without hegemony."[1] Whatever a foreign policy as usual might have meant before the 1970s, the United States government cannot return to it.

Vietnam and Watergate are ideal symbols in this regard. Vietnam involved the world outside America's borders. It demonstrated that the probabilities surrounding the exercise of successful influence had changed and that the global political agenda could no longer be dominated by the state-centricity of containment doctrines or falling dominoes. Watergate's significance was more internal in the sense of shedding light upon the decision-making process. The relationship between the United States government and the American society has now become so complex that what was perhaps the ultimate attempt to centralize leadership failed, no matter how often "the national security" might have been (artificially) invoked.

Too much can be made of symbols, however, and the symbolic watersheds which Vietnam and Watergate represent do not mean that the history of American involvement in global politics has ceased to be important analytically. Substantive themes like isolationism or the uniqueness of the American democratic mission continue to be evoked in the framing of foreign policy issues, although less so than the explicit ideological formulations employed by Marxist countries. Despite ongoing institutional tinkering, which may be inevitable and is probably desirable, structural arrangements relevant to the ways foreign policy issues arise and are disposed of stay very much the same. Most important, the United States remains a very polyarchic and highly advanced industrial democracy.

Historically commentators have pointed to democracy as no better than a mixed blessing for foreign policy purposes. There are at least two schools of thought on the question, the first associated with Federalists like James Madison and Alexander Hamilton. It views democratic government as a distinct disadvantage in foreign policy.[2] This "inefficiency argument" was given its most eloquent expression by Alexis de Tocqueville:

> For my part, I have no hesitation in saying that in control of society's foreign affairs democratic governments do appear decidedly inferior to others. . . . Foreign policy does not require the use of any of the good qualities peculiar to democracy but does demand the cultivation of almost all that it lacks. . . . [A] democracy finds it difficult to coordinate the details of a great undertaking and to fix on some plan and carry it through with determination in spite of obstacles. It has little capacity for combining measures in secret and waiting patiently for the result.[3]

The second school of thought, closely identified with President Woodrow Wilson, is variously labeled "idealism" or "legalism-moralism." It stresses the inherent goodness of democratic government, asserting that democracies naturally pursue peaceful foreign policies and enter into conflict only for self-defense. This "goodness argument" gained limited adherence even in Wilson's own time, and reaction against it formed a cornerstone of political realism's triumph as the dominant approach to American foreign policy following World War II. Walter Lippmann, for example, argued that placing foreign policy in "the people's hands" was of dubious virtue:

> The people have imposed a veto upon the judgments of informed and responsible officials. They have compelled the governments which usually

knew what would have been wiser, or was necessary, or was more expedient, to be too late with too little, or too long with too much, too pacifist
in peace and too bellicose in war, too neutralist or appeasing in negotiation
or too intransigent.[4]

Both the "inefficiency" and "goodness" schools are essentially normative, and neither has found widespread support in recent empirical
literature.[5] Moreover, political realism, which continues to dominate the
rhetoric and execution if not the analysis of American foreign policy,
appears increasingly at odds with the world it purports to explain. Incorporating much of the inefficiency argument, realism sees a unitary and
sovereign United States government as totally dominant over American
society. Like other national governments vying for position on a global
chessboard, the United States is supposed to possess an identifiable national interest which can be defined in terms of power. Thus, because the
United States has nuclear weapons that can annihilate any potential opponent, all possible issues are thought to be somehow ultimately reduci-
ble to military-security concerns.

Yet the issues in current global politics are not only military-security
matters, no matter how broadly defined or aggregated. National interests
and legalisms grounded in sovereignty are of limited value for understanding a world in which nonstate actors abound.[6] The analytic task has
become enormously complicated for scholar and policy maker alike.
Stanley Hoffmann suggested recently that "the single most striking feature of America's conduct in the world in 1978 was fragmentation."[7] This
comment need not be confined to 1978; fragmentation resulting from the
diversity of the issues composing the global political agenda has typified
the post-Vietnam/post-Watergate era. Comprehending its effects on
American foreign policy requires several theoretical perspectives.

Theoretical Perspectives

When ordering the issues on the global political agenda was largely an
American prerogative, analysis that explicitly took into account the comparative method may have seemed less necessary. Considered as unique,
the United States could be dealt with largely in descriptive terms—its
foreign policy the outplay of manifest destiny, crusades to make the world
safe for democracy, and so forth. From a comparative perspective like
the Rosenau pretheory, however, the United States is merely representative of a logical categorization: a large country with a rich economy and
an open polity.[8]

Using such categories provides us with an initial push in the direction
of explanation. Because the United States is a large, rich, and open soci-

ety, the relative weights of different variable types important for explaining foreign policy should exhibit a particular ranking. Least important are those "individual" characteristics exhibited by political leaders. The psychological differences between one American decision maker and another, even at the highest levels of the government, are associated largely in marginal ways with variations in patterns of foreign policy behavior. Consider, for example, that the well-studied rigidity of John Foster Dulles's perceptions of the Soviet Union exhibited "only a very moderate correlation" with actual American actions.[9]

Such individual variables may have profound impacts in particular situations like crises, but they are of less relevance for understanding the roles played by various issues in the creation of foreign policy patterns. Thus our analysis of American foreign policy will treat issues as "given" rather than as creations of individual decision maker perception, differing from those "subjective" approaches according to which issues "must be perceived as relevant to policy by people with influence over policy." [10]

Issues, actors, and *systems* are the three concepts that constitute a model with reference to which American foreign policy can be analyzed. *Issues* represent what behavior is about, and are defined as subject matters concerning which actors, the second concept, can desire a diversity of possible outcomes.[11] *Actors* are identified because of their ability to initiate autonomous behavior. They undertake purposeful actions which cross the frontiers of the United States or have an impact beyond them, even if the nature of the impact is not what is originally intended. This leads us to the kind of variables which Rosenau suggests to have the most significance for American foreign policy, those of the "societal" variety. These characteristics are typically operationalized in terms of indicators like degree of urbanized population or social homogeneity, but they take on a somewhat different meaning within the present context.

Societal variables highlight the extent to which the United States provides an arena for actors of various kinds. With advanced modernization has come a proliferation of nonstate actors representative of American society at large—interest groups, multinational corporations, the media, and so forth. The vast number of actors originating within the geographical confines of the United States engage in practically all issues in world politics. This means that virtually any organized group, be it part of the government or not, is relevant to the analysis of American foreign policy.

Most often, of course, the actors with which we are concerned are governmental in their origins. Yet individual governmental bureaucracies, or factions within them, can also meet the above criterion and be regarded as actors in their own rights. The impact of societal variables on American foreign policy thus becomes quite complementary with those of a governmental nature, and it can even be argued that "there is no difference in the relative importance of societal and governmental variables in accounting for foreign policy behavior."[12] Even though Rosenau's pretheory specifies "governmental" variables as secondary in significance to those of a societal nature, such a distinction may well be somewhat arbitrary. So many American actors, both governmental and nongovernmental, have autonomous impacts across the panoply of global issues that their product cannot really be aggregated. A single national interest pursued in the foreign policy of a unified United States Government simply does not exist.

One can make the same point about the extreme decentralization of the United States in contrast with other industrial democracies by approaching the question from a governmental as well as a societal perspective. American foreign policy involves executive agencies and governmental bureaucracies, not to mention Congress with its committees and issue-oriented cleavages that do not necessarily correspond with partisan divisions. The American political system in the view of Samuel Huntington is "antique," bearing "a closer approximation to the Tudor polity of the sixteenth century than does the British political system of the twentieth century." He continues: "In America, Tudor institutions and popular participation are united in a political system which remains as baffling to understand as it is impossible to duplicate."[13] The key is that authority is diffused throughout the American government in a number of somewhat multifunctional political structures. From a consideration of purely "domestic" politics (if such a thing may still be said to exist empirically rather than in the abstract), this may be an appropriate reflection of American society. For foreign policy purposes, however, this encourages participation from American nonstate actors on matters that otherwise might remain in governmental circles. The multifunctionality of governmental structure becomes an open invitation to the activities of nonstate actors which tend to be more functionally specific.

This profusion of actors and issues could make the subject of American foreign policy prohibitively complex were it not for the final analytic concept constituting our model. *Systems* are the highest level of abstraction useful for understanding American foreign policy and can be defined as unique concatenations of actors and issues recognizable through behavior. This definition emphasizes the primary analytical importance that issues have for discussing American foreign policy because it reveals the other facet of what is a dual theoretical role. Not only are issues related to the behavior of foreign policy actors, but the actions which issues elicit also facilitate the identification of global systems. In Rosenau's terms, "systemic" variables are third-ranking in importance for understanding American foreign policy, meaning that indicators based on trade patterns or alliance characteristics are of significance for explaining American foreign policy behavior because they convey a sense of systemic effects. Rosenau's suggestion that systemic variables are only third-ranking in importance behind societal and governmental ones therefore can be taken to imply the profound impact that the behavior of American actors have on the configuration of various global systems. What American actors do is far more critical to systemic patterns than systemic patterns are to American actors.

Juxtaposing issues, actors, and systems with the Rosenau pretheory raises questions of the overall logical fit the various concepts have with American foreign policy behavior. Basically, societal, governmental, systemic, and individual factors serve as the independent variables for explaining the foreign policy behavior of American actors. This behavior and the actors who undertake it become the components of global systems once issues are added to the picture. According to later work by Rosenau, foreign policy behavior can also be classified into patterns based upon the relative potency of one variable cluster rather than another.[14] Given the ordering, two overall strategies can be pursued by a large, developed, and open country—"preservative" and "intransigent." The basis for the distinction is the imperatives exhibited by an overall pattern of foreign policy behavior. In the case of the former, behavior reflects societal variables, being virtually determined by the internal composition of an actor. For the latter, foreign policy behavior can involve a high potency for any of the variable clusters other than the individual. It exhibits the attempt by an actor "to live within the limitations that its present structures and its present environment impose on each other (i.e., by preserving the existing equilibrium between them)."[15]

If we link the independent variables of American foreign policy behavior to the overall patterns that such behavior should exhibit, then the role of issues is essentially that of intervening variables. In other words, the nature of a given issue should be important in determining whether American behavior will exhibit the characteristics associated with intransigent or promotive foreign policy. Whereas no widely accepted and relatively straightforward approach to issue-typing exists, one dimension that continues to crop up is the extent to which the political goods related to an issue are predominantly tangible and subject to being divided.[16] Let us assume that the intervening variable of issue-type can have values of being either exclusively tangible or including aspects that are intangible and symbolic (having characteristics usually associated with public goods and collective benefits). This dimension can then be combined with Rosenau's suggestion that the dependent variable of American foreign policy actions will exhibit either intransigent or preservative patterns. The result is shown in Table 2.1.

The interesting thing about Table 2.1 is that it can be employed to derive the more common categories used by analysts to describe the kinds of issues with which American foreign policy is concerned. These categories are not exclusive because specific issues may well involve

Table 2.1
Nature of Issue and Foreign Policy Type

		DEPENDENT VARIABLE *Type of Foreign Policy*	
	TANGIBLE	INTRANSIGENT	PRESERVATIVE
		P	Economic
		o	
		l	
		i	
INTERVENING VARIABLE *Nature of Issue*		t	
		i	
		c	
		a	
	INTANGIBLE	Security	l

more than one such label or combination of intervening and dependent variables. Minimizing conflict with regard to food exports, for instance, has both an "economic" and a "political" side. The latter has to do with the pressures that may be exerted by actors within the United States to dispose of foodstuffs regardless of the most advantageous price, an intransigent strategy based upon treating the issue as purely tangible. Nonetheless the foodstuffs and the price they bring may also be looked at in more purely economic terms because adjustments have to be made for global marketing conditions as well as the value of the dollar.

A similar point can be made with regard to "security" issues. Such matters as the long-run strategic balance with the Soviet Union involve ideological contexts reflecting persistent concerns emanating from past Cold War environments. At the same time, when such issues are viewed within a more preservative light, they involve differential impacts of one weapons system as opposed to another, the reactions of NATO allies to more particularistic bargaining relationships, and so forth. In this way intangible concerns of security are transposed into a political context in which grand strategies can become subservient to short-run bargaining advantages.

It is noteworthy that the political category cuts across both types of issues and includes foreign policy behavior of the intransigent as well as the preservative variety. This predominance of politics in American foreign policy can be supported by examining how the world looked from a systemic perspective to American foreign policy decision makers in the 1970s. A little more than half of the issues discussed in the journal *Foreign Policy* throughout the 1970s were posed in terms involving their political ramifications.[17] Roughly 30 percent were economic in nature. What is at first surprising is that security issues appeared to merit so little attention, only 13 percent in 1978 and 20 percent across the decade. Yet Table 2.1

suggests a reason why this may be so—the relatively less probable combination of issues with intangible aspects and foreign policy behavior manifesting intransigent patterns. That America's physical security appears to be lacking in salience for analysts of United States foreign policy only begins to suggest the changing nature of the issues on the global political agenda. Before dealing with these issues themselves, however, the current situation of the United States in world politics merits our examination.

Involvement in the Global System

The United States remains the government most heavily involved in the host of issues that make up the global political agenda. Nor is such heavy involvement limited to the government. Nonstate actors with American origins continue to make their presence felt, particularly in economic terms. As a result, the dominant theme in the relationships to the outside world this heavy involvement entails seems best reflected in the chant of sports fans: "We're Number 1." This feeling has a historical basis. So-called isolationist periods have been infused with a sense of superiority reminiscent of the early Puritans, and similar emotions are also shown when internationalism predominates, giving interventionist experiences the character of moral crusades.

By the early days of the Cold War, of course, isolation from global responsibilities was no longer considered a viable option, something about which a widespread consensus existed for more than two decades. Yet whether or not a "neo-isolationism" emerged in the aftermath of the Vietnamese quagmire, in recent years the inherent belief in American superiority has been challenged. The world has changed, and even the characteristic chant appears to have lost its verve:

> The optimistic view of America's current situation in the world is really a valid one only if Americans can be made to recognize the truths in the pessimistic view. There is an urgent need to impress on Americans that we are part of a small island of immensely talented and productive people living in a quite poor and populous world, and that the ratio is daily changing against us. . . . If, as the pessimists say, our condition is steadily worsening, then we must solidify ties with our friends before entering the fray with our adversaries.[18]

The list of friends and adversaries of the United States has remained largely unchanged since the inception of the Cold War, but the connotations relevant to each term have become increasingly murky. Vincent Davis has suggested that two of the fundamental questions asked by American decision makers at the close of World War II were: "(1) Are there any new enemies?—and, if so, who or what are they? (2) Are there friends?—and, if so, who or what are they?"[19] The answer to both questions was easy initially. "The enemy" was the Soviet Union, to which was added within a matter of months the communist states of Eastern Europe, China, and Korea. The ensuing decade brought a similar status for North Vietnam and finally Castro's Cuba. "Friends" were the former great powers, France and Great Britain, the other industrial democracies of Western Europe, the recently vanquished enemies, Japan and what would become the Federal Republic of Germany, as well as the host of other then extant states, especially those in Latin America and Asia which professed "anticommunism."

The breakup of the colonial empires in the late 1950s and early 1960s and the creation of a host of new, and potentially unstable, states in its wake was not all that complicating for the identification of friends and enemies. The newly independent Third World merely provided a different arena for the globalization of the Cold War, as in the Congo. The main contestants, the United States and the Soviet Union, would continue to face each other on opposite sides of the East–West cleavage wherever one or both was heavily involved, the Middle East being a notable example. "Nonalignment" was basically to be ignored or scoffed at, the former for states with little perceived value as coalition partners and the latter for those who would find out who their friends really were if the chips were down.

The bankruptcy of such dichotomized thinking was later shown in the Vietnam war's minimal effect on détente with the Soviet Union, and the beginnings of normalization with the People's Republic of China. By now, at least insofar as military-security issues are concerned, it is difficult to disagree with the assessment: "The second question—do we have any reliable allies?—is fairly easy to answer on the face of it, and the answer is no, and the answer is probably the same for the USSR. The key word here is *reliable*."[20] Or, as former Senator Eugene McCarthy put it, "the fact is that the United States has few, if any, true allies. What it has instead is a number of nations that it maintains in a dependency relationship."[21] Even if such observations overstate the case somewhat, changes in global politics have rendered the United States relatively less dominant vis-à-vis its allies. The accoutrements of being "Number 1" are no longer a foredrawn conclusion.

Trying to identify the current friends and adversaries of the United States has become a complicated task because the list differs according to the nature of the foreign policy issues under consideration. Since the Cuban missile crisis it has become increasingly unlikely that a nuclear war will erupt between the United States and the Soviet Union, and East–West confrontations have almost come to resemble ritualized behavior. This provides at least a surface explanation for the lack of reliable allies

—American friendship just does not seem to be as needed as at the height of the Cold War. Indeed, even if not overwhelmingly successful, superpower consultations about matters such as nuclear proliferation and arms limitation have a high symbolic value. Furthermore, establishment of diplomatic relations with the People's Republic of China represents the crumbling of another pillar of the Cold War environment, indicating that even interaction with adversaries is becoming less strident. In a more moderate global political climate friendship and enmity are not as clear-cut.

Despite this, there can be little doubt that major affinities exist among the United States and the industrial democracies of Western Europe, as well as Japan. Yet the existence of affinities does not mean that relationships will be purely cooperative. It is noteworthy also that the United States remains identified to a greater or lesser extent with various "pariah states," Israel, South Africa, South Korea, and Taiwan, although the possibilities of future American involvement for security reasons appear greater in the cases of the first and third. What has most complicated the identification of American friends and adversaries, however, is that military-security issues are no longer the sole stuff of foreign policy.

There are two interrelated aspects to this problem. The first is the emergence of the North–South cleavage, the division of the world into the relatively well-off countries north of the equator and the less developed world south of it. This cleavage cuts across the Cold War division of East and West because comparatively the economic lot of the Soviet Union and its Eastern European allies has improved. By 1976 the per capita GNP of the Soviet Union was a mere $280 less than that of the United Kingdom, and the average for the countries of Eastern Europe only $500 less than the Soviets.[22] This means that various actors on both sides of the East–West cleavage have certain common interests above and beyond the prevention of mutual assured destruction. Whereas the Pentagon may still have its budget "made in Moscow," American farmers are more concerned with grain sales, and Soviet advocates of greater consumer good production attempt to acquire American technologies. These kinds of exchanges of goods and services could not characterize interaction between societies at very disparate levels of modernization. Vodka and cola are a fair trade only when markets exist in which they can be consumed.

The second aspect is much more complex: the increased importance of economic and what may be referred to loosely as developmental issues. Whether such issues have become the major concern for the American foreign policy agenda need not involve us, but the importance of economic issues is readily understandable. The United States contributes almost one-fourth of the world's total GNP, but its annual rate of growth since 1964 is roughly 2 percent below the total for six other developed countries.[23] The dollar remains the world's standard currency, although its value has declined dramatically and with it American trade balances. The 1971 Smithsonian Agreement, which accepted the dollar's inconvertibility into gold but attempted to preserve some semblance of a fixed rate exchange system, was a shambles within two years. The situation worsened with successive increases in the price of oil, and 41 percent of the total deterioration in United States bilateral trade balances from 1975 to 1977 was attributable to the oil exporting countries.[24] By 1976 the international reserves held by the United States were less than they were in 1960, and, while they recovered somewhat from the depths of 1971–1973 these figures do not reflect the impact of inflation.[25]

Such dismal economic performance has been another profound shock to America's image of itself. Part of the reasons for the shock are historical and reflect faulty generalization from traditional and virtually total predominance in the Western hemisphere. The Monroe Doctrine may originally have been enforceable only through the good graces of the Royal Navy, but as years passed it was seen as a formula that could be globalized. When America looked outward at the turn of the century it seemed to be assumed that even economic competition would lead inevitably to triumph, something reflected in the Open Door Notes regarding China.[26] Since then the United States has had great difficulty adjusting to rivalry not just in economic terms. This is no better illustrated than the intensity of public reaction to Castro's Cuba or Allende's Chile, or the recent vociferous debate about the Panama Canal Treaties. Yet the evolution of the American position in the current global political economy has meant that certain rivalries are now inevitable, affecting relationships with friends and potential allies as well. Marina Whitman has suggested:

> [T]he postwar international economic system, created under the unchallenged leadership of the U.S., grounded in the American principles of economic liberalism, and dependent on the special roles played by this country in several different dimensions, appears to be in disarray. And there are pressures for the United States to forswear not only dominance but leadership as well. . . . But any special U.S. role must be grounded in a clear understanding of the changed international realities; a leadership position created under conditions of military and economic dominance can continue effectively only if it can be successfully adapted to an environment in which more and more countries have made the transition from dependence to partnership, and to partnership's other face, rivalry.[27]

The difficulty the United States government has in adjusting to changing conditions in the global economy is illustrated well by American behavior with regard to the negotiations surrounding the New International Economic Order (NIEO). The subject itself demonstrates the extent to which the two aspects of military-security issues are interconnected. The spur for NIEO emanates from actors on the south side of the North–

South cleavage, the Group of 77, and the issues concerned are economic ones. While the United States government continues to express dissatisfaction with the global state of economic affairs, in these negotiations it has advocated no more than tinkering. In fact, the United States appears less willing to endorse change than some of its northern partners like Canada or the European Economic Community, prompting some analysts to view American policy with almost an air of disbelief: "The US still hopes to break apart the 77 coalition. . . . [T]he adaptations to the existing order proposed by the US are designed to preserve the essential characteristics of the post-World War II economic system, not alter them."[28]

NIEO reveals the dilemmas surrounding the American role in the current global economy. It has become almost dogma to attribute these dilemmas to the American inability to cope properly with a rise in global "interdependence." Like the NIEO, interdependence is supposed to describe an overall situation. Emphasis on overall conditions, however, fails to take into account particular circumstances. This is one reason for the American expectation that the Group of 77 will succumb to factionalism and the tremendous diversity in the economic circumstances of its members. In the American case, interdependence implying a greater partnership with others actually masks the specifics of the American stake in the global economy becoming more concentrated.[29] There is a continued reliance on a few suppliers of certain raw materials at the same time that the United States has become more sensitive to the economies of other developed countries in terms of manufactured goods.

These dilemmas have both a philosophical and a practical side. Philosophically, the United States in the post-World War II period has been the staunchest supporter of free trade policies based upon economic liberalism. Accordingly, market conditions are supposed to reign supreme as goods and services move across state boundaries with minimal restrictions. Direct governmental roles should therefore be minimal, except for participation in the kinds of international organizations like the International Monetary Fund (IMF) or the later General Agreement of Tariffs and Trade (GATT) envisioned by the creators of the Bretton Woods international economic regime. Such international organizations represent the institutionalization of assumptions based on the belief that all countries have a stake in a stable international economic order. Even if the prelude to World War II revealed the flawed assumptions on which collective security had been based, analogous assumptions about economic affairs were obviously still alive and well in its aftermath. Today the dominant American attitude remains that philosophically everyone is in the same boat, exacerbating tensions on both sides of the North–South cleavage. For example, Robert Keohane and Joseph Nye maintain that "management of a stable international monetary system comes close to being a public good, that is, all states can benefit from it without diminishing the benefits received by others. To the extent that states perceive a public good from which they all gain, they tend to be more willing to accept leadership."[30]

Practical dilemmas, however, surround American ability to exercise the kind of leadership it did for the establishment of the Bretton Woods regime, no matter how willing various others might be to accept it. The causes are complex, although the dilemmas' aspects can be summarized quite succinctly. In Whitman's words, "the events of 1978 suggest a sharpening of the tension between our commitment to these long-term principles on the one hand and our pursuit of specific short-term economic and political goals on the other."[31] These short-term goals involve the tradeoff that American political leaders are willing to make between inflation and unemployment. Tracing the historical origins of this situation can bring about an almost infinite regress. Suffice it to say that the 1973 quantum jump in the price of oil (and other commodities as well) plunged the world into a recession, from which recovery has been extremely uneven. The United States was plagued by inflationary pressures during this recovery period, although somewhat less so than other industrialized countries like Great Britain or Italy. Initially the American response was to tolerate higher than desired levels of unemployment in order to curb inflation. Yet conditions of "cost-push" and "price-push" have continued to persist, and, as John Pinder argues, this necessitates "some control of prices and incomes."[32] The Carter Administration, and one would suspect any other American administration as well, found such wage and price controls politically impossible.

The effects have not only been dislocations in the domestic American economy but also, more importantly, the persistent abysmal performance of the dollar on foreign exchange markets. Nor are these two phenomena unconnected, as the strong performances of such currencies as the West German mark and the Japanese yen illustrate. These strong performances have taken place despite the greater initial impact of the oil crisis on these two economies. Indeed, this provides a certain amount of implicit support for Pinder's position. American attempts at recovery have produced higher economic growth rates, thus spurring inflationary pressures, while the slower growth rates of Germany and Japan indicate economies subject to greater control. American decision makers have been left in a somewhat anomalous position. While seeking to preserve preeminence in the global economic system, something that even continued poor performance of the dollar cannot remove because the United States remains the world's largest economy in gross terms, American decision makers have nonetheless tried to entice other countries to take the lead in economic recovery.

In a sense, therefore, the practical difficulties of the American economic position are philosophical also. They have to do with the ways that

American actors view the world, namely, in moralistic terms based on a special position for the United States. Juxtaposed with a symbolic assumption of American superiority, an unsound dollar becomes extremely difficult for some to comprehend. Just as American actors continue to be those most heavily involved in the many issues in global politics, the dollar, even if unsound, persists as the world's standard of exchange. If there is a single overall generalization to be drawn from America's economic woes, it is that the unique requirements of the American polity are out of step with global circumstances. In order to gain a greater insight into what is perhaps this ultimate dilemma, the American political system and the ways in which foreign policy issues percolate through it merit examination.

Sources of Issues

In an ideal sense, foreign policy is always a *response* to circumstances in global politics. Traditional analysts of foreign policy may have found that they could argue for ignoring its "domestic context," although current circumstances reveal that such a separation from "the international" is surely arbitrary; foreign policy action represents a variable mixture of both. Issues and events might exist "out there" for American governmental foreign policy decision makers, but unless they are cloaked in secrecy (as at the inception of the Cuban missile crisis) they are likely to be recognized by some domestic nonstate actors before the wheels of the government itself begin fully to turn.

The extent to which "the public," rather than the government alone, becomes involved in American foreign policy is determined by the nature of the issue. All other things being equal, the greater the tangibility of an issue, the larger the public role. The overall magnitude of this involvement is difficult to estimate, although a recent study suggests that "a segment of the general American public has sufficient interest in and adequate knowledge about foreign policy that the individuals within that segment can maintain considerable control over foreign policy. We have seen that as much as 30 percent of the public (although generally a smaller percentage) fits into such a category."[33] Yet such findings should not be taken as *prima facie* evidence against elitist interpretations of the foreign policy process because it is not an amorphous public that acts. The public is "represented," albeit circuitously, in the behavior of identifiable actors. Many of these actors are nonstate in origin, such as interest groups and multinational corporations. Their behavior does not necessarily have to be directed toward or even channeled through the United States government. In this sense, any actor can have *its own* foreign policy.

A provocative attempt to demonstrate public involvement in American foreign policy by Barry Hughes focuses not only on issue type but also on decision time and the locus of governmental decision-making activity.[34] While the latter two variables could well be related to the first, Hughes does evolve a fairly workable eightfold typology by dichotomizing the importance of economic considerations, the security/nonsecurity quality of an issue, and short/long decision time. Public involvement in gross terms was found to be greatest when economics were important for security issues with long decision time (defense budget size). It was less but still somewhat significant for similar issues with short decision time (Marshall Plan) or longer term, nonsecurity issues for which economic considerations were important (tariffs). Put somewhat differently, these basic findings suggest that public involvement tends to be highest for foreign policy issues on which there is significant Congressional impact.

Impact, however, is quite distinct analytically from the assumption of a Congressional role as a major source for foreign policy issues. To be sure, there are occasions when individual legislators take the lead in crystallizing positions. Most often, though, these occasions merely reflect the peculiarities of a given constituency or the special relationships certain legislators maintain with particular nonstate actors. Congressional activities remain essentially reactive, despite the fact that the last several years have witnessed something of a resurgence by the Congress in the foreign policy process.

Even the causes for Congressional resurgence have been essentially reactive. The imperial presidency simply went too far. The effects are more difficult to judge.[35] In an ideal sense, the circumstances of the post-Watergate era might have increased the possibilities for more meaningful Congress–Executive partnership in the rebuilding of foreign policy consensus. Congressional weakness was thought to have provided too great a temptation to imperial presidents, so measures were taken to bolster congressional resources. Staffs were increased, the Congressional Budget Office created, and various other specific measures enacted—among them the 1973 War Powers Act, the 1976 National Emergencies Act, and the creation of Select Intelligence Committees in both the House and Senate. The common rationale was that Congress's primary need was more information, much of it thought to reside in arcane recesses of the Executive branch. Once greater access to information was assured, Congress's role could become more equal.

Reality proved not to correspond with this ideal, something which can be highlighted in at least three ways. First, greater access to information was not a magical solution and in the opinion of some merely ended up revealing the extent to which "Congress has been constipated by an inefficient decision-making structure and process."[36] This was particularly true for intelligence oversight functions. Despite attempts at centralization, intelligence agencies, the CIA in particular, remained leery of allowing the Congress to "know too much." Given the altered institutional circumstances, reports abound of malaise in the intelligence community, prompting its Congressional champions to call for a reversal of the trend to greater oversight in the wake of "the loss of Iran."

Criticism of too much actual and/or potential oversight illustrates a second consideration, the extent to which greater access to information may serve only to provide more fuel for partisan fires. The postwar norm of bipartisanship may have served as something of a sham, a political bludgeon wielded by the Executive to keep Congress in line. Nonetheless, before the peak of Vietnam dissension the bipartisan norm could be employed with relative ease by granting greater access to relatively few influential legislators. By 1979, however, influence in Congress had become more diffuse, and this was complicated by the continuing precipitous decline in party discipline. One of the few things Republican legislators could agree on in the late 1970s was eschewing the bipartisan norm in the face of a Democratic President who appeared vulnerable on significant foreign policy questions. As usual, their Democratic counterparts could not agree on analogously banal generalities. If greater congressional access to information might have been supposed to nudge the American polity in a slightly more parliamentary direction, its real effects have been to place its peculiarities in ever starker relief. Lacking a substantive "rationale" with which the various strands of foreign policy can be woven together, the Congress has fostered greater American "incoherence":

> [S]ecrecy remains essential for diplomacy, especially in dealing with regimes that insist on it and in the expeditious resolution of conflicts—but secrecy and congressional consultation are mutually exclusive. . . .[D]iplomatic agreements are usually deliberate exercises in ambiguity, each side agreeing to leave certain conflicts in the dark, with the intention of reaping immediate gains from what could be agreed upon, and the hope of later resolution to its own advantage: witness Camp David or the subtle formula adopted by Washington over Taiwan. But Congress prefers floodlights to the delicate flashlights of diplomats, and tends to insist on the immediate clarification of issues.[37]

Despite its resurgence, therefore, this penchant for issue clarity serves to reinforce the conclusion that Congress will continue as essentially reactive rather than as a source for foreign policy issues. This leads to a final point concerning the issue-specificity of the Congressional role and its relationship to the behavior of American nonstate actors. The involvement of the "average" Congressman or Senator in the foreign policy process, like that of most nonstate actors, takes place on an issue-by-issue basis. Many of those most involved, for example, in issues related to American support for Israel will not be very much in evidence with regard to Panama Canal Treaties or Strategic Arms Limitation Talks (SALT). As a result, the White House or the foreign affairs bureaucracies can manipulate access to the decision-making process in order not only to reinforce their own preeminence but also to build cross-issue coalitions. The lower salience of foreign affairs makes such coalitions more difficult in the Congressional context. Congressional mechanisms, like public hearings, provide more open forums in which nonstate actors can have greater impact, although they may have other disadvantages.

When more actors, both governmental and nongovernmental, become involved with a foreign policy issue, coalitional possibilities proliferate and the likelihood of outcomes satisfactory to nobody increase. This creates a disincentive for legislators to get out front on foreign policy issues too soon, because it serves as an open invitation to make them easy targets. Congressional involvement becomes cautious, often muddying the waters, exactly the opposite of what a desire for issue clarity would demand. These overly compromised outcomes are stressed by critics deprecating the effects of democracy in American foreign policy-making. The alternative to Congressional impact such critics seem to have in mind is the true "commander-in-chief," the archetypical "strong President," who can bend others to his will, setting a national issue agenda and mobilizing virtually all of American society at the same time. In the post-Watergate United States, however, such a figure would more likely than not breed suspicion rather than compliance.

Moreover, bureaucratic politics also result in compromises. Even the strongest of presidents have had their difficulties navigating bureaucratic waters, something illustrated by President Franklin Roosevelt's apocryphal remark that dealing with the Navy was "like punching a feather bed. You punch it with your right and you punch it with your left until you are finally exhausted and then you find the damn bed just as it was before you started punching."[38] This raises the question of bureaucratic responsiveness and the effects of the bureaucracy as a source of issues in American foreign policy. Nelson Polsby has pointed out the extent to which the make-up of the original Carter cabinet manifested a "curious neutrality" to political forces in a position to place demands on it, something which illustrates yet another peculiarity of the American system:

> Presidents and their political appointees have frequently puzzled over making the enormous apparatus of the executive branch responsive to their will. The legitimacy of this claim is based upon the results of the last election; presumably a president is elected and makes appointments, at least in part, to carry out his promises with respect to the future conduct of public policy, and the necessary instruments of that conduct reside in the unelected agencies of the executive branch.[39]

Those bureaucracies with the greatest relevance for foreign policy (State, Defense, Treasury, and the National Security Council), even under President Carter's cabinet staffing strategy, largely remained the preserve of specialists. As such, they continued as a durable source for foreign policy issues for at least two reasons. First, at the bureaucratic levels below those of presidential appointment are individuals whose tasks include the day-to-day monitoring of foreign policy issues regardless of who comes to power. Expertise therefore becomes a source of issues. The second reason is more overtly political in a traditional sense. Not only must a president find ways to persuade bureaucrats to accept whatever departures he may advocate, but in the event he is unsuccessful in doing so, bureaucrats may increase the salience of particular foreign policy issues. This is usually accomplished through forging coalitions with similarly inclined bureaucrats, legislators, or nonstate actors.

The overall result is that, despite their positional advantage, the White House and the bureaucracies may also become prisoners of issue-specificity. The ostensible reason for bureaucratic preeminence may well be that there are no real challengers, and American bureaucratic dominance does appear somewhat diffuse in comparison with other industrial democracies like Great Britain or France. Defining issues constitutes a first round in the bureaucratic game. If a foreign policy issue can be defined initially so that it falls within the purview of one bureaucracy rather than another, the probability of an outcome increasing that bureaucracy's budget or prestige is raised. Whatever order exists comes from the fact that everyone is playing a similar game in which the central participants all practice disjointed incrementalism.

Furthermore, it is questionable whether any meaningful alternatives exist to disjointed incrementalism with its attendant reinforcement of issue-specificity. When the best predictor of tomorrow is what is taking place today, the world can be full of surprises—as events in Iran or the Chinese invasion of Vietnam surely illustrate. The only solutions offered amount to institutional tinkering with wistful glances often cast in the direction of more "planning." The argument in favor of increased planning suggests that the bureaucracy could be a more orderly source of foreign policy issues, especially for the medium or long term. Lincoln Bloomfield doubts this, and his comments on the inherent structural limitations involved deserve to be quoted at length:

> First, "successful" planners are those considered most "relevant" by the secretary of state and other policy makers. Second, whether planning ever approximates the ideal model is entirely up to the secretary. Third, to be "relevant," and thus "influential," planners simply cannot (or will not) get too far out of line with established policies. Two supplemental points: Inside information is a form of power in bureaucracies and therefore, to be in the know, planners have to remain close to operations. And to foster that relationship, they eschew experimental, theoretical, or methodological unorthodoxies, or flights into the future that in the foreign service subculture would invariably brand them as unsound.[40]

The combination of issue-specific actor involvement and disjointed incrementalism means that the ways in which issues actually evolve into occasions for American foreign policy action are manifold, but some bases for generalization can be found. Certain categories are composed of specific issues that, when they become part of the psychological environments of policy makers, are the occasions for decisions. The public at large, what Johan Galtung has referred to as the "periphery" away from the decision-making "center,"[41] sees the categories rather than specific issues. Thus there is public awareness of a Soviet-American strategic relationship (category), which may be viewed as improving or worsening, but Soviet naval capabilities, NATO preparedness, or tradeoffs involving cruise missiles and Backfire bombers (specific issues) enter the consciousness of only more "attentive" publics.

Understanding the sources of American foreign policy issues requires a scrutiny of dynamics in these center-periphery connections. Elections, even presidential ones (1968 being the exception proving the rule), are contested on grounds that are relatively close to home, leaving little incentive for candidates to become involved with foreign policy issues. Candidates remain more concerned with their images vis-à-vis issue *categories*—"hard-liner," "dove," and so forth. Thus cosmetics triumph over substance because mass public consciousness is filtered in evaluative rather than cognitive terms.[42] Once in office, presidents find that the impression of "movement" with reference to a given issue category is more important than the specifics of foreign policy action; presidential popularity rises after any kind of decisive behavior.[43] When attempts are made to communicate with the public in specific terms, the filtration process takes so much time that it is inherently part of postelectoral politics. The permanent foreign affairs bureaucrats and nonstate actors thus find that they are overwhelmingly advantaged in attempting to define specific issues because the limitations imposed by American politics are on their side.

Domestic peripheries, then, are not a source of specific issues for United States foreign policy, and those issue categories recognized in the peripheries constitute largely simplified reflections of the American position in the world. The only way in which the peripheries continue to make their presence felt is passive: as those closer to the center define the specifics of foreign policy issues, they attempt to anticipate reactions in the peripheries. An example of this anticipated reaction can be found in Carter administration maneuvering with regard to public acceptance of SALT-II. Senate approval of the Panama Canal Treaties was more difficult than had been expected in part because of right-wing success in mobilizing mass opposition. This success was built by using issue categories to paint the treaties as an act of American self-abnegation. Because of recent Soviet and Cuban behavior in Africa (specific issues), it would seem that the intricacies of SALT-II could be painted in a similar light. Anticipating this possible public reaction, the Carter administration has been attempting to decouple SALT-II from other aspects of the American–Soviet relationship.

The sources of issues in American foreign policy therefore do not lend themselves to a single neat description. Specific issues on the foreign policy agenda are not fixed, and the categories into which they may fit are subject to slow evolution. Even if nonstate actors and the public at large add a certain haphazard quality to the process by which issues are defined, those closer to the center of decision-making typically get their way, at least insofar as establishing the substantive nature of an issue affects the eventual outcome. It remains by and large an insiders' game. Ideally what should most affect decision makers' perceptions, no matter how idiosyncratic, is what transpires in the world at large, although the individuals involved may have previously had a hand in creating it. Yet in the American case such perceptions are uniquely shaped by the parochial concerns of bureaucratic and other loyalties. As we shall see, the nature of the currently defined American foreign policy agenda tends to engender conflict and a lack of consensus not only among bureaucrats but also in much of the government and society.

Major Contemporary Issues

In understanding the specific issues on the American foreign policy agenda an initial task is to identify the "categories" into which they fit. Alternative techniques of doing so exist and might include reliance on the State Department organization chart or interviewing participants in the policy process. I have chosen a less direct (but I hope more discrete) method of identifying these categories, a largely inductive classification of articles by foreign policy analysts.[44] Table 2.2 gives the percentage of article titles reflective of each issue category and Figure 2.1, though somewhat impressionistic, attempts to specify the linkages among them.

One initially impressive aspect of the American foreign policy agenda treated in this way is that almost two-thirds of it represents categories of issues broadly conceived. The first five categories are not limited to an interactive context involving specific countries; this may suggest an increasing concern with conceptual substance above and beyond more simple day-to-day American relationships. Referents to particular actors can be found within these categories, however, and the remainder of the foreign policy agenda comprises countries with whom the nature of American interactions itself constitutes an issue. The linkages between the various categories are identifiable by the ways in which the issues are related to particular actors.

It is noteworthy that more than one-fifth of the American foreign policy agenda is concerned with issues derived from what takes place

Table 2.2
Issue Categories for the American
Foreign Policy Agenda

CATEGORY	% OF TITLES
Domestic Actor Context	11
American Attitudes and Ideology	10
Global Security and Strategy	11
Economic and Developmental	26
Oil	6
American-Soviet Relationship	7
Western Alliance	6
Japan	3
American-Chinese Relationship	3
Middle East	6
Peripheries	11

within the United States. There are two interconnected categories here, the first of which is the "Domestic Actor Context," referring to particular actors, most often governmental, which are capable of undertaking their own foreign policy behavior. Although formally part of the governmental structure, an individual bureaucracy's peculiarities and its relationships with other actors can have profound effects on American foreign policy. Whether or not these real and potential rivalries within the United States government render foreign policy less efficient than citizens should expect poses questions which merit attention and sometimes can be pursued to almost obsessive lengths. Is the State Department inherently inefficient because of its bureaucratic norms or because of the type of people it recruits? Does the overwhelming budgetary impact of the Pentagon mean that it is the preeminent foreign affairs bureaucracy? What is the appropriate role of Congress: a minimalistic and reactive oversight of those for whom foreign affairs is a daily preoccupation or the provision of operational policy guidelines? Should the CIA be restricted to intelligence gathering and analysis, eschewing covert operations and submitting to overt public scrutiny?

Answers to such questions are most often colored by opinions drawn from the larger context of "American Attitudes and Ideology," the second of the major issue categories. The distinction between the two is based on the latter's reference to more amorphous beliefs which are not directly operationalizable in the behavior of specific actors. Whereas the existence of a distinct "American ideology" is arguable, governmental actors particularly can find themselves constrained by perceptions of the overall nature of opinions held in the public at large or those attributable to an "establishment." Specific concerns here include the apparent crumbling of the post-World War II consensus on containment. Whether various policies remain budgetarily feasible and what effects a vanishing

Figure 2.1.
Linkages among Issue Categories
for the American Foreign Policy Agenda

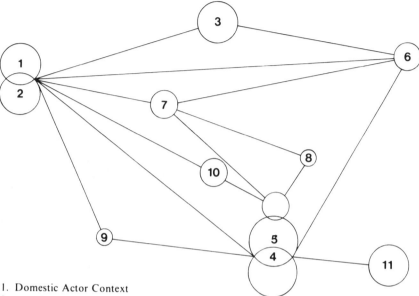

1. Domestic Actor Context
2. American Attitudes and Ideology
3. Global Security and Strategy
4. Economic and Developmental
5. Oil
6. American-Soviet Relationship
7. Western Alliance
8. Japan
9. American-Chinese Relationship
10. Middle East
11. Peripheries

consensus may have on the foreign policy middle ground traditionally occupied by "liberals" of course can be seen only by probing the public consciousness. In the aftermath of Watergate specific issues have surfaced also about the ways particular actions may relate to overarching American beliefs such as freedom and democracy as well as about the effects of the mass media on the foreign policy process.

Explicit linkages exist between American actors and those issue categories that refer more to events outside the United States. "Global Security and Strategy" presents an excellent example. Assessing the current state of the Soviet–American strategic arms race and deterrent relationship involves not only methodological considerations of divining intentions but also the realization that certain American actors can gain or lose ground depending on the nature of the assessment. If the current

political utility of military power requires global scrutiny, then notions
related to security and defense policy (as well as budgets) also come in
for review. Interestingly, almost 15 percent of the specific issues composing this category are susceptible to interpretation according to more
broadly developmental rather than interactive considerations. For example, the arms trade and nuclear proliferation bear importantly on the
evolution of the global political structure.

If the future of world politics constitutes a minimal part of global
security, this is maximally apparent in the next and largest category on
the American foreign policy agenda, namely, the "Economic and Developmental" issues, of which 55 percent can be posed outside particular
state-to-state interactions. The boundary between economic and developmental issues is admittedly somewhat hazy and is complicated because
economic issues are often expressed in developmental terms. Such complications, however, are not as apparent in human rights and ecological
concerns, which directly link developmental aspects of global politics to
"American Attitudes and Ideology."

The difficulty of separating economic from developmental questions
can be demonstrated by considering some of the particular issues this
category entails. American foreign economic policy relates to balances of
payments, the value of the dollar, special drawing rights, exports, foreign
aid, investment abroad, and foreign investment in the United States. All
have connections with developmental questions concerning international
monetary reform and a new economic order, as well as with threats implied by Third World positions on such issues. The ability of the United
States government to manage economic developmental issue fixes is complicated by an additional factor: certain significant American actors are
not easily subject to governmental control. Preeminent here is the impact
of American-based multinational corporations on the global economy.
Also important are the possibilities of American labor exerting its influence internationally (or attempting to protect jobs within the United
States), and the entire relationship between public debt and private profit
in the Third World.

To complicate matters further, the gamut of economic and developmental issues cannot be easily uncoupled from those related to "Oil."
When formulated in explicitly separable terms, Oil adds another 6 percent
to the set of Economic/Developmental issues, making them almost three
times more salient for the American foreign policy agenda than Global
Security and Strategy. Each specific issue included in Oil is very closely
linked to Economic/Developmental concerns. Oil prices have had profound effects on the American and global economic situation. American
multinational oil companies, the behavior of OPEC, and the possibilities
of cartels affecting other key raw materials mean that Oil has a developmental as well as a narrowly economic aspect. Moreover, this category

allows for linkages to others through various actors' behavior. Just as oil production and trade with Western Europe place certain Soviet policies within an Economic/Developmental context, Chinese oil resources allow for a similar connection. Last, and far from least, the foreign policies of the Arab oil giants cannot be considered in isolation from American policy toward Israel and the entire complex of Middle East issues.

Throughout the most intense years of the Cold War nothing was more central to United States foreign policy than the "American-Soviet Relationship." The fact that it now composes only 7 percent of the American foreign policy agenda as a distinct issue category suggests the extent to which the Cold War has moderated. Indeed, the symbols of such moderation, détente and SALT talks, are specific issues important to the definition of this category. A residue of the hotter days of Cold War interaction exists nonetheless, and other issues involve what containment may have meant, the internal politics of Moscow and its relationship to Eastern Europe, and American-Soviet strategic rivalry, including the effects of increasing Soviet power at sea.

Rivalry with the Soviet Union, of course, had provided the rationale for the formation of the "Western Alliance." This partly explains its interconnection with the previous issue category, but it is also noteworthy that an explicit linkage between NATO (an obvious specific issue here) and the broader state of global security is *not* apparent. The changing nature of the American foreign policy agenda is nowhere better reflected than in the specific issues composing the Western Alliance. Concerns about an overall European malaise brought about by dependence on foreign oil and the resurgence of Eurocommunism indicate that America's relationships with its closest allies are no longer grounded in purely strategic terms. The state of the Anglo-American "special relationship," as well as concerns related to the survival of Canada in the face of regional separatism, contribute to overarching questions about constraints that may be imposed on foreign policy by America's allies.

Another such problematic ally is "Japan," less salient than Europe in overall terms, but critical in terms of linkages with the foregoing category and the complex of Economic/Developmental/Oil issues. The guarantee of Japanese security still constitutes the linchpin of American relationships with Asia, even given the post-Nixon Doctrine conception of the United States as a Pacific rather than an Asian power. Thus our ally's internal developments constitute a focus for American scrutiny as does Japanese dependence on external oil, which may suggest the need for a concerted Atlantic-Japanese trilateral energy policy. Yet Japan's most significant impact on the American foreign policy agenda is due to its status as an economic giant. By 1978 American trade with Japan reflected a gross surplus of imports over exports, causing the dollar to fall to a post-World War II low compared to the yen.

The "American-Chinese Relationship" takes up another 3 percent of the foreign policy agenda, although it appears only indirectly linked to Japan through various connections with Economic/Developmental/Oil issues. It might also have been expected that China would form part of a complex of issues connected with the Soviet Union and global security, but this was not found to be the case. Hence the American relationship with China seems more interactive than developmental. Specific issues involve concern with China's internal politics as well as the possibilities of increased trade. The overall impact of continued Sino–Soviet rivalry and a more outward-looking Chinese leadership have not yet been synthesized into a coherent American vision of China's role in the emerging structures of world politics.

The "Middle East" accounts for another 6 percent of the American agenda. The core issues composing this category have to do with prospects for an overall Arab–Israeli settlement, as well as the possibilities of American actions encouraging doves on both sides. Complicating the regional picture are inter-Arab rivalries, focused particularly on the Palestinians, and potential ideological threats to conservative regimes like Saudi Arabia and Jordan. There are two significant linkages of the Middle East to other issue categories. First, traditional support for Israel plus the activities of Jewish nonstate actors in the United States means that *both* intra-American issue categories become connected with the Middle East. Second, there is the entire question of energy in the complex of Economic/Developmental/Oil issues, and the possibility that a regional flare-up could spill over into a broader "oil war."

Finally, a not insignificant 11 percent of the American foreign policy agenda is oriented toward what can loosely be termed the world's "Peripheries." To the extent that commonalities can be found among the extremely diverse set of specific issues composing this category they would appear to be twofold. First, linkages with the more central aspects of the American foreign policy agenda arise largely in terms of issues having some bearing on Economics/Developmental/Oil. Examples are American relationships with Latin American and African countries. Inclusion of Southern Africa here at first might seem to be stretching a point, but questions of majority rule can be seen to be ultimately developmental, even if only loosely so from an American perspective. Second, the specific issues composing this category are all to a large degree time-bound in the sense that they appear to take on great importance for a year or two and then fade into the background, perhaps reappearing cyclically. Such specific issues would include Cyprus, Portugal, and the Indian Ocean.

If the substantive nature of the American foreign policy agenda we have just described is compared with the day-to-day concerns of the policy-making community, certain differences emerge. Employing National Security Council documents for the years 1970–1977 (National Security Study Memoranda in the Nixon and Ford Administrations, Presidential Review Memoranda under President Carter), Stephen Walker finds that the subjects covered were three times *less* concerned with Economic/Developmental issues. In contrast, Western Alliance was two-and-a-half times *more* salient to the NSC decision makers, who were also one-and-a-half times *more* concerned with Global Security and Strategy and Peripheries.[45]

Such differences are not as puzzling as they might seem at first, and they underscore comments made earlier about the difficulties of planning on the part of decision makers. The structure of the policy-making community is inherently retrospective, allowing for constituencies that must be served to develop around more time-worn issues. Moreover, some would argue that these bureaucratic tendencies were uniquely shaped for most of the 1970s by the predilections of a single individual, Henry Kissinger. Vincent Davis suggests that Kissinger prevented the establishment of a Council on International Economic Policy because he "was not about to tolerate the existence of a new 'economic NSC' that would clearly rival his own 'political-strategic NSC,' " further exacerbating "Kissinger's failures to understand any economics."[46] Whatever Kissinger's personal contribution, comparison of the American foreign policy agenda we have considered with that of the NSC uncovers a larger problem: when American foreign policy has not been overgeneralized, as in the halcyon days of containment, it has been too mired in detail. Some of the reasons for this have to do with the ways issues are processed.

Issue Processing

Identifying issues does not automatically translate them into foreign policy behavior. American action (or inaction) comes about only after various actors have in one way or another *processed* an issue. Depending upon the nature of issues and their situational contexts, foreign policy processes will vary accordingly. If American foreign policy were a rational and tightly coordinated activity, it might in a certain hypothetical sense be "all up to the president." The fact that even presidents are constrained in terms of their ability to persuade only begins to suggest the complexity of the American decision-making process.

Considering sources of issues suggested the preeminence of American foreign affairs bureaucracies, and a similar conclusion is even more true for issue processing. The complexity of the decision-making process, however, does not derive merely from bureaucratic structures, something which is illustrated by those who are organizationally closest to the president. It remains impossible for a president to exercise anything approaching total control whether the NSC and the White House staff are set up according to formal chains of command as during the Eisenhower years (a style carried to excess by Nixon), or whether they are more loosely run as in the Kennedy administration. Furthermore, even though the top levels of the bureaucracy are titularly the president's men, this is no guarantee that bureaucratic processes end up producing foreign policy outcomes that accord with the president's wishes.

The essence of issue processing therefore derives from the nature of the American foreign policy bureaucracies. Although they do exhibit certain unique peculiarities, many of their characteristics represent more general bureaucratic phenomena. For one thing, bureaucracies are hierarchically structured and have a recognizable division of labor. This results in pressures against innovation because the responsibilities of a position are already established before the arrival of any given role occupant. Also, individuals at the next level of the hierarchy by and large expect that channels and routines previously established will continue to be observed. This is not only because a bureaucracy attempts to socialize its members, but also because those at each successive bureaucratic level usually owe their advancement to having followed such channels and routines. The pressures to "think organization" become virtually irresistible, and one of their most important effects is that fairly consistent expectations are built up both within and outside an organization as to how its representatives will behave. As one study of the Military Assistance Program reports:

> First, stereotypes of agency positions can be applied to an agency quite independently of specific personalities. . . . Second, these attributed preferences are predictive. . . . Third, they were reliable. . . . Fourth, and most surprising, the positions were independent of the issue at hand. . . . Fifth, the stereotyped positions can be represented in terms of policy dimensions.[47]

Ultimately, a bureaucracy is a blunt instrument that, in the words of Henry Kissinger, "is efficient if the matters which it handles routinely are, in fact, the most frequent and if its procedures are relevant to their solution."[48] The way this is supposed to be accomplished is through the use of standard operating procedures (SOPs). SOPs are designed to fragment issues into component problems, and are the main source of the incrementalism attached to the foreign policy process. The fragmentation which SOPs introduce into the processing of issues may have a psychological basis as well. John Steinbruner argues that, from a cognitive perspective, individuals exhibit "general tendencies to set up decision problems conceptualized in terms of a single value, to associate but a single outcome with the available alternatives, and to restrict information utilized to a relatively limited number of variables."[49] This casts doubt upon the model of the individual decision maker as a "rational man," weighing the costs and benefits of alternative courses of action according to a more integrated set of goals and values. It also serves to exacerbate the bureaucratic tendency to deal only with that which can be processed through already established channels according to extant routines. Such considerations lead Charles Hermann to point out that a

> difficulty arises because search routines, decision rules, and standard operating procedures by definition focus the search for potential foreign policy problems toward some cues or particular kind of signals. The unavoidable question becomes: What about critical problems that do not have the characteristics established by the specialized search routines? Searching for the unexpected will always pose major challenges to foreign policy organizations.[50]

These general tendencies can be illustrated with reference to the State Department, traditionally regarded as a major repository of bureaucratic vices. Such vices have become more apparent as the issues on the American foreign policy agenda increasingly have come to imply "complex decision problems" involving tradeoffs between two or more values, environmental uncertainty, and dispersed decision-making power.[51] The backbone of State is its geographic divisions, tied directly to American embassies overseas. Despite the existence of functional bureaus dealing with economics, politico-military affairs, and so forth, developmental or transregional issues inherently engender difficulties in coordination and translating behavior from staff to line. Yet such issues make up much of the American agenda, and even those that seem geographically limited often have linkages that produce rippling effects.

The State Department, of course, is only one of the bureaucracies engaged in processing issues in American foreign policy. Although its formal responsibilities for the day-to-day conduct of foreign affairs might be taken to imply its preeminence, virtually every governmental organization can become involved in certain foreign policy issues at one time or another. This leads to what Michael O'Leary has called "the dilemma of the foreign ministry today"; issues are so complex and the involvement of other actors has become so likely that not even "countries with conditions most strongly favoring large diplomatic services" like the United States may be able to process them adequately.[52] Thus issue complexity serves to increase the notable tendency toward bureaucratic conflict that was virtually built into the American system in the first place.

Indeed, the State Department's role in processing issues has been subjected to continuing assault by bureaucratic rivals. Perhaps the most flagrant instance occurred during the Nixon/Kissinger years when the NSC staff virtually overwhelmed State's impact on the conduct of American foreign policy. Nor was this totally without precedent. During the

Kennedy administration, "the lament was frequently heard in Washington that [National Security Adviser McGeorge] 'Bundy's State Department' had become the real locus of effective decision-making power on foreign policy issues."[53] The NSC notwithstanding, State Department officials can count on regular clashes with representatives of the Department of Defense and the Central Intelligence Agency, both of which benefited greatly from the more interventionist activities of the Cold War period. Defense enjoyed years of unprecedented budgetary booms, especially during the Vietnam escalation, and CIA influence expanded in an appropriately covert fashion. Yet at the end of the 1970s both the Pentagon and the CIA felt a bit of a pinch. In the case of the former, the Carter administration's early attempts at greater fiscal restraint caused interservice rivalries to surface. The latter, disgraced by association with Watergate and subsequent revelations, was barely beginning to recoup its bureaucratic losses when events in Iran suggested that they might well not be recoverable.

Furthermore, this is not to deny the impact of conflict *within* a given bureaucracy. In theory, SOPs should be able to keep the lid on intrabureaucratic conflict, but this has other effects on issue processing. When one organization is attempting to forge compromise among its members and other actors are trying to do the same, issues necessitating coordination across bureaucracies become especially problematic, taking days even to reach a stalemate. There are two means typically used to break such stalemates. The first is decision by committee, which has the virtue of probably not offending anyone's bureaucratic sensitivities, even if nobody really wants the outcome produced. The second is to keep kicking decisions upstairs until they may eventually reach the Oval office, although this violates another bureaucratic norm: "When issues get that far, one of the fundamental rules has already been violated: keep issues away from the President. Bureaucrats prefer to be left alone to do their own thing."[54] As Kissinger has remarked, "All of this drives the executive in the direction of extra-bureaucratic means of decision," which are justified because:

> Faced with an administrative machine which is both elaborate and fragmented, the executive is forced into essentially lateral means of control. Many of his public pronouncements, though ostensibly directed to outsiders, perform a perhaps more important role in laying down guidelines for the bureaucracy. The chief significance of a foreign policy speech by the President may thus be that it settles an internal debate in Washington (a public statement is more useful for this purpose than an administrative memorandum because it is harder to reverse).[55]

Even this cursory summary of bureaucratic characteristics suggests that issue processing in American foreign policy is not only incremental but also disjointed, complex, and curiously decentralized within the government, let alone when the society as a whole is added to the picture. The incentives for innovation are not very high, and attempts at even marginal change have apparently little chance for success. This has been shown by the long series of commissioned reports about streamlining the foreign affairs bureaucracy.[56] The tendency for the whole process simply to lumber along is irresistible, except in crises. Crises appear to be the only circumstances in which significant changes are possible, meaning that some decision makers almost crave them, and this creates further complications.

Crises represent merely one particular kind of situation in which issue processing occurs.[57] It was suggested earlier that issues serve essentially as intervening variables in American foreign policy, and the situational context they represent when they are processed can be considered from a similar logical perspective. Although bureaucratic considerations are not necessarily absent,[58] crises represent occasions for decision with the most far-reaching effects. Normal bureaucratic procedures are not nearly as significant as they are on a day-to-day basis because crisis decisions are typically made by the president surrounded by a small circle of close advisers cutting across and sometimes working outside of more normal bureaucratic lines. Crises thus present the opportunity for true innovation in the substantive direction of American foreign policy if not its procedures.

More normal bureaucratic procedures are of increased significance for the issues making up the current American foreign policy agenda because the entire sense of what constitutes a crisis is subject to reinterpretation. The word "crisis'" itself conjures up emotional connotations nurtured by the military-security issues of the Cold War period. The bureaucratic machinery does not easily yield to "low" economic and developmental issues becoming the "high politics" of the current agenda because such issues represent a new set of incentives.[59] As it begins to do so, however, bureaucrats may discover that fresh outlets exist for old procedures due to the fact that economic and developmental issues are more representative of "complex interdependence" in which multiple channels connect societies, issues demonstrate an absence of hierarchy, and military force is less evident.[60] It is especially this last factor that suggests the ambiguity which now clouds the meaning of crisis.

If incentives existed previously for top decision makers to try to get the bureaucracy moving by billing virtually everything that came close as a "crisis," such characterizations have come to take on an appearance of "crying wolf" for the bureaucracy and public alike. The reason is that decisions taken in the here and now may have a devastating potential for the longer term that is difficult to judge. Previous crises had parameters which could be defined more clearly. Yet spectacular and unanticipated plunges in the value of the dollar somehow are not as decisive as the invasion of South Korea by the North. Lengthy and highly technical negotiations over matters like SALT lack the drama of the Cuban missile crisis. The "moral equivalent of war" regarding energy just isn't Pearl Harbor!

The way issues are processed in American foreign policy has therefore come to manifest a new form of immobility extending to all levels of the decision-making hierarchy. Its causes extend beyond the peculiar characteristics of a bureaucracy conditioned to enshrine pragmatism and deprecate planning. The traditional ways in which Americans process foreign policy issues have virtually ensured that the system would appear to grind along on its own inertia. There are so many bureaucratic advocates that issues ultimately come to be processed and managed according to a sort of survival ethic in which outcomes favor those who are most persistent. The only time the pattern breaks is in crisis when bureaucratic channels can be short-circuited. Otherwise, the political and the manipulative dominate the diplomatic and analytic. This may not necessarily be a bad thing. It even appears to induce in Richard Holbrooke "a sense of drift, a time for calm."[61] Whether we should join him in this state, however, depends upon the judgments reached by considering issue management.

Issue Management and Performance

Foreign policy processes produce decisions that are eventually expressed in behavior designed to have an impact on the resolution of issue(s) in some global system(s). This represents an issue's "management," and successive decision processes and behavioral undertakings may be necessary because issue management is rarely if ever accomplished with a single stroke. Unambiguous criteria for judging just what constitutes "successful" issue management are difficult to ascertain, as will become apparent when we consider American foreign policy within the broad interactive categories of security, political, and economic issues.

As I pointed out earlier, explicit questions of physical security somewhat surprisingly appear to be lacking in salience for the American foreign policy agenda. Adding the category of Global Security and Strategy to that of the American–Soviet Relationship accounts for less than one-fifth (18 percent) of the total issues, although I also suggested that such concerns are of greater significance to decision makers. Whatever the precise weight, this does not necessarily mean Americans and their foreign policy leaders are feeling "secure." A more apt characterization might well be that over time Americans have come to live with the insecurity bred by the fact that, even if nuclear deterrence continues to "work," the mutual assured destruction on which it rests is not a naturally comforting idea. In this way successful management of some security issues has in an ironic way contributed to American unease.

To appreciate this irony more fully, a bit of historical perspective is in order. Initially, the Cold War was punctuated with possibilities of all-out hot war, spurring developments that could bring victory on the part of both the Soviet Union and the United States. With the hardening of strategic forces in the early 1960s, however, occurrence of such conflict, if not totally "unthinkable," came to be recognized as too destructive, especially when its specter was raised during the Cuban missile crisis. This led to certain halting steps which produced superpower agreement first in banning atmospheric testing and later regarding nuclear proliferation, both of which represented a successful but limited management of particular security issues.

Most important, though, was the 1972 SALT-I accord, continued in the Vladivostok Agreement of 1974. SALT had a peculiar impact upon American security policy. It committed both the United States and the Soviet Union to the *principle* of arms limitation, but by allowing the development of a common evaluative framework it could also contribute to perceptions of insecurity and bad faith. If the former constituted successful issue management, the latter cast doubt on the success by calling into question the exact purposes of each weapons system. Under such circumstances it would seem difficult enough to judge whether SALT constituted satisfactory American management of security issues, but there were additional complications. SALT became the most visible symbol of "détente," now passé as a word if not as a concept. Although primarily a security matter, SALT was interwoven with the entire fabric of the American–Soviet relationship. Little wonder that by 1979 American public opinion data revealed "the presence of ambivalence, ambiguity, and conflict. . . . While there remains a strong public support for agreements between the two superpowers on strategic arms limitations, weapons testing and trade, one also finds a rising concern for stricter reciprocity on any new accords."[62]

Since 1964 the United States has been spending relatively less on defense than the Soviet Union, but the significance of this datum for "handicapping the arms race," as Barry Blechman points out, still depends on whether one assumes a "minimalist" or "maximalist" position.[63] The former stresses that Europe has largely been removed as a focal point for war, that apparent crises in the Third World do not necessarily concern the superpowers, and that it is the overall deterrent relationship rather than momentary advantages in the balance of forces that counts above all. Possibly conceding these points, maximalists still can argue that the Soviet penchant for control is so great that their belief in nuclear restraint is inherently less than that of the United States. Therefore, although grounded in security considerations, SALT ultimately can become a *political* question, as in the Spring 1978 face-off concerning whether SALT-II should be linked with (National Security Adviser Brzezinski) or uncoupled (Secretary of State Vance) from Soviet behavior in Africa. Thus management of American security issues concerns not only calculating *ultima ratios* but also divining intentions, something noted by Alton Frye:

> The military capabilities of a state are more or less observable, while a nation's intentions tend to elude objective assessment. Optical and electronic surveillance can provide extensive information regarding weapon systems and deployments, but, as Fred Inklé put it so aptly, not even the best camera can detect an intention from 50,000 feet.[64]

All of which brings us to the specific considerations bearing upon SALT-II. One set of problems is largely military in nature and concerns the rationales employed by American defense officials in assessing overall force postures. Since 1974, in both Nixon's ideas about "strategic sufficiency" and Carter administration doctrines of "essential equivalence," counterforce strategies have assumed a renewed importance. Originally introduced during the Kennedy administration as a means of suggesting that a limited use of nuclear weaponry does not necessarily have to escalate into the deliberate destruction of population centers, counterforce currently implies precise comparisons between various forms of Soviet and American weaponry. Whether or not a limited nuclear exchange could actually be confined to producing destruction which by a macabre calculus might be deemed "acceptable," counterforce creates incentives for pursuing the arms race according to more qualitative strategies. The ultimate meaning of neutron bombs or cruise missiles is that they would transfer the onus for the ultimate escalatory step to the other side, and analogous Soviet technological innovations would serve a similar function.

SALT-II is therefore quite a bit more ambitious than SALT-1 because certain of its provisions attempt to begin controlling more qualitative aspects of the arms race. This is particularly true where multiple independently targeted reentry vehicle (MIRV) missiles are concerned. Moreover, if SALT-II appears in approximately the same form that current reports suggest, it will contain restrictions on technological innovations such as those related to transforming the American Minuteman into some sort of mobile launch system to protect against possible Soviet direct hits. SALT-II is no panacea, though, because it will not by itself limit the arms race, or create significant budgetary savings, or serve as a "cornerstone" for a new relationship between the superpowers.[65]

In addition, a successful SALT-II has ramifications for American relationships with its NATO allies. Certain Soviet weapons not covered by the treaty and thought to be more relevant to the Sino–Soviet relationship (like Backfire bombers or intermediate SS-20 missiles) could also be used to place Western Europe in jeopardy. Intercontinental strategic parity between the United States and the Soviet Union means that forces in the European theater become functionally equivalent to qualitative advances in the arms race, presenting short-term advantages which transfer final commitment to the opponent. This poses the old question of whether the United States would actually risk global nuclear warfare for the sake of Europe, a question raised so often by General de Gaulle. Although no final answer can be given, Jan Lodal suggests that "the 'nuclear umbrella' can only go so far in providing adequate security for Europe. The best way to enhance European security is to improve Europe's own conventional capability, and any available additional European defense resources should be allocated principally to this task."[66]

Finally, there are political considerations, sometimes based on strategic assumptions but too often not, which could end up proving crucial for eventual Senate ratification. Serious military questions exist as to whether the Soviet Union could develop a first-strike capability by the mid-1980s, although the answers can become virtual certainties for nonstate actors like the Committee on the Present Danger. More purely political concerns appeared to be at the root of President Carter's somewhat intemperate March 1977 proposals regarding SALT-II which were rejected out of hand by the Soviets. On the whole, though, a SALT-II agreement would seem to represent a successful management of some strategic issues for reasons detailed by Bruce Russett and Bruce Blair:

> Failure to sign or ratify SALT II could (a) terminate a useful strategic arms dialogue, (b) stimulate the spread of nuclear weapons to other countries, (c) destroy the chances of success in arms control efforts, such as chemical weapons control, a comprehensive test ban, and mutual and balanced force reductions in Europe, (d) render impossible the control of dangerous new technologies, such as antisatellite weapons and lasers, (e) lead to the abrogation of existing agreements such as the ABM treaty, (f) seriously strain Soviet–American relations, and (g) unleash the most furious arms race to date.[67]

From an overall perspective it would seem that the United States has been relatively successful in managing security issues. Because it cannot be seen as part of a communist monolith, the People's Republic of China is no longer judged as a physical threat, especially in the wake of full diplomatic recognition. Also, improving relationships allow for the possibility that the so-called "China card" can be played, hypothetically encouraging greater American–Soviet cooperation because of fears in the latter that a *de facto* alliance could crystallize between the United States and Russia's ideological rival. A China card requires a great deal of finesse, however, because overplaying it could boomerang, causing Soviet positions to harden.

Consideration of the American–Soviet and Sino–American relationships raises a larger point about the management of security issues: the meaning of "security" in American foreign policy is in the final analysis a "political" issue. Even if greater Sino–American cooperation is in the cards, specific circumstances can appear to place the United States in overly compromised situations. This was illustrated by the fact that Deng Xiao-ping had barely left the United States when the Chinese invasion of Vietnam commenced. Mention of Vietnam also provides a reminder that Indochina would not have become a major security issue for Americans had they not gone there in the first place to have their security threatened. This lesson appears applicable to possibilities of future American involvement in the Middle East or Southern Africa.

As far as interactive political issues go, American foreign policy management is more mixed. Such issues most often bring increased actor involvement, encouraging decision by compromise rather than design. Primary political issues include those important to the American agenda on their own terms (Middle East), as well as those which, having been relatively peripheral previously, might in the future develop into fairly central concerns through the actions of others (Southern Africa). Both kinds of issues present difficulties for issue management in the American political system.

The 1973 Yom Kippur war in the Middle East set the stage for what have been some of the more dramatic successes of United States foreign policy in recent years. At the same time that Americans were recoiling from the effects of the Arab oil embargo, Henry Kissinger embarked on what at least in retrospect appears to have been a grand design. Step-by-step negotiations culminated during his days of shuttle diplomacy in the 1975 Israeli–Egyptian Sinai disengagement accord. The underlying key to Kissinger's strategy was to center possibilities for an overall settlement in President Anwar Sadat's Cairo. Kissinger's approach bore initial fruit when Sadat ended the Soviet presence in Egypt and cast his regime's fate with the United States. The United States found itself with an implicit coalition of Arab "moderates": Egypt along with the ever cautious King Hussein and the conservative Saudis.

The Egyptian linchpin held when Kissinger was forced into retirement, although two factors changed. First, President Carter, even as an "outsider" among Democrats, became more dependent on electoral support in the American Jewish community than any Republican. Second, the 1977 Israeli elections broke the hold the Labor Party had had since the state's founding, although Menachem Begin was elected on domestic issues rather than on those related to a peace settlement. When Sadat made the unprecedented move of going to Jerusalem in November 1977 the result was drama, awakened hopes, and a series of rather rapid stalemates. The United States was expected to play the "honest broker" because initial successes in managing more limited issues created expectations; future inability to match them can easily come to be considered failure.

The Carter administration then bore up to this responsibility well, although the unexpected success of Camp David soon created new logjams as the two sides came closer. Among the specific stumbling blocks are Egyptian defense commitments to other Arab nations and the particular procedures to be followed for establishing some kind of Palestinian "autonomy." Both involve delicate questions of the Egyptian role in the Arab world, which is shown by the fact that even the moderates have proved highly critical and extremely reluctant to become enmeshed in the peace process up to this point.

Two things seem clear. First, a major Arab–Israeli war along the general lines of the four previous conflicts is increasingly unlikely because Arab forces are simply not militarily viable without Egyptian participation. A second point is perhaps even more important. With the overthrow of the Shah of Iran, what was regarded by Americans as the underpinning for strategic stability in the region has been eliminated, although the configuration of the revolutionary forces does not necessarily suggest increased Soviet influence. Yet the Shah's overthrow was a major setback, and more tranquil relations between Egypt and Israel would present new prospects for some stability as well as restore lost American prestige. John Campbell summarizes well the factors bearing on the prospects for successful American long-term management of Middle Eastern issues.

> The problem of management is essentially one of adaptation without losing sight of hard interests. If the United States is to be able to cope with the persistence of conflict (as between the Arabs and Israel and among the Arabs themselves) and with the disintegration of regimes (as in Iran), it will have to arrive at a deeper appreciation of both surface and subsurface forces in those countries. It will have to do more than stand with a series of friends (e.g., Israel, Sadat's Egypt, Saudi Arabia, the Shah of Iran) without taking full account of the currents of Palestinian nationalism, inter-Arab rivalry, social unrest or Islamic fundamentalism swirling around them. The fragility of governments, no matter how rich they may be, is endemic in the Middle East.[68]

The Middle East has been linked in the eyes of some with events in Southern Africa. American nonresponse to Soviet/Cuban presence in newly independent Angola appears to have encouraged more of the same. The result has been a similar Soviet/Cuban presence in Ethiopia which in the chesslike scheme of geopolitics can be seen to be potentially threatening to Saudi Arabia and its oil on the other side of the Red Sea, and hence the Middle East. It may well be, however, that the failure of Congress to give a sympathetic hearing to pleas for a more overt American presence is an appropriate step in the management of this issue. Rather than a feint at the Middle East's "underbelly," the Soviet presence may be a jockeying for position with the black regimes of the area in an attempt to undercut Chinese influence that is fraught with possibilities of overcommitment. What all this activity has to do with really is the white supremacist regime in South Africa. Even if the United States wanted a greater say in an eventual outcome, there seems little that can be done short of obvious intervention, which does not appear likely.

On the whole, discussion of how interactive security and political issues have been managed in American foreign policy has prompted assessments reflecting a certain amount of equivocation. Political issues are most important to the management and performance of American foreign policy. If, as was suggested in the last section, issue processing in American foreign policy is somewhat immobile, this is true of the management of political issues conceived in the broadest terms. For largely similar reasons evaluation of the management of economic issues is even more clear-cut and can be expressed in a single word—dismal. This is not to say that those involved in the management of American foreign economic policy have not tried mightily, but it is to suggest that they continue to fail. Following World War II it was the United States which virtually created economic order, so, even if suffering, American foreign policy must accept blame.

Some of the causes for the American failure to manage foreign economic policy adequately are structural in nature. Despite the tremendous impact of the American economy in global terms, the government can gain access or attempt to control the resources it represents only with extreme difficulty. This is because so many of these resources are concentrated in private hands, particularly those of nonstate actors like multinational corporations (MNCs), which can prove highly resistant to governmental attempts at mobilization and regulation. Stephen Krasner has proposed that such mobilization potential is a function of two factors: (1) the structure of the domestic political system—"the domestic weakness of the American state"; (2) the convergence between private and public interests, which in the American case has been subject to change over time.[69] A number of considerations bearing on the first factor have already been discussed within the context of issue sources and processing, so it will be the second that primarily concerns us here.

Although the global predominance of the American economy was virtually total at the end of World War II, the incentives for nonstate actors contained in the liberal principles enshrined at Bretton Woods took a while to become apparent. The cause was simply that American actors spent some time adjusting to active global economic involvement. Krasner suggests that the watershed year for American economic policy turned out to be 1960 because by then a consensus finally had come to exist around liberal principles. At the same time, parts of the American economy began to feel a pinch due to imports, and the effects of increased imports during the 1960s brought differential effects for various nonstate actors. While some MNCs plunged wholeheartedly into the acquisition of foreign subsidiaries, in other basic manufacturing industries adjustment was much more difficult. Labor was held hostage by the entire process and became a part of pressures for protection in certain industries like textiles or footwear and eventually iron and steel.

It would not be fair to suggest that the behavior of American nonstate actors or the United States government willfully plunged the global economy into its currently depressing state. Indeed, past coalescence of those with more particularistic concerns in support of liberal economic policies may itself have been something of an aberration, reflecting the unique circumstances of the Cold War period. With the economic dislocation brought about by the Vietnam war and subsequent American disengagement, the potential for conflict came into starker relief. Governmental insistence on liberal economic principles was no longer a guarantee that nonstate actors capable of their own foreign policy behavior would act in accord with it. Krasner notes:

> During the 1970s, the fundamental objective of foreign economic policy for American central decision makers has remained the maintenance of a liberal international economic regime. This goal is now most frequently explained in terms of interdependence, the notion that at least all non-Communist countries are locked into a complex network of relationships whose rupture would be extremely costly for everyone. While this rationale is different from the anti-Communism of the late 1940s and 1950s, the policy implications are identical. However, American leaders have found it increasingly difficult to implement their preferences.[70]

Liberal economic principles apparently are not a sufficient basis on which the United States government can rebuild consensus with nonstate actors. The result has been various fits and starts in managing American foreign economic policy which have had a profound bearing on relationships with the closest allies of the United States, the industrial democracies. Major problems in trilateral relations became overt during the Nixon administration when Treasury Secretary Connally's "Texas poker" with a declining dollar infuriated Japan and Kissinger's "year of Europe" did not materialize. Since then, at least trilateral governmental relations have largely been on the mend. Recognition that problems of energy, inflation, unemployment, and so forth are common throughout the developed world has brought more serious attempts on the part of the United States to manage such issues on a more multilateral basis. Whether efforts at multilateral management of interactive economic issues will ultimately succeed, however, is dependent on two things. First, American nonstate economic actors, even if not in wholehearted agreement, must at least provide implicit support for those trilateral arrangements that may be reached. Second, the United States and its allies must somehow face the economic implications posed by developmental issues.

Foreign Policy Performance and Developmental Issues

Use of the term "developmental" entails hidden difficulties. At most, it connotes a situation in which individuals possess both human dignity and the ability to control their environment to the greatest possible extent. At least, development implies a relatively high per capita GNP, hence the intimate connection between economic issues and the developmental. American foreign policy has come to reflect a profound ambivalence regarding developmental issues. Emphasis on America as a revolutionary metaphor for a newly independent Third World has given way to the suggestion by Senator Daniel Moynihan when he was Ambassador to the United Nations that the United States "go into opposition."[71] Having initially encouraged the growth of international organizations like the United Nations, American foreign policy now reflects uncertainty. Third World rhetorical predominance at the United Nations represents something of an embarrassment—a potentially high-rent property in New York City which now provides a forum for denouncing the titular landlord.

The strains that may exist regarding various interactive issues largely fade into the background when the United States and its industrialized allies are placed into the common category of "developed." This represents the North–South cleavage in its boldest relief because across a wide variety of issues the concerns of the less developed amount to suggestions for a restructuring of privilege in current global politics. While NIEO has come to represent the focus for such suggestions, it is significant to note that if it is compared with "the UN Conferences on the Environment, Population, Food, Law of the Sea, and the like, several interesting similarities are apparent":

> This collective decision-making mode is increasingly intersectoral, and no longer simply confined to the atomistic sector-by-sector approach to socio-economic issues of the past. Furthermore, since it is concerned with relationships among several sectors, *this mode of decision making seems to put an incremental strategy at a disadvantage,* as it necessitates the construction of more holistic perspectives and the formulation of broader policy bundles on the basis of which to calculate trade-offs. . . . [T]he

functionally-specific and technocratic system of international socio-economic decision-making constructed after World War II is increasingly superseded by a more integrated and directly political mode.[72]

NIEO and what we shall consider its related issues therefore presents a serious challenge because American foreign policy is the paradigmatic case of incrementalism for issue sources, processing, and management. This can be demonstrated in several ways. First, NIEO-related issues raise massive problems of coordination across bureaucratic structures. By one count there are at least nine separate governmental actors with specific responsibilities for economic issues, not including Congress or the president.[73] Second, American governmental regulation of nonstate actor activities poses enough difficulties on an incremental basis. Placing MNC behavior in a global context across the broad variety of economic issues increases the problems geometrically. Indeed, the perspective among some of the less developed which sees the multinational corporation as the concrete manifestation of capitalism's evils is almost too facile because it fails to take into account the challenges posed for home governments. This leads Robert Keohane and Joseph Nye to challenge implicitly the underpinnings of a NIEO by suggesting rather pessimistically: "If bargains between rich and poor are struck, they will have to be largely self-enforcing."[74]

While the origins of the NIEO negotiations are somewhat complex, from the perspective of a developed country like the United States they emerge from the attempt to establish a dialogue between oil producers and consumers in the wake of the 1973 oil embargo. This in itself is of some interest, reinforcing the point made earlier that events of virtual crisis proportions are often necessary for inducing the processing of new issues by American foreign affairs bureaucracies. Be that as it may, the oil producer-consumer discussions at Paris in 1975 became stalemated over the insistence by the LDCs, backed strongly by OPEC, that the substantive topics covered by the dialogue be broadened. The United States and its developed partners acceded, and the NIEO was taken up at the Seventh Special Session of the U.N. General Assembly.

The call for a NIEO is composed of several substantive themes,[75] each of which presents unique problems for those who make United States foreign policy because the themes violate major principles of maintaining an economic regime based upon liberal principles. First, the LDCs insist that they should receive larger amounts of resources and technology from the industrialized world. The ways in which this is to be accomplished are several. One is increasing developmental aid on the part of the industrialized countries to 0.7 percent, and eventually 1 percent, of total GNP. Whatever position the American foreign affairs bureaucracies assume on this proposal, Congress has become increasingly stingy with foreign aid, suggesting that this target could become a source of increasing political conflict. Another proposal by the LDCs is that they be allowed to link the prices they charge for exported commodities to the costs of manufactured goods from the industralized world. American opposition to this proposal has been quite vehement, arguing that this kind of indexing is a violation of the free market envisioned by liberal trading principles.

A second desire of the LDCs is that they be treated as a special case because of past "exploitation." Whereas this term can be imbued with various meanings bordering on the pedantic, Richard Cooper offers the following definition for "nonexploitive" economic transactions: "They must be undertaken voluntarily and they must not involve persistent above-normal profits, normal profits being reckoned with respect to each of the trading economies." [76] Of course, the precise meaning of "normal" is debatable in and of itself. Operationally, Third World countries insist that past exploitation serves as a justification for exercising full control over those natural resources they may possess, as well as for protecting themselves from future exploitation through the formation of commodity producers' cartels. These suggestions represent what may be a faulty generalization from the OPEC case, although cartels could possibly hold the economies of more developed countries captive, charging exorbitant prices for raw materials or attempting to deny them altogether.

Needless to say, the United States has resisted such proposals. On the one hand, the United States argues against the claim that certain governments should be treated as exceptions simply because they may have been exploited, and that general rules for industrialized countries are applicable in the Third World too. On the other, the United States denies the applicability of general rules, insisting that each country or commodity must be treated on a case-by-case basis. Furthermore, general rules such as those envisioned by the Third World could interfere seriously with the MNCs' abilities to operate in less developed contexts, something which could have significant effects for economies like that of the United States.

A final theme of the NIEO is revision of the international mechanisms themselves that govern the global economy, giving a greater say to the less developed. In this way trade barriers could be removed, and the structure of preferential tariffs in the industrialized world could be altered. The overall effect would be to allow poorer countries to increase their relative standing in the global economy because they would still be allowed to manipulate such items as export incentives to their own advantage. In a sense, these proposals could have the effect of standing the current international economic structure on its head. Instead of industrialized countries having a greater say in the global flow of currencies because of their larger proportionate impact, it would be the Third World because of its greater numbers. Here again the United States has attempted to resist Third World pressure, arguing that marginal increases in responsiveness will prove sufficient within the current international framework.

All in all, United States foreign policy with regard to developmental issues appears to accept the possibilities of a philosophical legitimacy for claims like those raised by the NIEO. At the same time, however, American behavior often seems to deny that it is actually worth bothering about such principles by attempting to play one country off against another. The entire notion of development rests on a metaphor between processes of political change within states and what may or may not be happening in global politics. Whereas this metaphor has some heuristic value, it could well be misplaced. This is not to say that issues of participation, institution building, and legitimacy are not to some extent characteristic of global politics. It is to suggest that as the United States becomes less disorganized with regard to developmental issues the actual behavior for which the sometimes lofty rhetoric serves as underpinning should be scrutinized. Before one discusses the normative in foreign policy the empirical must be taken into account.

Conclusions

I have pointed out that issues have a twofold importance in world politics. Issues are related to, and represent incentives for, actor behavior, at the same time that they serve as the components of the global systems in which such behavior succeeds or fails. Since there is no global system of which the behavior of American actors does not form a part, governmental orchestration becomes a profound problem because of this high level of involvement. The United States remaining the most important country in the world, the initial successes of American foreign policy following World War II have created expectations on the part of many that can be met only with great difficulty.

Actor proliferation as well as issue-specificity are largely a reflection of modernization. Since the United States serves as the model for modern society, its government finds that the more actors involve themselves in a given issue, the higher the probability that foreign policy will reflect compromise and incrementalism. In this sense societal and governmental variables are quite complementary in their effects on American foreign policy. The result is that authority becomes increasingly diffuse and decision-making often disjointed. The president can rarely if ever command. The likelihood of his being successful in doing so declines with the tangibility of various issues because of the more widespread actor involvement they engender. As a result, political considerations predominate in American foreign policy.

Less than a decade ago the effects of U.S. foreign policy were a day-to-day concern. At the beginning of the 1980s it appears that most Americans, acknowledging that their country should by and large have an active foreign policy, would rather not be bothered by it. Perhaps this response is not all that surprising because the issues with which American foreign policy has to deal have become increasingly complex. It is easier to deal with a world of greater physical comforts in the short run than to search out the threats lurking just beyond the horizon. There are adequate occasions to criticize the views of the world held by decision makers, but this is the point at which the task of the foreign policy analyst becomes critical. Too often, foreign policy analysis in the United States spares decision makers from being brought fundamentally to task about their basic theoretical assumptions in dealing with foreign policy issues and hence politics.

If the American foreign policy community has been far from perfect, and perhaps even less than satisfactory, it should be reported in fairness that the United States has *not* committed national suicide. Efforts are made to cope with foreign policy issues of both the interactive and developmental variety. Yet the conceptual frameworks into which these issues are placed prevent those responsible for dealing with them from getting beyond particularistic conceptions of a national interest. Students of bureaucratic behavior know that the best predictor of future action is the past. American foreign policy had muddled through up to now. It is fairly safe to predict that it will continue to do so in the future.

Notes

1. Marina V. N. Whitman, "Leadership without Hegemony. Our Role in the World Economy," *Foreign Policy,* 20 (Fall 1975), 138–60.
2. See *The Federalist Papers,* Nos. 42 and 66 (New York: Mentor, 1961), pp. 264–71 and 401–407.
3. Alexis de Tocqueville, *Democracy in America* (J. P. Mayer, ed., translated by George Lawrence) (Garden City, N.Y.: Doubleday, 1969), pp. 228–29.
4. Walter Lippmann, *Essays in the Public Philosophy* (Boston: Little, Brown, 1955), p. 20.
5. See, for example, R. J. Rummel, "Dimensions of Conflict Behavior within and between Nations," and Jonathan Wilkenfeld, "Domestic and Foreign Conflict," in Wilkenfeld (ed.), *Conflict Behavior and Linkage Politics* (New York: McKay, 1973), pp. 59–123.
6. These arguments and some of those which follow are developed more fully in Lawrence S. Falkowski, Donald E. Lampert, and Richard W. Mansbach,

Beyond the National Interest (Englewood Cliffs, N.J.: Prentice-Hall, forthcoming).

7. Stanley Hoffmann, "A View from at Home: The Perils of Incoherence," *Foreign Affairs*, 57 (America and the World 1978), 463.

8. James N. Rosenau, "Pre-Theories and Theories of Foreign Policy," in R. Barry Farrell (ed.), *Approaches to Comparative and International Politics* (Evanston, Ill.: Northwestern University Press, 1966), pp. 27–92. The subsequent discussion follows Rosenau's lead in dispensing with the "role" variable and is based in part on analysis contained in Patrick J. McGowan, "Problems in the Construction of Positive Foreign Policy Theory," in James N. Rosenau (ed.), *Comparing Foreign Policies* (New York: Sage/Halsted, 1974), pp. 25–44.

9. See the discussion of Ole Holsti's findings regarding Dulles in Michael P. Sullivan, *International Relations: Theories and Evidence* (Englewood Cliffs, N.J.: Prentice-Hall, 1976), pp. 45–46.

10. Robert O. Keohane and Joseph S. Nye, *Power and Interdependence* (Boston: Little, Brown, 1977), 64.

11. See Donald E. Lampert, Lawrence S. Falkowski, and Richard W. Mansbach, "Is There an International System?" *International Studies Quarterly*, 22 (March 1978), 143–166.

12. Patrick J. McGowan and Howard B. Shapiro, *The Comparative Study of Foreign Policy* (Beverly Hills, Calif.: Sage, 1973), p. 117.

13. Samuel P. Huntington, *Political Order in Changing Societies* (New Haven, Conn.: Yale University Press, 1968), pp. 98, 122.

14. See James N. Rosenau, *The Adaptation of National Societies: A Theory of Political System Behavior and Transformation* (New York: McCaleb-Seiler, 1970).

15. Ibid., p. 4.

16. See William Zimmerman, "Issue Area and Foreign-Policy Process: A Research Note in Search of a General Theory," *American Political Science Review*, 67 (December 1973), 1204–1212.

17. These figures were determined through a content analysis of the titles and subheads of the first thirty issues of *Foreign Policy* beginning with Winter 1970–1971 and ending with Spring 1978. Using the definition of an issue employed herein (see Note 11 above), the individual titles and subheads were coded if they evoked a recognizable specific issue. For example, "Security or Confrontation: The Case for a Defense Policy" (a title in *Foreign Policy*, 1) was *codable*, as was "The Claims of National Security" (a subhead in the same issue). "Half Past Nixon" (a title in *Foreign Policy*, 3) or "A Critical Reappraisal" (a subhead in this article) were *uncodable* because they did not evoke a specific issue. A total of 77 percent of the total titles and 19 percent of the total subheads for the thirty issues proved codable in this manner. Based upon the average number of subheads per article, each title was weighted by a factor of 5. The scores for titles and subheads were then summed, with the following results for the total of weighted titles and subheads for all issues: Political: 51 percent, Economic: 30 percent, Security: 20 percent. The respective figures for the last year (four issues) were then computed, yielding: Political: 55 percent, Economic: 37 percent, Security: 13

percent. A Chi Square was calculated for the last year in comparison with an average based on the data for all years, and a significant difference ($p < .05$) did emerge which appears to be based on a further declining importance of security issues.

18. Paul Seabury, "Thoughts on a New Foreign Policy Agenda," *Orbis,* 20 (Fall 1976), 578.

19. Vincent Davis, "The Changing International Environment and U.S. Military Policy in the 1980s: Some General Observations" (paper presented at the Regional Conference of the Inter-University Seminar on Armed Forces and Society, Southern Methodist University, April 1978), 6. Used by permission.

20. Ibid., 50. (Emphasis in original)

21. Eugene J. McCarthy, "Look, No Allies," *Foreign Policy,* 30 (Spring 1978), 3.

22. Central Intelligence Agency, *Handbook of Economic Statistics 1977* (Washington: ER 77–10537, September 1977), 19.

23. Ibid., 1, 2.

24. Richard N. Cooper, "Testimony before Subcommittee on Trade of House Committee on Ways and Means" (3 November 1977), *Department of State Bulletin,* 77:2009 (26 December 1977), 904.

25. Central Intelligence Agency, *Handbook,* 38.

26. The classic statement of this position may be found in William Appleman Williams, *The Tragedy of American Diplomacy* (New York: Delta, 1962).

27. Whitman, "Leadership without Hegemony," 138–39.

28. Branislav Gosovic and John Gerard Ruggie, "On the Creation of a New International Economic Order: Issue Linkage and the Seventh Special Session of the UN General Assembly," *International Organization,* 30 (Spring 1976), 325.

29. See Richard Rosecrance and Arthur Stein, "Interdependence: Myth or Reality," *World Politics,* 26 (October 1973), 1–27.

30. Keohane and Nye, *Power and Interdependence,* p. 162.

31. Marina V. N. Whitman, "A Year of Travail: The United States and the International Economy," *Foreign Affairs,* 57 (America and the World 1978), 554.

32. John Pinder, "The Reform of International Economic Policy: Weak and Strong Countries," *International Affairs,* 53 (July 1977), 349.

33. Barry B. Hughes, *The Domestic Context of American Foreign Policy* (San Francisco: W. H. Freeman, 1978), p. 197.

34. Ibid., pp. 198–201 and 218–19.

35. See Lee H. Hamilton and Michael H. Van Dusen, "Making the Separation of Powers Work," and Douglas J. Bennet, Jr. "Congress in Foreign Policy: Who Needs It?" *Foreign Affairs,* 57, (Fall 1978), 17–50.

36. Harvey G. Zeidenstein, "The Reassertion of Congressional Power: Curbs on the President," *Political Science Quarterly,* 93 (Fall 1978), 401.

37. Hoffman, "A View from at Home," 482.

38. Cited in Marriner Eccles, *Beckoning Frontiers* (New York: Knopf, 1951), p. 336.

39. Nelson W. Polsby, "Presidential Cabinet Making: Lessons for the Political System," *Political Science Quarterly,* 93 (Spring 1978), 17.

40. Lincoln P. Bloomfield, "Planning Foreign Policy: Can It Be Done?" *Political Science Quarterly,* 93 (Fall 1978), 378.

41. Johan Galtung, "Social Position, Party Identification, and Foreign Policy Orientation," in James N. Rosenau (ed.), *Domestic Sources of Foreign Policy* (New York: Free Press, 1967), 161–93.

42. See William A. Scott, "Psychological and Social Correlates of International Images," in Herbert C. Kelman (Ed.), *International Behavior: A Social-Psychological Analysis* (New York: Holt, Rinehart and Winston, 1965), pp. 71–103.

43. See John E. Mueller, *War, Presidents and Public Opinion* (New York: Wiley, 1973).

44. This inductive classification was based upon the 248 codable article titles for the thirty issues of *Foreign Policy* beginning with Winter 1970–1971 and ending with Spring 1978 (see Note 17). Whereas it might readily be admitted that this analysis therefore reflects no more than the editorial perspective of *Foreign Policy* rather than a "foreign policy agenda," there are a number of reasons that this seemed an appropriate data source. As a new journal started during the 1970s, it appears likely that this "agenda-setting" was exactly what the editors of *Foreign Policy* had in mind. The editorial board reflected a higher degree of academic input than comparable journals, and one would hopefully look to academics for more of a sense of "the long view." *Foreign Affairs* was deemed to have the drawback of a greater policy maker input with a corresponding attentiveness to the day-to-day. Also, articles by foreign writers seemingly give it less of an explicitly American orientation than the design of *Foreign Policy* suggests. *Orbis,* which does have academic input, manifests a certain fixation with security problems. Furthermore, the flavor of *Foreign Policy* in the early 1970s was that of an "in-house journal of a government-in-exile" concerned with just the kind of agenda-setting of interest herein. Since the advent of the Carter administration this has been reflected in a number of people associated with *Foreign Policy* moving into government positions. It would obviously be of some interest to compare the results of a similar analysis based on *Foreign Affairs* and/or *Orbis,* but for present purposes the procedure employed was deemed appropriate. The categories were decided upon by the investigator. In order to qualify as a "category," at least 3 percent of the codable titles had to be accounted for, and all titles did prove classifiable. In the discussion which follows reference to "specific issues" can be read as reflecting particular substantive titles within the categories.

45. Stephen G. Walker, "Trends, Decisions, and Issues in American Foreign Policy," In David Berman and John Stookey (eds.), *American Government: A Public Policy Approach* (Pacific Palisades, Calif.: Palisades Publishers, forthcoming), Table 2. Professor Walker's results, which he generously shared with me, were based on an adjustment of the issue categories employed herein, eliminating the Domestic Actor Context and American Attitudes and Ideology. Walker suggests that the discrepancies which emerged may mirror the extent to which Economic/Developmental/Oil issues crosscut bureaucratic divisions (27–29).

46. Vincent Davis, "Henry Kissinger and Bureaucratic Politics: A Personal Ap-

praisal,'' (University of South Carolina: Institute of International Studies, Essay Series No. 9, 1979), 40, 39.

47. Robert Axelrod, "Bureaucratic Decisionmaking in the Military Assistance Program: Some Empirical Findings," in Morton H. Halperin and Arnold Kanter (eds.), *Readings in American Foreign Policy: A Bureaucratic Perspective* (Boston: Little, Brown, 1973), 163–64.

48. Henry A. Kissinger, "Domestic Structure and Foreign Policy," in James N. Rosenau (ed.), *International Politics and Foreign Policy,* rev. ed. (New York: Free Press, 1969), p. 263.

49. John D. Steinbruner, *The Cybernetic Theory of Decision* (Princeton, N.J.: Princeton University Press, 1974), p. 138.

50. Charles F. Hermann, "Why New Foreign Policy Problems Might Not Be Met: Constraints on Detecting Problems and Setting Agendas," in Charles W. Kegley, Jr. and Patrick J. McGowan (eds.), *Challenges to America: United States Foreign Policy in the 1980s* (Beverly Hills, Calif.: Sage, 1979), p. 281.

51. Adapted from Steinbruner, *The Cybernetic Theory,* pp. 16–18.

52. Michael K. O'Leary, "Foreign Policy and Bureaucratic Adaptation," in Rosenau (ed.), *Comparing Foreign Policies,* p. 69.

53. Cecil V. Crabb, Jr. *American Foreign Policy in the Nuclear Age,* 3rd ed. (New York: Harper & Row, 1972), p. 64,

54. Leslie H. Gelb and Morton H. Halperin, "The Ten Commandments of the Foreign Affairs Bureaucracy," in Steven L. Spiegel (ed.), *At Issue: Politics in the World Arena,* 2nd ed. (New York: St. Martin's, 1977), p. 359.

55. Kissinger, "Domestic Structure and Foreign Policy," pp. 265–66.

56. The latest in the series was chaired by Robert D. Murphy. See *Commission on the Organization of the Government for the Conduct of Foreign Policy* (Washington: U. S. Government Printing Office, June 1975).

57. See Charles F. Hermann, "International Crisis as a Situational Variable," in Rosenau, *International Politics,* pp. 409–21.

58. This is a major implication of Graham T. Allison, *Essence of Decision: Explaining the Cuban Missile Crisis* (Boston: Little, Brown, 1971).

59. This distinction was originally posed in Stanley Hoffmann, "Obstinate or Obsolete? The Fate of the Nation-State and the Case of Western Europe," *Daedalus,* 95 (Summer 1966), 892–908. By now even Hoffmann appears to have at least implicitly conceded. See his "No Choice, No Illusions," *Foreign Policy,* 25, (Winter 1976–1977), 97–140.

60. Keohane and Nye, *Power and Interdependence,* pp. 24–25.

61. Richard Holbrooke, "A Sense of Drift, A Time for Calm," *Foreign Policy,* 23 (Summer 1976), 97–112.

62. Daniel Yankelovich, "Farewell to 'President Knows Best'," *Foreign Affairs,* 57 (America and the World 1978), 678.

63. Barry M. Blechman, "Handicapping the Arms Race," in Spiegel (ed.), *At Issue,* pp. 273–77.

64. Alton Frye, "Strategic Restraint, Mutual and Assured," *Foreign Policy,* 27 (Summer 1977), 14.

65. See Aaron L. Friedberg, "What SALT Can (And Cannot) Do," *Foreign Policy,* 33 (Winter 1978–1979), 97.

66. Jan M. Lodal, "SALT II and American Security," *Foreign Affairs*, 57 (Winter 1978–1979), 261.
67. Bruce M. Russett and Bruce G. Blair, "SALT II: Limited Negotiations: Introduction," in *Progress in Arms Control?* (San Francisco: W. H. Freeman, 1979), pp. 120–21.
68. John C. Campbell, "The Middle East: The Burdens of Empire," *Foreign Affairs*, 57 (America and the World 1978), 631.
69. Stephen D. Krasner, "U.S. Commercial and Monetary Policy: Unravelling the Paradox of External Strength and Internal Weakness," *International Organization*, 31 (Autumn 1977), 641–56.
70. Ibid., 665.
71. See Daniel P. Moynihan, "The United States in Opposition," *Commentary*, 59 (March 1975), 31–44.
72. Gosovic and Ruggie, "On the Creation of a New International Economic Order," 345. (Emphasis added.)
73. Krasner, "U. S. Commercial and Monetary Policy," 648.
74. Keohane and Nye, *Power and Interdependence*, p. 235.
75. Richard N. Cooper, "A New International Economic Order for Mutual Gain," *Foreign Policy*, 26 (Spring 1977), 67.
76. Ibid., 82.

3

Issues for Global Actors: The U.S.S.R.

Andrzej Korbonski

Theoretical Perspectives

To say something original and/or interesting at the beginning of the 1980s about the Soviet Union's involvement in international relations is not an easy task. It may be argued that by now all the important aspects of Soviet behavior on the global scene have been sufficiently examined. This can be said of many features of the U.S.S.R.'s conduct in the international arena, such as the role of ideology in determining foreign policy, the influence of geographical factors, the impact of Russian history and of the traditional political culture, and last but not least, the part played by the Soviet ruling oligarchy. Finally, the impact of the behavior of the other global actors vis-à-vis Moscow has also been examined at various levels, as has been the influence of technological progress, especially with respect to the development and impact of the modern weapons systems.

The literature dealing with the above issues is quite extensive, and the level of analysis is impressive and often highly sophisticated. Any student of Soviet affairs attempting to gain some new insights into Soviet behavior on the international scene or to use a new analytical framework for the study of Soviet external politics therefore must approach the task with considerable caution if not humility: there is an excellent chance that most of the things he or she intended to say have already been said or written—often better—by others.

It is the great virtue of the framework adopted by the editors of this volume that it implicitly assumes the existnece among the readers of a considerable reservoir of knowledge about the individual global actors and their foreign and domestic policies, and that instead of going over the ground made familiar to us by at least one generation of scholars since the end of World War II, it focuses on two issues: the foreign policy formulation and its linkage to the level of political development. The latter variable in particular has been largely neglected in the literature dealing with communist international relations, and except for the pioneering work on the whole question of national-international linkages initiated by James Rosenau, the cupboard has remained bare.[1]

In his perceptive study of the contemporary Soviet political system, John Reshetar distinguishes six different "systemic models" which he examines for the purpose of explaining how the Soviet system works: the totalitarian, the authoritarian, the bureaucratic, the oligarchic, the modernization, and the imperial model.[2] It is clear that no one of these models taken alone explains satisfactorily the performance of the Soviet polity, and it is equally obvious that some of the above models tend to be obsolete and are of little relevance in the contemporary context.

Because of that we shall consider the totalitarian model as .naving little applicability for the analysis of the present Soviet system. Much has been written about the totalitarian syndrome and little if anything would be gained by repeating the familiar arguments and clichés. The same may be said to be true for the imperial and the authoritarian models, which leaves only three paradigms as apparently relevant for the study of the contemporary Soviet political system: the bureaucratic, the oligarchic, and the modernization model.

The bureaucratic model has always been closely identified with Alfred G. Meyer and his "USSR, Incorporated."[3] Although there is little doubt that Soviet reality does not resemble closely the "company town" and is in fact much more complex, the intellectual clarity and analytical strength of the model have not really been seriously challenged and weakened since its appearance almost twenty years ago. The concepts of "administered society" and of "totalitarianism without terror" also continue to perform the highly useful function of explaining if not the input then at least the output of the Soviet polity.[4] Bureaucratic politics and conflicts among different categories of bureaucracies—party, government, and military—seem to dominate the Soviet domestic scene, including the decision-making processes, in the early 1980s as much as they did twenty years earlier.

The main virtue of the bureaucratic approach is that it permits, albeit in a somewhat revised form, the retention of all "totalitarian" variables except for the presence of arbitrary terror which for many scholars represented by far the most crucial condition of totalitarianism. Moreover, many western observers of the Soviet and East European scene, especially since the 1960s, have become convinced that "the tenuous distinction made between politics and administration in Western pluralistic societies completely disappears in Communist politics" and that "the political process of Communist states can best be understood by a consideration of the same kinds of issues and problems that are evident in all highly bureaucratized states."[5]

One does not have to believe in the validity of the "convergence theory" to realize the impact of economic development on the political system, and especially on the character and quality of political leadership. The ruling elite, including the bureaucracy, must sooner or later respond to the imperatives of industrialization by coopting increasing numbers of experts and specialists to deal with the growing complexity of the economic and social systems.[6] At the same time the new generation of more pragmatic and better educated younger technocrats has already begun to move into the middle and even some top decision-making positions, displacing the conservative old guard.[7]

In essence, both the totalitarian and bureaucratic approaches or models were designed or invented specifically for the study of nondemocratic societies, and they assumed by implication that the generalized or universalistic models, approaches, and paradigms customarily used for the study of all political systems—democratic and authoritarian, developed and nondeveloped—were not suitable for the study of communist systems. Today, however, the assumption no longer commands much support among political scientists and it is generally recognized that there may be other approaches that could yield more useful results than the models discussed earlier. The two analytical schemes or frameworks— the oligarchic or group conflict, and the modernization or developmental —have one basic assumption in common: they assume explicitly or implicitly that there is no fundamental difference between the communist and noncommunist systems, and that the same approaches, paradigms, and techniques can be used for the study of both.

While some may object to the identification of the oligarchic model with that of group conflict, a good case can be made for the argument that conflict among groups may be seen as a conflict among oligarchies representing particular groups and articulating their interests and demands. Thus one can view the political process in the Soviet Union as essentially a contest between different oligarchies or groups, each representing a specific interest and each insisting on being consulted, if not formally included, in the decision-making process. The role of the government is seen as basically that of a more or less passive arbiter or broker trying to achieve a workable compromise by reconciling divergent interests.

Despite the surging popularity of the approach, especially in the East European context, the question still remains whether the model has any validity for the analysis of communist political systems. As with the other approaches the answer is both yes and no. There is little doubt that the growing complexity of communist economies and societies has produced specialized groups that are beginning to hoard and monopolize expert knowledge. The respective governments, including that of the Soviet Union, are gradually forced to seek advice from these groups, thus increasing their stature in the system. This in itself tends to strengthen the groups by endowing them with a sense of identity that sooner or later is bound to lead to further demands for participation.

The critics of the group theory approach feel that whereas incipient pluralism may be observed in several East European countries, this has not been the case in the Soviet Union. Moreover, the approach is considered largely meaningless as a researchable category, and the application of this approach, developed as it were, for the study of genuinely pluralistic societies, is felt to have little or no validity for analyzing communist systems.[8]

From a rigorous point of view the critics are undoubtedly right and in the strictly formal sense pluralism has no place in communist societies. It can be argued, however, that the above view is too restrictive to be of much value for research purposes and that a compulsive adherence to rigidly defined categories may prevent us from gaining useful insights into the working of the Soviet system. To quote a recent suggestion, "in order to push on with various studies of interest group politics in the Soviet Union we must first rid ourselves of the constricting belief that group theory applies only to groups that operate openly and straightforwardly within a political culture which not only tolerates, but celebrates, pluralism."[9] Enough empirical evidence has been accumulated over the past several years to indicate that there is considerable group activity going on in the Soviet Union and that interest articulation has become (or is in the process of becoming) legitimized by the ruling party. This phenomenon led one of the authorities on the U.S.S.R. to come up with a concept of "institutional pluralism" as a possible way out of the dilemma,[10] and there have also been growing references in the literature to the "pluralism of elites" as an alternative to, or a variant of, the group conflict approach.[11]

Judging by the amount of research it has stimulated, one would conclude that the group conflict approach filled a void in research strategy. Perhaps one of its greatest attractions lay in its responding to an easily observable phenomenon which could not be easily explained by any of the hitherto accepted analytical frameworks. Moreover, it appealed to the supporters of the "convergence theory" by confirming their faith in the common industrial or postindustrial culture giving rise to identical or similar political and social processes regardless of the character of the political system.

Nevertheless it can be argued that the approach raised almost as many questions as it answered. It was one thing to study pluralistic tendencies in communist societies and another to disregard, explicitly or implicitly, the fact that these societies were after all communist and hence nondemocratic. So far at least, there has not been any evidence of the complete disappearance of either the communist ideology or the ruling communist party—both of which still continue to make communist countries, including the Soviet Union, different not only from the democratic but also from other authoritarian systems.

As suggested earlier, one of the foci of this volume has been the level of political development of the various global actors. In a sense, this determines the choice of the basic analytical framework for the study of the Soviet system, which is the modernization or developmental approach. This has been widely discussed, analyzed, praised, and criticized in the literature and at this stage there is no point in summarizing once again the major arguments, except very briefly. This is also not the place to deal with the problem of defining "development" or "modernization" or with the merits of the respective concepts: both have also been ably analyzed in the profession and the discussion is far from over.

It can be said that there are two major variants of the developmental approach as applied to the study of the Soviet society. One is based on the assumption that communist systems are simply a genus in the family of industrializing or modernizing nations and as such they are not essentially different from other noncommunist regimes bent upon economic development. In the words of the chief proponent of the approach, John Kautsky, "Communist phenomena are not distinguished from non-Communist ones by any particular characteristics,"[12] and hence the approach appears especially attractive for the study of those communist systems that exhibit systemic features similar to those shown by the less developed countries throughout the world. Whether this includes the Soviet Union is difficult to say.

The other variant of the developmental approach is associated with Gabriel Almond and Bingham Powell.[13] The major advantage of this variant is that it can be applied to the analysis of the *whole* system. Whatever the merits of the bureaucratic and the oligarchic-group conflict approaches, their main drawback is their *micro*-character which means that they can be used only for the study of individual, albeit important, segments of society.

The modernization framework avoids another problem faced by at least two of the approaches mentioned earlier. The totalitarian and the bureaucratic paradigms were "invented" by and large exclusively for the study of communist societies. The other approach—the group conflict one—claimed to be of a more generalized nature but, as suggested above, that claim has been under considerable criticism by those who believe that communist systems *are* different from all other political systems. Similar criticism can be directed against Kautsky's developmental model, which according to some critics has gone too far in its neglect of ideology as a systemic variable.

Does this mean that the Almond approach is totally free of drawbacks and disadvantages? Obviously not. The criticism can be divided essentially into two parts: that dealing with the theoretical underpinning of the approach—systems theory and structural functionalism—and that concerned specifically with the application of the developmental framework to the analysis of the communist systems. The former criticism is quite familiar and needs not be elaborated on here; the latter is of greater interest. Its exponents castigate the approach for neglecting the importance of leadership and personality and for not paying sufficient attention to the influence of exogenous factors,[14] for being culture-bound,[15] and for generating "unduly optimistic general theory of political development."[16]

The first two points are well taken. Clearly there is a difference between Stalin, Khrushchev, and Brezhnev and between their respective influences on the Soviet political system. However, as with the number of other concepts, the importance of leadership and personality should not be exaggerated. It was obviously greater under Stalin when it formed part of the totalitarian syndrome but its role today is not as easily ascertained. The same applies to the influence of the outside factors on the Soviet system.

In the final analysis, the impact and weight of leadership and of the international environment—neither of which can be easily operationalized—depend on the perception of the researcher. On the one hand there is always the temptation to explain nearly everything that has been happening in the U.S.S.R. with reference to either the personality of the current leader or leaders or to the influence of other global actors, or both. While certainly valid at certain periods in recent Soviet history, this assumption ignores many interesting internal socioeconomic developments occurring spontaneously and autonomously in the U.S.S.R.

Ultimately, regardless of the approach chosen, an analytical study of the Soviet political system and its linkage to foreign policy-making must be largely couched in intuitive and impressionistic terms, and the various conclusions, generalizations, and hypotheses must necessarily be highly subjective. Nevertheless, even though they must be surrounded by the standard caveats and treated with considerable reserve, it may be argued that the conclusions emerging from this chapter represent another modest step toward increasing our knowledge of this area.

Interpreting the external behavior of any actor is a function of many variables: the amount of past and present information and intelligence about the actor's domestic and foreign policies; knowledge of the actor's history, political culture, and political system; success of failure in interpreting and predicting the actor's past behavior on the international scene; and, last by not least, the biases and prejudices of the interpreter.

The amount of sheer factual knowledge about Soviet internal and external policies is impressive. The level and quality of analysis have been high and are rising. Whereas the United States and Canada have been generating most of the information, analysts and experts in Great Britain and West Germany have also been making important contributions. Thus our knowledge and understanding of Soviet history and its political system should make it possible to interpret Soviet external behavior in a more sophisticated fashion than in the past. The revival of interest in the concept of communist political culture and its impact on policy has added a new dimension to our analysis.[17]

Insofar as our ability to interpret and predict past Soviet behavior is concerned, the record seems to be generally positive, whether it was related to the Sino–Soviet conflict, Moscow's policy in the Middle East, or Kremlin activities in Eastern Europe. Whereas Soviet behavior in the various parts of the globe may have been misunderstood now and then and in the short run, the overall thrust tended to be generally interpreted correctly.[18]

I am prepared to argue that the major problem in interpreting Soviet global behavior and in explaining it to a wider public lay with the interpreters and that furthermore the perception or misperception of Moscow's policy which led to its being understood and interpreted in a certain way has been frequently influenced by United States domestic and foreign policy considerations. In other words, American policy makers, often for reasons of their own, preferred to interpret Soviet policy in a way that benefited them politically at home, even though the basis for such an interpretation was often highly questionable.

One could cite many examples of such faulty interpretations, frequently made with the full knowledge that the opposite interpretation was, in fact, much more probable or correct. Thus throughout the entire "Prague Spring" of 1968, both the White House and the State Department studiously managed to withhold any positive comment regarding the process of liberalization in Czechoslovakia for fear that this would greatly antagonize the U.S.S.R. whose friendship the United States attempted to cultivate in order to use Moscow's good offices to bring North Vietnam to the peace conference table in Paris. Why it would have been in Moscow's interest to terminate the war in South East Asia that was proving increasingly burdensome for Washington was difficult to explain in light of the history of U.S.–Soviet relations in the post-World War II period.

Henry Kissinger's public interpretation of Soviet behavior in the late 1960s clearly was motivated by factors which had to do less with an objective analysis and evaluation of the actual situation than with his own preferences and the interests of the Nixon administration and the Republican Party. The whole concept of the U.S.–Soviet détente, which culminated in the exchange of visits by Brezhnev and Nixon in 1972–1974 and in the SALT I Treaty, was based on the premise that the U.S.S.R. had become a peace-loving country, interested in maintaining and safeguarding the global status quo and deterred by the U.S. strategic dominance from trying to change in any significant fashion the existing boundaries of the respective spheres of influence. Détente, according to Kissinger, implied the end of the Cold War, mutual recognition of each other's status as global power, and the beginning of a new era of collaboration rather than confrontation on a variety of fronts.

Other examples abound. The emergence of the "revisionist school" among the modern historians who blamed the United States rather than the Soviet Union for the outbreak of the Cold War was clearly caused by the Vietnam war and had little if anything to do with the discovery of new, hitherto unknown facts. Soviet policy in the Third World and in Europe has also be interpreted frequently in accordance with the requirements of American domestic policy as perceived by the administration in power at a given time.

The correct perception and interpretation of Soviet external behavior is obviously crucial for policy makers throughout the world. In the past such a perception has been strongly influenced by ideological considerations which at times sharply distorted that behavior. It was only recently that Western observers have been able to shed the ideological baggage and view the U.S.S.R. as an important global actor whose actions and behavior in the final analysis did not differ fundamentally from the behavior of other global actors. To be sure, as suggested earlier, the presence of communist ideology could now and then make a difference at *a margin* but, by and large, one of the major assumptions underlying this essay is that at the beginning of the 1980s the Soviet foreign policy is basically no longer influenced by ideology but by a variety of factors held in common by all great powers, which in turn make up the given country's concept of national interest, usually defined and interpreted by its leaders.

The question to be asked next is what are the major issues in the Soviet foreign policy today and how does one analyze them? Whereas it is relatively easy to list the major issues that dominated Soviet foreign policy in the late 1970s, the list itself and especially the hierarchy and order of importance of the various issues lie in the eye of the beholder. In other words, the identification of the problems that need to be solved by

Soviet foreign policy makers interested in reaching certain concrete objectives, must be somewhat subjective. One of the purposes of this chapter is, after all, the analysis of Soviet global objectives and priorities. At this stage, however, all we can do is to suggest some of them, in no particular order of importance or relevance.

One of the questions that ought to be addressed is the issue of Soviet national interest. In other words, what is the Soviet national interest in the last quarter of the twentieth century? Is it primarily defensive in the sense of preserving the existing status quo which, after all, appears to quarantee the U.S.S.R. at least second place in the global configuration of forces? Or is it basically offensive, attempting to change the present state of affairs by expanding Soviet influence, especially in the Third and Fourth Worlds, and by overcoming or neutralizing the U.S. strategic superiority. In analyzing the Soviet national interest, should we focus on regional or global objectives: Eastern Europe and China, or also Angola, Cuba, and Ethiopia? Should we concentrate mostly on political and military issues as the only relevant ones or should we also consider economic issues which are becoming increasingly important on a global scale?

This is just a small sample of issues that this chapter will discuss, however briefly. By now, any analysis of Soviet foreign policy first has to get rid of veritable cobweb of conventional wisdoms accumulated over the years if one is to get a clear and uncluttered picture of that policy. For example, one of the oldest clichés presupposed that Soviet external behavior was aggressive and expansionist *ex definitione*. Thus any authoritarian, nondemocratic country was bound always to conduct a dynamic foreign policy, party to compensate for the lack of success at home and partly to increase its influence abroad. In the case of the Soviet Union the extra ingredient, absent in other global actors, was the existence of communist ideology and party, which tended to be viewed as playing a major role in influencing and formulating that policy in an expansionist and even revolutionary mode. Yet one can also argue—as China did in the 1960s—that the U.S.S.R. has lost its revolutionary elan and that it has become a strongly status quo-oriented, conservative, and satisfied power, no longer willing to use its military might to oppose capitalism and to support liberation movements throughout the world.

Another form of conventional wisdom which seemed to gain considerable currency in the 1960s, contributing greatly to the popularity of the "convergence theory," assumed a close linkage between the level of economic development and the character of the political system. In the Soviet context this implied a kind of linear relationship between industrialization and liberalization, first economic and then political.

Although this causality if not automaticity has been adequately criticized in the literature, the "convergence theory," which may be seen as the ultimate logical culmination of the socioeconomic processes in both the communist and noncommunist countries, refuses to die.[19] A corollary to this theory is that by becoming more developed, the U.S.S.R. has simultaneously become more peace-loving since for the first time in its sixty years it is now relatively prosperous and thus reluctant to engage in unnecessary violent conflicts for fear of losing the accumulated wealth. In other words, the U.S.S.R. has become a "has" country increasingly unwilling to risk its status and wealth for the attainment of some nebulous and ill-defined goals.

Although there is probably more then a grain of truth in the above hypothesis, an equally plausible case could be made by arguing that the linkage between industrialization and liberalization is at best a tenous one, that developed countries are not necessarily more peace-loving then the developing ones, and that highly industrialized states possessing large arsenals of weapons may in fact be quite aggressive.

Soviet Involvement in the Global System

How does the Soviet Union appear in the global system's patterns of societal and political affinities? One way of looking at the U.S.S.R.'s role in the international system is to view it as the second most powerful global actor today. This has not always been the case. Although with the disappearance of Germany and Japan in the wake of World War II the Soviet Union had beome the second most important military power in the world, its influence at that time was somewhat limited, covering only Europe and parts of Asia. In both of these areas the Kremlin has been in a position to present a formidable challenge to the United States, yet until recently Moscow was powerless to influence substantially the course of events in Africa and Latin America, and even the Middle East.[20]

This is obviously no longer true today. The Soviet Union has become a global political and military actor. This has been due to several causes. One was the rapid progress in weapons technology which put the U.S.S.R. ahead of the rest of the world in the development of long-range strategic arms and enabled it to exert powerful influence a long distance away from its Eurasian bases. This process was further strengthened through the rapid buildup of a Soviet bluewater navy and strategic air force, both of which made it possible for the Kremlin to challenge its enemies for the first time throughout the world.

Another reason for the development of a strong Soviet global role was a major decision on the part of the United States not to stop the process of Soviet globalism. The Cuban Missile Crisis of 1962 was probably the last clear-cut case of U.S.–Soviet confrontation which resulted in a bitter Soviet defeat, and it had very serious implications for the future course of U.S.–Soviet relations and for the Soviet foreign policy in general.

There is enough evidence suggesting that it was the Cuban debacle that provided the impetus for the rapid Soviet strategic buildup which culminated in reaching parity with the United States some ten years later. For reasons of its own, Washington decided not to match the Soviet buildup and to opt instead for the initiation of the arms limitation talks, thus acknowledging that the U.S.S.R. had become an equal partner on a global scale.

Has the Soviet ruling oligarchy had an expansionist policy? There is no evidence that this has actually been the case. The decision to match U.S. strategic strength was presumably made by Khrushchev in the wake of the Cuban disaster but it is not clear that its purpose was offensive rather than defensive. The Soviet interest in pursuing East–West détente by way of SALT, MBFR, and the Helsinki Conference might be viewed as an expression of peaceful intentions on the part of the present Soviet leadership.

As suggested by Brzezinski, the fact that both the Soviet Union and the United States are global actors means that their relationship even in the era of détente is bound to be a mixture of conflict and collaboration.[21] The global interaction between the two superpowers is being made even more complex by the fact that neither is acting alone or in a complete vacuum but that both are leaders of politico-military alliances which influence their behavior and policy. The apparent symmetry is further complicated not only by the presence of disintegrative tendencies within both camps but also by the serious challenge to the Soviet leadership of the international communist movement posed by China. While the United States has had problems with its European allies, the Sino–Soviet conflict for about two decades has been a major factor on the international scene introducing an additional complication for the Soviet foreign-policy makers.

To sum up, insofar as the global matrix of political affinities is concerned, the Soviet Union continues to view itself as the leader of the international communist camp despite being challenged, on the one hand, by China and, on the other, by some Eurocommunist leaders. Whether this role continues to be politically meaningful or whether it is primarily symbolic is difficult to say. The same is true for the societal context. In the past the U.S.S.R. proclaimed itself the first truly revolutionary society, a model to be emulated throughout the world, but particularly by the developing countries and especially those under the colonial rule of the West. That exalted status has become somewhat tarnished in the past two decades as a result of the challenge posed by China, yet the recent Soviet and Cuban inroads in Africa suggest that the role has not been abandoned entirely.

Moving from the network of societal and political affinities to that of economic power, here again the role played by the Soviet Union has changed rather substantially in the last decade or so. Until the mid-1960s Soviet participation in the international economic order was unimpressive, to say the least. This was due to several reasons. One was the traditional Soviet preference for economic autarky. Another was the sheer size of the Soviet economy which minimized the country's dependence on foreign trade. A third one was the economic Cold War which reduced East–West trade to a trickle during the 1950s and 1960s.[22]

The Western embargo on trade with the East contributed to the creation of the Council for Mutual Economic Assistance (CMEA) which initially at least was a major economic asset for the U.S.S.R., satisfying some of its most important economic needs and obviating the necessity to seek closer economic contacts with the rest of the world.

The last decade witnessed a major change in Soviet foreign economic policy. To begin with, the U.S.S.R. decided to enter in a massive way the realm of international trade, which was seen as a source of modern technology and know-how badly needed to modernize the Soviet economy. Undoubtedly the success of Moscow's East European allies in expanding their trade with the West and in attracting a large volume of credit provided a strong incentive. Another reason was most likely the change in the international markets caused by global inflation, especially in the area of energy and raw materials, that benefited the Soviet Union, which long has been a major producer of both. Soviet exports of oil and other raw materials to the West commanded high prices and permitted importation of modern technology.

Has greater Soviet involvement in the international economic order resulted in a higher degree of Soviet dependence on the outside world? I do not think so. I would also be prepared to argue that Moscow's involvement in the international division of labor was the result of special circumstances and not the outcome of a major policy decision. Except for oil and some other raw materials, the U.S.S.R. has had little to offer to the outside world and even its future as a major oil exporter has recently been questioned.[23] This means that the Soviet Union will not be able indefinitely to sustain the large balance of payments deficits, and sooner or later it will probably reduce its participation in East–West trade and rely once again on CMEA.

Thus far there has been no indication that the Soviet Union has used its newly discovered economic power for its own political advantage. For example, there was some apprehension in the West that the U.S.S.R. might reduce its oil exports to the West in the mid-1970s, following the Arab oil embargo, and that it might in fact use its influence in the Arab world to persuade the OPEC countries to continue the boycott in order to extract additional concessions from the West. The fact that this did not happen may be taken as another proof of growing Soviet political sophistication, reflected in Moscow's continuing concern for maintaining international stability and avoiding crisis situations.

The same appears to be true for Moscow's economic relations with its junior East European partners. Initially CMEA was used by the Kremlin as an instrument of economic exploitation in Eastern Europe. For the first postwar decade or so that area was clearly viewed as an economic asset for the U.S.S.R., supplying it with a variety of commodities at prices well below world market levels. This one-sided relationship began to change in the 1960s, and today it can be argued that Eastern Europe has in fact become an economic burden for the Soviet Union.[24] Although the U.S.S.R. has recently raised the prices of raw materials, including oil, exported to CMEA members, the latter have been receiving for many years a substantial subsidy from Moscow which again represented another good testimony of the Kremlin's willingness to pay the price of being a leader of an important regional alliance.

What about the Soviet role in the global and regional strategic balances? Much has been written about the former and no useful purpose will be served repeating the standard arguments.[25] As suggested earlier, the Soviet desire to achieve strategic parity with the United States is understandable in view of the agreement between Washington and Moscow to initiate the process of détente by focusing on the limitation of strategic arms. While the apparent current Soviet eagerness to conclude the SALT II agreement is viewed with suspicion in some circles in the United States, one possible interpretation is that Moscow has become firmly committed to the doctrine of peaceful coexistence with the West and that it no longer feels threatened or encircled by the capitalist camp. This, after all, has been the recurring theme in Soviet official pronouncements all the way from Malenkov's proper inferences from the successful Soviet testing of the H-bomb, through Krushchev's willingness to sign the Nuclear Test Ban treaty, to Brezhnev's eagerness to conclude SALT I and the Vladivostok agreements.

In the final analysis, the Soviet strategic posture can be viewed as a function of the overall western perception of Moscow's intentions. Those who perceive the U.S.S.R. as an essentially unchanging aggressive and imperialistic power are bound to question the Kremlin's sincerity in seeking to conclude the SALT II Treaty with the United States and they point instead to the Soviet-Cuban involvement in Angola and Ethiopia, to Moscow encouraging Vietnam's invasion of Cambodia, and to the continuing Soviet conventional military superiority in Central Europe. Those who see the U.S.S.R. as firmly committed to a policy of relaxation of international tension will focus on Soviet behavior at Helsinki and Belgrade, on Moscow's willingness to settle the German problem, including the vexing

Berlin issue, and on the Kremlin's continuing participation in the MBFR talks in Vienna.

Moving from the global to the regional strategic balance, the Soviet Union continues to lead the Warsaw Treaty Organization (WTO). By now the literature dealing with WTO is quite extensive although the organization itself has not been very active and visible since the Soviet intervention in Czechoslovakia in 1968. As in the case of CMEA, the Soviet domination of the Warsaw alliance has been repeatedly challenged by Rumania which since the early 1960s has continued to emphasize its autonomy in foreign policy. There is little doubt that the main value of the Warsaw Pact lies in its legitimizing the presence of Soviet troops on the territory of member countries. Until now there has been little effort to integrate the military establishments of the treaty members, and the WTO High Command has been totally dominated by the Soviets. There is no evidence of Soviet willingness to equip the East European armies with the most sophisticated weapons which, interestingly enough, have been given to Soviet allies in the Middle East and elsewhere. This could be taken as a sign of Soviet mistrust of the reliability of the WTO armies in the event of a confrontation with NATO. Recent events suggest that although most of the members pay lip service to the Soviet leadership of the alliance, Rumania's challenge to Moscow's hegemony may enjoy considerable support among the other East European countries.[26]

The other region where the Soviet Union has been facing a conventional if not yet a strategic challenge has been the Far East. Some forty Soviet divisions have been stationed along the Sino–Soviet border for close to twenty years, and the 1979 conflagration in Indochina, where Moscow's client Vietnam invaded Peking's ally Cambodia, has dramatized the sharp competition between the Soviet Union and China for influence in East Asia.

Apart from the global strategic confrontation with the United States, Central Europe, the Sino–Soviet border, and Afghanistan are the only areas of Soviet strategic and conventional military involvement. Although there are Soviet military advisers in Angola, Ethiopia, and some Middle Eastern countries, their presence does not constitute a major threat to the existing global and regional balances.

To conclude, the Soviet involvement in the global patterns of interaction appears to be primarily in the political and strategic areas and it concerns mostly the relationships with the United States and, to some extent, with China and some of Moscow's East European allies. Soviet involvement in the international economic order has been on the increase but so far has not reached a significant level, especially as compared with such major actors as West Germany or Japan. However, it may be argued that in contrast with the past, the Soviet Union has been more and more willing to play a role in the international environment, possibly to assert its growing role as an important global actor.

Sources of Issues in Soviet Foreign Policy

How do foreign policy issues originate within Soviet domestic foreign policy inputs? This is not an easy question to answer, if only because of the perennial difficulty in gaining information about Soviet policy inputs in general. We still have only a rather vague notion of how decisions are made in the Kremlin.

In light of the previous discussion it could be argued that today the domestic sources of Soviet foreign policy making are not greatly different from domestic sources of foreign policy making of any important international actor. The U.S.S.R. is no longer a revolutionary or even a fast changing society. It has gone through the period of rapid modernization and change and some of the domestic factors that tended to have a major influence on foreign policy formulation in the past are either no longer present or are present only to some degree.

Does ideology make any difference insofar as the formulation of Soviet foreign policy is concerned? Although I would be tempted to respond in the negative, I am persuaded that at least for the time being ideological considerations should not be entirely discarded, especially with regard to Soviet policy toward China and Eastern Europe. To be sure, it has been a long time since the last major ideological pronouncement *ex Kremlin cathedra* that had some relevance to the Soviet conduct of international relations. I have in mind here Khrushchev's declarations concerning the question of inevitability of war between the two camps, the problem of the peaceful transition to socialism, and the validity of the doctrine of many roads to socialism—all of them made at the famous Twentieth Congress of the Community Party of the Soviet Union in 1956. All of these pronouncements paved the way toward relaxation of tension and the ending of the Cold War: the denial of the principle of inevitability of war put substance in Khrushchev's concept of peaceful coexistence between East and West and the admission that communism could come to power in a peaceful, nonrevolutionary way contributed to greater international stability. The same was true for the doctrine of "many roads to socialism" which succeeded in defusing serious popular discontent in Eastern Europe—although clearly not in China.

However, all this took place some twenty-five years ago, and since then the only supposedly original theoretical declaration originating in the Kremlin was the so-called Brezhnev Doctrine issued to justify and legitimize the Soviet intervention in Czechoslovakia in 1968. Other than that, the ideological boxes remained strangely empty and in the early stages of the Sino–Soviet conflict, which were dominated by ideological differences between Moscow and Peking, the former found itself clearly on the defensive. Interestingly enough, no attempt was made to justify the war between communist states in South East Asia in ideological terms.

Still, although ideology no longer plays an active part in Soviet foreign policy making, it does retain some importance. Its influence has been admirably summarized and analyzed by Vernon Aspaturian who sees it primarily as a prism or an analytical tool which conditions the reasoning and perception of the Kremlin leaders and foreign policy makers.[27] Ideology to a large extent shapes mass and elite attitudes toward politics in general and international politics in particular. However, the value of ideology as a common language and a symbolic "glue" linking the various communist countries with the Soviet Union seems less and less important as time goes by. In fact, at times ideology appears almost as a handicap and an obstacle to better relations as illustrated by the conflict between the U.S.S.R., China, and Cambodia.

Reference has already been made to the influence of the domestic economic situation on the conduct of Soviet foreign policy. Whereas we should not fall into the trap of economic determinism, Khrushchev's proclamation of the era of "goulash communism," translated into a commitment to raise the standard of living of the Soviet population, obviously had an impact on the state of East–West relations. The decision to start importing large amounts of grain from the United States and other Western countries could be viewed as a milestone in that respect since it could only be interpreted as a public admission of the inability of the Soviet Union to feed its own people. Similarly, the decision to modernize the Soviet industrial base by importing the know-how and the technology rather than by developing it slowly and painfully at home was another manifestation of the growing maturity and sophistication of Soviet leadership, no longer afraid to acknowledge openly its failure to keep up with the other advanced countries around the world. The innovative decision to take advantage of the opportunities for international trade was a good example of increasing rationality in Soviet behavior—yet interestingly enough, it was not matched by a similar rational behavior at home where the internal economic system has shown few if any signs of liberalization and reforms, especially when contrasted with the situation in Eastern Europe. It may be presumed that bureaucratic vested interests, particularly in the central planning apparatus, were simply too strong and deeply rooted to yield to reforms that would have been linked with the expansion of Soviet economic contacts with the West.

How important the economic factors were in modulating Soviet foreign policy is difficult to say. There is no evidence of the U.S.S.R. using its economic power to impose its will on the East European allies: on the contrary, there are indications that Moscow provided economic aid to

East European regimes facing popular discontent caused by economic difficulties. Whereas economic factors may have been at least partly responsible for the grudging Soviet acceptance of the West German *Ostpolitik* of the late 1960s, there is no sign of economic considerations playing a significant role with respect to U.S.–Soviet relations. Although the Soviet Union has long been interested in receiving the Most-Favored-Nation treatment from the United States, its interest was not strong enough to ignore or disregard the Jackson-Vanik amendment which tied the whole question of U.S.–Soviet trade to a more liberal Soviet policy with respect to Jewish emigration. Altogether a reasonable case can be made for asserting that economic considerations, although probably more important than ideology, have not been exerting a crucial influence on Soviet foreign policy.

What about the different elites or oligarchies and their impact on foreign policy formulation? Here again only some tentative guesses can be offered. There is no doubt that the Soviet elites today are better educated, less doctrinaire, and more pragmatic than their counterparts of a generation ago. Although this may not necessarily be true of the gerontocracy in the Kremlin, many signs point to a growing intellectual and analytical sophistication on the part of the second-echelon decision makers at the level of ministries, functionally specialized state committees, and research institutes which provide expert advice to top policy makers. Most if not all of them seem to be well aware of the increasing complexity of international relations, including the area of international strategic and security affairs which until relatively recently was a *tabula rasa* in the Soviet Union. As suggested by Alexander Yanov in his perceptive study, many of the apparatchiki and government functionaries have become strong supporters of the policy of détente for reasons having little or nothing to do with their training or background.[28] At the same time it may be assumed that some of the better educated younger elites, aware of the likely consequences of a nuclear exchange between the Soviet Union and the United States, would also favor SALT agreements and other negotiations leading to arms control and disarmament.

What about the Soviet military and their influence on foreign policy? Again, very little can be said about this particular issue. We know on good authority that it was the Soviet military leaders who played a major if not a decisive role in the intervention in Hungary in 1956 and in Czechoslovakia in 1968.[29] It may also be assumed that it is the military in their role as an important interest group that has insisted on maintaining a large conventional military establishment, including the huge concentration of troops and weapons in Central Europe with all its foreign policy implications. While the military clearly gave their imprimatur to SALT I and II, they are obviously not giving in easily with respect to the mutual force reductions in Europe being negotiated in Vienna.

So much for the key domestic factors and actors linked with the formulation of Soviet foreign policy. It stands to reason that one of the crucial variables in determining the course of that policy originates outside the Soviet system. It is equally clear that not only the exogenous events and processes but also—and perhaps more importantly—the perception and interpretation of these developments by the Soviet leaders play an important part in providing the main thrust of that policy.

For example, it may be assumed that the Kremlin's decision to seek bilateral negotiations with the United States in the late 1960s was strongly influenced by a number of events and processes: the Vietnam war, which was becoming more and more unpopular, was dividing the American people and weakening the general will to resist Soviet encroachments on what was assumed to be the U.S. sphere of influence in Europe and elsewhere; the resulting American preoccupation with South East Asia at the expense of Europe; the growing polarization of American society, giving birth to a series of racial riots and student demonstrations against the Johnson administration; and finally, an increasingly unpopular president losing support and opening the way to a long and bitter domestic political struggle. As seen from the Kremlin, these were favorable developments that could facilitate attempts to extract major concessions from an impotent America.

Whereas it may be argued that Soviet perceptions of a paralyzed United States were important in the formulation of Moscow's foreign policy, the reverse may have been true for Moscow's relations with Peking. It is not inconceivable that Moscow viewed the Sino–Soviet conflict at least partly as a by-product of a personality clash between Khrushchev and Mao Zedong. All that is known is that one of the first major policy initiatives undertaken by the Brezhnev-Kosygin regime after Khrushchev's ouster in 1964 was an attempt to patch up the conflict, albeit without success. In general, the history of the Sino-Soviet schism is a history of misperceptions and misunderstandings, mainly on the Soviet side. Ultimately, the traditional Russian dislike and distrust of China began to assert itself at the expense of supposedly more sophisticated ideological explanations.

What about the Soviet perception of Eastern Europe in the late 1970s? It would appear that over the years Moscow has learned some lessons from events in the region during the 1950s and 1960s, and that at some point it began to see itself more as a leader of a conventional politico-military-economic alliance than as a *vozhd* of an ideological camp engaged in a sharp doctrinal struggle with the capitalist world. This new self-image meant that the Kremlin realized that the leadership of an alliance represented an obligation to provide aid and support for its members instead of exploiting them. Hence, as suggested earlier, the Soviet willingness to supply the Warsaw Pact countries with oil and raw materials at favorable prices and to ship grain to Eastern Europe even at times when a poor Soviet harvest made such shipments highly burdensome.

To put it somewhat differently, it may be said that in the past few years the Soviet Union has become much better informed about the situation in the individual East European countries, and as a result its perception of the various changes and processes in the region has acquired greater depth and sophistication. For example, again as mentioned above, Moscow has been aware for some time of the potential linkage between economic well-being and the system's legitimacy, and it has provided economic aid to regimes such as the Polish one which was unable to cope with economic difficulties. There is also some evidence pointing to a somewhat greater tolerance by the Kremlin of the various dissident movements, if not at home than at least in some of the East European countries. Altogether it seems that Moscow has learned some lessons from the Czechoslovak crisis and desires to avoid a repetition of that experience.

There is one final aspect of the Soviet–East European relations in which the problem of perception and images appears crucial. It concerns the reliability of the East European armed forces in the event of an East–West confrontation and the willingness of the East European military to resist a possible Soviet intervention à la Czechoslovakia.

Both questions are not readily answered. The former one was briefly discussed above with reference to Moscow's reluctance to supply its junior partners with the most advanced weapons. The latter question can only be speculated upon. One can hypothesize that one of the reasons for the Soviet decision to intervene in Czechoslovakia in 1968 was the Kremlin's belief that the Czechoslovak government and its armed forces would not resist. Similarly, the reluctance or unwillingness of the Soviet Union to intervene in Poland in 1956 and later, and in Rumania in the 1960s, might well have been due to the realization on Moscow's part that both countries would fight. The same seems to be true for Yugoslavia, which has long enjoyed a reputation as a country that would fiercely resist any Soviet attempt to intervene following Marshal Tito's death. It is this image that may prove decisive in determining future Soviet policy toward Belgrade.

It seems that the Soviet perceptions of the situation in Western Europe and the Third World have also become much more sophisticated. For example, the Soviet policy makers have had to steer a middle course between the communist parties of France and Italy—both flirting with Eurocommunism—and the respective national governments with which Moscow intends to have good relations. Although that policy has not always been successful, it still shows increasing Soviet awareness of subtleties of domestic conditions in the individual West European countries.

The same can be said about Soviet willingness to establish closer diplomatic contacts with the Vatican, which has been visited by Foreign Minister Gromyko, who had a long conversation with the then newly elected Polish Pope, John Paul II.

Insofar as the Soviet attitude toward the developing countries is concerned, here again the last decade has witnessed a major change in Moscow's policy. Whereas in the past the U.S.S.R. almost invariably distrusted the local regimes and insisted on the creation of separate communist parties, in the 1970s the Kremlin found the local nationalist regimes frequently more amenable and more easily managed than governments established and dominated by Marxist-Leninist parties.

Finally, what can be said about the personality and psychological makeup of Soviet decision makers and their impact on policy? Unfortunately not very much beyond some broad hypotheses. It was suggested earlier that there is a considerable difference between a Khrushchev and a Brezhnev, a Malenkov and a Molotov. How do these differences become translated into policy? Again, the last two decades have witnessed a significant change in this respect. With the emergence of collective leadership it has become increasingly difficult for the top leader to impose his own policy preferences on his colleagues in the Politburo and the Party Secretariat, although in the final analysis his views most likely predominate. If this is the case, the psychological profile of the leaders is of some relevance. A cursory glance at the last two Soviet leaders confirms it rather well. Khrushchev, although a product of the Stalinist system, was by nature an innovator—dynamic, impatient, emotional, even "hare-brained" to use a Soviet epithet. There is little doubt that Soviet foreign policy in the late 1950s and early 1960s bore a strong imprint of his personality starting with the announcement of the policy of peaceful coexistence, through destalinization, the Sino–Soviet conflict, all the way to the Cuban missile crisis and the Nuclear Test Ban treaty. Whether the policy ultimately benefited the U.S.S.R. is difficult to say: it was clearly a radical departure from Stalinist policy and as such it was welcomed by the West, which saw in it the possibility of sincere negotiations.

Leonid Brezhnev also started his career under the Stalinist system but it took him longer to reach the pinnacle of power and the path he took was typically bureaucratic: cautious, conservative, and devoid of risk and experimentation. The same can be said about his foreign policy, which has been characterized by conservatism, caution, and cold calculation. There is some evidence that Brezhnev's style and approach to foreign policy has been shared by his colleagues in the top and middle-echelon decision-making bodies, which would explain the rather dull and conservative character of that policy.

Major Contemporary Issues

Some of the major contemporary issues in Soviet foreign policy have been referred to earlier. At this time it may be useful to bring them together and discuss their thrust and content, albeit briefly, in a somewhat more systematic fashion.

There are obviously many ways of analyzing policy issues. In line with the overall approach adopted by this volume I propose to look at the issues in terms of their outreach: some of them can be seen as global, others as reaching beyond a single region and spanning more than one continent, still others concern only one region or only the Soviet Union itself. In this sense the various issued can be analyzed along a certain continuum—from the global to the local arena or focus, each of which corresponding to what Kenneth Jowitt calls "overlapping" memberships or "identity reference."[30] The Soviet Union, together with numerous communist and noncommunist countries, shares membership in many of these reference groups: global actors, postindustrial societies, communist countries, nuclear weapons club, single party regimes, etcetera. Each category of membership carries with it certain obligations and responsibilities, as well as benefits and costs, and gives rise to certain problems and issues.

Soviet involvement in the global system has already been discussed at some length and there is little that can be added to the conclusions reached earlier. It can be shown that although the U.S.S.R. became a global actor quite recently, it has quickly and fully understood the awesome responsibility that goes with this particular role, and from the beginning its global behavior has been essentially moderate and rational. This has been particularly true with respect to the strategic arms control and disarmament negotiations both at the bilateral and multilateral levels which Moscow has approached in a serious and responsible fashion.

The above generalization can be challenged by pointing to the Soviet and Cuban engagement in Africa and the Soviet forays in the Middle and Near East. Nevertheless, it is one of the basic premises of this essay that being a global actor carries with it certain imperatives which imply that the actor's interests are global rather than regional or parochial, and that this can mean changing the status quo in a given part of the world. Obviously such a change involves the risk of retaliation by the other global actor or actors but it is not necessarily tantamount to reckless behavior on Moscow's part. Soviet aid to Luanda and Addis Ababa carried a risk of an American reaction but it was clearly not irresponsible, although it was branded as such by Washington. Similarly the lenghty and at times close Soviet relationship with Egypt which came to an end in 1972 simply reflected traditional Russian interest in that particular area reinforced by the presence of the Soviet fleet in the Eastern Mediterranean and Moscow's ability to resupply its Arab allies with modern weapons.

Being a postindustrial society carries different responsibilities. Although at times Moscow liked to identify itself, or at least some of its Asian republics, with the Third World or the developing countries in general, there is little doubt that the Soviet Union has reached the postindustrial stage. Although the most visible consequences concern domestic politics, there are also some important foreign policy considerations which, in fact, are likely to become even more important in the foreseeable future. I have in mind here further Soviet participation in the international division of labor and Moscow's growing involvement not so much in the East–West as in the North–South confrontation and conflict over the distribution of the world's shrinking natural resources. Although this is likely to be hotly denied by both the Soviet leadership and the Russian masses, in the eyes of the Third and especially the Fourth World, the U.S.S.R. is a "has" country whose interests are diametrically opposed to the "have not" countries. This identification of the Soviet Union with the developed capitalist world adds a new dimension to the Kremlin's foreign policy, if only by undermining its credibility vis-à-vis the developing countries. Whatever the way out of this dilemma, it is bound to be quite costly at a time when the U.S.S.R. can ill afford to commit a large share of its resources to foreign aid.

The leadership of the international communist movement also entails heavy burdens and responsibilities. To be sure, the international communist camp today is much less integrated and much more loosely structured than in the 1930s and 1940s; nonetheless it is still hierarchically organized with its leadership vested in Moscow. As mentioned earlier, that leadership—which entails also the monopolization of ideology in the name of proletarian internationalism—has been under strong challenge from various sides, to mention only China, Yugoslavia, Rumania, and the Eurocommunist movement.

We shall not concern ourselves here with the origin of China's challenge but only with its consequences. The direct attack by Peking forced Moscow to seek allies among communist countries throughout the world but mostly in Europe and in Asia. It may be hypothesized that the East European communist countries took advantage of the Soviet predicament and demanded (and received) greater autonomy in return for siding, at least formally, with Moscow against China. Outside of Europe the Kremlin appeared successful in persuading Cuba and Vietnam to join the anti-Peking camp, although the price was most likely quite steep in both cases. While North Korea continued its policy of neutrality, another communist country, Cambodia, clearly sided with China, which eventually led to a bloody war.

What is the likely Soviet response to this disintegration of international communism? It may be argued that there is very little that the Kremlin can do at the present time, short of going to war with China for the purpose of forcing Peking to cease challenging Moscow for the leadership of the communist camp. Despite some earlier bloody skirmishes on the Sino–Soviet border the chances of an armed confrontation are not very high, and the most likely outcome is the maintenance of the status quo and perhaps a creation of some *modus vivendi* acceptable to both sides. It may be speculated that any shooting war between the U.S.S.R. and China—whether strategic or conventional—would prove much more costly to the Soviet Union, which thus has little choice but to live and let live with its Chinese challenger.

What about the Eurocommunist challenge? From the perspective of the late 1970s it may be said that the seriousness of that challenge has been greatly exaggerated for at least two reasons: despite a number of highly emotional and volatile statements uttered by their leaders, neither the French nor the Italian parties appear ready to stage a frontal attack on Soviet ideological hegemony over the communist camp. Secondly, there is good reason to believe that Moscow at no time took the Eurocommunist challenge very seriously. There is no indication of Soviet foreign policy having been visibly affected by Eurocommunism in the way it was influenced by the persistent attacks by the People's Republic.

The major issue the Soviet Union faces as an important European actor and leader of a European alliance is the question of European security. The salience of that particular issue to the U.S.S.R. is illustrated by the fact that it took the Kremlin about twenty years of incessant efforts to bring the European countries, the United States, and Canada to the conference table at Helsinski in August 1975. There seems to be general agreement that the main objective of Moscow in calling the conference was to have the latter ratify the existing division of Europe, thus *ipso facto* legitimizing the Soviet hegemony in the eastern part of the continent. The Kremlin's insistence on approval of the principle of inviolability of the postwar European frontiers was a clever move designed, on the one hand, to gain the gratitude and support of those East European countries whose borders had been challenged in the past and, on the other, to make the division of Germany final and thus to weaken the chances of West Germany to regain its traditional status and importance on the European continent.

It may be added as a footnote that although the initial impression of the Helsinki Conference has been that of a major Soviet victory, the ultimate result was far from clear and, in fact, could be interpreted as a defeat for Moscow. I have in mind here the great impetus given by the Helsinki "Final Act" to the human rights and dissident movements throughout Eastern Europe. There is little doubt that the U.S.S.R. managed to draw proper conclusions from the emergence of this phenomenon and at the follow-up European Security Conference in Belgrade it successfully blocked any extensive discussion of human rights violations in the Warsaw Pact countries.

Perhaps the most burning contemporary issue for the Soviet Union in its regional environment is its role as the leader of the Warsaw Pact, of the Council for Mutual Economic Assistance, and of what is also called the "Socialist Commonwealth of Nations" in Eastern Europe. Some aspects of Moscow's "triple crown" have already been discussed earlier and only a few additional points can be made at this stage.

Soviet leadership of the Warsaw Treaty Organization involves two sets of interactions: one vis-à-vis NATO and one vis-à-vis the membership of the Warsaw alliance. The relationship with NATO revolves essentially around the question of abolishing both treaties at some point in the future. Although NATO preceeded WTO by roughly six years, both alliances are not only similar on paper but have also been undergoing similar crisis and challenges posed by their respective members. It may be argued that from the Soviet point of view the greatest value of the Warsaw Pact lies in its being a sort of a bargaining chip that could come in handy in East–West negotiations aimed at dissolving both NATO and WTO. The traditional Soviet obsession with maintaining parity vis-à-vis the West was reflected in the creation of WTO whose actual military strength and reliability have been seriously questioned for some time.

Soviet leadership of the Warsaw alliance enables Moscow to engage in East–West negotiations concerning the mutual reduction of forces in Central Europe. In contrast to other multilateral negotiations the Soviet attitude toward the MBFR talks in Vienna is not easily explained. The incontrovertible fact is that the WTO has for many years maintained a striking numerical superiority in manpower and conventional arms over NATO in the European theater. Initially this could be viewed as an attempt at offsetting U.S. strategic superiority over the Soviet Union but this argument lost its validity in the 1970s, especially after the signing of the SALT I Treaty which de facto recognized the U.S.–Soviet strategic parity. In these circumstances the maintenance of large Soviet military detachments in East Germany is not easily explained unless their ultimate purpose is either to influence domestic politics in Western Europe in the direction of closer relations with the East to the point of eventual "Finlandization" of Europe, which has often been cited as the final objective of Soviet policy, or to prop up the shaky East German regime. The Soviet reluctance in pushing the Vienna talks forward may be an indication of continuing interest in keeping large conventional forces in Central Europe for bargaining purposes. The latter hypothesis may have been strengthened by the lengthy discussion of the so-called "confidence building measures" at the follow-up Conference on European Security in Belgrade which aimed at further relaxation of tension in Europe.

Insofar as Moscow's relations with the junior WTO partners are concerned, the main requirement is to maintain a modicum of political stability in the alliance and to deal with the expressions of dissatisfaction with Soviet domination articulated with increasing frequency by Rumania. There is no doubt that it has been the Soviet military threat which has preserved the existing state of affairs in the region. As mentioned earlier, in the past twenty-five years the Soviet army was deployed to prevent the collapse of a communist regime (Hungary, 1956) and to halt what Moscow perceived as a far-reaching qualitative change in the nature of a communist political system (Czechoslovakia, 1968) which threatened to extend beyond the confines of a single country.[31]

The actual or implied Soviet military threat to Eastern Europe raises certain interesting questions. To begin with, there is the question of the threshold beyond which the Kremlin will no longer tolerate a course of action taken by an East European country without recourse to arms. Obviously such a threshold is likely to change over time with shifts in the Soviet leadership, in the general international environment, and in the overall "correlation of forces," especially between East and West. The relationship between the Soviet Union and Eastern Europe may be seen as a game in which one of the players is also the empire capable of changing the rules at any time. Accordingly, it is virtually impossible to identify a situation that may trigger Soviet armed intervention.

The question is often asked why Moscow invaded Czechoslovakia but not Rumania despite the latter's highly erratic and frequently challenging behavior toward the Soviet Union. The only sensible answer is that President Ceausescu, though clearly a maverick on the international scene, maintained a tight and perhaps even a neo-Stalinist control over the domestic political processes in Rumania. By contrast, at least from Moscow's viewpoint, the internal situation in Czechoslovakia in 1968 showed signs of getting out of hand, undermining the foundations of communist rule in that country and extending in a threatening manner into the neighboring countries. It was the perceived danger to the communist regime in Prague, including the threat to the leading role and monopoly of power exercised by the ruling party, that finally convinced the Kremlin that armed intervention was inevitable.

The crucial factor in the decision to intervene was, of course, Moscow's perception of the events supposedly threatening its hegemony in the region. Despite many linkages between the Soviet Union and its client states, some evidence points to a misperception by the Soviet leadership of the meaning of certain processes in Eastern Europe. The situation in Czechoslovakia in the summer of 1968 was interpreted by the Soviet Embassy in Prague as leading to a collapse of communist rule which had to be stopped at all cost. The fact that this perception was wrong did not prevent the intervention from taking place.

By and large, however, Soviet behavior in the region, even in times of crisis, had been cautious. Undoubtedly, part of Moscow's caution has been due to the belief that the threat of armed intervention has often had an opposite effect from that intended, as in Stalin's experience with Yugoslavia in 1948, when the threat of an impending Soviet invasion succeeded in submerging national and regional conflicts and in mobilizing the country behind Marshal Tito. The overwhelming popularity of Gomulka in Poland in the late 1950s and of Ceausescu in Rumania a decade later stemmed largely from the respective leaders' attitude toward a threat of Soviet intervention.

The threat of violence can thus be seen as the Kremlin's weapon of last resort. The continued presence of such a threat graphically illustrates the overwelming failure of Moscow's East European clients to achieve even that modicum of legitimacy and popular acceptance that would make such a threat largely redundant. Since the local regimes are a long way from becoming legitimate, the stationing of Soviet troops, supposedly sanctioned by the provisions of the Warsaw pact, represents a constant reminder to potential rebels in the region that any serious attempt to change the status quo in Eastern Europe would meet with a violent Soviet reaction.

Even though the development of the modern weapons systems has made at least some of the initial Soviet objectives in Eastern Europe less valid or relevant in the late 1970s than thirty years earlier, it is clear that the region has continued to be a piece of valuable real estate for the U.S.S.R. and that the latter intends to maintain its hegemony, barring all other global actors from the area. This, among other things, explains the almost hysterical Soviet reaction to the visit of Chinese Party Chairman Hua Guofeng to Rumania and Yugoslavia in the summer of 1978. Once before the Soviet Union made a mistake in soliciting China's aid in restoring stability in Eastern Europe in 1957, and one of the results was the defection of Albania. Any new attempt by Peking to establish a foothold in the area is bound to arouse strong suspicions in Moscow.

Soviet Foreign Policy Performance

What has been the Soviet Union's level of achievement in foreign policy? Before answering we should settle on the method of evaluating policy performance and on the choice of the yardstick to measure the success or failure of that policy. One possible way is to contrast the actual achievements of the Soviet Union with the expectations articulated by its leaders. Another approach would be to compare the accomplishments of the U.S.S.R. with those of other powers at the same or a similar level of economic and sociopolitical development. Still another method would be to conduct a cost-benefit analysis of Soviet foreign policy in order to see whether the different objectives have been reached at the least possible cost, thus making the Soviet policy performance relatively efficient.

The other issue that ought to be decided is that of the time dimension. I propose here to focus on the last fifteen years which coincide roughly with the period of the Brezhnev leadership which began in October 1964. Inevitably references will be made to earlier periods in Soviet history but the main focus will be on the last decade and a half.

Has the U.S.S.R.'s foreign policy met the expectations of its makers? It may be argued that at the time of Krushchev's ouster in 1964 the Soviet Union was on the defensive throughout the world. The new regime took over almost exactly two years after the Cuban missile crisis, which without a doubt represented the most serious Soviet setback since the end of World War II. Moscow's leadership of the international communist movement had been seriously challenged by China and, to a lesser degree, by Rumania and Yugoslavia. The Soviet bridgehead in Egypt was being maintained but its cost was growing rapidly without any visible gain. The U.S.S.R. appeared to have been effectively shut off from Africa and Latin America and even its influence in Asia had lost some of its earlier luster: Soviet unwillingness to become actively engaged in supporting North Vietnam in its struggle against the United States reduced Soviet credibility among actual and potential allies. Insofar as the relations with the United States were concerned, the Cuban debacle was followed by the signing of the Partial Nuclear Test Ban Treaty, which could be interpreted as a major step in the direction of rapprochement between the two superpowers. Finally, de Gaulle's challenge to the American hegemony in Western Europe was clearly welcomed by the new Soviet leaders who obviously favored the resulting division in the Western camp. To sum up, the overall situation as viewed from the Kremlin must have appeared somewhat mixed although on balance the overall Soviet posture vis-à-vis the United States and China was clearly defensive.

The incoming Soviet leaders must have made a number of major foreign policy decisions soon after taking over. One of them was the decision to continue the rapid buildup of strategic weapons with the ultimate goal of catching up with if not overtaking the United States. Another decision concerned China and was followed by an effort to come to an understanding with Peking. Also, it appears that Moscow agreed to step up its military aid to North Vietnam. Elsewhere, the Soviet Union continued rearming Egypt and some of the other Arab countries while at the same time attacking West Germany as a major threat to peace in Europe. Nevertheless Moscow decided to continue the policy of incipient détente with the United States by continuing discussions on nonproliferation and, eventually, on control of strategic arms.

Have the various decisions proved successful in the intervening years? Here again, the answer is mixed. Starting with the region closest to its own territory, the Soviet domination of Eastern Europe appears, at least on the surface, as strong as ever. The U.S.S.R. has managed to cope with the Czechoslovak crisis, Rumania's challenge, Albania's defection, Poland's perennial economic and political instability, and East Germany's weakness. To be sure, the cost of hegemonial control has been rising rather dramatically but the degree of Soviet control appears unimpaired.

Whereas Moscow managed to weather successfully the various crises on its western flank, this clearly was not the case with its Far Eastern neighbors. The Sino-Soviet conflict has shown no signs of abating despite the deaths of Mao Zedong and Chou En-lai, often identified as Moscow's chief enemies. If anything, the new Chinese leadership has demonstrated more than ever before its determination to maintain the pressure on the U.S.S.R. by attacking Vietnam and continuing to improve relations with the United States and Japan.

On another hemisphere Soviet relations with Cuba have not changed greatly in the past decade or so except for the common venture in Africa. Even in this case it is not entirely clear where the initiative to send Cuban troops to Angola and Ethiopia came from. Although conventional wisdom would have suggested that it was the Soviet Union that ordered the Cubans to Africa to underscore Moscow's growing importance as a global actor, an equally good case can be made for the supposition that the Cuban involvement in the war of liberation in Angola was, in fact, the result of the revolutionary ethos that had characterized Fidel Castro's activities ever since his seizure of power in Havana twenty years ago. It appears that the Soviet-Cuban involvement on the African continent represented one of the few bright spots insofar as the Soviet foreign policy was concerned. The fact that it was so strongly condemned and criticized by the West speaks for itself: in the American eyes it clearly amounted to a Soviet victory in the global competition for influence. Needless to say, the victory came at a price: the Kremlin's success in Africa effectively derailed the U.S.-Soviet détente of the mid-1970s—at least in the short run—and made the American public much more suspicious of Moscow's intentions in seeking a rapprochement with Washington.

Another region where the Soviet Union has lost ground in the past fifteen years was Egypt. Although the Soviet presence remains visible in Syria and Iraq, it hardly compensates for the forced withdrawal of Soviet advisers from Cairo. Although Moscow's involvement in Egypt was very costly and most likely opposed by many Soviet policy makers who viewed that Middle Eastern country as a highly unreliable ally, the psychological cost of the withdrawal was quite staggering.

What about Western Europe? Here again the record is mixed. On the one hand the U.S.S.R. clearly benefited from the disarray in the ranks of

NATO caused by de Gaulle and his successors. Economic difficulties experienced by the two "sick men of Europe"—Great Britain and Italy —have also weakened Europe's will to resist, and it is to Moscow's credit that so far, at least, it has not used the economic crisis to its own political advantage. Although NATO was having difficulties, it still managed to maintain a surprising degree of cohesion, due undoubtedly to the presence of large Soviet forces across the demarcation line in Germany. The invasion of Czechoslovakia gave some new life to the dormant Atlantic alliance and the recent strengthening and modernization of the Warsaw Pact military establishment was followed by an agreement to increase NATO defense spending by 3 percent. In this respect there has been little or no change as compared with the early 1960s.

A rather striking change occurred in Soviet-West German relations. As recently as 1968 the German Federal Republic was being officially branded as a hostile power seeking revenge and restoration of territorial losses suffered as a result of World War II. Less than five years later, following a series of treaties involving the U.S.S.R., the U.S.A., Britain, France and the two German states, relations between Bonn and Moscow could only be described as cordial. Soviet eagerness to come to terms with West Germany cannot be easily explained: the Kremlin was so interested in normalizing relations with Bonn that it was even willing to sacrifice to a significant degree the interests of East Germany, long recognized as one of Moscow's most faithful clients. One could argue that the rapprochement between Bonn and Moscow represented a plus for the Soviets: whereas the U.S.S.R. did not make any major concessions, the Federal Republic not only recognized the existence of two separate German states and the Oder-Neisse Line as the new western boundary of Poland, but it also offered to supply the Soviet Union with generous credits for the purpose of modernizing the country's industrial base.

Soviet efforts to cultivate better relations with the other West European countries became stymied in the mid-1970s by the emergence of Eurocommunism. As suggested earlier, the Eurocommunist bark was worse than its bite, and by hindsight it must be admitted that its importance and lasting power tend to be somewhat exaggerated. Although at times the shrill Eurocommunist declarations must have strongly irritated the Soviet leaders, Moscow maintained an admirable control over its reactions, and eventually Eurocommunism began to peter out leaving Moscow largely in control of the communist movement, at least in Europe.

Throughout this chapter I have made frequent references to U.S.-Soviet relations as clearly being the lynchpin of Soviet foreign policy. On balance the Kremlin did rather well in its encounters with successive American administrations over the past fifteen years or so, and whatever difficulties and challenges were faced tended to originate in environments other than the United States and its closest allies. This was a rather striking departure from the previous era of frequent sharp confrontations in different parts of the globe.

What about the future? Predicting the future is always a hazardous exercise, and even more so in the case of Soviet foreign policy which, as suggested throughout this chapter, has been dependent on many domestic and external factors: systemic changes, leadership succession, perceived behavior by Moscow's adversaries and competitors, and developments in the global economy. None are easily predictable, and the best that can be done is to investigate some probable options and to postulate some broad hypotheses.

Insofar as Soviet systemic change is concerned, Zbigniew Brzezinski writing in 1970 examined five possible options available to the policy makers in the Kremlin: oligarchic petrification, pluralist evolution, technological adaptation, militant fundamentalism, and political disintegration. His own feeling at that time was that in the decade of the 1970s "the Soviet leadership will seek to strike a balance between the first and third variants" and that "in the short run, development toward a pluralist, ideologically more tolerant system does not seem likely." [32] From a perspective of the last decade Brzezinski's prediction appears remarkably prescient and it may be hypothesized that a similar pattern will also be followed during the 1980s.

What is the likely impact of this pattern on the conduct of Soviet external relations? It may be argued that a synthesis of oligarchic conservatism and technological adaptation produces a form of technocratic rule which could become more pragmatic and less ideological than its predecessors, yet more cautious and possibly more conservative. This could easily be translated into a policy of status quo maintenance or at best slow, incremental change. Whereas this would not mean abdicating the role of an important global power, it could mean a tendency toward reducing Soviet international commitments and involvements, trying to settle some long standing conflicts such as the Sino–Soviet schism, and hoping to tie some vexing loose ends such as the irritating challenge by Rumania and the highly visible albeit minor scuffles between Moscow and some Eurocommunist leaders. The above is not meant to imply a Soviet trend toward isolationism: the U.S.S.R.'s current stature as a global actor simply would not permit it. It simply means that the new ruling oligarchy may prefer, at least in the short run, to cut its losses and focus its attention on domestic problems.

As always, leadership succession presents a major unknown insofar as Soviet foreign policy is concerned, and it appears that Moscow is bound to experience another changeover at the top in the near future. Whereas in the past turnover in the Kremlin was usually followed by a sometimes drastic change in the direction of Soviet foreign policy, this may not necessarily be the case after the departure of Leonid Brezhnev. For reasons having much to do with the current state of Soviet political and socioeconomic development as well as with Moscow's status as a global actor, there is clearly an awareness on the part of the Soviet ruling elite that the system cannot well afford another lengthy succession crisis, comparable to that of the 1920s and 1950s. The new emphasis on maintaining continuity and avoiding sharp departures from past policy patterns was already clearly visible in the aftermath of Khrushchev's ouster in 1964, and one can surmise that a similar effort would be made the next time there is a vacancy in the Kremlin. This may also mean that the next succession at the top would not result in any radical departure from the current major thrust in Soviet external behavior.

Another process which is likely to propel Soviet policy along a middle-of-the-road path is the probability of growing economic interdependence vis-à-vis the capitalist and the Third and Fourth Worlds.[33] The Soviet Union is bound to move further into the postindustrial stage with the help of the scientific-technological revolution. The entry into the postindustrial stage is likely to be closely linked with an increase in Soviet participation in world trade which, in turn, would lead to the U.S.S.R. becoming more tightly interwoven into the fabric of international economic contacts and dependencies.

On the other hand, the impending global economic polarization between the North and the South is likely to put the Soviet Union in the same Northern camp as its erstwhile capitalist adversaries. This may well be followed by the establishment of even closer economic links between the U.S.S.R. and the industrial West, starved for energy and raw materials and willing to invest heavily in the development of Soviet natural resources. This would also mean that a high premium would be put by all participating actors on maintaining political stability and avoiding unnecessary confrontations.

Finally, what about the actual or perceived behavior of Soviet adversaries? As suggested above, there is a good chance that the U.S.-Soviet relations in the 1980s will continue to exhibit the mixture of conflict and collaboration with the latter in ascendance.

As in the past fifteen years, the major challenge is likely to come from China and possibly from the smaller East European countries. Future Chinese behavior—both at home and abroad—is totally unpredictable and the safest course is to assume that China's relations with the Soviet Union will continue to be hostile without necessarily leading to an armed confrontation. Rumania's attitude toward the U.S.S.R. is largely a function of the volatile personality of President Ceausescu, and here again no easy predictions can be made. It may be speculated that Moscow itself will move in the direction of defusing the challenge which has become more than just a minor nuisance. Insofar as the other Balkan countries are concerned, contrary to some earlier expectations the probability of

Soviet intervention in Yugoslavia following Tito's death appears to be quite low. Similarly, Moscow may seek resumption of diplomatic and perhaps even of party-to-party relations with Albania, which appears to have severed its Chinese connection.

One interesting aspect of future Soviet-East European relations concerns a possible Soviet reaction to continuing internal political opposition, including the human rights movements, in some of the smaller countries, particularly Poland. Until now there has been no evidence of Soviet pressure on the East European governments to curtail dissident activities through coercive measures. However, the question remains whether in the event of a major challenge to the existing regimes in Warsaw or Budapest, Moscow would entertain the notion of another armed intervention *à la* Hungary and Czechoslovakia. Thus far there is no indication that this would be a likely course: on the contrary, the public Soviet reaction to expressions of popular discontent among Moscow's junior allies could be characterized as that of benign neglect but it is equally clear that this may change quickly in the event of a perceived imminent collapse of communist rule in any of the East European countries.

The major conclusion that emerges from this chapter is that in the course of the past fifteen years the U.S.S.R.'s external behavior has undergone considerable change. From being largely defensive and reactive, frequently highly personalized and unsystematic, Soviet foreign policy seems to have acquired a much greater confidence and sophistication, and it has clearly become more forward-looking and pragmatic, albeit still cautious and largely averse to taking unnecessary risks. Throughout this chapter I have made an effort to analyze and explain the reasons for this rather dramatic transformation and I have concluded that some of the changes stem directly from changes in the Soviet political system while others originate either in the changing behavior of other global actors or, autonomously or spontaneously, in the drastic changes in the global economic and social environments. In the final analysis all this means that despite declarations to the contrary the Soviet Union is rapidly becoming modernized like all other global actors, regardless of the coloration of their respective political systems, and that the process of *Gleichschaltung* is likely to continue in the future.

Notes

1. James N. Rosenau, ed., *Linkage Politics* (New York: Free Press, 1969).
2. John S. Reshetar, Jr., *The Soviet Polity,* 2nd ed. (New York: Harper and Row, 1978), pp. 336–61.
3. Alfred G. Meyer, "USSR, Incorporated," *Slavic Review,* 20 (September 1961), 369–77.

4. Allen Kassof, "The Administered Society: Totalitarianism without Terror," *World Politics,* 16 (July 1964), 556–75.

5. Lenard J. Cohen and Jane P. Shapiro, eds., *Communist Systems in Comparative Perspective* (Garden City, N.Y.: Anchor Press-Doubleday, 1974), p. xxix.

6. For an interesting discussion of the concept of "cooptation," see Frederick J. Fleron, Jr., "Toward a Reconceptualization of Political Change in the Soviet Union: The Political Leadership System," *Comparative Politics,* 1 (January 1969), 228–44.

7. For an analysis of the intergenerational conflict, see Zygmunt Bauman, "Twenty Years After: The Crisis of Soviet-Type Societies," *Problems of Communism,* 20 (November-December 1971), 45–53.

8. Probably the most telling criticism of the application of the group-conflict approach to the analysis of communist societies is that of Andrew Janos in his "Group Politics in Communist Society: A Second Look at the Pluralistic Model," in Samuel P. Huntington and Clement H. Moore, eds., *Authoritarian Politics in Modern Society* (New York and London: Basic Books, 1970), pp. 437–50.

9. David E. Langsam and David W. Paul, "Soviet Politics and the Group Approach: A Conceptual Note," *Slavic Review,* 31 (March 1972), 136–37.

10. Jerry F. Hough, "The Soviet System: Petrification of Pluralism," *Problems of Communism,* 21 (March-April 1972), 27–29.

11. For a recent example, see Carl Beck et al., *Comparative Communist Political Leadership* (New York: McKay, 1973.)

12. John H. Kautsky, "Comparative Communism versus Comparative Politics," *Studies in Comparative Communism,* 6 (Spring-Summer 1973), 141.

13. Gabriel A. Almond and G. Bingham Powell, Jr., *Comparative Politics: A Developmental Approach* (Boston: Little, Brown, 1966).

14. Gabriel A. Almond, "Toward a Comparative Politics of Eastern Europe," *Studies in Comparative Communism,* 4 (Summer 1971), 76–77.

15. Charles A. Powell, "Structural-Functionalism and the Study of Comparative Communist Systems: Some Caveats," *Studies in Comparative Communism,* 4 (Fall-Winter 1971), 58–62.

16. William E. Griffith, "The Pitfalls of the Theory of Modernization," *Slavic Review,* 33 (June 1974), 247.

17. See, for example, Robert C. Tucker, "Communism and Political Culture," *Newsletter on Comparative Studies of Communism,* 4 (1971), 3–12; and Alfred G. Meyer, "Communist Revolutions and Cultural Change," *Studies in Comparative Communism,* 5 (Winter 1972), 345–70.

18. For an interesting discussion of pitfalls in analyzing and predicting Soviet political developments, see Alexander Dallin, "Bias and Blunders in American Studies on the USSR," *Slavic Review,* 32 (September 1973), 560–76.

19. The best critical discussion of "convergence theory" can be found in Zbigniew Brzezinski and Samuel P. Huntington, *Political Power USA/USSR* (New York: Viking Press, 1963), pp. 409–36.

20. For details, see W. Raymond Duncan, ed., *Soviet Policy in Developing Countries* (Waltham, Mass.: Ginn-Blaisdell, 1970); and Alvin Z. Rubinstein, ed., *Soviet and Chinese Influence in the Third World* (New York: Praeger, 1975).

21. Zbigniew Brzezinski, *The Competitive Relationship* (New York: Columbia University Research Institute on Communist Affairs, 1972), pp. 37–39.

22. For one interpretation, see Gunnar Adler-Karlsson, *Western Economic Warfare 1947–1967* (Stockholm: Almqvist and Wiksell, 1968). See also Franklyn D. Holzman, *International Trade under Communism: Politics and Economics* (New York: Basic Books, 1976).

23. For an interesting discussion, see "The Soviet Oil Situation: An Evaluation of CIA Analyses of Soviet Oil Production," Staff Report of the Senate Select Committee on Intelligence, United States Senate, 95th Congress, 2nd sess. (Washington, D.C.: U.S. Government Printing Office, 1978).

24. Paul Marer, "Has Eastern Europe Become a Liability to the Soviet Union? III. The Economic Aspect," in Charles Gati, ed., *The International Politics of Eastern Europe* (New York: Praeger, 1976), pp. 59–81.

25. For a recent analysis, see John M. Collins, *American and Soviet Military Trends Since the Cuban Missile Crisis* (Washington, D.C.: The Center for Strategic and International Studies, Georgetown University, 1978). See also Thomas W. Wolfe, "Military Power and Soviet Policy," in William E. Griffith, ed., *The Soviet Empire: Expansion and Detente* (Lexington, Mass.: D. C. Heath, 1976), pp. 145–209.

26. Apparently in November 1978 at a meeting of the Warsaw Pact Political Consultative Committee in Moscow, attended by all top WTO leaders, Rumania rejected a Soviet demand to increase defense spending supposedly to counter the increase in the NATO defense budget. Rumania's opposition was apparently shared by other WTO members. Charles Andras, "A Summit with Consequence," Radio Free Europe Research, *RAD Background Report/271 (Eastern Europe)*, 14 December 1978.

27. Vernon V. Aspaturian, "Soviet Foreign Policy," in Roy C. Macridis, ed., *Foreign Policy in World Politics*, 5th ed. (Englewood Cliffs, N.J.: Prentice-Hall, 1976), p. 171.

28. Alexander Yanov, "Detente after Brezhnev: The Domestic Roots of Soviet Foreign Policy," Institute of International Studies, University of California, Berkeley, *Policy Papers on International Affairs*, No. 2, 1977.

29. For an interesting account of the Soviet decision to invade Czechoslovakia, see Jiri Valenta, "Soviet Decisionmaking and the Czechoslovak Crisis of 1968," *Studies in Comparative Communism*, 8 (Spring-Summer 1975), 147–73.

30. Kenneth Jowitt discussed these terms in Sylvia Sinanian, Istvan Deak, and Peter C. Ludz, eds., *Eastern Europe in the 1970s* (New York: Praeger 1972), pp. 180–84.

31. For a discussion of the meaning of the Soviet military threat to Eastern Europe, see Andrzej Korbonski, "Eastern Europe and the Soviet Threat," in Grayson Kirk and Nils H. Wessell, ed., *The Soviet Threat* (New York: The Academy of Political Science, 1978), pp. 67-69.

32. Zbigniew Brzezinski, *Between Two Ages* (New York: The Viking Press, 1970), pp. 167.

33. For a recent discussion, see Walter C. Clemens, Jr., *The USSR and Global Interdependence* (Washington, D.C.: American Enterprise Institute, 1978).

4

Issues for Global Actors: The European Community

John Pinder

THE ROLE OF THE EUROPEAN COMMUNITY in the international economy is second only to that of the United States.[1] The Community's trade is bigger than that of the United States, and in trade negotiations the Community is probably the more important. Yet the Community lacks cohesion in monetary affairs, has no strategic identity, and is in many respects a political dwarf. Why this immense disparity between its economic, strategic and political roles?

The answer is in the special character of the Community, which lies somewhere between a regional economic association and a federation of states. It is not surprising that the Community has evoked a rich theoretical literature which tries to explain why it has taken this form, how it works, and what the consequences are. These questions must be answered if we are to understand what global issues are important to the Community and how it deals with them. Beyond that, the answers may help us to understand some elements of the global system itself and the way in which it may develop. For it can be argued that the forces that have pushed the Community toward integration are also at work in the global system.

Theoretical Perspectives

After 1945, the first task for European statesmen was to rebuild their countries' economies which had been shattered by the war. The second concern, for many, was to make quite sure that no such war among them should ever occur again. In the six founder members of the European Community, the view was strongly held that this would be best done by establishing a federation of the democratic states of Western Europe[2]; the European Coal and Steel Community (ECSC) was launched with the explicit aim of being "the first concrete foundation of a European federation which is indispensable to the preservation of peace."[3] The successful establishment of the ECSC in 1951, with supranational institutions to control the coal and steel industries of France, Germany, and the other member countries, led to high hopes that the federation would be completed before too long.[4] These hopes were reflected in the original thinking of the neofunctionalists, who expected that the attachment of interest groups to new supranational institutions would facilitate the "spilling over" of integrative activity from one sector to another, in what might become an almost automatic process.[5] At the same time the proposal for making the union indissoluble through a merger of the member states' armed forces, in a European Defense Community (EDC), encountered fierce opposition in France, so that the EDC treaty, signed by all six member governments of the ECSC in 1952, was rejected by the French parliament in 1954. Whereas this demonstrated that the nation-state was still a formidable obstacle to full federation, the movement toward unity revived with the establishment of the European Economic Community (EEC), and Euratom in 1958. The member countries thus created institutions which they could use for cooperation or common action across almost the whole field of economic affairs. Thses structures, comprising an independent Executive Commission, an intergovernmental Council of Ministers holding the main power of decision, a European Parliament which was for the most part consultative, and a Court of Justice, fell short of the federal model on which so many postwar hopes had been placed, but they were much stronger than those of any other international organization. Their functions were broadly defined for most aspects of economic policy, with agreement on detailed action to be filled in as and when the member governments wished. The program for establishing a customs union with a common external tariff and common commercial (that is, external trade) policy, however, was settled in detail in the EEC Treaty; the common agricultural policy, with its tough regime of price supports, import levies, and export subsidies, was laid down in the early years of the EEC.

The dynamism of the period was again reflected in the literature, with a further development of neofunctionalist theory.[6] There was more talk of the forthcoming United States of Europe. But French nationalism again cut the ground from under it. In 1963 President de Gaulle antagonized his partners and stalled the Community's development by vetoing the entry of Britain[7]; in 1965 he shook the Community to its foundations by withdrawing French representatives from the meetings of the Council of Ministers until it was fully understood that Paris would not accept majority decisions on matters it regarded as significant French interests.[8] This led to a new period of uncertainty, reflected in the title of the last major neofunctionalist book.[9]

An attempt to promote further integration after de Gaulle's demise by setting up an economic and monetary union failed, partly because of French and German differences on monetary policy and Community institutions and partly because of the monetary storms associated with the floating of the dollar in 1971.[10] This seemed to block further development in a supranational or federal direction, and theoretical works began to focus on the Community's intergovernmental and transnational aspects.[11] The enlargement in the 1970s to include Britain, Denmark, and Ireland strengthened the antifederalist forces (even if Ireland was an exception) and the establishment of the European Council, in which the heads of government of Community countries meet three times a year, added a weighty intergovernmental element to the Community institutions.

The concerns of this chapter are the Community's ability to act as a unit in world affairs and the possibility that it will acquire the capacity to do this in further fields, beyond those of external trade policy where it is already strong. I have argued elsewhere that the possession of a common instrument is the crux in providing the Community with a capacity for common action.[12] Despite the complex interplay of member governments and Community institutions in an extrememly pluralistic and unwieldy decision-making process, experience with the common external tariff and the common agricultural policy shows that the Community does actually decide and act when the member states give it an instrument for action. The countries' attempts to coordinate the use of instruments which they have retained under their national control have usually, in contrast, been largely ineffective, as has been shown time and time again in the field of monetary policy.[13] The Community's significance as a collective actor is now to be enhanced by the establishment of a European Monetary System, which will attempt to coordinate the exchange rates of members' national currencies, and set up a new European Currency Unit and eventually a Community Reserve Fund, in which a substantial proportion of the member countries' currency reserves are to be placed.

The purpose of combining the perspectives of theory with those of recent history has been to show how the development of theory and of Community institutions has reflected alternating emphasis on both integration and national autonomy, but there is a reason to focus on Community cohesion rather than on national reaction against it. Contemporary economic forces are rendering the member governments less and less able to deal with their economic problems without the use and the development of Community institutions. The common instruments proposed for the European Monetary System and the direct elections to the European Parliament in June 1979 can thus be seen as indicators of a prevailing trend toward the further development of Community instruments and institutions.[14]

Technological Factors

The peculiar political conjuncture of the early postwar years, with the deeply felt need for Franco-German reconciliation in a context of Soviet threat and American hegemony, might appear a sufficient explanation of the creation of the European Community. But it would hardly explain the durability and vitality that the Community has shown over a period of a quarter of a century.

Western economists, for the most part, have failed to break out of the elegant cage of static neoclassical analysis, with its bias against investigating the causes and effects of growth. It has been left to East European economists to stress the incremental need for integration as a consequence of what they call the scientific-technological revolution.[15] Technological progress causes specialization of production and enlargement of the market; because this is a continuing process, the economy is continually becoming more internationalized. It is not necessary to accept other elements of Marxist theory in order to perceive the implications of this for the European Community and for the wider international economy.

Trade among the member countries now accounts for one-tenth of the gross Community product. Whereas this is a lower level of interdependence than is usual among the regions of an industrialized nation, it is much higher than has been normal among a group of such states. This reflects the need of the West European countries to integrate their markets if they are to exploit the potential of modern technology, and it pushes them toward common economic management, or policy integration, because so many of the economic forces with which policy must deal are now escaping the control of national governments.

Technological progress is also changing the form of management needed for the modern economy. Specialization and the division of labor have become so intense that oligopoly or monopoly in the myriad product and factor markets has become the norm, and these markets and producers in a given economy are extremely dependent on one another. Higher capital intensity and skill intensity augment the costs of changing from one activity to another or of leaving production facilities idle. New policies are required to deal with the social costs and the oligopolistic or monopolistic bargaining power that result from this degree of market imperfection. These include manpower policies, industrial policies, and price and income policies: in short, sectoral and microeconomic interventions and even global demand management.

Whereas the need for such public interventions in the economy increases, the cost of excessive constraints on the initiative of enterprise or production units rises too, for many of the feasible changes in technology are so complex that their application can be understood only by those who are directly concerned. Thus the management of a modern economy is a delicate problem, and none of the existing "systems" can claim to have a well-articulated solution.

The comprehensive new methods of economic management involving manpower and industrial policies have profound implications for Community and global politics. Policy integration can no longer be confined largely to the creation of a common market by suppressing distortions of trade, nor can external economic policies be focused mainly upon trade liberalization. Either national micro and sectoral policies will disintegrate the international market back into separate national markets or those policies will be coordinated and integrated to an extent sufficient to deal with the movement of economic management issues to an international level. Policies there will certainly be on matters such as agricultural prices, oil supplies, steelmaking capacity, subsidization of shipbuilding, and the production of aircraft. The question is to what extent these policies will be national and disintegrative or international and integrative.[16] Policy (or "positive") integration has become a condition of market (or "negative") integration through the liberalization of trade. It is difficult to draw sufficient policy guidance from the current theoretical literature on this, but if the links between technological development, micro and sectoral policies, and international interdependence are as strong as has been suggested, the costs of failure to achieve common policies will continue to increase; and this will push the Community, even against the grain of some of its member states, toward more effective common action, both to manage its internal economy and to promote the international economic interests of the member countries.

Involvement in the Global System

The involvement of the Community in the global system has been primarily economic. The member countries play their strategic roles on

other stages, particularly NATO, and they coordinate their foreign policies through the intergovernmental machinery of European Political Cooperation.[17] The results are significant but in no way compare with the
impact of the Community on global politics when it is wielding a common
instrument of policy—which applies, so far, only to certain economic
issues.[18]

The Community is deeply and widely involved in the world economy.
One-tenth of its gross product is exported, and a similar proportion is
spent on imports. This trade is spread extensively among the main regions
of the world, with North America ranking first.

Links between the West European neighbors are particularly close.
Trade with the United States is reinforced by the use of the dollar as the
principal international currency and by the heavy involvement of American multinationals in Europe and, increasingly, of European multinationals in America; this dense economic network is underpinned by the
strategic relationship, in which Western Europe depends on the United
States for the military balance with the Soviet Union, while the United
States needs to prevent any possible absorption of Western Europe into
the Soviet bloc. Trade with the Soviet Union and Eastern Europe, though
less, is not far short of 1 percent of gross Community product, in the
context of the converse strategic relationship. While Japan's primary relations among the other industrial countries are with the United States,
its trade with the Community has been growing fast. Australia and New
Zealand have longstanding links with Britain and other Community countries, in which the trade of food and materials against manufactures plays
an important part. Africa, Latin America, the Middle East, and Southeast
Asia each account for trade equal to about 1 percent of gross Community
product, as well as a significant share of overseas Community investments; and the Community has become heavily dependent on Middle
East oil. Trade with China is still relatively slight, but this may change
with the new policies of China after Mao.

The Community, since the member countries have transferred to it
the function of external trade policy, including the right to levy the common external tariff on imports from outside countries, is represented in
the General Agreement on Tariffs and Trade (GATT) as a single unit by
the Commission. In the International Monetary Fund (IMF) the Community's member countries are still represented separately, although they
try to coordinate their monetary policies. Both the member governments
and the Commission are involved in the meetings of the OECD, where a
wide range of economic issues are discussed by the industrial countries,
and of the U.N. Conference on Trade and Development (UNCTAD),
where the less developed countries make demands on the more advanced
both in monetary affairs, where the Community's individual members are
primarily responsible, and in trade, where control has passed to the Com-

munity. Beyond its participation in these international organizations, the Community has developed a web of bilateral and regional agreements. These include free trade arrangements with most other West European countries; agreements and associations with Mediterranean countries and with over fifty African, Caribbean, and Pacific countries under the Lome Convention, which provide for aid as well as trade preferences; and cooperation agreements with other developing countries such as Brazil, India, Mexico, and members of the Association of South East Asian Nations.

Trade liberalization, or negative integration, through the GATT has been the most important aspect of the Community's involvement in international organization and a major theme of the postwar international economic policies of industrial countries. Positive integration, for example, the coordination of industrial and other sectoral policies, is much less developed. Yet the process of technological development has increased the need for policy coordination over a wide range of international economic issues as it has outside the Community.[19] Although the degree of interdependence, or market integration, is generally less between the Community and other economies than it is among the Community members themselves, its interdependence—and indeed dependence—is very great with respect to certain countries, in particular the United States and Saudi Arabia. Its overall level of international interdependence has tended to increase, and the costs of a failure to coordinate or integrate policies have risen correspondingly.

These costs tend to be incurred. Policy integration is more difficult to achieve internationally than it is in the European Community, because economic, political, social, and cultural differences are so much greater.[20] Yet the differences are not so great between the Community and its closest partner, the United States, or most of the other advanced Western countries, and differences with Japan are being reduced. Moreover, underlying political forces may work toward more compatibility between the Community, some of the East European countries, and eventually the Soviet Union. There is a convergence of economic levels and perhaps systems between the Community and the newly industrializing countries, where growth rates are now much faster than those of the already industrialized. It is not unlikely, then, that a multipolar world economy will emerge revolving around a number of major units such as the United States, the European Community, Japan, the Soviet Union, China, India, and Brazil, in which the disparities of economic level, weight, and perhaps system will be reduced, and among which better communications will cause the common cultural elements to increase.

This would not lead to any smooth or automatic process of policy integration. Integration is hard enough among similar countries, and the many divergences make it still more difficult. The difficulty is compounded by the weakness of all systems in dealing with the problems of the contemporary economy. If economic management is generally inefective, integration may be no more use than the blind leading the blind, and the integrating countries will not persist with it. If some countries manage their economies effectively, they may invoke measures of separation in order to retain their independence to do so. If a group such as the Community countries pursues effective policy integration, it may separate collectively from instabilities in the international economy. Yet the costs of international disintegration are a powerful incentive to avoid it, and the various trends toward convergence or at least the reduction of disparities offer the conditions for some international policy integration, alongside the elements of disintegration that will certainly also be present.

The Community has a strong interest in the stability of the world economy. It can be argued that a polity which is itself integrating will at the same time provoke disintegration in its relations with others,[21] or that a group as powerful as the Community will not be coooperative in its relations with the less powerful.[22] The analysis later in this chapter, however, suggests that Community behavior tends to promote cooperation rather than disintegration in the international economy.[23]

Behind any particular global economic issue, there is the more general issue of whether the approach of each major global actor contributes to international policy coordination and to the development of international capacities for policy coordination. We might call this general issue the "issue of issues." The particular global issues considered in this chapter are analyzed, then, so as to evaluate the role of the Community and its member countries, as regards this issue of issues, in relation to both policy coordination in the international economy and policy integration within the Community itself.[24]

Sources of Issues

The ability of the Community's members to confront global issues in common depends on the general capacity of its institutions and the policy instruments of which these dispose. This capacity has evolved largely in response to external factors, such as the postwar Franco-German reconciliation, American support for community integration, and the threat of Soviet domination. The Community has shown itself more likely to act as a unit, and to strengthen its capacity to do so, when it has been stimulated by external challenges. For example, the creation of the ECSC followed the communist takeover of Czechoslovakia in 1948; the EEC was established after the Soviet occupation of Hungary; the project for an economic and monetary union and the successful enlargement of the Community followed the occupation of Czechoslovakia in 1968. The collective behavior of the Community in the world economy results partly from challenges such as these, although other sources, such as the impact of economic events, have often been more important.

EXTERNAL SOURCES

The crucial global issues for the Community in the 1970s have arisen because of shocks in the world economy: the oil crisis that followed the quadrupling of prices at the end of 1973; the monetary storms associated with the instability of the dollar and the payments disequilibria that followed the oil price rise; the inflation and unemployment provoked by these events (sustained by failures of domestic economic management); and, on top of the world recession, the inroads of Japan and the newly industrializing countries into a variety of product markets. The consequent policy issues have been the security and cost of energy supplies, monetary stability, general economic management in the United States and Japan, and the crisis in hard-hit sectors of industry.

Over the whole period of its existence, however, the pressure of demands from its trading partners has been the most prominent external source of issues for the Community. Whereas this pressure came from many countries and took many forms, the substance was mainly the question of trade liberalization: a demand for better access to the large and rich Community market. The most influential source of such pressure has been the United States, demanding reductions, through GATT negotiations, in the Community's industrial and agricultural protection and in its special preferential arrangements with numerous less developed countries. When the EEC was established, the other West European countries, led by Britain, sought a free trade area with the six founder members of the Community; after the Community, as required by de Gaulle, rejected this and the subsequent British attempts to achieve membership in the 1960s, the applications of Britain, Denmark, and Ireland were accepted, resulting in their membership in 1973 and the parallel negotiation of free trade agreements requested by almost all the other countries of Western Europe. To the south, Greece and Turkey earlier secured far-reaching association agreements; they were followed by almost all the other Mediterranean countries. The original source of the preferential association of Francophone African countries was France's insistence; its extension included, under the Lome Convention, the Commonwealth countries of Africa, the Caribbean, and the Pacific, as demanded by Britain. Latin Americans and Asians have also sought better access through bilateral trade and cooperation agreements with the Community and by pressing in UNCTAD for more general arrangements, such as generalized preferences for their industrial exports and benefits in commodity stabilization and credit terms.

Few countries have failed to press the Community for measures of import liberalization. In a small number of cases, the economic relationship has also been used as a means to political ends. Thus Arab countries have used oil as a lever to influence the policies of the Community and its member governments toward Israel; the Chinese have secured their trade agreement with the Community to further their opposition to the Soviet Union as well as for economic reasons. The Soviet Union, for its part, has sought to impede the development of the Community and has up to now required its East European allies to refuse it diplomatic recognition.

INTERNAL SOURCES

At the same time that the Community faces external demands for import liberalization it is pressed for economic advantages by internal industrial and social groups. In some cases, of which agriculture is the prime example, these internal pressures have been deeply entrenched against the external ones, so that negotiations on agricultural trade have been blocked for long periods. The farm lobbies have been very strong in most member countries; the French government has made the defense of its agricultural interests a top priority. German industry, with its drive for exports, which would be helped if outside countries sold farm products to the Community and thus earned currency that could be spent on the purchase of manufactures, has preferred a more open Community policy toward agricultural imports; the German government has chafed at the amount of German money going to support Community agriculture, to the special benefit of France. But the German farm lobby itself has had leverage out of proportion to its numbers, exploiting the narrow majorities of its federal governments.

The balance between agricultural interests, fiercely championed by the French, and industrial interests has, however, been changing in favor of a more open agricultural policy. The work force on Community farms has been halved since the EEC was established, and the British government has been demanding cheaper food and agricultural imports. Meanwhile, agricultural trade has become one of the major subjects for bargaining between the Community and other countries in the Tokyo round of GATT negotiations, and the Community is likely to be more accommodating than it has been in the past.

Among the Community's manufacturing industries, textiles were for a long time an exception in securing a large measure of quota protection against imports from less developed countries. The recession of the 1970s and the exporting thrust from Japan and from the newly industrializing countries have, however, stimulated many other sectors such as footwear, steel, shipbuilding, and automobiles to press for protection or for subsidies and measures of job preservation. This follows not only the external threat of intensified competition but also the Community's internal problem of stagnation and the growing demand of its citizens for job security. The response of the Community and its member governments to this domestic problem and this demand can hardly fail, where production of tradable goods is concerned, to be externalized through policies that affect imports.[25]

The Community, however, has a big surplus in its external trade in manufactures. Since the Community is not well-endowed with primary products, this is necessarily a structural surplus: the export surplus in manufactures has to pay for the imports of primary products that are needed by the Community's industries and consumers. Although imports of manufactures have hit hard in particular sectors, the Community in general has a stronger interest in facilitating exports than in protecting itself against imports. Lobbies with a particular sector to defend often exert influence, just as Community agriculture has done, out of proportion to the sector's importance when compared with a general interest spread across a large number of sectors or a whole economy. The Community offers them much scope to do so because of the blocking power that can be exerted by any member government. But the Community and its member countries would lose so heavily from a collapse of world trade that they seek to avoid precipitating a movement toward general protection. The support for industries under pressure has, therefore, tended to take the form not of a cut in imports but of control over the rate of growth of trade, price stabilization measures, or other orderly marketing arrangements discussed or negotiated with the exporting countries rather than imposed unilaterally. In short, the industrial export interest, which during boom years has been a powerful force for freer trade, has been strong enough to ensure that the demands of protective lobbies are channeled into measures for the control rather than the reduction of trade, and that as far as possible these interests are negotiated with the Community's trading partners.

Interests such as agriculture and industry, which raise issues of liberal, protected, or organized trade, are distributed across the whole Community, even if with uneven incidence. A number of issues stem, however, from the national histories and perceptions of national interest of the different member states. Some of these national positions reinforce the general interest in keeping open the channels of international trade. Most of the member countries have a stake in maintaining trade relations with the countries overseas with which they have historic economic links: France with its former African colonies; Britain with the Commonwealth covering large parts of Africa, the Caribbean, South and South East Asia, as well as Australia and Canada; the Netherlands with Indonesia; Germany and, when they become members, Spain and Portugal with Latin America. This was the impulse behind the preferential arrangement of the Lome Convention and agreements with countries such as India, Sri Lanka, and Malaysia.

Divergent national reactions often cause conflicts between member countries, affecting the issues to which the Community attaches importance and the Community's approach to them. Differences between France and Germany became, during de Gaulle's period, a classic conflict between opposing positions on basic questions of foreign and economic policy. France pulled out of the NATO command structure, opposed a wide range of American foreign policies, backed gold against the dollar, and blocked British entry into the Community. Germany, completely dependent on the United States for its security and adhering to a similar liberal economic ideology, supported the United States on most issues, was the most loyal member of NATO, backed the dollar against gold, and tried to promote British entry into the Community. These divergences hindered policy integration in the Community and prevented it from taking any effective action in relation to most global issues other than trade, where de Gaulle's policy was relatively liberal. After the death of de Gaulle, the attitude of French governments on most issues became less extreme. Later, the German government moved some way toward French positions, reacting to some of the earlier actions of the Carter administration in the monetary and strategic fields. This rapprochement led to the Franco-German initiative in 1978 to launch a European monetary system.

The British and most other Community governments have usually stood somewhere between the French and the Germans on issues of economic, monetary, foreign, and defense policy, so that Franco-German agreement has been a most important condition for the launching of any Community action. Behind the national positions on particular economic and foreign policies, however, lie national attitudes toward policy integration as such. Gaullist France developed a systematic ideology to oppose any measures of policy integration through supranational or federal institutions, insisting that any cooperation be achieved by strictly intergovernmental means. This was a source of conflict with Germany and all the other members of the Community until the entry of Britain and Denmark, for Germany and the others argued that effective decision-making would not be possible without using the supranational provisions of the Community treaties and moving further in a federal direction.

On entering the Community, Britain joined France in resisting supranational developments such as majority voting on decisions in the Council of Ministers or giving more scope and authority to the Commission. Yet this did not block the decisions to hold direct elections to the European

Parliament and to establish a European monetary system. The nationalist reflexes are balanced by the tendency of pluralist democracies to behave cooperatively,[26] giving scope to further policy integration within the Community, just as the demands by special interests for protection and the Community's preoccupation with its internal conflicts and development are balanced by its tendency toward cooperative behavior in the international system.

Major Contemporary Issues

Behind the issues in particular fields, such as trade, money, or energy, and in the Community's relations with trading partners is the general structural-functional problem of the international economic system. This problem has a considerable history.

When the Community was founded in the 1950s it was part of a coherent economic system, led by the United States and inspired by liberal or even laissez-faire principles. Trade was to be liberalized through the GATT, and exchange rates stabilized by the adjustable peg method in the IMF. Although the treaties establishing the Community contained many clauses that foresaw social democratic as well as liberal policies, the main purpose was to form a customs union, and the most important subsequent policy initiatives aimed to launch either a common currency or an exchange rate regime for the member countries somewhat similar to the model of Bretton Woods. In external policy, the major element was the cutting of the common external tariff by about half in successive GATT negotiations.

The Community's attachment to a neoclassical form of liberal doctrine was never unqualified. Although postwar Germany was deeply influenced by neoliberalism and by American policy, the French had opposite inclinations. French governments under de Gaulle became more liberal in trade policy, with the major exception of agriculture in which they insisted on Community protectionism, but they were opposed to American leadership. The Community's stance toward developing countries became a mixture of preferential favors toward former colonies and protection against imports of cheap manufactures. Imports from Eastern Europe were controlled to some degree to guard against possible disruption from a system with different methods of price formation and economic development. But none of this called in question the Bretton Woods system or the Community's participation in it.

In the later 1960s, however, the Bretton Woods system began to be shaken by turbulence in the international economy.[27] American external deficits through the 1960s led to successive dollar crises and to the floating of the dollar in August 1971. A synchronized boom throughout the industrial world in the early 1970s generated a surge of commodity prices in 1972–1973, capped by OPEC's quadrupling of oil prices at the end of 1973. Following this impulse to inflation, most of the industrial countries found the pay/price spiral, sustained by labor's bargaining power, very hard to control. Their efforts to overcome it caused heavy unemployment. Their differing success in reacting to the new energy costs and inflation left them with enormous deficits and surpluses in their balance of payments; and this caused steep fluctuations in their exchange rates. Buttressed by the stabilizers of Keynesian economics and the welfare state, the industrial countries withstood these shocks but confidence in the capacity of the neoliberal policy system to produce stability and growth was shaken.

Domestically, global demand management, having failed to maintain full employment and price stability, was supplemented in most countries by an industrial policy to rescue or develop problem sectors, a manpower policy to improve employment by training and job creation or preservation, and an income policy to combat cost push. This growth of sectoral and micro policies reflected, according to the argument earlier in this chapter, not only a temporary conjuncture of turbulence and shocks in the 1970s but also the character of the specialized, capital-intensive and skill-intensive economy in which we now live; hence the correspondingly altered conditions and policy needs in the international economy assumed a permanent character.

The rise of new micro and sectoral forms of economic management, as has been seen, must lead either to separation of the national markets under autonomous policy systems, or to international policy cooperation with respect to these new forms of policy. The general issue of the type of economic policy that is to prevail in the global system resolves itself, then, into the question whether there will be enough agreement in the global system as a whole, or in regional groups, on matters such as industrial policy and the control of inflation to enable a clear and coherent new system to replace that of Bretton Woods, or whether divergent national or regional policy systems will lead to increasing separation among national markets and fragmentation of the international economic system.

The United States is not, as at Bretton Woods, the midwife for the birth of a new system. The United States no longer has such predominant economic strength; its capacity for political leadership has been reduced since the Vietnam war and American adherence to neoclassical economic doctrine is too strong to allow innovative development of new methods of economic management. But no other power has emerged with the capacity to lead the development of a new international economy. The system therefore remains polycentric, with the United States, the Community, and Japan as the principal powers among the advanced industrial countries, the Soviet Union in the communist bloc, and China, India,

Brazil, and Saudi Arabia the most influential among the developing countries. The divergences of economic situation and policy concepts among these centers of power obstruct the emergence of an international policy system, on top of the centrifugal force of separate sovereign polities; and the Community itself, although united enough to qualify as one of the main centers of economic policy-making, contains enough of these divergences and centrifugal force to limit its own capacity for action.

Since 1973, the main substantive achievement of the industrial countries has been the negative, though important, one of refraining from reversion to wholesale protectionism. They have been able to agree on this partly as a result of their major institutional achievement of starting regular summit meetings among the leaders of government of the seven biggest industrialized economies: the United States, Japan, Canada, Britain, France, Germany, and Italy. Together with the heads of government of the four latter, which are its largest member countries, the Community is represented at these meetings by the President of the Commission. Apart from trade, however, the Community has not been effective in promoting a common policy on most of the other subjects at these summit meetings, such as general economic management (efforts to get Germany and Japan to reflate) or exchange rates (pressure on Germany and Japan to revalue and on the United States to strengthen the dollar). Divergences among the member countries, particularly between Germany, with its low inflation and powerful external position, and the others, which are less strongly placed, have been too great, and there is no collective instrument as a focus for common policy, such as the common tariff provides with respect to trade. More fundamentally, the seven governments have not developed a positive and realistic design beyond the maintenance of an open trading system. The "Group of 77" developing countries have promoted a more positive concept in their demand for a new international economic order. This consists largely of demands for transfers of resources and other concessions from the rich to the poor, and the Community has been able to negotiate fairly effectively about this, as many of the demands relate to trade, where the Community has adequate powers and instruments.

The discussion of particular issues that follows, however, will show how the Community has moved unsteadily toward the evolution of new types of economic policy, the acquisition of common instruments, and the development of wider international cooperation. The unsteadiness should not cause surprise. The new economic conditions have presented a challenge to economists, political scientists, and statesmen to find the appropriate response. Economists must develop the ideas on which to base new policies, which will not be derived readily from the existing neoclassical or Marxist models. Political scientists must show how national and international institutions can be adapted to produce the necessary policy output, which is likely to require more radical thinking than has come so far from the functionalist, neofunctionalist, or transnationalist schools. Statesmen will have to apply new ideas about economic policy and political institutions within a complex and unwieldy Community polity and an even more complex world system, both at different unprecedented stages of international integration.

TRADE: LIBERAL, PROTECTED, OR ORGANIZED

In line with the philosophy of Bretton Woods, the Community has used its principal common instrument, the common external tariff, in bargaining for mutual tariff reductions in the framework of the GATT. The United States, as the other market economy of similar size, has been the major partner, and it seems unlikely that Americans would have been motivated to cut their own tariff by one half had they not been confronting a partner of equivalent importance.

The tariff reduction began with the Dillon round (1960–1962), when the Community, soon after its establishment, made cuts to compensate trading partners for any diversions of trade that might ensue from the customs union. This was followed by the Kennedy round (1963–1967), with cuts of about a third implemented toward the end of the 1960s. Further substantial reductions were negotiated during the Tokyo round (1973–1979).[28]

The logical end of the liberalization envisaged within the GATT would be the complete removal of tariffs by industrial countries. This would at the same time liquidate the Community's main policy instrument. Already in the 1960s, however, groups within the industrial countries began to resist this form of economic logic; and an initial result was the Long-Term Cotton Textile Arrangement, which later became the Multi-Fibres Arrangement, whereby the Community and other industrial countries imposed quotas on their imports of textiles and clothing from low-wage developing countries.

In the 1930s such protection was used to enforce deep cuts in the volume of trade, but in the 1960s and 1970s the textile arrangements were negotiated to allow controlled annual increases. Although the exporters negotiated in the knowledge that the Community and the other importing countries would probably impose unilateral restrictions if they did not reach multilateral arrangements, the importing countries wished the negotiations to succeed and thus avert the risks of general unilateral protectionism and of a confrontation with the developing countries. The multilateral negotiations had some substance, therefore, as an example of international policy coordination for a controlled growth of trade.

The pressure of imports from Japan, followed by the newly industrializing countries such as Hong Kong, South Korea, and Taiwan, caused the United States to secure the exporting countries' agreement to bilateral orderly marketing arrangements, which also restrained the growth of trade in a number of other products; and the Community has reacted to imports from Japan in a similar way. After the recession that followed the oil crisis in the mid-1970s, the Community, like the United States, took measures to control its imports of steel and thus stabilize prices and production in its hard-hit steel industry. As with textiles, these measures were far from the savage protectionism of the 1930s. Both the Community and the United States set a floor to import prices at the level of Japanese production plus transport costs, calculated in cooperation with the Japanese; and agreements to stabilize prices were made with East European and other industrializing countries. At the same time the Commission tried to enforce the price floor on Community steel producers and to secure the agreement of member governments to a Community plan for reductions of capacity and restructuring of the industry, although concerted Community action proved hard to achieve. Even without an effective industrial policy designed to help the industry to adapt to a new pattern of international commerce, however, the Community sought to stabilize the trade, not reduce it, and to maintain policy cooperation with the trading partners.

In recent years, with the swift inroads into particular sectors by imports from Japan and the newly industrializing countries on top of the general recession, West European industries have suffered severely. Hence the Community has pressed for an amendment to the GATT clause which provides that if quotas are imposed to protect a sector suffering from market disruption, they must affect imports from all sources indifferently. Since the disruption is usually caused by imports from specific newly industrializing countries, the Community wishes to control them without restricting trade flows that cause no trouble. In return, it is expected that quotas would be supervised by a GATT committee to ensure that they were justified by market disruption and phased out as the disturbance was reduced, and to encourage the use of industrial and manpower policies to help adjustment.

Altogether the Community has played a major part in trade liberalization; and, with the new economic conditions of the 1970s, it has controlled the growth or stabilized the prices of imports that compete with some of its troubled industrial sectors. Reflecting its heavy involvement in the international economy, the Community has generally tried to do this in cooperation with its trading partners, or at least with minimum conflict. It has also taken some industrial and manpower measures to help its industries to adapt to new patterns of import competition. It has funds to support manpower and industrial adaptation, some powers of price control in the coal and steel industries, and competition laws, which could be used to encourage industrial objectives such as capacity reduction but which on the whole are not. These instruments, however, are modest compared with the national instruments of member governments. Moreover, the views of member governments over the proper use of industrial policy differ enough to inhibit the full use of existing Community instruments or the creation of new ones. Although it would be logical, therefore, to supplement measures for organizing trade with measures to impel industry to adapt to new trade patterns, the Community has concentrated rather on the organization and controlled growth of trade through negotiated international policy-making.

AGRICULTURE

For agriculture, as for external trade, the Community has a policy backed by common instruments. As in many other economies, the Community underpins its farmers' income by means of price supports: buying farm products when prices fall below intervention levels, imposing levies to prevent imports from undermining the internal price structure, and subsidizing exports to get rid of surpluses.

Unlike the common external tariff on industrial imports, the agricultural import levies and export subsidies insulate the Community's price level from international market forces and promote Community self-sufficiency. The common agricultural policy has been regarded as a major national interest by the French, who wanted agricultural gains to match the industrial benefits expected for Germany. France therefore insisted on an organized common market for Community agriculture; the prices were set high to cover the higher costs of German farmers. With surpluses generated by these high prices, and France reluctant to allow the Community to negotiate internationally on agriculture for fear that some French advantages would be bargained away, the Community's agricultural policy has tended to be internationally disruptive. For the exporters of temperate agricultural products, led by the United States, and including Australia, Canada, New Zealand, Argentina, Hungary, and Poland, this agricultural protection and the export dumping which has resulted have been a major issue in their relations with the Community; and some developing countries have been at odds with the Community over products such as sugar.

The forces that have moved the Community to seek international accommodation rather than separation with respect to industrial trade, however, have also moved it toward negotiations on agricultural trade.[29] The industries that export one-tenth of the gross Community product are damaged by the agricultural protection which deprives foreign exporters of money which they could spend on Community manufactures. Britain has entered the Community with a tradition of cheap food imported from overseas. Consumers have become a more vocal lobby. On the other side, the French farm population has been halved since the establishment of the EEC, and the agricultural lobby has lost some of its strength.

The first practical sign of an intention to move beyond autarky in agriculture came as early as 1964, after the start of the Kennedy round negotiations, when the member of the Commission responsible for agriculture proposed that there should be international agreements on the levels of protection for different agricultural products. The Americans did not wish to negotiate about this at the time, although it has since become a major subject of discussion regarding the international organization of agricultural trade.

In the course of the negotiations for British accession to the Community, guarantees were made for access to the enlarged market for agreed quantities of New Zealand dairy products and of sugar from the Commonwealth developing countries. Meanwhile, the Community became more open than the United States to proposals for commodity agreements from developing countries in UNCTAD. The first major international negotiation in which the Community has participated with agriculture as a major subject was the Tokyo round, where agreements on major products such as wheat were negotiated. Thus the Community has begun to use its powerful instruments for the organization of its domestic agricultural market in negotiations designed to contribute to the regulation of international agricultural markets as a whole.

ENERGY

In contradistinction to agriculture, the Community has few instruments with which to organize the energy market.[30] The ECSC provided for Community action relating to coal prices, investments, and production, but with the decline of the coal industry in the 1950s and 1960s the member governments tried to deal with the problem themselves and deprived the Community of much of its role. Foreseeing an eventual shortage of energy, Jean Monnet promoted Euratom more actively than the EEC,[31] and when the two were established together in 1958, it was hoped that Euratom would play a big part in developing civil nuclear power. But de Gaulle, jealous of French nuclear sovereignty, reduced Euratom to a minor role. Through the 1960s and up to the oil crisis in 1973, there was divergence between the French, who envisaged an organized Community energy market, and other member countries, notably the Dutch, who wanted the Community to maintain a free market system. There were some warnings that the Community was becoming extremely dependent on imports of oil from OPEC countries;[32] but political inertia combined with general faith in free market forces prevented the Community from taking any action to anticipate the quadrupling of prices and the threat of an oil embargo at the end of 1973.

An embargo on their oil supplies would have brought the economies of the Community countries to a standstill. Not being bound by any common instrument, most of the member governments reacted by trying to make their own arrangements with the suppliers.[33] The embargo on oil supplies to the Netherlands was quietly dealt with by the multinational oil companies, with no expression of solidarity by the other member governments. Thus the Community economy survived that crisis without major disruption.

Despite the danger of a recurrence and the Community's need to secure its supplies by agreement with the producers, the Community made little progress toward a common energy policy in the subsequent five years. Eight of the member countries joined the International Energy Agency, established in the OECD on American initiative, but the French stood aside. The Community tried to improve its political relations with the Arabs by means of a modestly successful intergovernmental "Euro-Arab dialogue," which started in 1975. The stability of the oil trade thus has depended mainly on the American relationship with Saudi Arabia. Britain, since 1973, has developed its North Sea resources and is now more or less self-sufficient, but it has used this to guard its separation from the Community in energy policy, not to promote a common measure. In short, the Community has done little to defend its own collective interests in the security of energy supplies.

MONETARY POLICY

The instability of the international monetary system has been aggravating for the Community as for other trading economies. Much of the fluctuation of exchange rates has reflected economic forces such as differing rates of inflation in various countries or price trends in energy and other commodity markets. But these trends have been exaggerated by waves of speculation, which distort exchange rates and endanger economic stability. Whereas in trade policy the Community has become the equal of the United States, in money it has no common instrument with which to challenge the primacy of the dollar, the dominant international currency for both official and commercial use. The Community has a strong interest, therefore, in improving the stability of the international system and securing influence in it equivalent to that of the United States.

The Community has made major efforts to advance its integration in the monetary field, which would result in the creation of common instruments with which it could negotiate internationally.[34] Through the 1960s, progress was almost impossible because of the divergence between France under de Gaulle, who backed the role of gold in order to attack the dollar, and Germany which cooperated with the United States in supporting the dollar. When Pompidou succeeded de Gaulle, however, he quickly agreed with the other heads of government of the Community countries that a plan for economic and monetary union should be launched. The first step, taken in February 1971, was to hold the exchange rates within a narrower band of fluctuation (the "snake") than applied to those within the international system as a whole. This was a small move toward greater stability, but the aim was to follow it by larger steps, leading by 1980 to the centralization of monetary policy in the Community institutions and the replacement of member countries' currencies by a common currency (or at least the permanent locking of their parities, which amounts to much the same thing). The Community currency would then rival the dollar as a dominant force in the international system.

Later in 1971, however, the weakness of the dollar led to its floating; and monetary instability forced the Germans and the Dutch to float their currencies only four months after they had put them into the Community's snake. Subsequent efforts to promote economic and monetary union were frustrated, partly by continued international monetary upheavals, partly through divergent French and German reactions to American policy and to the dollar, and partly through differences between France and its partners about supranational control of monetary policy in the Community. The Community did manage to negotiate as a unit with the United States, and reached the Smithsonian agreement about exchange rates in December 1971; but these exchange rates too were soon swept away by tides of speculation. After three further years of turbulence, the Community shelved its bold plan for monetary integration.

The inconvenience of an unstable international system dominated by a weak dollar caused the Community to return to its efforts of monetary unification. By 1978 the Germans were strongly motivated to link the other Community currencies to the mark so that they would share the strain of speculative flights from the dollar; the French wanted to tie the franc to the mark in order to reduce inflation. On Franco-German initiative, therefore, a project to establish a European monetary system was agreed. Although its launching was troubled by discord between France and Germany about the effect on agricultural prices, and by Britain remaining outside the system for a time at least, the new system had features that made it better adapted than the earlier plan for economic and monetary union. The arrangement for exchange rates was more flexible, with a wider band for fluctuation by weaker currencies and allowance for adjusting the parities of those that get out of line. A European Currency

Unit (ECU) was created, in terms of which credits would be available to keep exchange rates within the band, with the intention of pooling one-fifth of the member countries' reserves in a common reserve fund after two years. The more flexible exchange rate arrangement seemed better adapted to a period of differing rates of inflation and turbulence in the market for dollars; and the parallel instruments would give the Community greater weight to influence monetary policies both in member countries and in the international system. The persistence of the efforts to promote monetary integration shows that the Community members understand the need for more stability in their monetary relationships, in line with the secular trend toward greater economic interdependence. Success in meeting this need would provide the Community with the monetary instruments it requires to pursue an effective common policy in the international system and to move toward a more equal relationship with the United States.

RELATIONS WITH THE UNITED STATES

The United States is the Community's largest trading partner and the dominant source of international money, multinational companies, and transferred technology; the Community countries are also largely dependent on the United States for their nuclear defense. Numerous questions concerning trade, agriculture, energy, and money are posed in this relationship, and it raises fundamental policy issues for the Community.[35]

The interaction has been vexed by the opposing views of Germany and France. In the early postwar period the French, like other West Europeans, rebuilt their economy with the help of Marshall aid but then began to contest American policies. This reached a climax through the late 1950s and 1960s, under de Gaulle, when France left the military organization of NATO, waged its campaign against the dollar and vetoed British entry into the Community, partly on the grounds that Britain would act as America's Trojan horse. Although French policies became steadily less anti-American after de Gaulle's demise, Paris refused to join the International Energy Agency in 1974, because it would be led by the United States, and there are still substantial differences between France and the other Community countries in their attitudes toward the United States.

Throughout the period of Gaullist opposition to America, Germany remained one of the most loyal supporters of the United States in both the military and the economic fields, and this impeded the formation of common policies and the development of the Community in many ways. The other Community countries generally sided with Germany, as did

Britain after its entry into the Community in 1973. The importance of attitudes to the United States was again shown in 1978, when the German government's espousal of the idea of a European monetary system was caused partly by frustration with American hesitations in both defense and monetary policy, while the British government's doubts about the plan were due partly to a desire to link it more closely with the dollar.

Where the Community has already established its common instruments, its member countries' options are no longer confined to the alternatives of either frustrated opposition to America or loyal support. As the experience with trade and agricultural policy has shown, the common instruments enable the Community to display its united strength, and so to choose between the alternatives of equal partnership and policy cooperation (as with trade) or in some fields self-sufficient independence (agriculture). France accepted the trade partnership while Germany accepted the policy of self-sufficiency in agriculture. As we saw, economic interdependence has been pushing the Community toward negotiation and policy cooperation on agriculture, too, again on an equal basis because of the effectiveness of its policy instruments; and if the Community develops common monetary instruments, the same may be confidently predicted with respect to eventual monetary cooperation.

This would give the Community the capacity to be an equal partner of the United States in the major fields of international economic policy. But the Community's use of this capacity would be constrained by strategic dependence on the United States. If linkage between the new fields is brought fully into play, the Community's bargaining strength in economics can be overridden by its weakness in defense. The Americans regard such linkage as legitimate,[36] but they have been fairly restrained in its use, partly because they too have a powerful interest in the security of Western Europe and its independence from Soviet influence—strong enough, French governments have argued, for the potential of linkage to be ingored altogether by the Community. A safer way to reduce the influence of U.S. linkage, of course, would be for France to agree with other Community governments on steps toward defense integration, which would strengthen the European bargaining position.

If economic integration in the Community continues, the Community will emerge as a major force in the international economic system, particularly in new fields such as monetary policy. Conflicts with the United States may be caused not only by the usual rivalries between sovereign partners but also by differing views of the new economic and industrial policies appropriate to deal with the problems of the modern economy. But interdependencies with the United States are likely to increase, and these will continue to pull the Community toward cooperation with the Americans in international policy-making.

RELATIONS WITH THE SOVIET UNION

Fear of Soviet military strength has been an important motive for integration in Western Europe. The establishment of the ECSC and the plan for a European defense community followed the communist takeover in Czechoslovakia; and the Soviet interventions in Hungary (1956) and Czechoslovakia (1968) reinforced the urge toward integration, in the first case with the establishment of the EEC and in the second with the revival of the Community's development, after de Gaulle, through enlargement and the plan for economic and monetary union. Yet this had not led to any significant interactions between the Community and the Soviet Union.[37]

The Soviet Union has deliberately minimized its relations with the Community institutions, while expanding its trade with member countries. On both ideological and political grounds, the Russians have opposed integration among capitalist countries. They have used diplomatic and political pressure to hinder integration and enlargement of the Community, have reacted extremely sharply against moves for defense integration within Western Europe, and have sought to deter the Community from developing a common commercial policy toward its eastern neighbors. The U.S.S.R. has refused to "recognize" the Community and has prevented East European countries from undertaking general trade negotiations with the organization.

Initially, the Community countries responded by keeping their trade relations with the Comecon countries in the hands of the Community member governments, at least as long as the Treaty of Rome made it legally possible. By 1975, however, they could no longer conduct separate trade negotiations without being in breach of the treaty, so the Comecon countries and other state-trading partners were invited to start trade negotiations with the Community. The Chinese reacted positively by negotiating a trade agreement with the Community, but the Soviet Union and its allies refused to do so.

This primacy of politics over economics does not harm the Soviet Union's interest, because the bulk of its exports to Western Europe are raw materials—oil and gas—which are not subject to Community tariffs or trade restrictions. The East Europeans, on the other hand, export agricultural products and low-technology manufactures, which encounter stiff protection from the Community's common agricultural and commercial policies. Their need to negotiate with the Community about these problems has been evident to the Soviet Union. They have in fact been able to negotiate about tariffs in the GATT, of which the Czechs, Hungarians, Poles, and Rumanians are members; agreements have been allowed in specific problem sectors such as textiles and steel, and the Community for its part leaves its member governments free to negotiate economic cooperation agreements with the Comecon countries, provided that these do not concern tariffs, quotas, or agricultural levies that come under the common commercial policy. But the East Europeans still feel the need for general trade negotiations. The Soviet Union, since its 1968 intervention in Czechoslovakia, has promoted integration in Comecon as a more convenient way to maintain stability within the group; and it has pressed the East Europeans to negotiate collectively, as a Comecon group, with the Community about trade. The Rumanians have resisted this strongly, and some other East European countries have done so more quietly, as it would entail greater Soviet influence, perhaps control, over their external trade.

The Community has rejected Comecon proposals to negotiate about trade. Its explicit reason has been that Comecon does not possess the powers, as the Community does, to negotiate on behalf of its member states. Behind that lies the reluctance of a number of Community governments to act in a way that could strengthen Soviet dominance over the East Europeans. The Community has therefore repeated that it remains open to general trade negotiations with the several Comecon states; it has declined to accept, for negotiations with Comecon, any more than a reference to general principles of trade policy which have already been agreed in the Conference on Security and Cooperation in Europe (CSCE).

The Community is thus an influence on East–West economic relations when it uses common instruments in a way that affects other countries. Its external tariff, quotas, and agricultural levies affect the exports of East European countries, which therefore want to negotiate. This influences Soviet policy, although the Soviet Union itself is hardly affected. Since the Soviet Union is so predominant in Comecon, the relationship between the Community and Comecon or its member countries has developed at a pace the reflects Soviet rather than East European interests, that is, very slowly, with scant progress between 1974 and 1980.

Apart from the political reasons for this, there is an unsolved problem relating to differing methods of economic management. The tariffs, which are so central to trade negotiations between market economies, have little importance in Comecon countries where prices are still, for the most part, determined administratively. Whereas the East Europeans have been clear in their requests for lower tariffs or levies and relaxation of quotas, the Western countries have not yet discovered what reciprocal demands to make on their eastern partners. While negotiations between Western firms and eastern trading entities involve normal give-and-take, the negotiations between Western and Eastern governments have usually concentrated one-sidedly on Eastern demands and Western concessions, without much reciprocation based on Western demands. Official negotiations are consequently not very important to the Western countries.

This asymmetry in trade negotiations may be reduced, however, as methods of economic management respond to modern needs. Enterprises in advanced economics need scope for initiative to handle the complex problems in their sectors. This is pushing the Soviet group toward greater use of market mechanisms, which may eventually enable it to offer some reciprocity to the Western countries in terms of access to Eastern markets. The market economies for their part, as they develop industrial policies and organized markets for commodities, may become able to request and offer concessions relating to investment plans, market shares, and long-term contracts for particular products, in terms which are meaningful for directively planned economies.

Insofar as the Community develops sectoral and micro policies to deal with its industrial and commodity problems, therefore, it may be able to pave the way for new forms of cooperation with the directively planned economies. The relationship between the Community and its Eastern neighbors is not likely to develop rapidly, however, unless there is a change of policy by the Soviet Union, either to evolve a more positive relationship itself or allow the East Europeans more autonomy in dealings with the Community. In the longer run, the Russians will be influenced, as other countries are, by the pressures of technological development toward modern methods of economic administration and interdependence management.

THE DEVELOPING COUNTRIES

Stemming from its world-wide links, the Community has a wider spread of economic relations than any other global actor. Since the Community disposes of major instruments of statecraft toward the developing countries, in the form of the common commercial policy and a proportion of the aid budgets of the member countries, it has the opportunity to use its collective weight in a very important segment of the world economy.

When Britain stood aside from the foundation of the Community in the 1950s, the member country with the strongest overseas links was France, which still had a dozen African colonies. The French insisted that these African countries be associated with the Community, which accordingly provided, in Part IV of the Treaty of Rome, for an association of member countries' colonies (mainly the French African colonies, Madagascar, and Zaïre, which was then the Belgian Congo), on terms that gave them free access to the Community market and aid from a European Development Fund.

Germany and the Netherlands did not like this and secured some concessions in the external tariff on products imported from Latin America. But the association arrangement remained intact. France fought hard to retain the privileges of the associated countries through the 1960s when they were independent, although this was strongly criticized by the majority of developing countries as well as the United States and some other industrial states and became an issue in UNCTAD and the GATT. The Community did extend somewhat similar favors to most of the Mediterranean countries, but this did not help relations with the big majority elsewhere.

In the 1970s, however, the Community widened its policies toward developing countries, to reflect better the width of its trade and investment links.[38] In 1971 it introduced its Generalized Scheme of Preferences, to benefit imports of manufactures from all developing countries. On the enlargement of the Community to include Britain, the association arrangement was replaced by the Lome Convention, covering not only the existing associates but also the Commonwealth countries in Africa, the Caribbean, and the Pacific. Over fifty countries, comprising almost all of black Africa and the Caribbean islands, plus a few islands in the Pacific, now share the advantages of free access to the Community market for most of their products, aid from the European Development Fund, guaranteed sales from the sugar exporters among them, and compensation for price falls in their commodity exports under the Community's Stabex scheme. The Community has also negotiated economic cooperation agreements with India, Bangladesh, Sri Lanka, Malaysia, Pakistan, Brazil, Mexico, and some other countries, and has set up a development fund for Asia, although on a modest scale. A Euro–Arab dialogue has sought ways of further developing links between the Community and the Arab countries; the Community has discussed with the Association of Southeast Asian Nations (ASEAN) the possibility of a formal relationship with that regional group; and a trade agreement with China has come into force. Thus the Community's external policies now deal with almost all developing countries and it has special agreements of one kind or another with the most important ones.

On the issue of global versus regional links with developing countries, then, the Community has moved quite a long way in the global direction. At the same time, the developing countries have articulated a wide range of demands for a New International Economic Order (NIEO). The Community was the first major industrial economy to respond to the UNCTAD proposal for generalized preferences; its record is at least not much worse than that of the others in its liberalization of imports of labor-intensive manufactures, although the agricultural exports of developing countries have not made much headway when they have come up against the protective measures of the common agricultural policy. The aid budgets of the Community and its member countries comprise, moreover, a larger proportion of their gross product than do the aid budgets of the other global actors.

The NIEO demands call for greater use of some of the mechanisms of organized markets, notably in commodity trade. Here the Community has been more inclined than the United States to respond positively, although its position has been weakened by divergent attitudes among the member countries, with Germany resisting interference in free markets and France better disposed to accommodate. The Community has also gone beyond traditional liberal policies with a provision for industrial cooperation under the Lome Convention and some related bilateral agreements, although the mechanisms for such cooperation are still embryonic. Thus the Community seems readier than the United States to adopt new methods of economic management to deal with problems in its relations with developing countries, even if it is far from quick or decisive in doing so.

The NIEO proposals express a desire to shift the balance of economic power in the direction of the developing countries. Changes in that balance are occurring, as a result of the quicker growth rates of the newly industrializing countries, which together with the OPEC members have a fifth to a quarter of the population of the developing countries as a whole. If China and India are added, this classes about three-quarters of the population of the developing countries among those whose economic strength is both significant and growing. It is this rather than the proposals of the NIEO that is likely to change the global balance of economic power. When the Community concentrated its favors upon a few small associates among the developing countries, it could justly be accused of turning its back on some of the most important trends in contemporary world economics. The widening of its policies has given it a better chance to evolve new forms of policy cooperation with those Asian, Latin American, and African countries that will play a growing part in the organization and management of the international economy.

Issue Processing, Management, and Performance

The Community, unique among the major global actors, lacks the political structure of a state. Its system for processing and managing issues is extremely pluralist, complex, cumbersome, and slow. The participants include the government of each member, the "European" institutions (Commission, Court, Parliament, Economic and Social Committee) and numerous unofficial actors such as political parties and interest groups.[39]

The most striking peculiarity of the Community is the dominant role of the member governments in taking all the main decisions. This is done mainly in the Council of Ministers, supported by their cohorts of officials, with different ministers taking part in the meetings according to the subject in question (agriculture, energy, finance, trade, transport, etcetera). The heads of government of the members during the past decade have had fairly frequent meetings, which have been institutionalized into a European Council meeting three times a year.[40] The meetings of the European Council are rather informal, but important decisions have been made at them, including new departures such as the direct elections to the European parliament and the launching of a European monetary system, as well as the resolution of problems which have been stuck in the Council of Ministers, such as the renegotiation of the terms of British membership in 1975.

Because the decisions in the Council of Ministers are usually taken by unanimous agreement, the views of each government, and particularly those of the larger countries, are crucial. For a big decision, active support of at least one major government is necessary. The creation of the common agricultural policy was promoted, for example, by France, while both France and Germany were behind the launching of the European monetary system (whose start was, however, jeopardized by disagreement between the two governments). Nor can a big decision be taken if it is opposed by a major government (for instance, British entry in the 1960s opposed only by France) or even, sometimes, by a minor one. The unwieldiness of the system is evident when one considers that behind the ministers are large and complicated national government machines,[41] and behind each of them the parliaments and polities of nine pluralist democracies, any of which, if there are strong interests or feelings in relation to an issue, can upset the Community's decision-making process. It is not surprising that the Community often fails to reach any decision on proposed new developments. When it does manage to do so, this is often after long delays: the Community took two years to prepare itself for the Multi-Fibre Agreement, to the detriment of all its textile industries, for the governments were unable to agree on how to divide the quotas among the member countries; as many as fourteen years were needed before a common form of added-value tax was adopted in the member countries.[42] Once a decision is taken, it is hard to alter: the structure of the common agricultural policy is an obvious example.

Yet numerous decisions have been taken by the Community, some very important, not least in its external relations: the Kennedy round; the Generalized Scheme of Preferences; the enlargement to include Britain, Denmark, and Ireland; and the Lome Convention. It was suggested earlier that this is possible where the Community has a common policy instrument; and a number of the Community's most important instruments relate to its external policies. These include the common tariff, the agricultural levies and subsidies, the European Development Fund, and the power to make agreements and treaties with other countries with respect to all aspects of commercial policy. Where the Community has lacked such common instruments, as in energy and monetary policy, it has been much less effective; the members' foreign policy coordination in the "political cooperation" machinery, which does not dispose of common instruments, has only modest achievements to its credit.

In bringing the governments to their decisions, the "European" institutions have played an important part. Up to now the Commission has been the most significant, with its role as initiator of policies, executor of decisions, negotiator with trade partners, and watchdog over the application of the Community treaties. Although it has been weakened by the member governments' jealousy over their sovereign prerogatives, the Commission can, when it is politically skillful, tilt the balance in favor of Community action. Well-researched examples have been the part of Commissioner Rey in the final stages of the Kennedy round[43] and that of a small group of officials in the adoption of the Generalized Scheme of Preferences.[44] The Court has extended the scope of the common commercial policy by ruling that export credit policy is a part of it. The Parliament, directly elected in 1979, may help to fill the vacuum caused by the absence, hitherto, of a European political focus in the Community.[45]

The neofunctionalist literature has laid much stress on the integrative role to be expected of nonofficial bodies such as interest groups in pressing upon and providing support for Community institutions.[46] Although interest groups have been active, particularly in relation to the agricultural policy, the neofunctionalists have been disappointed in their expectation that such political forces would help integration to spill over from one field into another, with the common interest being "up-graded" through expansion of the functions and authority of the European institutions.[47] After the initial great decisions to give the Community its power and instruments in agricultural and external trade policy, the Community's achievements have related mainly to the use of these instruments rather than the creation of new ones.

The weakness of the neofunctionalist argument may have been its expectation of further integration as a spillover from existing policy integration rather than by the economic policy needs of the member countries resulting from their growing interdependence. As we have seen, the motive behind the initiative to set up the European monetary system lay in the member countries' economic needs rather than in any tension between their unintegrated monetary policies and the integrated policies in agriculture or trade. Given the Community's doubtful record in the creation of new instruments, we should not be surprised if it develops common monetary instruments incrementally or with stops and starts, or even if this particular initiative has no lasting results. Nor should we be surprised if the Community makes only halting progress in developing common instruments of industrial policy, especially as long as Germany takes a more laissez-faire view of the desirability of such instruments than most of its Community partners. If the assumptions made earlier about technological development and its implications for interdependence and for methods of economic management are justified, the Community's continued vitality in monetary as well as trade matters give grounds to suppose that the necessary instruments are likely to be created eventually; the Community's record in the use of its common instruments shows that, despite the defects that will doubtless remain in its capacity to process and manage issues, it is likely to perform fairly effectively as an actor in the international economy, probably over a widening range of subjects.

The European Community and Global Development

As with the United States and Japan, the substance of the Community's activities in the global economic system is in the hands of autonomous companies or other economic agents, and not in those of public authorities. History, as we have seen, has endowed the Community with a more dense and widespread net of such links than any of the other global actors. Unlike in the United States and Japan, the responsibility for official economic relationships that provide a framework for this immense autonomous activity is divided in the Community between the European institutions and the member governments, which also retain responsibility for general foreign policy and defense. The Community's official involvement in the global system therefore takes the form of a complex interplay between member governments and European institutions, whether in the international institutions themselves or in the bilateral and regional agreements which the Community has made with so many countries.

The thread which has been used, in this chapter, to guide us through this complex web of relationships is the possession by the Community of common instruments of external policy. Where it has such instruments, the Community has been able to act as a collective force in international affairs; where it does not, the several member governments have usually acted independently and the Community's collective performance has been poor.

This has been strikingly demonstrated in relations with the United States. With its common tariff, the Community has emerged as the only economy able to negotiate about trade on level terms with the Americans. This has swung the balance of economic power away from American domination in both the Atlantic system and the GATT. Thus the Community has played the key part in the movement toward a multipolar global economic system. On the other hand the Community has failed to match American bargaining power in other important sectors of economic policy, such as money and energy. Although the Commission as well as member governments are represented in organizations such as the OECD and its International Energy Agency and in summit meetings of the seven major advanced industrial states, the Community's role in these bodies is less significant than that of the governments of its major member countries. The Community governments have tried to adopt common lines in the IMF and in other monetary negotiations, but this has seldom borne much fruit.

The failure of member governments to agree to the complete adoption of the common commercial policy before the mid-1970s deprived the Community of a significant role in relations with the Soviet Union and Eastern Europe until then, although trade increased rapidly on the initiative of individual firms, with some help through bilateral agreements concluded by the Community's members. Since 1975 the Community has performed more effectively by offering to negotiate commercial agreements with each state-trading country and refusing to negotiate with Comecon as a group. The Community is represented, along with the Comecon countries, in pan-European organizations such as the U.N. Economic Commission for Europe and the Conference on Security and Cooperation in Europe (both of which also include the United States); and the Community has played an effective part not only in the economic negotiations in the latter but also in maintaining a united front, through its political cooperation machinery, in political matters. The Community refused to allow the CSCE negotiations to begin until the Soviet Union had agreed to the inclusion of contacts and information, that is to say some aspects of human rights, on the agenda. The divergence of political attitudes and economic systems is, however, still a formidable obstacle to the development of relations between the two groups.

The Community's official relations with less developed countries, by contrast, have been quite prolific. It has the Lome Convention with most African, Caribbean, and some Pacific countries, and has agreements with almost all the Mediterranean countries, which are of substantial significance to the Community's partners. The regional and bilateral agreements have been, perhaps, more important for policy cooperation with less developed countries than the Community's participation in international bodies such as GATT and UNCTAD. The Community's performance in such bodies, nevertheless, has often been more positive than that of other major global actors in its response to the developing countries' demands. For example, the Community was the first to adopt a Generalized Scheme of Preferences; it has generally been readier than the United States to consider proposals for commodity support schemes; and it has been fairly constructive in the North–South dialogue. It has thus contributed to policy cooperation with the developing countries in international organizations as well as in its network of regional and bilateral agreements.

The Future

Three broad possibilities have been projected for the Community: somewhat more integration followed by an "overall equilibrium state," transformation into a "federal or quasi-federal pattern," or "spillback" into "a reconfirmation of national decision-making patterns." [48] Although there is no inevitability about it, the consequences of technological development are likely to press the Community toward the acquisition of new common instruments, and hence toward an impact on global affairs similar to that of a federal system. If this does not happen, the member countries will face growing difficulty in managing their own interdependent economies or holding their own in bargaining with the world's economic giants.

Similar pressures will apply to the relations between the Community and the other advanced industrial countries. Among the Community's neighbors in Western Europe, Greece has now joined, Portugal and Spain are likely to become members in the early 1980s, and others may follow later. The Community and the United States are already closely interdependent, through monetary and multinational company links as much as through trade; and the pressures toward policy integration will not diminish. If the Community achieves an effective common currency, a formal system of economic policy integration between the Community and the United States will not be out of the question. But both sides would be reluctant to cut across their links with other economic partners. Japan, for example, whose economic level and system place it among the advanced industrial countries, has a cultural pattern and national orientation different enough to be a severe obstacle to formal policy integration for a long time ahead. The Community and the United States would fear that if they went too far with a formal system, they would isolate Japan as well as other major countries which might by then be joining the ranks of the industrially advanced.

Were it not for divergences of political attitudes and economic systems, the Soviet Union and the East European countries could have a relationship with the Community similar to that of the United States and the other West European countries. Whereas such a development cannot be expected for a long time, the East Europeans might fairly quickly form a close relationship if the Soviet Union were to allow them. The Soviet Union itself is not, in the long run, likely to find any alternative other than to satisfy its technological needs by responding to the growing pressures for interdependence; this could reach the point where it would both reform its economic system and change its political attitude toward the West. The logic of interdependence would then point to a rapid growth of policy cooperation.

With the less developed countries, the Community is likely to continue evolving its bilateral and regional links, but the relationship will remain uneasy as long as the less developed have greatly inferior bargaining power. The irruption of the oil producers and the newly industrializing countries as important forces in the world economy has begun to tilt the balance of power, however; and if our argument about the fast growth rates of the newly industrializing was justified, this process is likely to continue. China, India, Brazil, Mexico, and a number of other countries, now classed as less developed, by the twenty-first century could become partners on a much more equal footing with the Community and the United States. Any such change in the global balance of power is, of course, painful for those who are now more powerful; but the mutual interest in an accommodation is substantial enough to weight the scales in favor of a more or less constructive relationship; and experience even in the difficult period of the 1970s tends to bear this out.

A global system would, in these circumstances, emerge with perhaps seven major economic powers (the United States, the Community, the Soviet Union, Japan, China, India, Brazil), each of them with a web of bilateral relationships, and playing leading roles in the various international organizations. The differences of economic levels and growth rates, of economic and political systems, of cultural patterns and security interests are enough to make progress toward policy cooperation difficult and uncertain. But the underlying advance of technology and hence of economic interdependence is likely to remain as a constant pressure toward a convergence of economic levels and systems, and hence to a reduction of some of the barriers to policy cooperation. The Community's focal position in the international economy, its own experience as a most advanced form of policy cooperation and integration, and its record in the international arena seem to justify the belief that it could play a pivotal part in the movement of the global system through an increasingly intense process of policy cooperation, toward a form of integrated economic management which alone could satisfy the needs of the future world economy.

Notes

1. The European Community (EC) comprises the European Economic Community (EEC), the European Coal and Steel Community (ECSC), and the European Atomic Energy Community (Euratom). The ECSC was established in 1951, the EEC and Euratom in 1958. The founder members of the Community were Belgium, the Federal Republic of Germany, France, Italy, Lux-

embourg, and the Netherlands. In 1973 it was enlarged to include Denmark, the Republic of Ireland and the United Kingdom. Greece became a member in January 1981. Portugal and Spain have applied for membership.

2. The most important theoretical works on which the European federalists drew were written by British federalists in the period 1938–1941, in particular W. Ivor Jennings, *A Federation for Western Europe* (Cambridge: At the University Press, 1940); L. Robbins, *The Economic Causes of War* (London: Cape, 1939); P. Ransome (ed.), *Studies in Federal Planning* (London: Macmillan, 1943). The early development of this thinking on the Continent is documented in W. Lipgens, *Europa-Federationsplane der Widerstandsbewegungen 1940–45* (Munich: R. Oldenbourg Verlag, 1958); W. Lipgens, *Erster Teil 1945–47* (Stuttgart: Ernst Klett Verlag, 1977). Subsequent literature is reviewed in Charles Pentland, *International Theory and European Integration* (London: Faber and Faber, 1973), chap. 5.

3. Text of the statement made by M. Robert Schuman, French Foreign Minister, on 9 May 1950, cited in Roy Pryce, *The Political Future of the European Community* (London: Marshbank for the Federal Trust, 1962), p. 97.

4. Note, for example, the title of Jean Monnet's *Les Etats-Unis d'Europe ont commencé* (Paris: Robert Laffont, 1955).

5. The foundation work for this school was Ernst B. Haas, *The Uniting of Europe* (London: Stevens, 1958).

6. Leon N. Lindberg, *The Political Dynamics of European Economic Integration* (Stanford, Calif.: Stanford University Press, 1963).

7. See Miriam Camps, *Britain and the European Community: 1955-1963* (London: Oxford University Press, 1964).

8. See Miriam Camps, *European Unification in the Sixties: From the Veto to the Crisis* (New York: McGraw-Hill, 1966).

9. Leon N. Lindberg and Stuart A. Scheingold, *Europe's Would-Be Polity* (Englewood Cliffs, N.J.: Prentice-Hall, 1970). The state of the various theories on European integration in the early 1970s—pluralist, functionalist, neofunctionalist, and federalist—is fully analyzed in Pentland, *International Theory and European Integration*.

10. See Loukas Tsoukalis, *The Politics and Economics of European Monetary Integration* (London: Allen and Unwin, 1977).

11. A recent review of the various theories is to be found in Carole Webb, "Variations on a Theoretical Theme," in Helen Wallace, William Wallace, and Carole Webb (eds.), *Policy-Making in the European Communities* (London: John Wiley, 1977).

12. John Pinder, "Europe as a Tenth Member of the Community," *Government and Opposition,* Autumn 1975; and "Das extranationale Europa," *Integration* (Bonn: Institut für Europäische Politik, 1978).

13. See Tsoukalis, *The Politics and Economics of European Monetary Integration.*

14. For an analysis of the significance of the directly elected parliament, see David Coombes, *The Future of the European Parliament* (London: European Centre for Political Studies, Policy Studies Institute, 1979).

15. See, for example, M. Maximova, *Osnovnye Problemy Imperialisticheskoy Integratsii* (Moscow: Mysl, 1971).

16. This dichotomy is analyzed in John Pinder, "Economic Diplomacy," in James N. Rosenau, Kenneth W. Thompson, and Gavin Boyd (eds.), *World Politics* (New York: Free Press, 1976), pp. 316–17.

17. The word political is used in a peculiar sense to distinguish the main field of work of ministries of foreign affairs from that of economic departments. Students of politics will know that economic affairs are just as political.

18. For an analysis of the structure and results of "political cooperation" see William Wallace and David Allen, "Political Cooperation: Procedure as a Substitute for Policy," in Wallace, Wallace, and Webb (eds.), *Policy-Making in the European Communities.*

19. The need for closer international policy coordination was considered in Richard N. Cooper, *The Economics of Interdependence* (New York: McGraw-Hill, 1968), and in Miriam Camps, *The Management of Interdependence* (New York: Council on Foreign Relations, 1974).

20. The conditions for integration are discussed in Pinder, "Economic Diplomacy," pp. 317–19.

21. Gunnar Myrdal, *An International Economy* (London: Routledge and Kegan Paul, 1956).

22. John Galtung, *The European Community: A Superpower in the Making* (London: Allen and Unwin, 1973).

23. See Roger Morgan, "The Foreign Policies of Great Britain, France and West Germany," in Rosenau, Thompson, and Boyd (eds.), *World Politics,* pp. 175–76; and Joseph Nye, *Peace in Parts: Integration and Conflict in Regional Organization* (Boston: Little, Brown, 1971), cited in Rosenau, Thompson, and Boyd (eds.), *World Politics,* pp. 613–14.

24. This focus may be compared with that of the neofunctionalists when they use their concept of "upgrading the common interest" to describe the parties concerned with an issue "redefining their conflict so as to work out a solution at a higher level, which almost invariably implies the expansion of the mandate or task of an international or national government agency." Ernst B. Haas, "International Integration: The European and the Universal Process," *International Organization,* 15 (1961), 368, cited in Lindberg, *The Political Dynamics of European Integration,* p. 12; Lindberg uses the concept throughout.

25. For a discussion of the concept of externalization in relation to the Community, see Philippe C. Schmitter, "Three Neo-Functional Hypotheses about Regional Integration," *International Organization* 23 (Winter 1969); and Werner J. Feld, *The European Community in World Affairs* (Sherman Oaks, Calif.: Alfred Publishers), chap. 9.

26. Both Morgan, "The Foreign Policies," and Nye, *Peace in Parts,* argue that cooperative behavior is normal within such regional organizations as well as between them and other countries.

27. See T. Peeters and W. Hager, "The Community and the Changing World Economic Order," in M. Kohnstamm and W. Hager, *A Nation Writ Large?* (London: Macmillan, 1973).

28. The Community's part in GATT rounds is described in Feld, *The European Community in World Affairs,* chap. 5; W. J. Feld, *The European Common Market and the World* (Englewood Cliffs, N.J.: Prentice-Hall, 1967), chap. 6;

and P. Coffey, *The External Economic Relations of the EEC,* (London: Macmillan, 1976), pp. 23–30 and 82–84.

29. The case for international accommodation in agriculture is made in A. Zeller, "European Agriculture in the World Economy," in Kohnstamm and Hager, *A Nation Writ Large?*

30. The attempts to form a Community energy policy are described in R. A. Black, Jr., "Nine Governments in Search of a Common Energy Policy," in Wallace, Wallace, and Webb (eds), *Policy-Making in the European Communities.*

31. Camps, *Britain and the European Community 1955-1963,* pp. 55, 56.

32. See, for example, J. Hartshorn, "Europe's Energy Imports," in Kohnstamm and Hager, *A Nation Writ Large?*, p. 106.

33. These events are described in Feld, *The European Community in World Affairs,* pp. 277–92.

34. Community efforts toward monetary integration are analyzed in G. Magnifico, *European Monetary Unification* (London: Macmillan, 1973); Tsoukalis, *The Politics and Economics of European Monetary Integration;* and R. W. Russell, "Managing Europe's Money," in Wallace, Wallace, and Webb, *Policy-Making in the European Communities.*

35. For discussion of this issue see G. Mally (ed.), *The New Europe and the United States* (Lexington, Mass.: Lexington Books, 1974); J. R. Schaetzel, *The Unhinged Alliance* (New York: Harper and Row, 1975); and Feld, *The European Community in World Affairs,* particularly pp. 325–30.

36. See, for example, McGeorge Bundy, "Europe Still Matters," in Mally, *The New Europe and the United States,* p. 101; and Feld, *The European Community in World Affairs,* p. 320 and chap. 5.

37. The relationship between the Community and the Soviet Union, together with the East European countries, is analyzed in J. and P. Pinder, *The European Community's Policy towards Eastern Europe* (London: Chatham House and PEP, 1975); J. Pinder, "Economic Integration and East–West Trade," *Journal of Common Market Studies,* September 1977 [also in F. Alting von Geusau (ed.), *Uncertain Detente* (Leiden: Sijthoff, 1979)]; and J. Pinder, "Integration Groups and Trade Negotiations," *Government and Opposition,* Spring 1979.

38. For a review of the Community's relations with developing countries in the 1970s, see Feld, *The European Community in World Affairs,* chaps 4 and 7. On the respective positions of the former associates and the other developing countries, see J. Pinder, "The Community and the Developing Countries: Associates and Outsiders," *Journal of Common Market Studies,* September 1973.

39. The literature on the Community's political system includes Coombes, *The Future of the European Parliament; Feld, The European Community in World Affairs,* chaps 1, 2, and 9; Haas, *The Uniting of Europe;* Lindberg, *The Political Dynamics of European Integration;* Lindberg and Scheingold, *Europe's Would-Be Polity;* G. G. Rosenthal, *The Men behind the Decisions* (Lexington, Mass.: Lexington Books, 1975); Wallace, Wallace and Webb (eds.), *Policy-Making in the European Communities;* and A. Spinelli, *The Eurocrats* (Baltimore: The John Hopkins Press, 1966).

40. The experience of the European Council is analyzed in A. Morgan, *From Summit to Council: Evolution in the EEC* (London: Chatham House and PEP, 1976).
41. See H. Wallace, *National Governments and the European Communities,* (London: Chatham House and PEP, 1973).
42. D. J. Puchala, "Fiscal Harmonisation and the European Policy Process," in Wallace, Wallace and Webb (eds.), *Policy-Making in the European Communities.*
43. David Coombes, *Politics and Bureaucracy in the European Community,* chap. 8.
44. Rosenthal, *The Men behind the Decisions,* chaps 3 and 8.
45. Coombes, *The Future of the European Parliament.*
46. See in particular Haas, *The Uniting of Europe.*
47. See Haas, *The Uniting of Europe;* Lindberg, *The Political Dynamics;* Lindberg and Scheingold, *Europe's Would-Be Polity.*
48. Lindberg and Scheingold, *Europe's Would-Be Polity,* p. 279.

5

Issues in China's Global Policy

Gavin Boyd

CHINA IS A MODERNIZING STATE and thus differs significantly from the other major actors in the global system, who account for important contributions to the world product. The Chinese industrial establishment is somewhat larger than India's and, although it is growing with the use of indigenous resources and with substantial imports of Western and Japanese technology, it will probably not be sufficiently advanced and diversified to rank among those of the leading countries in the international economy before the end of this century.

The Chinese leaders strive to overcome the limitations of economic backwardness by intensive political activity in the global system. This is directed toward the mobilization of broad international support for a campaign against Soviet ambitions for global hegemony, and the encouragement of revolutionary change in the developing areas. The principal targets of the anti-Soviet campaign are the industrialized democracies, headed by the United States. The Chinese stress that they see a grave danger of large-scale warfare by the U.S.S.R. against noncommunist states and against their own regime. The encouragement of revolutionary change in the developing areas is a secondary concern, but it has long-term significance, for an ultimate objective is the establishment of a world socialist system in which China, it seems, will be the leading member. The scale of all the anti-Soviet and revolutionary activity is the principal reason for designating China as a global actor. Another reason, of somewhat lesser importance, is that China has modest strategic forces that would be capable of devastating some industrial centers and military bases in Soviet Central Asia and in the Soviet Far East, and is thus a factor on the periphery of the central balance. As such, China has considerable significance for the United States and also attracts West European interest, which for the present is expressed in small-scale transfers of military technology that are contributing to the modernization of the Chinese armed forces.

China's international activities entail more serious risks than those faced by other global actors and are affected by greater uncertainties, because the Chinese leadership is divided. The risks are encountered because large Soviet forces are deployed along the common border, and Soviet emotional hostility tends to be kept high by Chinese denunciations of Moscow's global ambitions. Meanwhile, the degrees of emphasis to be given to the struggle against the U.S.S.R. and to cooperation with the United States appear to be matters of dispute within the Chinese ruling elite, which is split by opposing ideological views and preferences and by personal conflicts. The divisions have serious implications because the regime has experienced severe high-level antagonisms for more than two decades and because the present dominant faction is a group of aged revolutionary leaders whose grip on the system is likely to weaken over the next half decade.

As a global actor the Chinese regime confronts choices associated with the immediate and anticipated future utility of its current international activities, and its decision makers face options posed by their own internal differences. Examination of the ways in which foreign policy issues are resolved or evaded is difficult, but the decisions reached on many of these questions will probably have important consequences for the global system.

Analysis

The study of China's foreign policy issues can be aided by insights from the main streams of international relations literature, and from works on comparative communism and on political change and development. The utility of such insights depends on their adaptation for analysis of the political psychology of the Chinese leaders and their secondary elite, their decision processes, and the significance of various aspects of their regime that provide resources for or impose constraints on their statecraft.

The examination of issues in China's behavior as a global actor encounters difficulties because the explicit recognition of foreign policy choices is largely precluded by the long established style of formulating international objectives and courses of action as "correct" applications of revolutionary wisdom. This is done in terms which imply that alternative aims and methods are always unrevolutionary and do not deserve consideration, and that accordingly there is no *comparative* justification for foreign policy choices, in terms of costs and benefits. Further, it is implied that there is no necessity for foreign policy debate, because the correct revolutionary prescriptions are provided by authoritative formulation, based on the ruling elite's superior ideological knowledge and dedication.[1]

The study of choices in Peking's external behavior thus requires understanding of processes of symbolic interaction in which authoritative definitions of roles and situations, to build solidarity and give direction, preclude multiple advocacy and bargaining while tending to emphasize commitment at the expense of instrumental rationality. Overall, this type of decision-making could facilitate holistic foreign policy management, but some of its practical consequences evidently limit the primary elite's recognition of and engagement with foreign policy questions and tend to lower the sensitivities of the secondary elite and the middle echelons in the foreign affairs structures to external problems and opportunities.

The difficulties are cognitive and structural. The established patterns of authoritative symbolic interaction in which policy is prescribed are based on information-processing which maintains an elite psychological environment that is heavily ideological and strongly influenced by the cultivation of revolutionary optimism, especially through the contemplation of claimed successes by affinitive revolutionary movements. Political discipline imposed on the officials limits the scope for critical evaluation of new knowledge and hinders objective recognition of new factors.[2] Some external activities, including especially the development of trade with the West and the absorption of selected elements of Western strategic thinking, are evidently bringing Chinese leaders into closer contact with the operational environment, but the degree of closure which protects the content of their psychological environment from cognitive challenge remains rather high.

The political psychology of the Chinese elite is authoritarian, revolutionary, nationalist, and modernizing, but it is also factional. The mix tends to generate some conflict and stress, although there is a considerable basis for consensus and stability.

The authoritarian quality of the Chinese leadership has an ideological basis. Communist doctrine, and especially its Leninist component, is a source of convictions that the revolutionary movement which controls the regime must be given firm direction by an elite that has virtually absolute power, and that this power must be made effective through repeated political campaigns against individuals suspected of insufficient loyalty. Operationally, such convictions have been greatly influenced by personal ambitions, intensified in the course of numerous contests for domination of the regime. Members of the ruling elite thus exhibit strong needs for power, distrustful attitudes toward suspected critics and opponents, and orientations toward conflictual behavior. The most prominent figure in the primary elite, Deng Xiaoping, was disgraced and purged twice before his group was able to assert strong influence in 1977, following the death of Mao Zedong, and he has shown much determination to remove from office individuals who supported or condoned the purges that cut short his previous careers.[3]

All members of the Chinese elite, despite their differences, are revolutionaries, primarily in the sense that they have long internalized the concepts, values, logic, and language of Marxism-Leninism. Between them there is an unevenly shared consensus that the realization of Marxist-Leninist values in their system necessitates the exclusion of "bourgeois" influences, and, on the positive side, the maintenance of intensive socialization processes throughout Chinese society. This perspective on state building and the development of the political culture influences orientations toward the regime's international objectives, especially because there is a compulsion to express revolutionary values in external behavior. The imperative to build up the national revolutionary order, however, is understandably given much higher priority than the provision of support to foreign Marxist-Leninist movements. Yet there is a history of conflict over the relationship between revolutionary values and technocratic concerns in the development of a modern socialist economy.[4]

The revolutionary beliefs and commitments of the Chinese leaders have a strong nationalist ethos. This derives from the nation's political tradition, its humiliating experiences of Western imperialism, especially in the nineteenth century, and the recent history of conflict with the U.S.S.R., particularly since the withdrawal of Soviet aid in 1960. The nationalist ethos emphasizes the realization of great power ambitions in the course of international activities that are, in principle, revolutionary, and evidently can have a strong influence on perceptions of ideological obligation. Yugoslavia, slighted in the 1960s as a "revisionist" state, is now viewed as a partial ally because it is seen to be threatened by the U.S.S.R. Another effect of the leadership's nationalism is stress on self-reliance in economic growth; this remains quite strong, despite the present leadership's recognition of the need for advanced foreign technology.[5]

The Chinese elite consists of modernizers determined to build their nation into a powerful advanced socialist state. Some of them, especially those who were formerly closely associated with Mao Zedong, evidently have some fears that economic growth, particularly if aided by extensive contacts with the West, will contribute to a process of deradicalization, through the *embourgeoisement* of officials and their concentration on technocratic matters.[6] The dominant group in the leadership shows a very active concern to promote full recognition of the practical requirements of modernization. Its procurements of foreign technology are matched by efforts to have large numbers of Chinese students trained in the West— partly because the Chinese education system was severely affected by an extreme emphasis on revolutionary consciousness during the last decade of Mao Zedong's rule.

The revolutionary, nationalist, and modernizing elements of Chinese elite psychology are logically compatible, but there have been tensions between them since the mid 1950s, principally because of a deep cleavage within the leadership between figures who have given high importance to ideological motivation and others who, while sharing much of that concern, have had a somewhat pragmatic understanding of the administrative and technological requirements of economic growth. In numerous conflicts over this matter, personal rivalries within the leadership, of the kind to be expected in any closed system, have intensified, and there has been a growth of factional politics, which tends to erode ideological and institutional loyalties. Leaders tend to build up factions as informal bases of support, and these intrigue against each other.[7] Factionalism, of course, distracts leadership attention from substantive policy issues, and engagement with these tends to be affected by biases imparted by personal antagonisms that are roused in factional conflicts.

Military figures appear to be particularly active in high-level factions. Army leaders have strong representation in the Politbureau and in the Central Committee of the Chinese Communist Party, and several of them appear to provide most of the support on which the present ruling group depends for its control of the regime. Some army leaders, including the Commander of the Peking Military Region, have been purged in recent years by the dominant faction that is headed by Deng Xiaoping. Under the latter's direction, especially in his capacity as Chief of the General Staff, the high level command structure is being reconstituted, and its more prominent members will be able to assume new party or governmental responsibilities as replacements have to be found for the older revolutionaries who presently hold many top positions.[8] The strong political influence of the military establishment has been acquired mainly as a consequence of the weakening of the party apparatus during the Cultural Revolution of 1966–1969, during which under Mao Zedong's direction large numbers of party officials were purged.

Chinese elite psychology is the main source of inputs into the regime's foreign policy processes. Inputs deriving from this psychology are strongly *directive,* but they must activate or cope with other inputs deriving from the characteristics of the regime, several of which act as constraints on its international behavior. A low level of institutional development, together with the political discipline already mentioned, tends to limit the significance of inputs from the working levels.[9] At the same time the availability of resources for the support of external activities is limited by economic backwardness.

The primary elite's beliefs, values, perceptions, and calculations are expressed in an established and somewhat rigid pattern of international communications and activities. There are vigorous attempts at multilevel international symbolic interaction—the transmission of ideological meanings to foreign elites, societies, and revolutionary movements—in order to activate radical forms of political behavior and to promote hostility toward the U.S.S.R. Great urgency is given to the building up of general opposition to the Soviet Union in the developing areas and, more importantly, in the West. The conceptual basis for this is attributed to Mao Zedong,[10] but the ultimate consequences are left vague. An affinitive revolutionary elite is evidently expected to emerge at some stage in the U.S.S.R., and China, it seems to be understood, will have increasing influence on the establishment and development of new revolutionary states in the Third World as well as in the industrialized countries. China's transformation into a powerful modern socialist state, with technology transfers from the West and Japan, is to continue while the conflictual international communications are maintained. Trade and cultural exchanges with the industrialized countries strengthen ties that are intended to assist the anti-Soviet struggle. Meanwhile, the risks of provoking more serious Soviet hostility are accepted, while displaying a militantly defensive attitude, so as to keep high Soviet estimates of the costs of any aggressive moves against Chinese territory.

Regime Attributes

China is primarily an agricultural society. A high proportion of the very large population (totaling over 800 million) is engaged in relatively primitive collective farming. Agricultural output is increasing slowly, and this limits the rate of industrial growth, because technology imports are financed largely by exports of primary products. Other limitations on industrial growth are imposed by low education standards and a scarcity of skills as well as by managerial problems associated with the heavy centralization of economic controls. The scarcity of skills in particular limits capacities to absorb advanced technology.

Social energies are being mobilized for economic development, but the results are mainly of benefit to agriculture, although not sufficiently so to overcome serious production lags, and to low-technology manufactures, which unfortunately encounter protectionist barriers when exported to the industrialized democracies. Pressures are being applied from the highest levels to infuse more efficiency into the administrative structures, but the basic problems of bureaucratic inertia that seem to be inevitable in a command economy remain serious and indeed seem to be aggravated by the inhibiting effects of intra-elite conflicts on staffs at the middle and lower levels.

Social mobilization is facilitated by considerable racial and cultural homogeneity, although there is considerable provincial and regional consciousness, which can make for resistance to central control. Culturally, a rich Confucian tradition has been partially suppressed by a revolutionary value system, in which there is stress on loyalty to the regime rather than to the family or one's kin. The intense national pride which was fostered by the Confucian tradition, however, has been sustained and reoriented. Within the elite, this pride is a source of aspirations for high status in world affairs, as well as for the avoidance of dependency relationships.[11]

The political culture is revolutionary and thus fundamentally opposed to any tendencies toward deradicalization and liberalization. It is post-Maoist, however, in the sense that faith in the effectiveness of sheer ideological will-power has been modified by recognition of the necessity for institutionalized authority, material incentives, professional skills, relatively autonomous development in the intellectual disciplines, and technocratic direction of the modernization process. As most of the indications of differences within the leadership concern the relationship between ideology and economic growth, however, the orientation of the political culture is somewhat ambivalent. Official formulations of doctrine remain simplistic, express formal loyalty to Maoism, and continue to show hostility to revisionism as a dilution of revolutionary wisdom that can weaken a socialist state.[12] There is a manifest need for persuasive official formulations that will provide a coherent and credible new value orientation and produce an atmosphere of consensus, but there are no indications that this requirement will be met. The dominant technocratic group appears to be absorbed in its factional, support-building, and administrative activities. In addition, it appears to be constrained by felt needs to represent that its policies are in continuity with Maoist principles in order to maintain its own legitimacy and to avoid widening its differences with other elements in the leadership.

Structurally, the extreme centralization of power in a small self-perpetuating primary elite is sustained by strongly personal factional and client connections which enable each leader to draw support from segments of the secondary elite. These segments, it seems, rarely come into contact with each other, except at occasional formalized meetings, principally because members of the Politburo, the highest organ of the Chinese Communist Party, are unwilling to convene frequent meetings of its Central Committee to which they might become informally accountable, and at which groups within that committee might coalesce and adopt common policy positions.[13] There are grounds for believing that members of the Politburo itself tend to avoid encounters with each other because of their cleavages, and that each attempts to direct policy in his area independently, with much competition and overlap. The party and government bureaucracies appear to be managed through somewhat uncoordinated downward communications. Directives from the top, however, tend to be influenced by each leader's caution about engaging in the specifics of policy issues in order to avoid accountability in the eyes of the secondary elite. Information flowing to individuals within the ruling group, moreover, evidently does not provide sufficient challenges for high managerial performance because it stresses current successes and tends to avoid or minimize factors that would call for policy innovation. These are difficulties typical of what Etzioni would call an "overmanaged" society, in which officials operate under stresses imposed by communication restrictions and by generalized as well as unpredictably specific pressures for political conformity.[14]

The implementation of policy seems to be affected also by incrementalism at the secondary elite level, induced by caution and by the restrictive effects of political discipline on middle echelon autonomy, despite the need for this to complement the primary elite's chosen managerial role. The bureaucratic structures and state enterprises, moreover, remain burdened by officials of low competence who were appointed through the patronage of Maoists during and after the Cultural Revolution of 1966–1969. Large numbers of these, it seems, are being replaced by officials who had been purged during that upheaval, but who have been professionally inactive, to say the least, for a decade or more.[15]

Scientific and technological lag, low labor productivity, poor managerial creativity, and hesitation about implementing what may be reversible policies are the principal economic consequences of the regime's structural and functional weaknesses. These problems represent challenges to higher achievement, but there is a danger that frustrations with these may precipitate more serious differences within the ruling group. For Deng Xiaoping's faction, the somewhat Maoist policy orientation of Hua Guofeng evidently represents a major hindrance to the modernization program. To Hua Guofeng and his associates, however, the revisionist technocratic policies of Deng Xiaoping's group are threatening revolutionary beliefs and values.[16]

Estimation of the regime's economic performance is difficult, as the

Chinese publish very few statistics. Between 1957 and 1970 the average annual rate of growth is believed to have been about 3 percent, which is about one-third of Japan's and Taiwan's and less than half of Thailand's but roughly the same as India's. Grain production, which has been rising very slowly, is believed to have been 280 million tons in 1976, and during that year steel output probably reached 21 million tons, while oil production rose to an estimated 85 million tons. For the present, the rate of growth in industrial output is probably increasing, to the extent that imports of advanced technology are being suitably integrated into the economy and are thus more than compensating for indigenous weaknesses. Over the long term, however, the rate of industrial growth is likely to decrease, because of factors similar to those which have caused a decline in Soviet industrial development over the past half decade. Bureaucratic inertia in this command economy will tend to become a more serious obstacle to technological innovation as the intermediate stage of modernization is reached and the requirements of economic diversification will tend to reduce the proportion of investment funds available for industry.[17]

The current level of industrial development is facilitating slow modernization of the armed forces. The technological gap between these and the Soviet military establishment is probably widening, but the Chinese cannot increase their presently rather high allocations for the growth of their war potential without lowering their overall rate of development. Some sophisticated Western military equipment is being procured, but this is a slow process, and it seems that the main intent is to use such items as models for the improvement of local production capabilities, although the record, especially concerning the development of military aircraft, is poor.[18]

The army is a large infantry force, lacking transport, armor, artillery, and communications equipment. Vast improvements in equipment would be required for conventional parity with the Soviet units deployed along the common border and in Mongolia. Organizationally, moreover, the Chinese ground forces do not appear to be sufficiently integrated for major defense tasks: there is little troop rotation, no extensive maneuvers are held, and the regional commands seem to have some independence from the center. At that center, moreover, unified direction of the military establishment seems to be affected by factional conflicts, despite an unconventional arrangement whereby Vice Premier Deng Xiaoping has been concurrently Chief of the General Staff.[19]

The total strength of the army is about 2.5 million, but because of its equipment deficiencies and backward logistic system it is not capable of operating in force at a distance from the national territory. Its principal mission, for the present, is defense against a Soviet attack, with emphasis on mobile and guerrilla warfare from bases in the heavily populated provinces of the center and the East; the sparsely inhabited areas of Sinkiang and Inner Mongolia, in which Soviet mechanized units would move rapidly, could not be defended.[20]

The air force, which would be capable of modest defense efforts for a few days in the event of a Soviet attack, comprises several hundred outdated Soviet-type interceptors and medium bombers, and over one thousand quite obsolete fighters obtained from the U.S.S.R. in the 1950s. New military aircraft are being developed, slowly, and some will use engines manufactured in China under license from Rolls-Royce. Small strategic forces, comprising principally a few hundred liquid-fueled medium-range missiles, represent a vulnerable capability to inflict damage, with rough accuracy, on Soviet Far Eastern military and industrial installations. The navy is a large assortment of small craft, with outdated armaments, which could undertake coastal defense missions during the initial stages of a large-scale Soviet attack.[21]

There are factional divisions within the military elite, resulting in a large measure from personal and client ties that developed in service within the former five Field Armies, which constituted the regime's principal formations and between which there was little movement of personnel. These ties affect the attitudes of the various regional commanders toward each other and toward the center. Under the former Defense Minister, Lin Piao, purged in 1971, military figures who had served in his Fourth Field Army had strong influence at the center and in the regional commands, but now many key posts are held by veterans who had served in the Second Field Army. To the extent that unity is maintained under Deng Xiaoping leadership, the military elite is probably capable of having a strong voice in policy-making. Nearly half of the Politburo are senior military personnel; they include the Defense Minister, three regional commanders, and the army and air force commanders.[22]

China as a Global Actor

In the global pattern of affinities, interdependencies, communications, power relationships, and interactions, China is relatively isolated. Nevertheless, in some important respects the configuration of the global system favors Chinese policy. In particular, this policy is assisted by the U.S. administration's interest in exploiting Peking's adversary relationship with Moscow.

Culturally, China has affinities of a traditional character with Japan and, to some extent, with Vietnam. The bonds with Japanese society are the most significant, as a pervasive consciousness of these bonds in Japan is responsible for strong popular pressure to maintain friendly relations with Peking. In Vietnam, felt cultural affinities with China are more than offset by traditional anti-Chinese nationalism and by ideological antipathies, directed especially at Maoist elements in Peking's ideology. Ideologically, China has affinities with North Korea and with the small underground and insurgent communist movements in Burma, Thailand, Malaysia, Indonesia, and the Philippines, but not with any significant Marxist-Leninist movements in South Asia, or in any advanced democratic states.[23] There are no ideological bonds with any East European regimes but there are some political affinities with Yugoslavia and Rumania, based on common opposition to the U.S.S.R.'s international ambitions.

China has political ties of moderate strength, acquired through aid diplomacy, with Pakistan, Tanzania, and Zambia. These ties are of little use for the promotion of political change in those states, but they are maintained in order to obstruct Soviet penetration of their societies, and of their neighbors. Such links are sought on an extensive scale in Africa, but with limited success despite fairly substantial aid allocations.[24]

No significant political bonds link China with any advanced open state; no ruling elite in such a state accepts any important elements of the Chinese political philosophy, and neither do any of the major political parties in such states, with the important exception of the Japan Socialist Party, a leading opposition force.[25] In Western Europe, China seeks ties with ruling and nonruling parties, especially the conservative ones, in order to encourage stronger opposition to the U.S.S.R., again with little success.

In the global pattern of interdependencies China is of minor significance, with a small state's share of world trade (0.8 percent) and with no involvement in the North American-West European-Japanese-OPEC relationships which dominate international commerce. China also stands apart from the groups of developing countries that are seeking to establish a new international economic order, although generalized support is given in the form of ideological declarations about the dangers of imperialism and the need for revolutionary change in the Third World.[26]

The communication flows of the global system mostly bypass China and receive little Chinese input. Pervasive social controls ensure that international communication media have little impact on Chinese society; there has been some slight easing of restrictions on the import of foreign periodicals and books, but these restrictions remain severe. Efforts are made to spread Chinese literature in foreign countries, but these attract little interest in the industrialized democracies and their distribution is restricted in many of the Third World states. Broadcasts from Radio Peking are received by small audiences in the West and in most of the developing areas, but hold the attention of many Chinese in other Asian countries. Unofficial broadcasts on behalf of the Burmese, Thai, and Malaysian communist movements are directed at the inhabitants of border areas in northern Burma and Thailand, and at the Chinese in Malaysia, with considerable effect.[27]

For Third World audiences outside East Asia Chinese international media lack information and entertainment appeals, but there is some informal publicizing of the regime by visitors who go to China from many developing countries in considerable numbers, and by Chinese officials during stays in those countries and through encounters with their officials at other locations, especially the United Nations. In general, China's image is that of a dynamic socialist state which is in some respects a model for authoritarian modernization and which offers potentially useful friendship, especially to states resisting Soviet overtures.[28]

In the international strategic system China has an important secondary role as an adversary of the U.S.S.R. capable of threatening targets in the Soviet Far East, while discouraging if not deterring a Soviet attack. An important aspect of this role is Peking's cordial official relationship with the United States, which gives Washington incentives to pose a generalized threat that will deter any Soviet aggression against China and to contribute to China's military development. This is done by direct transfers of defense-related technology, including advanced computers, and by showing approval of British and French sales of military items to the Chinese.[29] A potentially complicating factor is China's support for the reunification policy of the North Korean regime, which appears to aim at a military conquest of South Korea, and the removal of U.S. forces from that state. In the event of a major conflict on the Korean peninsula, however, North Korea would be obliged to seek military support from the U.S.S.R. rather than from China.[30]

The major West European powers show interest in China as a regime whose military development can divert Soviet attention. Britain and France, however, are more willing than West Germany to provide China with defense equipment. Peking has sent several military missions to Western Europe in recent years and is seeking to develop exchanges with Britain, France, and West Germany on strategic questions relating to problems of defense against the U.S.S.R.[31]

China refuses to participate in arms control talks between the superpowers, arguing that the U.S.S.R. uses these for deception and that obligations of solidarity with the threatened peoples of the Third World, as well as the need for self-defense, oblige rejection of any restrictions on China's own military development. On the U.S. side, however, there is a tendency to view cooperation with China as a form of leverage against the U.S.S.R. to accept agreements for limitations on strategic arms. For their part, the Chinese warn the United States not to enter into arms control arrangements with the U.S.S.R., as they would give a false sense of security.[32]

Choices in Global Policy

Peking's global policy is formulated as an unswerving and comprehensive long-term endeavor, grounded in the revolutionary logic of current history, which is being steadily vindicated by successes in the support of radical social change and of struggles against the U.S.S.R. A style of authoritative prescription conveys impressions that a single line of correct action is always kept in view and that no basic choices have to be considered.

There is evidence, however, that some of the conflicts within the Chinese leadership in recent years have concerned foreign policy. Moreover, all members of the ruling group appear to take a Leninist approach to the management of external affairs, seeing this primarily as a conflictual process in which shifts of strategy and tactics are necessary to hold the initiative, immobilize potential adversaries, win over allies, and weaken the main enemy. Indications of tacit awareness of the necessity for choice between foreign policy options thus have to be expected. Further, on the constructive side of the regime's external relations, the development of productive interaction with the United States and Japan may be gradually opening the way for cautious debate about the possibilities for a more effective use of these relationships.

The main domestic sources of foreign policy issues, it is clear, are diverging views and preferences within the primary elite. These are value-based, in part, as Hua Guofeng and his associates evidently wish to see more struggle against imperialism and more support for revolutionary movements, whereas the group headed by Deng Xiaoping favors continuation of the tacit restraint on these elements of policy in order to increase the effectiveness of the anti-Soviet struggle and facilitate the acquisition of Western technology.[33] For Deng Xiaoping and his colleagues, who appear to dominate the upper levels of the regime, the significance of the rival group's preferences seems to be determined not by their relative merits but by the degrees of leverage with which they can be pressed, and these currently appear to be modest.

Foreign policy differences within the primary elite, because of its present internal tensions, evidently have to be settled by methods of political struggle, from the viewpoint of the leading faction or group of factions. As might be expected, however, there seem to be more negotiable issues that are posed, less urgently and more discreetly, by competing proposals and claims from government and party structures with international concerns. The numerous economic ministries and agencies that are involved in foreign trade are in many respects rivals as they attempt to influence allocative decisions, and their common organizational interests appear to make them competitors against the military establishment and the party's International Liaison Department, which manages relations with foreign communist movements. Underlying the allocative questions that evidently must be solved is the problem of balance between cooperative and conflictual activity in the regime's total international behavior, especially with respect to the West, but reference to this is probably not necessary in the bargaining which undoubtedly resolves the issues concerning the use of available resources.

The differing task orientations of the economic ministries, the military establishment, and the party's International Liaison Department probably result in diverging contributions to overall policy, especially because there seems to be little horizontal communication and exchange in the Chinese system. Foreign policy management, moreover, may be considerably less integrated than would appear from the regime's routinely expressed pronouncements on external relations. The degree to which coordination is a responsibility for the Ministry of Foreign Affairs is difficult to estimate, and it is not clear to what extent this ministry's task orientation is dominated by the management of co-existence relationships, to the exclusion of concerns with the local revolutionary movements that interest the International Liaison Department.

The external sources of foreign policy issues are more extensive than the domestic ones and, of course, necessitate much reliance on expertise and on the processing of information across social distances. In general, engagement with these external sources of issues sets demanding requirements for statecraft, and these requirements can be increased if the choices presented concern values of great magnitude and are posed with urgency and surprise.

Soviet behavior is the most prominent relational source of foreign policy issues. This behavior is intensely conflictual and poses a threat of large-scale aggression, together with generalized demands for abandonment of China's ideological opposition, acceptance of Soviet leadership of the revolutionary states and movements, and renunciation of Peking's links with the United States. To cope with this danger China needs a strong alliance with a major power,[34] but a military relationship with the United States could not be sought without giving serious provocation to the U.S.S.R. and might not be obtained because of Washington's basic interest in working out a comprehensive détente with the Soviet Union. Further, even if obtained, such an association could be of uncertain utility, because a U.S. administration could be willing to sacrifice the connection in order to reach an enduring settlement with Moscow.

There is no meaningful interaction with the U.S.S.R., and no possibilities for change in the Soviet system can be expected, except in the long term. Hence the influence of emotional factors on perceptions of the

Soviet regime and its behavior is probably high, to the detriment of cognitive factors. Stress, moreover, may be associated with the emotional factors because of the magnitude of the threat faced and because of frustrations in the struggle to build up adequate international opposition against the Soviet Union.[35]

Behavior received from the United States is the next major relational source of foreign policy issues for China. It presents substantial opportunities as well as problems because it is constructively oriented and is open to wide-ranging cooperative engagement. The affective factors stirred by this behavior are moderate and positive, but there are cognitive challenges, as this activity is at variance with ideological expectations concerning the expression of the U.S. administration's class character in its foreign relations.[36] There is evidently some openness to new knowledge about the United States, and there are incentives for innovative thinking about possibilities for increasing the utility of the relationship.[37] A serious problem, however, is seen in the U.S. pursuit of détente with the Soviet Union. The United States is seen as leaning toward acceptance of a dangerously inferior position in the central balance and toward toleration of Soviet gains in the developing areas.[38]

Japan ranks next as a relational source of issues for China's foreign policy. The Japanese government is more constructively oriented than that of the United States, is less interested in détente with the U.S.S.R., and is much more open to Chinese diplomacy and transnational activity. Japan, moreover, is a more unified and coherent actor, particularly on economic issues. Japanese foreign economic policy presents major opportunities because of the strong interest of the country's leading firms in the China market.[39]

The major West European states, separated from China by long social and geographic distances, are less open to interaction and penetration, and rank as secondary relational sources of foreign policy issues for Peking. In dealings with these states the Chinese have a relatively limited scope for bargaining, as their trade with China is a very small proportion of their total foreign commerce and as their policies are strongly influenced by hopes for secure détente with the U.S.S.R. Britain and France, however, are China's main sources of military technology,[40] which is supplied in modest quantities.

The Third World states, as relational sources of foreign policy issues, are less significant for China's principal foreign policy concerns. Almost all of them are friendly and are open to economic and cultural exchanges with China, but almost all, while in varying degrees receptive of Peking's warnings about the U.S.S.R., are reluctant to endorse the Chinese political campaign against the Soviet Union.[41] While potentially useful to the extent that they can thwart Soviet attempts to penetrate their societies, the administrations of these developing states are vulnerable to revolutionary violence and thus do not invite close engagement that would tend to identify China with their political fortunes.

External *situations* are also sources of foreign policy issues for the Chinese regime. These situations, of course, are closely linked with relational factors in Peking's holistic outlook, but understandings of them seem to be more simplistic and ideological and more strongly influenced by generalizations formulated at the primary elite level.

The central strategic balance is the most salient factor among the situational sources of foreign policy issues, because it has grave implications for China's security. The Chinese authorities show much awareness of the projections by Western analysts regarding the U.S.S.R.'s strategic capabilities over the next half decade, and they are clearly apprehensive that in a general war the U.S.S.R. would be able to devastate their regime while inflicting potentially decisive blows on the NATO powers. Soviet behavior toward China, it must be stressed, is understood primarily with reference to this strategic context.[42]

The state of the international economic system seems to be the next major situational source of issues for China's global policies. Attention focuses on the commercial competition between the industrialized democracies, which aids China's efforts to procure technology on favorable terms and which results in preferences for Japan and West Germany as the main sources of such technology. The interaction between the industrialized democracies and the developing states over questions of trade, aid, and investment is viewed as a form of international class struggle in which China must support the developing states, but there is an unacknowledged interest in evolving more effective methods of competing against them as exporters of primary products and low-technology manufactures to the industrialized democracies.[43]

The very complex configurations of political forces in the industrialized democracies and in the Third World are further situational sources of foreign policy issues, linked of course with many relational factors, since the behavior received from most foreign administrations is understandable primarily in terms of the political composition of those governments. In the industrialized democracies, conservative political parties tend to be viewed favorably because of their greater willingness to express opposition to the U.S.S.R. Whereas enthusiasm can be shown in greeting representatives of those parties on visits to China, however, it is generally not feasible to explicitly encourage voter support for those parties. In the developing areas, governments whose political weaknesses are being exploited by Soviet-oriented protest movements and revolutionary groups are sources of special concern, but in many cases there is little scope for effective Chinese involvement either to support the threatened administration or to aid the development of political groups opposed to those receiving Soviet assistance.

Major Contemporary Issues

The prominence of an issue for Chinese foreign policy makers depends on their perspectives, task orientations, information, designs, and preferences, and is affected by their mutual interactions. Most issues seem to be recognized indirectly, and slowly, in the course of primary and secondary elite interactions that are strongly influenced by the authority and status of dominant members of the leadership. Factional differences within the primary elite, while diverting attention from foreign policy questions, evidently tend to inhibit attempts by senior officials to raise such questions, especially because of the risks of being drawn into high-level controversies.

Even in conditions of relative elite stability, routine information flows to the Chinese leadership apparently tend to avoid identifying foreign policy issues. The political discipline imposed on officials obliges them to demonstrate revolutionary optimism and to show confidence in courses of international activity to which leadership prestige has been committed. If foreign policy issues were discussed, this could not only strain relations between high decision makers and officials but could also result in demands on the officials for appropriate solutions. At the primary elite level, capacities to probe incoming information are limited because this has considerable uniformity due to the ways in which it is processed and because alternative sources—principally western news media—are evidently not trusted. Whether there is a will to probe information from the regime's own agencies presumably depends on the intelligence and task interests of members of the ruling group. Their primary roles as managers who give general direction to external relations, operating at what might be called the level of high policy, evidently incline them to hold back from close engagement with foreign policy issues, as has been seen, and over time this probably limits their opportunities to acquire skills in foreign policy management.[44]

Tendencies toward continuity with established foreign policy endeavors appear to be quite strong in the Chinese system because of the apparent bias against innovation at the leadership and working levels. Changes in foreign policy behavior tend to be slow and incremental, with efforts to demonstrate that courses of action which have been implemented for some time remain basically correct and are not being drastically altered. The manifest concern with continuity reflects anxieties to preserve elite consensus in the Chinese system and to safeguard leadership prestige that has been committed to specific forms of international activity.[45]

Foreign policy issue recognition thus seems to be restricted in several respects by the dynamics of the Chinese system, but the media output of this system and its foreign policy behavior indicate much preoccupation with the external sources of foreign policy questions that have been identified in the previous section. Of these external sources, the superpowers, Japan, and the major West European states appear to receive much attention.

The U.S.S.R.'s perceived hostility poses problems of great dimensions because of the scale of Soviet deployments on the frontier and in Mongolia. It seems that the Chinese leaders are fully conscious of their regime's military weaknesses and of the apparent reluctance of the U.S. administration to make an explicit commitment to their defense because of the strains which this would impose on Washington's relations with Moscow. For Peking, then, there would seem to be a basic choice between continuing the present animosity toward the Soviet Union or seeking a rapprochement. If the first option continues to be regarded as an absolute imperative, China must accelerate its military development and meanwhile must secure military understandings with the West. What would seem to be the logical force of these conclusions, however, seems to be to some extent resisted or evaded. The armed forces are being modernized but not at a significant pace, and there is no active quest for firm military understandings with the United States. Cognitively, imbalance or dissonance seems to be limited by cultivating intense *commitment* to the ongoing struggle against the U.S.S.R.; absorption in this tends to preclude analysis of the underlying issues.[46]

Comprehension of the Soviet challenge in the Third World is evidently less difficult for the Chinese than analysis of the problems set by Soviet behavior in the direct relationship and by the state of the central balance. Peking's basic attitude, that threatened noncommunist governments in the new states must be supported, encounters problems because of the Soviet capacity to project military power more effectively than the United States in unstable parts of the Third World and because available Chinese resources usually cannot compensate for the weaknesses of administrations under pressure from Soviet-assisted revolutionary movements.

In the immediate environment the close Soviet relationship with Vietnam presents grave issues, to which China could logically respond by taking a conciliatory approach to Hanoi and endeavoring to exploit the frictions that are likely to develop between Vietnam and the U.S.S.R. There appears to be considerable anti-Vietnamese nationalist feeling, however, which prevents consideration of this option, despite the very serious danger that Vietnam's association with the U.S.S.R. poses because of the significant congruence of security interests. The probability that the Soviet presence in Vietnam will grow, at least for the time being, increases the significance of China's official links with the noncommunist Southeast Asian countries. Nevertheless there appears to be no disposition to strengthen those ties by reducing links with the local revolutionary movements, although these links cause much annoyance and anxiety to the administrations whose support is needed for the overall struggle against the U.S.S.R.[47]

The foreign policy issues relating to the U.S.S.R. are clearly seen to be linked with questions concerning the engagement with the United States. The most fundamental problem that appears to be perceived is that of persuading the United States to oppose Soviet expansionism more actively. Analysis of this problem and of the questions it raises does not appear to be as restricted by strongly willed commitment as the consideration of issues presented by the U.S.S.R., but significant limitations do seem to be in effect, although there are incentives to innovate, for the purpose of extracting greater utility from the connection. The main limitations on issue recognition and debate in this context appear to be the wishes of the dominant figures in the primary elite to maintain direction over basic policy toward the United States and thus to restrict the scope for the articulation of expert views by lower-level officials. This evidently explains why the level of sophistication in Chinese policy statements relating to the United States is not appreciably higher than in those concerning Third World matters, despite the greater incentives to evolve relatively pragmatic attitudes in dealings with Washington.[48]

The problem of influencing U.S. security policy is a matter of communications and inducements. The most basic difficulty is that the possibilities for rapport are seriously limited by the strongly ideological quality of Chinese communications, but perception of this by the leadership of the regime seems to be hindered by long internalization of the revolutionary belief system and of its concepts and language. Strategic inducements that would be sufficiently potent cannot be provided without major innovations in communication styles and would of course require drastic revisions of the ideology. There is indirect political support, in Chinese media output and foreign policy statements, for U.S. activities directed against the U.S.S.R., and this presumably could be increased; that, however, may not be considered feasible because it could be recognized as explicit collaboration with the imperialists.[49]

The manipulation of U.S. strategic interest in China as an adversary of the Soviet Union appears to be influenced by suspicions that the United States tends to view the relationship primarily as a means of leverage against the Soviet Union and secondarily as a factor that causes Soviet military decision makers to concentrate more attention on China. There is clearly an unwillingness to be manipulated by Washington, and this seems to affect perspectives on the question of strengthening ties and increasing cooperation with the United States, but these matters are given little clarification in Chinese official communications and information media. An understandable basis for concern is that any innovations in Soviet co-existence diplomacy that strengthen U.S. hopes for permanent détente will probably cause Washington to reduce its interest in the China connection. This possibility would seem to make it all the more important to devise ways of increasing the presently limited degree of influence on U.S. policy, but the ideological difficulties, it must be stressed, are likely to remain serious.[50]

More manageable questions, although of less magnitude, are presented in the relationship with Japan. The most important problem is to increase the effectiveness of the inducements and forms of persuasion that ensure high priority for friendship with China in Tokyo's policy and that limit Japanese interest in economic cooperation with the U.S.S.R. Peking does not wish to see Japan contribute significantly to economic and military development in the Soviet Far East; for the present, Japanese incentives to do so are not strong because Soviet behavior is on the whole unfriendly, but the danger of a favorable response by Tokyo to any shift toward friendliness by Moscow can be reduced by expanding China's economic ties with Japan. Large increases in Sino-Japanese commerce have been projected in a 1978 trade agreement which will run into the early 1980s and which will consolidate Japan's position as China's main source of capital goods.

A security issue of growing importance is posed by manifestations of reduced U.S. interest in Japan's security. The Chinese leadership has indicated to visiting Japanese political and military figures that common interests in relation to the Soviet threat must be served by the preservation of Japan's military ties with the United States and by Japanese rearmament, which is evidently expected to make possible some transfers of military technology to China. As the pace of Japan's military development is gradually increasing, the questions to be decided presumably are whether to associate Chinese policy more openly and more closely with this trend, and whether to give more explicit support to the continuation of Japan's military cooperation with the United States. Recognition of these practical questions is probably easier for the Chinese leadership than consideration of the issues posed in the relationship with the United States because the connection with Japan is closer, more active, has a longer history, and can be managed more easily, although the revolutionary ideology evidently remains a source of constraints on collaboration with this capitalist state.[51]

The major West European states, which are secondary sources of capital goods, clearly draw less Chinese attention because interaction with them offers little scope for leverage. The issues posed in relations with these states are economic and strategic and are of less consequence than those presented in the context of dealings with the United States and Japan.

China can increase imports of technology from the leading members of the European Community, but at the cost of reducing allocations for the politically more useful trade with Japan and of accepting deficits, because access to the Community market is more difficult than entry into the Japanese market. The Community has protectionist barriers which limit access for Chinese primary products and low-technology manufactures,[52] but Japanese foreign economic policy is strongly influenced by concerns to facilitate trade with China.

Britain and France supply China with some military technology, and the way is open for Peking to increase its orders, but there are signs of caution on the Chinese side. This hesitation appears to be due to unwillingness to give more serious provocation to the U.S.S.R. and to ideological and nationalist desires to avoid dependence on military support from capitalist states. There have been exchanges with Britain, France, and West Germany on strategic issues relating to the U.S.S.R., but the question of moving toward military understandings that would provide a basis for some security cooperation in future contingencies evidently remains undecided.[53] For the present the Chinese are visibly more concerned about the weaknesses of the NATO forces in Western Europe and seem to be frustrated by the difficulties of persuading the Europeans to strengthen their defenses. As in the dealings with the United States there are communication problems, yet there seems to be little awareness that these problems could be reduced to more manageable proportions by shifts toward ideological flexibility.[54]

The dominant preoccupation with struggle against the U.S.S.R., which strongly affects perceptions of issues relating to the industrialized democracies, also has a profound influence on the recognition of policy problems in China's statecraft toward the Third World. Peking's general encouragement of opposition to the U.S.S.R. by administrations in the developing areas necessitates caution in the support of local revolutionary movements, especially because the Chinese denounce the U.S.S.R. for attempting to subvert those governments. Yet the strategic interests of the Chinese regime and its revolutionary obligations cannot be served by allowing the Soviet Union to preempt opportunities for drastic social change in the Third World, and Chinese ideological support for revolutionary struggles cannot be abandoned, except in cases where the revolutionaries are totally committed to the U.S.S.R. The difficulty of choosing is likely to be greatest when a friendly Third World government exhibits serious vulnerabilities and is challenged by radical forces that look to both the Soviet Union and China for support.

Because of the uncertainties affecting present and likely future options in relations with the more unstable Third World states, Chinese efforts to further revolutionary objectives tend to be limited to generalized although vividly formulated expressions of ideological values, to inspire affinitive radical movements without involving Chinese state interests. This, however, leaves the way open for the U.S.S.R. to assume greater significance as the regime from which revolutionary movements must seek military and political aid.[55]

Issue Management

The shaping of China's foreign policy is, first, a process of authoritative symbolic interaction with officials in the external affairs structures through which the primary elite maintains its control and status by articulating what are accepted as superior understandings of the regime's external interests, problems, and opportunities. To avoid inviting critical evaluation in the light of subsequent events, the leadership evidently tends to make its authoritative declarations at a high level of generality, while indicating that foreign policy is basically a matter of political struggle in a highly complex and changing environment, that changes of course will often be necessary, and that reverses as well as gains will have to be anticipated, and should be viewed in the light of the ultimate successes promised by the ideology. The leadership, however, may engage quite actively with some external issues, and if successes are achieved within a reasonable period these will enhance its domestic standing. The present dominant technocratically oriented group in the primary elite, reacting against the Maoist style of leadership that is seen to have been too oracular and arbitrary, displays a significant degree of task orientation. This may well render its symbolic interaction with the secondary elite and the middle echelons more potent, while eliciting more professional inputs into the foreign policy process.[56]

Substantively, the shaping of China's foreign policy is directed toward the realization of external values. These can be sought only if the prime requirements for legitimating the leadership's decision-making roles, in terms of the regime's values, are met consistently. The linkage, however, is functional not only with respect to the continued mobilization of domestic support for the leadership, but also with regard to the transmission of meaning and purpose to foreign political groups, including revolutionary movements whose attitudes and behavior are to be directly affected.

Cognitively, the processing and management of foreign policy issues is a function of the assorted psychological environments of the Chinese leadership, in which ideology and idiosyncratic ideological constructs are dominant factors. These provide concepts, analytical approaches, and theory, and they concentrate and restrict attention, with significant consequences in elite communication processes.

The conceptual equipment of the Chinese leaders comprises the central ideas of Marxism-Leninism, the practical revolutionary wisdom of Mao Zedong, which appears to be awaiting critical evaluation, and the theoretical work of Liu Shao-chi, the most prominent victim of the Cultural Revolution, whose views are being tacitly validated by the policies of the relatively pragmatic new leadership. With this somewhat disorganized collection of ideas the outside world is seen as a large complex of states, in varying stages of class struggle, which relate to each other and to China with varying degrees of hostility and goodwill. The basic feature of the broad interactive pattern, however, is the polarity that is claimed to exist between the U.S.S.R. and all the other states, including China.[57]

Analytically, the main interest is an expected sharpening of antagonisms between the Soviet Union and the large number of states believed to be threatened by its hegemonic ambitions. Hopes of seeing noncommunist governments in the advanced democracies initiating stronger anti-Soviet policies draw attention away from the development of class conflicts in those democracies, especially as their radical elements are influenced by the U.S.S.R. rather than by China. In the nearby developing countries the presence of affinitive communist movements gives rise to a different perspective, but the principal focus of interest remains the fundamental conflict between the governments of those countries and the U.S.S.R.

For the present, the analytical approach is undergoing little development. No insights are being provided concerning the working out of revolutionary logic in the advanced capitalist states, where the communist movements do not respond to Chinese leadership, or concerning the evolution of developing states. This suggests that a relatively pragmatic, case-by-case statecraft is being evolved, and that in areas where this has not yet happened policy is continuing more or less according to precedent. Operationally, shifts toward less doctrinal and more searching studies of external situations would seem to be required by the complexities of the foreign policy questions now being posed, and the extent to which they appear to demand engagement with bourgeois political forces in other states for the strengthening of China's international position. Nevertheless, the ideology continues to have restrictive effects on the thinking and communications of the ruling group. The introduction of new concepts to facilitate the acquisition of new knowledge is evidently being restrained by the leadership's long-internalized ideological beliefs. The language of the regime's policy statements and theoretical pronouncements thus fails to convey any grasp of the dynamics of the U.S. policy process or of Japan's external policy, although the external behavior of both states has vital significance for China's domestic and external objectives. Yet this is understandable in view of the tendency of the leadership to orient foreign policy in general terms, avoiding close engagement with the issues, while restricting the autonomy of officials and staffs in the foreign affairs structures. It is also understandable in view of the leadership's considerable dependence on information-processing by its own strictly subordinated structures, which, as has been seen, causes misperceptions and slow recognition of new developments.[58]

Affectively, the recognition, definition, and processing or avoidance of foreign policy issues derives motivation from a strong, radical, modernizing anti-Soviet nationalism. This in certain major respects inclines the leadership toward ideological simplicity and rigidity in external as well as internal matters, because it gives rise to very basic concerns about maximizing political unity in the regime and giving forthright expression to its values externally. Revisionism and sophistication, in so far as they can weaken the national political will, are to be rejected, although the requirements of modernization have to be met by absorbing foreign knowledge at the cost of tolerating the introduction of some cognitive complexity into the elite culture.

Intense anti-Soviet feelings evidently restrict cognitive processes in the shaping of policy toward the U.S.S.R., especially at times of rising tension between the two regimes. These feelings as well as the compulsion to maximize internal solidarity on their basis, seem to preclude consideration of the possible benefits of an improved relationship with the U.S.S.R., which of course could open the way for more vigorous competition between the two superpowers. Affective factors, however, clearly have less restrictive effects on the consideration of options concerning the United States, Japan, the West European powers, and most of the developing states. Yet relations with all the advanced democracies from which technology is being secured are influenced by traditional and anticolonial antipathies toward advanced foreign cultures, which make for emphasis on self-reliance.[59]

Strong national pride is associated with the emphasis on self-reliance, and this is responsible for intense sensitivities to matters of status. This in turn contributes to caution about involvement in support of the interests of friendly Third World states, as their uncertain political fortunes could affect China's international prestige. On the positive side, status considerations motivate quests for upward interaction in the global system so as to demonstrate China's superior standing to Third World countries, especially the neighbors in Southeast Asia. For this purpose, the relationship with the United States is highly significant, especially in so far as U.S. interest in China's goodwill is made evident.

High international status, in the minds of the Chinese leaders, requires considerable aloofness, complemented by selective, potent, and decisive engagement. Magisterial aloofness, evidenced in generalized ideological pronouncements, is the response to issues in complex distant situations which discourage engagement, such as the Middle East, and in situations where Chinese capabilities are not adequate for potent involvement, as in the North–South confrontation within the international economy.[60]

Normatively, the management of foreign policy issues is a matter of expressing ideological and nationalist imperatives. There is a deep compulsion to transmit the values of the regime's political culture to foreign societies so as to foster the emergence of profoundly affinitive revolutionary elites that will always look to China for inspiration. But it is understood that there must be complex and protracted struggles, at the governmental and transnational levels, to overcome the Soviet threat and to exploit, weaken, and oppose bourgeois and deviant radical political forces in other states. Foreign policy choices are thus affected by tension between the drive to manifest and communicate revolutionary values through external symbolic interaction and the instrumental requirements of engagement with the variously oriented governments, counterelites, uncommitted elements, and revolutionary groups which must be influenced and utilized, discriminatingly, for short- and intermediate-term purposes. Emphasis on the manipulation of those external political forces, while demanded by the magnitude of the regime's international tasks, tends to relativize ideological values, reduces the capacity to inspire foreign revolutionary movements, and risks opposition from the less pragmatic elements in the Chinese elite. For the present, as has been seen, strain is evident concerning the accelerated introduction of Western technology and the close relationship with the United States.

Functionally, Chinese foreign policy issue management appears to be informal, weakly institutionalized, and determined very much by the configuration of relationships within the primary elite. Institutional development of the kind that might be expected in an established one-party state has been prevented by the severe intra-elite conflicts of the past two decades, and is now hindered by Deng Xiaoping's reliance on close associates to direct party, government, and army affairs and by the continued purging of Maoist elements. The relatively pragmatic orientation of foreign policy sets requirements for routine professional performance, but the style of high-level direction remains based on the Leninist concept of a revolutionary leadership that makes policy at will, nonaccountably, and unrestricted by procedural arrangements.[61]

Foreign policy issues appear to be decided in the light of design considerations, elements of strategy, and current task preoccupations, with some guidance from operational codes and variable degrees of engagement with specifics by the primary elite. Because of the partial repudiation of Mao Zedong there has been a shift away from notions of foreign policy design attributed to him, with suggestions of a new design for foreign policy in the service of modernization, on a basis of coexistence with the advanced capitalist states. Whereas all this derives urgency from the struggle against the U.S.S.R., it is a source of somewhat pragmatic orientations toward issues in relations with the United States, Japan, and

Western Europe. The operative strategic notions are mainly anti-Soviet and, because of the weaknesses of affinitive revolutionary movements in the Third World and China's lack of strong ties with developing states, the focus is on using Western and Japanese opposition to the U.S.S.R. This task orientation necessitates vast international "united front" methods, and the most critical choices concern the need to maximize anti-Soviet hostility in the advanced states.[62]

The influence of operational codes on Chinese decision-making is probably quite significant. The Leninist operational code, which is part of the regime's political tradition, seems to provide some of the motivation and guidance for efforts to gain international influence and assert leadership through mounting an unending succession of political campaigns against primary and secondary adversaries. These campaigns are seen as means of drawing support, holding the initiative, and shaping the attitudes and behavior of states and political groups that cooperate, and they are expected to be succesful eventually because of the persistence and resourcefulness with which they are waged. The methods of struggle employed against the Kuomintang and the Japanese, although devised and formulated by Mao Zedong, appear to represent a supplementary operational code that has some relevance for external policy. These methods emphasize the gradual destruction of the main adversary's will and resources through relentless political struggle and the infliction of a long series of defeats in localized engagements. For the present, of course, such defeats are not possible in the struggle against the U.S.S.R., but there appears to be confidence that they will be imposed as the persistent Chinese campaign against the Soviet Union grows in strength and as the U.S.S.R. reveals more of its negative features through its involvement in the developing areas.[63]

The two closely related operational codes provide less obvious guidance for the mainly constructive interaction with the United States, Japan, and Western Europe. In these contexts, however, the codes do concern Peking's anti-Soviet strategy, although for the present little progress is being made in the development of understandings with major political forces in the advanced democracies whose cooperation is needed against the U.S.S.R.

Innovative application of the operational codes, especially the first, may result from the strong task orientation of Deng Xiaoping. If his leadership gives way to a competitively collective ruling elite, however, weaker task orientation and a less innovative thrust may follow. The processing and management of foreign policy issues will then probably be guided largely by precedent, with medium to low levels of sensitivity to positive or negative results, and a weaker capacity for engagement with the problems and opportunities presented by the behavior of the advanced and developing states.

Foreign Policy Performance

China's foreign policy issues are managed in a statecraft that comprises various mixes of behavior, conflictual and cooperative, international and transnational, in regional and larger contexts. Much of this behavior is assisted by favorably oriented relational factors, of which the most important is the United States' East Asian policy. If these factors become on the whole less favorable, numerous foreign policy issues will be more difficult to manage.

Communications make up the most important element in Chinese statecraft, and its most significant feature is the emphasis on influencing and shaping fundamental layers of the political psychology of foreign elites and segments of their societies. As this is attempted through doctrinal statements, policy announcements, and news commentaries that are meaningful primarily in the domestic context, the intended international transfers of meaning and conviction are difficult. What the Chinese wish to develop are forms of international symbolic interaction through which their political culture can penetrate foreign societies, but this clearly would require some blending with the established values of those societies, for which Peking's communications evince little sympathy.

Linked with the vast endeavor to shape basic attitudes in other political systems is a large flow of more specific communications that are intended to promote hostile or cooperative behavior by administrations, individuals, and groups on a wide range of national and international questions. These communications, for example, encourage hostility to Soviet involvement in Third World states such as Angola and Ethiopia, urge the members of the European Community to move further toward political integration, and express desires for friendly relations with the states in the Association of Southeast Asian Nations, while responding, on a day-to-day basis, to news of labor unrest and cost-of-living rises in the capitalist countries and of agitation in developing states for a new international economic order.

The main thrust of all the generalized and more specific communications relating to the U.S.S.R. is directed at the legitimacy of the Soviet Union as an international actor. The Soviet ruling elite is portrayed as an aggressive social imperialist leadership that is suppressing its people and betraying their revolutionary aspirations. Yet there is little effort to identify with and encourage dissident elements in the U.S.S.R., and there is probably some awareness that most of the underground groups opposed to the Soviet authorities are not inspired by China.[64] Insofar as total hostility to the U.S.S.R. is expressed and is manifested as the general attitude of the Chinese people, the Soviet authorities are expected to be aware that a vast and relentless ''peoples war'' would be waged against any Soviet invading force. There are no explicit suggestions that the United States would take countermeasures in the event of a Soviet attack on China, but continual exhortations to the United States about the need for more resolute opposition to Soviet military development and to Soviet penetration of the Third World are intended to increase U.S. awareness of security interests that are shared with China.[65]

The need for more resolute responses to Soviet challenges dominates communications with the United States. These complications, as has been seen, do not sufficiently engage with the problem of transmitting concerns that are meaningful in terms of the instrumental political culture in which U.S. decision makers operate. The main result is to sustain awareness among those decision makers of the distinctive revolutionary nationalist psychology of the Chinese leadership and thus of the difficulties of developing rapport in the relationship and establishing a stable basis for cooperation. Accordingly, the U.S. administration's quest for an enduring superpower détente remains its highest priority.

Secondary communications with the United States encourage cooperation with Western Europe, evidence respect for U.S. interests in the developing areas, and seek to induce acceptance of an expanding role for China in East Asian affairs. All these matters are overshadowed by the Soviet threat, but what is transmitted does not add significantly to the limited persuasive power of the communications urging a stronger anti-Soviet policy. U.S. behavior toward Western Europe is quite unaffected by Chinese assertions about the need for Atlantic solidarity, and there is little disposition to be grateful for Chinese goodwill toward the United States' Third World interests. There are some indications of a U.S. willingness to accept a stronger Chinese role in East Asia, however, not because of Peking's persuasion but to take advantage of China's adversary relationship with the U.S.S.R.[66]

Somewhat less important but more effective communications are directed at Japan. A high proportion of these are addressed to the Japanese corporate elite, relating to the development of opportunities in Sino-Japanese trade and to the political context of this commerce. This transnational activity is much larger than a similar communication flow which is becoming a feature of the relationship with the United States, and it contributes to the maintenance of the relatively strong Chinese influence on Tokyo's foreign economic policy. On the Japanese side, the ruling Liberal Democratic Party's leadership sees a need to retain the domestic political advantages of a friendly relationship with China, and to further the nation's external security interests by helping to sustain Peking's determination not to accommodate with the U.S.S.R. Ideology presents less serious difficulties in communications directed at Japan than in those aimed at the United States because of the much greater salience of economic matters, the more favorable orientation of affective factors on the

Japanese side, and the apparently greater credibility, for the Japanese audience, of Chinese denunciations of the U.S.S.R.[67] The level of rapport on political and strategic issues, however, remains low, primarily because of China's communication style and the resultant failure to identify credibly with Japanese elite perceptions of external interests.

The major West European states, which are the other principal targets of Chinese communications, are less receptive than the United States, and their somewhat narrower perspectives, limited mainly to economic issues, are significant barriers to rapport on the strategic matters that dominate Chinese thinking. Efforts to increase West German, French, and British awareness of the China market for technology tend to have only moderate results because exports to China are small proportions of the foreign commerce of these Community members. Cultural dissimilarities and social distances moreover make it all the more difficult for the Chinese to use their heavily ideological communications with effect and, while limiting West European empathy for China as an adversary of the U.S.S.R., tend to incline the West Europeans toward perspectives in which the Chinese regime is seen as an alien and unstable counterforce to Soviet pressures, through which some leverage can be exerted against the Soviet Union but below potentially provocative levels.[68]

Chinese communications to all the industrialized democracies, of course, are intended to transmit revolutionary beliefs and values, but such transfers of meaning and commitment tend to be linked with Peking's operational and manipulative concerns and are made difficult by the absence of affinitive political movements in Western Europe and the United States. The imperative to spread the ideology is given more expression in communications aimed at the Third World and, as has been seen, there are incentives to manage these communications in ways that will avoid close involvement with potential client states and movements of doubtful viability.

The noncommunist countries in the immediate environment and particularly in Southeast Asia are the most important targets of Peking's attempts to spread its political culture and further its operational purposes. For the present, most of the noncommunist administrations seem to be made more averse than they might otherwise be to the development of economic and other links with the U.S.S.R., and are certainly unwilling to support Soviet proposals for an Asian security system directed against China, but their attitudes are attributable in part to the projection of Chinese power rather than to the persuasiveness of Chinese communications, and to the influence of the U.S. presence in East Asia. The pattern of Chinese communications does not resolve the question of choice in Peking's overall diplomacy between coexistence and subversion through the local revolutionary movements, but for the Chinese authorities these two forms of international behavior are in principle mutually supporting lines of strategy. In practice the mix does not feature sufficient emphasis on coexistence to induce high receptivity to Chinese cultural and other forms of statecraft in Southeast Asia, and the expressions of revolutionary purpose and solidarity, while potent, do not provide the inspiration that the Chinese-oriented communist movements in the area would need to develop into large revolutionary organizations.[69]

In the more distant parts of the Third World the potency of Chinese ideological and manipulative communications is affected by long geographic separation, a weaker projection of the regime's power, and major cultural and ethnic dissimilarities. Inadequate resources for aid diplomacy, moreover, prevent the establishment of a presence in the non-Asian regions of the developing areas that could help to make Chinese communications more persuasive. Peking's expressions of support for Egypt, the Sudan, and other states hostile to the U.S.S.R. can earn goodwill but do not invite close identification with the very prominent ideological dimension of China's campaign against the Soviet Union.

Forms of *bargaining,* for which the various communication flows set the stage and provide support, are substantive methods of engagement with what may be called the manipulative problems of Chinese statecraft. The economic issues are managed in moderately effective ways, especially in the relationship with Japan; the potential size of the Chinese market is a valuable bargaining asset. The regime's perceived external security issues, however, are not adequately resolved, because the available bargaining resources are not adequate and cannot be sufficiently used on account of the communication difficulties on the Chinese side that are caused by ideology.

The most productive interaction is with Japan, and this is facilitated by the factors that have been identified as aiding Chinese communications in this relationship. The perceived identities and complementarities of interest across the issue areas are substantial, China's bargaining resources can be used with considerable effect—more so than in any other area of Peking's foreign relations—and the outcomes are sufficiently gratifying for Japan to motivate further cooperation. Tokyo's important secondary interest in developing economic relations with the U.S.S.R., however, remains a difficulty. China's principal gains are large technology transfers on favorable terms, and a stimulation of Japanese military development which may begin to balance the Soviet military presence and contribute later to the modernization of China's armed forces.[70]

The interaction with the United States over more extensive but more difficult issues ranks next in terms of actual results. In this relationship, Chinese communications are less persuasive, and the identities and compatibilities of interest are more uncertain and are affected by greater complexities on the U.S. side, particularly because Washington is virtually committed to a broad strategy of interdependence with the Soviet

Union. China's economic bargaining assets are of much smaller significance than they are in the relationship with Japan, while politically and militarily China offers less to the United States than to Japan and is more dependent on U.S. goodwill, especially in strategic matters. In the highly salient security issues, China's bargaining resources are small in the context set by geography, social distances, the character of the Chinese regime, and its relatively dysfunctional communications. There is no question of gaining additional bargaining power through linking security matters with economic issues, on which the Chinese have a little more leverage because of their potentially large market; several factors preclude such linking, and the most important is the understandable desire of U.S. decision makers to manage security issues in the *superpower* relationship without any reference to economic matters under negotiation with China. China indeed cannot bargain effectively for U.S. military protection or for a more active U.S. anti-Soviet policy; these remain matters that must be handled primarily by establishing levels of rapport that would permit meaningful bargaining.[71]

The issues that appear to be in various stages of exploration and resolution in the relationship with the United States tend to be affected by situational and relational factors in China's immediate environment. The potentially most difficult problem is Vietnamese hostility, which the Chinese seem to view largely as a manifestation of Soviet animosity, although they themselves, through their support of the very oppressive former regime in Cambodia, initially antagonized Vietnam. A renewal of the fighting which China began by attacking Vietnam early in 1979 could provoke Soviet military actions along the Sino-Mongolian and Sino-Soviet borders. The United States, unwilling to see its vital interests affected, would then be obliged to affirm its primary commitment to détente with Moscow, and China's utility as a potential coalition partner for the United States would be reduced. It is not in China's interests to produce a situation in which Washington will have to demonstrate that détente with the Soviet Union is an objective of the highest importance, but it is in China's interests to raise as high as possible Soviet estimates of the risks of drastic U.S. countermeasures in the event of a Sino-Soviet conflict; consequently the U.S.S.R. should be denied an opportunity to probe the degrees of interest and commitment in U.S. policy toward China. Yet on the Chinese side strong emotional factors evidently limit appreciation of this logic with respect to both Vietnam and the U.S.S.R.[72]

The Vietnam problem has become a source of limitations on China's capacity to influence U.S. policy and thus would seem to call for conciliatory approaches to Hanoi for the sake of China's larger interests. But there may be more compulsive hostility on the Chinese side, especially if the U.S.S.R. begins to exert serious pressures which occasion stress in Peking.

The context of the Taiwan question has been affected by the Vietnam problem, because moves toward asserting sovereignty over the island that could have been considered reasonable by the United States before the aggression against Vietnam would now seem inappropriate, and China's capacity to bargain for acceptance of measures against Taiwan, without diminishing U.S. interest in Peking's tacit cooperation against the U.S.S.R., has been reduced. The logical course for Peking, in line with the need to avoid pushing the United States into an embarrassing choice between détente with the U.S.S.R. and friendship with China, is to defer initiatives concerning Taiwan. This, however, may not be possible without an intensification of differences within the Chinese ruling elite.[73]

The most serious internally posed foreign policy issues that have to be managed concern Vietnam, Taiwan, and the U.S.S.R. Positions taken by the dominant group on these matters evidently must be vindicated by achievements, otherwise high-level differences may increase. For the present no major gains are being realized at the expense of the U.S.S.R. or Vietnam or on the Taiwan issue despite the United States' full recognition of Peking, and it is uncertain whether feelings of dissatisfaction in the leadership are being sufficiently overcome by successes in procuring large transfers of technology from the West and from Japan. If these are not helping to generate adequate support for the dominant group it may express its frustration by more severe purging of its perceived domestic opponents and critics. Externally, that could have significant costs because it could make the United States quite hesitant about strengthening its ties with China, encourage applications of pressure by the U.S.S.R., and cause the Vietnamese to tighten their bonds with the U.S.S.R.[74]

The Chinese regime's interaction with the large West European countries does not appear to be of major significance in the context of its intra-elite differences, mainly because it tends to be confined to economic questions and because it does yield moderate results. In this interaction China's bargaining power is weak because of economic backwardness, geographic separation, and the regional focus of West European security policies; the levels of mutual understanding tend to be low, and Chinese communications have relatively little impact. The size of the Chinese market is Peking's main asset and is largely responsible for acquisitions of technology on favorable terms. The problem of West European military weakness, of course, cannot be taken up in Peking's bargaining, and the gradually expanding economic relationships with Western Europe of course cannot increase the credibility of China's warnings on strategic issues to the NATO members and France, or the persuasiveness of Chinese exhortations regarding the need for greater cohesion within the European Community.[75]

Outside the context of Peking's dependency relationships are the mixed forms of Chinese interaction with noncommunist Asian neighbors

other than Japan, in which there is considerable use of pressures, especially through the support of local revolutionary movements. In these
relationships the manifest asymmetries favor China, and the interaction
is sufficiently effective to ensure the preservation of cordial official connections. China's capacity to exert leverage for the development of closer
cultural ties with its noncommunist neighbors, however, has been weakened by the development of the Soviet presence in Vietnam. Since the
anti-Soviet struggle in Southeast Asia has become more urgent, it could
be advantageous for Peking to cut ties with the underground communist
movements in Burma, Thailand, Malaysia, Indonesia, and the Philippines, or urge them to negotiate for recognition as legal political parties,
seeking power by peaceful means. There are few indications, however,
that this possibility is being considered.[76]

Interaction with developing states outside adjacent parts of Asia tends
to be affected by weaknesses in Chinese bargaining power and by the
Chinese strategy of aloofness from the interests of friendly governments.
Issue management in this large area of foreign relations entails risks of
failure more significant than those in dealings with nearby states, because
of the active intrusions of the U.S.S.R. into the developing areas, particularly Africa, and the insufficiently competitive involvement of the
United States, as well as China's own difficulties in projecting and asserting a presence across long distances. The U.S.S.R., as has been stressed,
has ideological as well as economic and military advantages in its efforts
to develop bonds with radical antiwestern groups in Africa, Latin America, and Southwest Asia, because China's new degree of identification
with the United States and Western Europe tends to diminish Peking's
revolutionary appeal. While retaining its ideological advantage, moreover, the U.S.S.R. tends to benefit cumulatively from gains made in areas
of the Third World, particularly Africa, in that increased projections of
its military strength, facilitated by the acquisition of new client states,
tend to have a strong impact on the attitudes of uncommitted governments in nearby countries and to encourage Soviet-inspired revolutionary
movements that are planning or making bids for power.[77]

In the direct relationship with the U.S.S.R., China's strategy of intransigent political confrontation, refusing virtually all meaningful interaction,
does not encourage favorable political change in the Soviet Union but
rather makes the evolution of a conciliatory leadership in the U.S.S.R.
more unlikely. The principal intent, clearly, is to ensure that the Soviet
ruling elite remains very conscious of the hostility felt toward it throughout Chinese society, and that it will appreciate that any invading Soviet
forces would encounter bitter and determined resistance on a vast scale.
The main risk entailed is that Soviet emotional hostility tends to be kept
high, and that this could be responsible for rapid escalation of any frontier
conflicts. The most serious contingency to be planned for by the Chinese,

however, is an enthusiastic U.S. response to any new Soviet diplomacy of peaceful coexistence that would offer dramatic concessions to the United States and hold out appealing promises of enduring détente. U.S. interest in China would then be greatly reduced, and the danger of Soviet coercive moves against China would be increased. Anxieties on this score may well be giving urgency to Peking's warnings to the United States about the risks of seeking co-existence with the Soviet Union.

Prospects

Elements of continuity and change are evident in the patterns of externally and internally posed issues for Chinese foreign policy makers. The economic exchanges with the industrialized democracies will continue to expand unless extreme leftist figures displace the present dominant group, but there are likely to be increasing frustrations with Western protectionist barriers that hinder the growth of Chinese exports. The connection with Washington will tend to become more active, especially because of opportunities arising out of U.S. initiatives for the export of technology and for the development of a more effective leverage against the U.S.S.R., yet there may be growing disillusionment on security matters because of Washington's continuing quest for détente with the U.S.S.R. There are no indications of a likely change in Soviet behavior toward China, but the U.S.S.R. may well be inclined to make increasing political use of its growing strength in the central balance, and yet uncertainties may be introduced into its policy by the large succession issue now being posed for the Soviet leadership.

Of the externally posed issues, those resulting from Soviet behavior are tending to become more serious as the U.S.S.R. increases its overall military power in relation to the United States and remains committed to the acquisition of war-fighting rather than simply deterrent capabilities. An increased threat to Western Europe will have adverse implications for China, and Chinese objectives in the developing areas will be set further back by continuing Soviet gains, which seem very likely in Africa. Chinese estimates of Soviet capabilities will probably be high, partly because of increasing stress caused by Soviet achievements and Western failures, and the gravity of the issues presented by the U.S.S.R. could have disruptive consequences within the Chinese leadership, especially as its own succession problems become more serious with the departure of aged revolutionaries from the dominant group.

The issues in China's relations with the United States are becoming more significant and are demanding more bargaining skills and resources. The engagement is continuing to offer scope for the exploitation of U.S. competition against Japan and Western Europe in sales of technology to

China, and for the expansion of exchanges that can induce favorable U.S. attitudes toward the Chinese drive for modernization. The promotion of such attitudes, however, will require restraint in the expressions of antagonisms toward Vietnam. In the development of Sino-American commerce, moreover, China will have to devise ways of securing better access to the U.S. market for light manufactures, linking demands for this with procurements of U.S. plant and machinery. Chinese bargaining strength could be increased by active participation in the efforts of developing countries to negotiate a new international economic order, but such involvement does not seem likely. While China remains apart from those countries, it may be possible to secure more favorable U.S. consideration on tariff matters and nontariff barriers if Peking's trade promotion activities rouse wider interest in the Chinese market.

The most exacting requirements for Chinese diplomacy toward the United States will concern strategic questions. To the extent that U.S. anxieties about the danger of a Sino-Soviet conflict over Vietnam can be relieved, Washington's willingness to facilitate, directly or indirectly, transfers of military technology to China will tend to increase. Meanwhile, Peking's need for a military understanding with the United States will grow because of the strengthening of the Soviet position in the central balance, but such an understanding will be difficult to achieve because of hesitations and ideological factors on the Chinese side and because of the probability of protracted and inconclusive strategic debates on the matter in the United States. The danger of intra-elite conflicts arising out of frustrations with the problem of influencing U.S. security policy toward the U.S.S.R. will probably increase and may become more serious if unexpected events produce acute awareness that the psychological environment in which the Chinese leadership has been operating has fostered excessive optimism about what can be achieved through the connection with the United States. The rather subjective quality of that environment will remain a potential source of miscalculation in Chinese behavior toward the United States.

Issues in the relationship with Japan will remain more manageable unless Japan's Liberal-Democratic administration is replaced by a coalition government. The Liberal-Democratic party's interest in China's goodwill, especially because of its domestic benefits, will continue to be a major advantage for Peking, particularly regarding the terms on which primary products and light manufactures are traded for Japanese technology. The Chinese will almost certainly continue to be confident of their ability to secure benefits from the policy orientation of the Liberal-Democratic administration as well as of the Japanese corporate elite which is closely identified with that administration. In the security area, however, China will still have a strong interst in the preservation of

Japan's military links with the United States to offset the strong Soviet presence in Northeast Asia.

Britain and France will continue to be important sources of military technology, but West German interest in sales of arms to China will remain quite restricted because of the importance of maintaining the leading position which the Federal Republic has acquired in European Community exports to the U.S.S.R. The Chinese demand for nonmilitary technology from Western Europe will remain strong, but protectionist barriers to Chinese goods entering the European Community are not likely to be lowered appreciably. Peking may seek a special trading relationship with the Community, but it cannot expect to obtain terms better than those secured by the developing states associated with the Community under the second Lomé agreement.

In relations with the developing states outside the immediate environment no major opportunities are being presented, and few gains are likely in the struggle to enlist allies against the U.S.S.R. or in the endeavor to promote radical change under the leadership of Chinese-oriented groups. Yet in this large area of foreign relations China's policy is likely to be rather insensitive to cognitive and operational challenges and to be influenced more by optimistic expectations based on ideology. Beliefs in China's superior capacity to inspire and guide revolutionary movements in the new nations are likely to remain strong, despite the weaknesses of the pro-Chinese communist groups in most Third World states and notwithstanding the advantages enjoyed by the U.S.S.R. through the use of its larger resources on behalf of client governments and political movements.

Foreign policy choices for China in most of the Third World will not be urgent because of the general avoidance of close engagement with ruling elites and counterelites. In relation to Southeast Asia and Korea, however, difficult options concerning highly salient political and security interests are likely to be presented, in some cases with only short decision time. Vietnam, with Soviet encouragement, may well try to displace China as the main source of support for revolutionary groups in Thailand, thus obliging Peking to choose between responding to this competition and developing an active friendship with the Thai administration. For the Chinese a decision could be especially difficult because the Thai communist movement's organization has been expanding in the Northeast part of that country, and the army-dominated Thai government has many of the vulnerabilities that have invited revolutionary violence against its predecessors. Of course, in the immediate future Vietnam's main challenge may continue to be simply defiance of China together with the expansion of ties with the U.S.S.R., and this challenge may be felt quite acutely as a threat to Chinese status in Southeast Asia and as a factor in the U.S.S.R.'s encirclement or containment strategy which must be dealt with even at the risk of provoking countermeasures by Soviet forces against China. Renewed North Korean aggression against South Korea is a contingency to be considered in the general context of the Soviet threat, and of Soviet options relation to Vietnam, because the U.S.S.R. would become North Korea's prime source of military aid, and the conflict would impose severe strains on the Sino-American relationship, while portending a strengthening of the Soviet presence in Japan's immediate environment.

Any major external achievements or reverses will tend to affect the status of the dominant group in the Chinese leadership, while that leadership's capacity to manage foreign policy issues will be weakened if there are serious intra-elite conflicts. The probability of such conflicts over the next few years seems fairly high because of the magnitude of the succession issue, since so many of the prominent figures in the primary elite are aged revolutionaries, and the military establishment will probably seek to strengthen its influence by securing new party and government posts for some of its top personnel. High level tensions are also likely to increase as relatively more Maoist elements see threats to the regime and to themselves in the shifts of authority to senior technocrats, in the expansion of the drive for economic modernization, and in the penetration of bourgeois influence from the West. Meanwhile, although major economic benefits will continue to flow from the connections with the United States, Japan, and Western Europe, these and any strengthening of the tenuous security links with the United States may well have less impact, in the political atmosphere of the Chinese elite, than events signifying Soviet gains in Africa and other parts of the Third World. Hence the status of the present ruling group may be weakened by what are seen as American failures in the developing areas that reflect unfavorably on the wisdom of the link with Washington. The criteria for assessing achievements in foreign relations are affected by differences in high-level value orientations, but the emergence of any Soviet-assisted regime in a developing country will be recognized as an unambiguous reverse.

Theory

For more than two decades the Chinese system has experienced considerable political decay. The initial modernizing nationalist-ideological consensus for socialist nation-building was disrupted by severe repressions in the early and mid-1950s, after which institutional development was set back by the disruptions of the attempted acceleration of economic growth in the later 1950s and by the Cultural Revolution in the mid- and later 1960s. The emergence of a strong technocratic-military leadership in 1977 prepared the way for new consensus building and a more orderly government, but institutional development at the highest levels evidently has a lower priority than the purging of elements who prospered in the Cultural Revolution. The ruling elite, moreover, is affected by internal divisions which may well become more serious as the succession issue becomes more urgent.

The Chinese experience has in some respects been similar to those of other authoritarian new states. Charismatic and personalist leadership has been replaced by bureaucratic direction. The mobilization of popular enthusiasms has to a considerable extent given way to routine social organization. Anti-imperialist nationalism has been moderated to facilitate technology imports. The leadership has become significantly dependent on military support, and the party organization has been somewhat weakened on that account and because of the growing importance of the government structure in meeting the technocratic requirements of modernization. Destructive intra-elite clashes have been the main sources of instability, and the factionalism they have stimulated has tended to erode nationalist and ideological loyalties.

The international projection of the Chinese regime's image as a modernizing socialist state has been made less appealing by its internal changes, but its external behavior has exhibited greater instrumental rationality under its new leadership. Generalizing from its foreign policy record is difficult because of the absence of comparative material, but there do seem to have been significant limitations on the ranges of possibilities within which changes have occurred in the management of external relations, and the process has exhibited the working out of imperatives deriving from fairly stable factors in the political psychology of the Chinese leaders.

The Peking regime's experience has indicated that, for a modernizing revolutionary state, tight closure to the outside world entails scientific and technological costs and will tend to be moderated if its leadership recognizes a need for constructive, wide-ranging interaction with advanced nonrevolutionary states. The will to preserve closure may remain quite strong within the leadership, but the necessary political discipline will gradually become more difficult to maintain as modernization continues, especially if there are intra-elite conflicts associated with controversies over the basic values to be promoted as the economy develops.

The degree of closure, as affecting the elite, will to a large extent determine how subjective the psychological environment of the leadership will be, but this will also depend on the authority and task relationships between primary elite, secondary elite, and middle-echelon personnel. The subjectivity of the primary elite's cognitive maps and processes will be greater if this elite tends to confine itself to broad pre-scriptions for high policy and is separated by a large gap in status and authority from the secondary elite.

In general, closure to the outside world to facilitate the fully directed building up of the political culture makes for a compulsive expression of a revolutionary state's values in its external behavior, with high confidence in the effects but low sensitivity to the actual results. Courses of international activity, once initiated, are thus likely to remain in effect with little adaptation, especially because of the authoritative determination that these are appropriate expressions of revolutionary values. Such determinations, associated with matters of leadership status, will strongly influence the processing of information about the outside world.

Manifestly favorable external events, especially if they can be attributed to established lines of international activity, will tend to strengthen commitments to that activity as well as elite status and authority, while limiting receptivity to information that would indicate future problems. Searches for more rational and less ideologically or idiosyncratically based courses of external activity are more likely to result from grave outside threats, especially if these are posed by other revolutionary states and thus present cognitive challenges. Shifts away from ideological commitment, however, may entail intra-elite cleavages, and these may lead to incoherence and indecision in foreign policy.

If there is a pragmatic trend in a revolutionary state's external policy, keyed to higher priorities for domestic economic growth, the communication of radical values in external relations will tend to become less effective, less influence will be exerted over foreign revolutionary movements, and there will be fewer external achievements to reinforce commitments to revolutionary principles. This is not to deny that such commitments, if maintained in the face of challenges to shift to a more flexible and pragmatic external policy, might not ensure significant achievements for the radical reshaping of the international order; they may become dysfunctional, however, because of incapacities to identify with vital forces in foreign societies.

To the extent that leadership status and authority are threatened, a decrease in external revolutionary achievements may well cause the dominant group in a modernizing radical state to resort to purging in order to strengthen its power. If this happens, the regime's capacity to inspire and win the loyalties of foreign revolutionary movements will tend to weaken. A serious problem for a revolutionary leadership that has shifted to a less radical external policy is that achievements in the procurement of foreign technology will tend to produce less satisfaction in a political atmosphere that remains strongly ideological than advances in the promotion of revolutionary change externally.

The routine processing of information about outside events that makes for stability in the psychological environment of a ruling revolutionary elite can be challenged by happenings that because of their magnitude and degree of surprise have a direct impact on leadership thinking through bourgeois international communication media that normally receive staff evaluations for the guidance of the dominant group. The openness of a ruling revolutionary elite to information from such noncommunist sources will tend to be quite limited, but it is likely to increase if major external issues are posed suddenly and involve cognitive as well as operational challenges with respect to the regime's ideology.

If not facing serious external security problems, a modernizing revolutionary state will have as its principal foreign policy choice the setting of a balance between cooperation with democratic, technology-exporting states and a struggle to realize revolutionary values in the international environment, particularly in the developing areas. Whichever way this balance is struck, it will tend to cause tensions within the ruling group, especially as its members are likely to differ in their views concerning the expression of revolutionary principles in policy as well as in their personal and organizational interests concerning the implications of this matter. Existing conflicts within the leadership may prevent prescription and implementation of a balance between cooperative and conflictual elements in statecraft, but to the extent that one becomes established these elements are likely to be managed separately, with only limited high-level integration. That seems likely because the heavy concentration of authority in such a regime at the primary elite level tends to limit possibilities for lateral coordination between government ministries, and between them and the party organizations with external responsibilities.

The cooperative relationships of a revolutionary state with technology-exporting democracies can induce acceptance of dependencies and interdependencies. A revolutionary state tends to be oriented toward autarkic policies, primarily because of its leadership's ambitions to assert and maintain virtually absolute power, including total economic sovereignty, but modernization requires the acquisition of foreign plant and machinery, and substantial imports of these items can help develop politically and strategically useful relationships with foreign states. These can make dependence on imported technology less objectionable and can moderate resentment at the protectionist devices with which industrialized democracies limit imports of primary products and light manufactures from the developing areas. Revolutionary elites will have an interest in moving toward *interdependent* relationships by overcoming asymmetries in the dependencies which have been accepted, and for this they will need to maximize their bargaining power by linking trade and investment issues as widely as possible in bilateral dealings with the industrialized democracies. The basic autarkic imperative however is likely to remain strong, and resolution to make it effective over the long term may be made firmer by experiences in dealings with Western transnational enterprises, as well as in coping with western and Japanese protectionism.

Sustained, large-scale dependence on technology imports from industrialized democracies will tend to influence a ruling revolutionary elite's perspective on political and strategic issues and may well increase differences over these within the leadership. Maximizing the utility of bargaining power in the commercial relationships will be considered to require some moderation of explicit ideological attacks on the social systems of the industrialized democracies and some respect for their interests in the developing areas. Thoroughly expedient subordination of revolutionary principles to modernization requirements, however, will probably be precluded by the ruling elite's deeply internalized ideological values and by the high-level socialization processes that sustain those values and maintain leadership solidarity.

As a modernizing revolutionary state becomes increasingly involved in the international economy, its elite will tend to acquire a somewhat sophisticated awareness of the foreign policies of the industrialized democracies, but principally from the perspective of managing dependencies, with weak bargaining power over a protracted period during which the technological leads and relative overall economic strength of those democracies will probably increase. Hence the radical value orientation of the revolutionary leadership may well be strengthened, although its foreign policy behavior will exhbit more instrumental rationality. With the continued normative rejection of nonrevolutionary value systems, economic growth may well be seen as a process of building military strength for coercive restructuring of the external environment. Constructive global actors, then, must recognize the degree to which inequities and disorder in the international political economy can strengthen the cognitive and affective factors that sustain the radical outlooks of revolutionary elites. Whereas modernization may contribute to the deradicalization of revolutionary regimes, their increasingly substantive dealings with advanced states that dominate the international economy may well have the opposite effect on their leaderships.

Notes

1. See foreign affairs section of report on work of the Government by Hua Guofeng at National Peoples Congress, *Peking Review,* 10 (March 10, 1978), 7–40; and speech to U.N. General Assembly by Huang Hua, *Peking Review,* 40 (October 6, 1978), 12–17. See also references to foreign affairs in Stuart Schram (ed.), *Chairman Mao Talks to the People* (New York: Random House, 1974). On the Leninist derivation of foreign policy style, see Robert V. Daniels "Doctrine and Foreign Policy," *Survey,* 57 (October 1965), 3–13.

2. See references to pressures on the Ministry of Foreign Affairs by George P. Jan in "The Ministry of Foreign Affairs in China Since the Cultural Revolution," *Asian Survey,* 17 (June 6, 1977), 513–29.

3. See *China News Analysis,* 1146, January 19, 1979.

4. See Kenneth Lieberthal, "The Politics of Modernization in the PRC," *Problems of Communism,* 27 (May-June 1978), 1–17; and Allen S. Whiting and Robert F. Dernberger, *China's Future* (New York: McGraw-Hill, 1977).

5. See Lieberthal, "The Politics of Modernization."

6. Ibid.

7. See Andrew Nathan, "A Factionalism Model of CCP Politics," *China Quarterly,* 53 (January-March 1973), 34–66; and Lowell Dittmer, "Bases of Power in Chinese Politics: A Theory and an Analysis of the Fall of the 'Gang of Four'," *World Politics,* 31 (October 1978), 26–60.

8. See *China News Analysis,* 1146.

9. This can be argued in view of the stresses experienced in the Ministry of Foreign Affairs. See Jan, "The Ministry of Foreign Affairs."

10. See Michael B. Yahuda, *China's Role in World Affairs* (New York: St. Martin's Press, 1978); and Samuel S. Kim, *China, the United Nations, and World Order* (Princeton, N.J.: Princeton University Press, 1979).

11. See Robert C. North, *The Foreign Relations of China,* 3rd ed. (North Scituate, Mass.: Duxbury Press, 1978).

12. See Constitution of the Chinese Communist Party, adopted at 11th Party Congress, *Peking Review,* 36 (September 2, 1977), 16–22.

13. See *China News Analysis,* 1146.

14. See Amitai Etzioni, *The Active Society* (New York: Free Press, 1968), pp. 135–312. See also E. Feit, "Political Groups under Severe Pressure: A Comparative Study Based on the Communication Control Model," *General Systems Yearbook,* 1964, pp. 265–82.

15. See reference to new Central Disciplinary Commission, *China News Analysis,* 1146.

16. See Lieberthal, "The Politics of Modernization."

17. See Shannon R. Brown, "Foreign Technology and Economic Growth," *Problems of Communism,* 26 (July-August 1977), 30–40; and Joseph S. Berliner and Franklyn D. Holzman, "The Soviet Economy: Domestic and International Issues," in William E. Griffith (ed.), *The Soviet Empire: Expansion and Detente,* (Lexington, Mass.: D. C. Heath, 1976), pp. 85–144.

18. See Harvey W. Nelsen, *The Chinese Military System* (Boulder, Colo.: Westview Press, 1977).

19. See *China News Analysis,* 1146.

20. See Edward N. Luttwak, "Chinese Strategic Security after Mao," *The Jerusalem Journal of International Relations,* 2 (Summer 1977), 97–111.

21. See *The Military Balance, 1978/9,* International Institute for Strategic Studies, London.

22. See *China News Analysis,* 1146; and *China News Analysis,* 1093/4 (September 17, 1977).

23. See Jay Taylor, *China and Southeast Asia* (New York: Praeger, 1974); and William J. Barnds, "The USSR, China, and South Asia," *Problems of Communism,* 26 (November-December 1977), 44–59.

24. See George T. Yu, "China's Role in Africa," *The Annals of the American Academy of Political and Social Science,* 432 (July 1977), 96–109.
25. See Chae-Jin Lee, *Japan Faces China* (Baltimore: Johns Hopkins University Press, 1976.)
26. See Kim, *China, the United Nations, and World Order.*
27. See Taylor, *China and Southeast Asia.*
28. See Kim, *China, the United Nations, and World Order.*
29. See discussion of U.S. policy in A. Doak Barnett, *China Policy* (Washington: Brookings Institution, 1977).
30. See Fuji Kamiya, "The Prospects for Peace in Korea," in Franklin B. Weinstein (ed.), *US-Japan Relations and the Security of East Asia* (Boulder, Colo.: Westview Press, 1978), pp. 167–88.
31. See Gavin Boyd, "The European Community and China," paper given at Conference of Europeanists, Washington, D.C., March 29–31, 1979.
32. See Huang Hua, *Peking Review,* 40.
33. See Lieberthal, "The Politics of Modernization."
34. See Gavin Boyd, "Sino-Soviet Relations: The Future," *Asian Forum,* 8 (Autumn 1976), 1–32.
35. Ibid.
36. See *Chairman Mao's Theory of the Differentiation of the Three Worlds is a Major Contribution to Marxism-Leninism* (Peking: Foreign Languages Press, 1977).
37. See Barnett, *China Policy;* and William J. Barnds (ed.), *China and America* (New York: New York University Press, 1977).
38. See Huang Hua, *Peking Review,* 40.
39. See Chae-Jin Lee, *Japan Faces China.*
40. See Boyd, "The European Community and China."
41. See Kim, *China, the United Nations, and World Order.*
42. See Huang Hua, *Peking Review,* 40; and "Social-Imperialist Strategy in Asia," *Peking Review,* 3 (January 19, 1979), 13–16.
43. See Boyd, "The European Community and China."
44. See comments by Helmut Schmidt on Chinese understanding of the outside world, *German International,* 19 (December 1975), 9–15.
45. Mao Zedong's prestige continues to be linked with the strategy of uniting with Western Europe against the U.S.S.R. See *Chairman Mao's Theory of the Differentiation of the Three Worlds is a Major Contribution to Marxism-Leninism.*
46. See Boyd, "Sino-Soviet Relations: The Future."
47. See William L. Scully and Frank N. Trager, "Burma 1978: The Thirtieth Year of Independence," *Asian Survey,* 19 (February 1979), 147–56.
48. See Huang Hua, *Peking Review,* 40.
49. See Huang Hua, "Social-Imperialist Strategy in Asia."
50. For an indication of the problems faced by Peking, see brief reference to China in Richard J. Barnet, "US-Soviet Relations: The Need for a Comprehensive Approach," *Foreign Affairs,* 57 (Spring 1979), 779–95.
51. See Chae-Jin Lee, *Japan Faces China.*
52. See Boyd, "The European Community and China."
53. Ibid.

54. Ibid.
55. For a discussion of the scope for Soviet involvement, see Donald Zagoria, "Into the Breach: New Soviet Alliances in the Third World," *Foreign Affairs*, 57 (Spring 1979), 733–54.
56. See review of new directions in China's foreign relations in Chalmers Johnson, "The New Thrust in China's Foreign Policy," *Foreign Affairs*, 57 (Fall 1978), 125–37.
57. See Yahuda, *China's Role in World Affairs;* and Kim, *China, the United Nations, and World Order*.
58. See general comments on groups under pressure by Feit, "Political Groups under Severe Pressure."
59. See Boyd, "The European Community and China."
60. See Kim, *China, the United Nations, and World Order*.
61. Some aspects of the political culture which are related to this style are noted in Jack Gray, "China: Communism and Confucianism," in Archie Brown and Jack Gray, *Political Culture and Political Change in Communist States* (New York: Holmes and Meier, 1977), pp. 197–230.
62. See Boyd, "Sino-Soviet Relations: The Future."
63. Ibid.
64. See discussions of the anti-Soviet outlook in Yahuda, *China's Role in World Affairs* and Kim, *China, the United Nations, and World Order*.
65. See, for example, Huang Hua, "Social-Imperialist Strategy in Asia."
66. See comments on impressions conveyed to the Japanese in Bernard K. Gordon, "Japan, the United States, and Southeast Asia," *Foreign Affairs*, 56 (April 1978), 579–600.
67. See Bernard K. Gordon, "Loose Cannon on a Rolling Deck? Japan's Changing Security Policies," *Orbis*, 22 (Winter 1979), 967–1006.
68. See Boyd, "The European Community and China."
69. See Taylor, *China and Southeast Asia*.
70. See Gordon, both works.
71. The economic and military constraints affecting Chinese policy are discussed in Dwight H. Perkins, "The Constraints on Chinese Policy," in Donald C. Hellmann (ed.), *China and Japan: A New Balance of Power*, (Lexington, Mass.: D. C. Heath, 1976), pp. 159–96.
72. See Boyd, "Sino-Soviet Relations: the Future."
73. See comments on political uncertainties in China in Barnett, *China Policy;* and in Barnds, *China and America*.
74. Barnds, *China and America*.
75. See Boyd, "The European Community and China."
76. See reference to Chinese policy toward the Burmese communist insurgents in Scully and Trager, "Burma 1978."
77. See Zagoria, "Into the Breach."

6

Security Issues in Global Politics

Charles Lockhart

Theoretical Perspectives

In their efforts to bolster their security, statesmen of different nations regularly pursue incompatible objectives in the international arena. The resulting conflicts of interest vary in numerous ways. In some instances each party to a conflict has important interests at stake. In other cases one party may have far more important interests at stake than the other or others and so perceive graver issues in the conflict episode. Additionally, the fashion in which statesmen pursue their interests varies considerably. In some cases each party may bring immense resources such as large military forces, important allies, or embargoes of products crucial for others to the support of the issues it perceives to be at stake. In other instances the application of resources may be more asymmetrical. And it is not unusual for statesmen to be unable to find much in the way of resources which can be brought to bear on specific conflict episodes. The interests the parties perceive to be at issue and the resources they are able to bring to the support of these interests form what can be called the structure of a conflict.

The aspects of conflict structure that are of central concern here are how the interests threatened or opportunities afforded the various parties, as well as the resources which they find usable, create preferences for action. According to Glenn H. Snyder and Paul Diesing it is possible to dichotomize the choices available to each party into general options of escalation and acquiescence.[1] The issues at stake in a particular conflict of interest and/or the resources available for supporting these issues may be such that a party will prefer to stand its ground or if necessary escalate its conflict activity in order to secure its interests. If both parties have such preferences, the structure of the conflict resembles a situation which game theorists call Prisoner's Dilemma. This conflict structure is shown in Figure 6.1. Prisoner's Dilemma has been widely used by conflict theorists throughout the social sciences.[2] It has numerous characteristics which appeal to a variety of concerns. The feature of this matrix which is of most immediate interest here is that neither party will back down with

Figure 6.1.
Prisoner's Dilemma

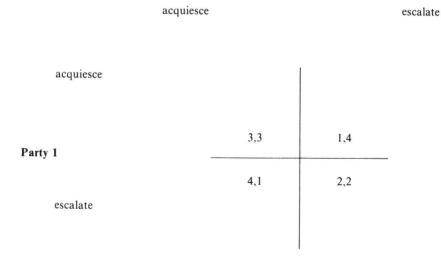

Party 2

acquiesce escalate

acquiesce

	3,3	1,4
Party 1		
	4,1	2,2

escalate

The numbers represent quantities of utility at the ordinal level of measurement. That is, 4 is the most desired outcome and 1 is the least desired outcome. The differences between outcomes— for instance, the difference between 1 and 2 or between 3 and 4—are unknown and are not assumed to be equal.

respect to what it perceives to be the central issues. If either insists on challenging the other on these issues, the other will stand its ground, and the conflict episode will persist and probably escalate.[3]

An alternative structure exists when a party does not perceive sufficiently important interests to be at stake in a conflict and/or does not have resources suitable for this particular instance and so prefers to acquiesce in the face of an adversary who appears willing to escalate. If each party to a conflict has such a preference, the conflict resembles the game of Chicken which is depicted in matrix format in Figure 6.2. In Chicken each party has the reverse preference of that in Prisoner's Dilemma on how to act with respect to the other party's challenge on the central issues in conflict. A party with Chicken preferences will swerve or give ground before an adversary who appears to be committed to winning its way on the contested issues.[4]

It is possible for asymmetries to appear in conflict structures as well. For instance, one party may have the preferences associated with Prisoner's Dilemma, and the other party may have Chicken preferences. These three structures—Prisoner's Dilemma, Chicken, and asymmetrical

Figure 6.2.
Chicken

Party 2

	acquiesce	escalate
acquiesce	3,3	2,4
escalate	4,2	1,1

Party 1

The numbers represent quantities of utility at the ordinal level of measurement.

Prisoner's Dilemma—Chicken—are not the only structures that underlie security issues in contemporary global politics, but they are particularly important in security relations among the great powers.[5]

As Robert Jervis has pointed out, all three conflict structures are found regularly in the relations among adversary nations.[6] Hence an extremely important problem for statesmen is the accurate identification of the structure underlying any particular conflict of interest. By drawing superficial historical analogies or by engaging in other questionable cognitive procedures, statesmen often misperceive the structure of conflict situations confronting them.[7]

Inaccurate identification of the structure of conflicts of interest is a particularly important problem because the various structures call for different strategies. Statesmen who find themselves on the Prisoner's Dilemma side of a Prisoner's Dilemma–Chicken structure can often successfully combine strong coercive pressure with a willingness to allow the adversary procedural concessions in order to soften the blow of defeat on the substantive issues. The statesmen on the Chicken side of this asymmetrical structure can reasonably entertain little more than stalling long enough to prompt some procedural concessions from the adversary before accommodating to his wishes on the substantive issues. Thomas C. Schelling has suggested that the symmetrical Chicken structure is a race to be the first to commit to a noncooperative (escalatory) strategy. Once one party has foreclosed other options, the second party has little choice but to follow the pattern mentioned above for the Chicken party in asymmetrical Prisoner's Dilemma–Chicken.[8] In international politics demonstrating such a commitment is often a lengthy process of bringing more resources to bear on a conflict of interest than the adversary is able or willing to match.

This strategy of protecting threatened interests or realizing new opportunities by bringing superior resources to bear on a conflict of interest will not work for a stable Prisoner's Dilemma structure. In this instance each party is able and willing to struggle for the matters at issue, and a clear-cut victory for one party is simply not possible within this structure.[9] Instead statesmen who find themselves in this situation must follow a different strategy. First, they need to signal their adversary that they will stand firm on the central issues they perceive to be at stake. This will normally require actions more dramatic than verbal statements. That is, actions such as military alerts, troop movements, or even a demonstrated willingness to initiate low-level military violence may be necessary. Second, each party must probe the fringes of the other's commitment to basic issues in the hope of finding small areas of compromise which will allow each party to come away from the conflict episode with its essential interests intact.

To review briefly, different conflict structures exist, and statesmen regularly have some difficulty correctly identifying the structures they face. These problems are extremely important, for various conflict structures require different strategies if they are to be managed and resolved successfully, that is, if particularly costly consequences are to be avoided and if the conflicting interests that separate nations are to be reduced. Another problem arises at this point. Just as statesmen have difficulties identifying the structure of particular conflicts of interest, they also have difficulty applying strategies appropriate for these structures. These latter problems arise from several factors. Incorrect identification of the conflict structure is one. Personal or organizational biases in favor of particular courses of action exacerbate these identification problems. And a nation's strategy may be muddled by compromises among different factions that disagree on the structure of a particular conflict, or that hold different predispositions toward strategy alternatives, or both.

From the perspective of the preceding paragraphs the basic problems facing the great powers in dealing with security issues are: correctly identifying the underlying structures of conflict situations and acting in an appropriate fashion once this identification has been made. These requirements sound simple enough, but meeting them is difficult. The individual signals that pass from one nation to another are often vague, and multiple signals tend to convey conflicting messages. So the "noise level" of international communications is high. Additionally, the differing perspectives from which statesmen interpret these messages hinder identification of the structure of a developing conflict.[10] Further, the biases for action which a statesman has developed over time in other international conflicts or in social arenas, in addition to the conflicting interests and action preferences of the statesman's colleagues, increase the difficulties of choosing a course of action appropriate for a particular structure.[11] Other problems exist as well. A nation's leaders may have an accurate perception of conflict structure but be unable to bring any influence to bear because of a lack of resources. For several years the United States and several other nations were relatively helpless with respect to terrorists who played havoc with commercial aircraft. Only gradually did these nations (whose general power was clearly greater than that of the terrorist groups) develop resources usable in the contingencies that the aircraft hijackers presented.[12]

Still broader problems may plague the perspective on conflicts of interest offered here. This perspective, like all others, presumes certain values, which may not be shared by all contenders. It is a perspective that stems from values of conflict management and resolution. Thus it presumes that statesmen will seek to avoid extensive destruction of lives, property, and national cultures or lifestyles. Although it may be impossible for statesmen to avoid such destruction in some instances, this perspective presumes that statesmen do not elevate values such as global hegemony to a position of higher priority. This perspective is based on a rough balance-of-power notion in which the statesmen of powerful nations are unwilling to pay the price of challenging the general status or national existence of other major powers. If these presuppositions do not accurately characterize the statesmen of an important power, then the security problems of these statesmen (and quite possibly of their adversaries as well) will be different. Another problem is that it may be impossible to resolve even some relatively modest issues without extensive violence. A Prisoner's Dilemma structure, for instance, may involve a severe overlap of interests such that neither party will be satisfied with the concessions the other can make. Several types of activity are associated with this predicament: stalling, gradually lowering expectations, and also the violence of war. This last option may increase the issues at stake for each party, and the conflict may even come to resemble a fight more than a game.[13] That is, the interaction may be based more on emotional criteria than deliberative strategy choices.

The Setting

The setting for contemporary global security issues is in a state of transition, and the changes that are occurring probably increase statesmen's problems in ascertaining the interests at stake in and the resources available for specific instances of conflict. This transition can be seen both in the nature of the issues raising security concerns and in the number of powers involved in global security issues. In terms of military power the setting is still bipolar, and the United States and the Soviet Union are still preeminent. They manifest this distinction in their strategic nuclear arsenals and in their ability to project their power beyond their territorial frontiers into neighboring spheres of influence and even into distant contested regions like the Middle East, Southeast Asia, and Africa. No other nation has an extensive strategic nuclear arsenal, and it is difficult for other states to project their military power beyond their borders unless they have the support of one of the two superpowers. This general inability to use military force beyond national frontiers arises in some instances from an absolute incapacity. Many developing nations and even some small advanced industrial nations simply do not have the economic and military resources to mount external military operations. In other cases the inability stems from the relative power of nations. West Germany, for example, has sufficient economic and military strength to engage in military operations beyond its frontiers. But the surrounding areas of Europe in which the Germans have traditionally been most interested are also of considerable interest to one or the other of the two superpowers, and the asymmetries of military power between West Germany and either of the superpowers are so great as to leave West Germany little opportunity for foreign military operations.

The superpowers have not always been successful in projecting their power abroad. In the recent war in Southeast Asia, for instance, the United States found the advantage of its vastly superior military power effectively countered by two factors. First, the Vietnamese enjoyed the advantage of having more important interests at stake—unifying the homeland. In Alexander George's terms the Vietnamese held a "favorable asymmetry of motivation." [14] Second, this struggle was waged far from the United States in a region that was plausibly of great interest to other regional powers—China—and even the Soviet Union. Under these circumstances United States leaders were interested in using selected and restrained military measures for political purposes. They hoped that restrained use of American military power would avoid provoking other interested parties into joining the conflict. The upper bounds on the United States' use of military force which these considerations erected created a situation in which the United States conducted military operations at a level at which the Vietnamese could effectively compete.

Other caveats to the notion of military bipolarity ought to be mentioned as well. Several regional powers—Israel and Egypt, for example—have found it relatively easy to gain at least short-term support from one of the two superpowers for their own military adventures. This support tends to be unpredictable in scope and duration, however, particularly in regions such as the Middle East in which each superpower has extensive interests which it does not wish to see disrupted by indigenous powers. Also, a small number of regional powers (France is the best example) are able to use limited military force beyond their frontiers under two general conditions. First, the force is used within a sphere of influence that does not attract much attention from the superpowers. And second, this force is used for purposes consistent with the purposes of the dominant interests indigenous to the region. That is, the force is used to stabilize the position of these interests.

The setting for contemporary global security issues extends beyond strictly military concerns. The issues that create conflicts of interest among nations are changing so that threats to economic goals are beginning to eclipse threats to territorial integrity and other traditional security matters. But the issues that generate conflicts of interest among nations are distinct from the various forms of conflict activity, and there is disagreement as to how the transition in issues will have an impact on conflict behavior.

It is possible that conflict activity arising from economic issues will create new security concerns. Economic issues could pose or contribute to global security issues in several ways. Some forms of economic conflict activity associated with international economic issues—embargoes, for example—might place resources for conflict in the hands of statesmen who have not previously enjoyed much in the way of conflict resources. Also, as Klaus Knorr has pointed out, conflict issues and the conflict activity arising from these issues may fall into different issues areas.[15] As economic resources for conflict activity become more broadly recognized, these resources may be used to influence the course of conflict episodes beyond those created by economic issues. The 1973–1974 OAPEC (Organization of Arab Petroleum Exporting Countries) disruption of oil flowing to Western Europe and Japan in an effort to shift policies toward Israel was economic conflict activity, used on a traditional high politics issue.[16] Another way in which economic issues can precipitate conflict activity is by prompting the traditional forms of coercion and military violence associated with high politics in the past. United States warnings that future disruptions of the flow of Arab oil to the West might lead to an invasion of Middle Eastern oil fields are an example of this possibility.[17]

Of course, economic resources are distributed more widely than military resources. The military bipolarity of the global setting and the resulting pattern of cohesion and conflict both dissolve when the point of reference shifts to economic resources. The Soviet Union is much less important economically than it is militarily because its economic base is proportionately smaller and, more importantly, because it is relatively isolated from the economic interaction of the First and Third Worlds. The Soviet Union essentially sits outside the global economy, and the well-publicized North–South conflict of interest is the redistributive struggle between the First and Third Worlds.

The First World has three general elements: the United States, the nations of Western Europe which are more or less organized by the EEC (European Economic Community), and Japan. The Third World is even less organized—a diffuse assortment of states, not yet a collective with significant power. OPEC (Organization of Petroleum Exporting Countries) and particularly OAPEC are clearly sources of economic power which hold implications for security issues. But the rest of the Third World is considerably less influential on such matters.

Resources for conflict activity are distributed asymmetrically between the First World and the Third World. Economic forms of severe conflict behavior are often difficult to organize and maintain as well as costly to implement. In order to pose serious threats to the First World, economic conflict activity by developing nations would have to be backed by more intensive efforts at international organization among these nations and greater domestic cohesion within them than currently appears possible. The OAPEC example of threatening the First World is an unusual circumstance in relations between these two groups of nations, and it is more an instance of vague threats of noncooperation than the use of extreme measures.[18] Frequent threats to the security of the First World do not appear to be likely consequences of the economic conflicts of interest between the First and Third Worlds for some time to come.[19]

This generalization, however, must be qualified because of the proliferation of nuclear weapons. Incredible resources for violence may be acquired by Third World nations, and some of the economic issues between the First and Third Worlds might generate severe conflict if nuclear proliferation provides resources for this activity. The acquisition of such resources, moreover, would raise possibilities for severe conflict on traditional security issues among Third World nations as well, and these might escalate to the global level.

Principal Actors

The preceding analysis suggests a ranking of major actors. The United States and the Soviet Union are still the most important, and essentially these two are adversaries. Each is the most important (perhaps the only important) single security threat to the other. The immediate basis for this danger in each case is the military power, particularly the strategic nuclear arsenals, these nations possess. Their value systems differ in important ways so that the triumph of one's values would mean substantial destruction to the other nation's values. Yet the United States and the Soviet Union have the crucial common interest of survival. Each is currently vulnerable to extensive destruction by the other. This predicament creates strong pressures for mutual understandings on a variety of security issues (peaceful co-existence) and some pressures for better relations generally (détente).

Western Europe (a *loosely* integrated collective on security issues) and Japan do not play active independent roles in the Soviet–American strategic rivalry. In essence both of these actors fall under the protection of the United States. This has become an increasingly difficult position for both Western Europe and Japan. The ability of the United States to deter Soviet attacks on the interests of these actors has declined as U.S. vulnerability to Soviet strategic forces has grown; the U.S. ability actively to defend the interests of these actors should a Soviet attack occur has declined as well. As the deterrence and defense value of these actors' relations with the United States has declined, both Western Europe and Japan have developed important rifts with the United States on security and other matters. These rifts have prompted desires for increasing autonomy in both Western Europe and Japan. Such desires have contributed to the expansion of the EEC (particularly British membership therein), West Germany's *Ostpolitik,* and Japan's increased ties with China and the Soviet Union. Yet on security matters relating to the Soviet Union there is not much scope for autonomy for either Western Europe or Japan. Both have differed from the United States on policies toward conflicts in regions contested by the United States and the Soviet Union, like the Middle East, and both are more concerned than the United States with deterring Soviet threats than defending against them, because active defense means general destruction for Japan and most of Western Europe. But on fundamental questions, such as their territorial integrity, neither Western Europe or Japan currently has any choice but to rely on the United States.

Western Europe and Japan have greater autonomy with respect to the security aspects of North–South economic issues. While the United States has the largest economy in the world, both Western Europe, particularly West Germany, and Japan have had extensive success in foreign markets. The larger United States economy is a domestic market to a far greater degree than are the individual economies of Western European nations and Japan, so these latter actors command greater influence on the global market than the size of their economies alone would suggest. Also both Western Europe and Japan are more dependent on developing nations for raw materials than is the United States, and this creates different interests.

On North–South economic issues the First World does not generally speak with a single voice. The only North–South issues which have to date raised immediate security problems for the First World have been the price and availability of oil. Yet the resulting interaction has been a standoff of mutual dependency, not a viable threat for either the First or the Third World participants. Severe conflict activity with respect to the oil producers even in the face of an embargo would be both dangerous and futile. Western violence in the Middle East would invite Soviet involvement and offer little likelihood of quickly turning on the oil spigot. For the oil producers dramatic tactics such as embargoes which would severely disrupt Western economies would have clear drawbacks. Western Europe provides most of the OAPEC oil revenues and offers the major investment opportunities for these revenues. Less severe disruptions of the flow of oil would still disturb profits for the producers, and whereas Saudi Arabia could surmount this problem easily, Iraq and other producers could not. Severe actions hold heavy costs for the sponsoring nations, and the oil producers would probably prefer to implement potentially drastic policies in a mild fashion as in 1973–1974 and leave escalation to the imagination of Western leaders. Additionally, OPEC and OAPEC and the power they wield are relatively unstable in comparison to the structure and the influence of the national actors considered in this section; it is difficult to predict whether these collectives will weather their internal strains over the long term.

Two final entries in this listing of major actors are regional powers.

These nations are important for global security issues because of the pressures their independent activities create for the superpowers. A large number of nations are relevant candidates for such a listing. One example is Israel, which probably has the capacity to bring the Soviet Union and the United States into military conflict. As an important power in a region in which the United States and the Soviet Union contest each other's influence, Israel can set in motion a chain of events which could culminate in a Soviet–American confrontation. China represents another sort of problem. The Soviet Union, in contrast to the United States, has a long land frontier lined with traditional adversaries—several European nations, Turkey, Iran, various nations in South Asia, and China. China is the most important single member of this group and raises for the Soviets the problem of a second front (in addition to Europe). This front contributes to global security issues in the following manner. In preparing for threats posed by the United States, the Western Europeans, and China (plus other lesser parties like Japan and Pakistan), Soviet security planners are apt to acquire theater forces and perhaps strategic nuclear forces that look extremely large to the United States and that cause its planners to suggest increasing its military strength. In other words the range of adversaries the Soviet Union faces creates pressures in Soviet-American arms competition.

Inputs

Characteristically for an anarchical milieu, the demands which each of the actors discussed above makes on the others sometimes surpass the level of supports they provide for anything which might be reasonably referred to as an international system of common diplomatic values and practices. Across these global actors the only clear basis for shared values arises from the fact that all are dependent in one fashion or another on others for their survival. This is an important system support or "glue," but the sort of cooperation that is apt to arise from this source alone has distinct limitations.[20]

For many years the most fundamental system glue has been the interest of the Soviet Union and the United States in avoiding mutual destruction. This has deterred each superpower from provoking the other either directly or through regional powers. The deterrent value of mutual destruction, however, has not been sufficient to prevent all provocation. Other interests have dominated in some situations. For the first two decades after World War II the German question was of sufficient interest to both superpowers to generate confrontations over Berlin.[21] The superpowers also clashed over the Soviet deployment of strategic nuclear weapons in Cuba in 1962, although this was probably unexpected by each party.[22] In all of these episodes (and in other less direct clashes[23]) each of the superpowers was sufficiently concerned about escalation to exercise considerable restraint.

Clashes of regional powers with ties to the superpowers have raised the possibility of a confrontation in the central balance. This danger was evident during the Middle East crises 1956, 1967, and 1973. In these situations there were growing dangers of superpower involvement, although each superpower was willing to act abruptly and forcefully to curb dependent regional states and thus avoid escalation.[24]

Other regional powers have viewed with increasing suspicion the Soviet-American domination of forums such as the SALT (Strategic Arms Limitation Talks) and to a lesser degree MBFR (Mutual Balanced Force Reductions). The West Europeans and the Chinese show concern that the discussions and occasional agreements of these forums neglect their interests while furthering those of the superpowers in the short run. In Western Europe there is concern to ensure that the United States will maintain a strategic posture to deter the expansion of Soviet influence in Europe. The United States and the Western European nations have reverse preferences on the content of the signal that the U.S. force posture sends to the Soviets. For Washington it is crucial that, if deterrence fails, the resulting active defense of interests along the European front be as limited as possible, especially to avoid expansion of the conflict to United States territory. For the nations of Western Europe it is absolutely essential that the Soviets see extensive damage of their homeland (damage apt to lead to extensive damage of the United States) as the immediate payoff for severely challenging the security of Western Europe.[25] The Western Europeans focus on deterrence since, for much of Western Europe, active defense means destruction. The military weakness of the Western European nations (individually or collectively) in comparison to either the Soviet Union or the United States leaves these nations unable to put together the deterrent force their needs demand. And it has also been politically impossible for the United States adequately to separate the European and North American theaters. The United States problem stems both from Western European resistance to such a separation and from the fact that the United States wishes to deter aggressive Soviet actions toward Western Europe as fervently as do the Western Europeans. The difference between the United States' and West European perspectives lies in desirable courses of action if deterrence fails. A strategy optimal both for linking the destruction of the Soviet homeland to Soviet aggression in Western Europe (as the Europeans wish) and for fighting a struggle limited to the non-Soviet portion of the European theater if Soviet aggression occurs (as the Americans wish) is difficult to devise and implement.

China's situation is different from that of Western Europe. China is not allied with a superpower. Nor does China yet possess the sort of limited nuclear threat that France and Great Britan do or the sophisticated conventional forces that France and West Germany have. While China could fight an impressive defensive action against any nation that violated its territory, for the moment it has little hope of projecting its power beyond its frontiers against highly mobile, heavily armed Soviet forces backed with theater and strategic nuclear weapons. This situation can change, but slowly, and until significant change does occur, China is likely to desire sufficiently good relations with both Western Europe and the United States so as to create some Soviet doubts about the consequences of Soviet attacks on Chinese interests, and to acquire sophisticated military equipment. But these relations are a matter of convenience for all concerned. The security of each party, particularly China, may be furthered by good relations. But it seems unlikely that a bond based on common values will develop between either of these parties and China.

Japan's concerns are focused on the credibility of the United States' deterrent even more than Western Europe's, and with little comfort. Tokyo's options are even more modest than Western Europe's, for there can be no pooling of resources with others in a similar predicament. There are no others. And given the caliber of the competition, it is unclear what security purpose Japan would serve by expanding its small national defense force. Japan cannot hope to match the Soviet Union, and whereas China's nuclear arsenal might be equaled after a period of years, Japan will continue to be more vulnerable to nuclear weapons than China. Its small size and highly concentrated population and industry make deterrence the most desirable choice for Japan. Yet deterrence may be beyond reach. Japan faces an unpromising array of security choices. The current response—working to improve relations with China and the Soviet Union —appears eminently reasonable under the circumstances. If Japan cannot deter or defend itself from its enemies, it must try to live in greater harmony with these powers.

From the Third World regions, then, two types of inputs affect global security issues. Both come disproportionately from the most prosperous developing nations. One is the threat of withholding raw materials necessary for the economic prosperity or military activities of others. Although this matter has not been studied so thoroughly as to leave no room for surprises, it appears reasonably safe to say that the probability of important global security issues arising from this source is low. Cartel action aimed at raising prices may have some chance for success for several products, but oil would appear to be the only one for which the control of distribution might be used as a political weapon. And, as was discussed above, this use is highly dangerous for all concerned and is apt to be limited to vague threats which deter undesirable initiatives by the major oil consumers as opposed to specific actions which would impose severe costs on Western Europe or Japan.

A second possibility is the threat of nuclear proliferation. The gravest danger here comes from the so-called pariah states—South Africa, Israel, Taiwan, and a few others. These nations share the characteristic of being outcasts in the sense of not fitting well in their immediate surroundings. All in fact face neighboring states that desire their destruction. Fifteen years ago when U.S. actions resembled those of a global policeman, most of these outcast nations had little to fear. Now that the United States has "retreated from empire,"[26] these nations—in a fashion similar to Japan —must fend for themselves. And for some of them nuclear weapons are both plausible and possible. Many Americans found the global policeman role undesirable at least in part because it led to the support of nations notorious for civil rights violations. Many of these same people are upset, understandably so, by the prospects of nuclear proliferation. But in all likelihood the United States cannot avoid one of these two possibilities. The most basic interests of the outcast states are severely threatened. These states have resources to bring to the support of their interests. And regardless of what others think of the values on which these interests rest, these nations will do whatever they can and need to do in order to defend their interests. In the absence of credible U.S. support, some of these nations will turn to nuclear weapons.

Nuclear proliferation is not limited to international outcasts. It is possible that other Third World nations will follow the example of India and acquire nuclear weapons for a variety of reasons including deterrence of regional adversaries and prestige. But neither the threat to national security nor the ability to produce nuclear weapons is so pronounced among Third World nations generally as among the outcasts.

Issues

The most fundamental issue raised by the actors discussed in this chapter is the degree to which mutual interdependence (due largely to the vulnerability of each actor's interests to the actions of others) will make for deterrence. The Soviet-American strategic balance is the most important factor lying behind this issue. For roughly the first decade and a half of the nuclear era, the strategic nuclear arsenals of both the United States and the Soviet Union were relatively small and vulnerable to attack. During this period the United States held a numerical advantage over the Soviet Union in terms of nuclear weapons and delivery systems. This advantage continued through much of the 1960s although for two reasons any strategic benefit associated with it was reduced. First, both the Soviet and the American arsenals grew so that the damage each could wreak on the other increased. Second and more importantly, each superpower began to rely on delivery systems which were invulnerable to attack— SLBMs (Submarine-Launched Ballistic Missiles) and hardened land-based ICBMs (Intercontinental Ballistic Missiles). For several years the United States enjoyed a lead in invulnerable strategic nuclear weapons. But by the early 1970s the two superpowers had large (roughly 2,000 delivery systems), reasonably well-protected arsenals of roughly equivalent size.

In the United States the manner in which nuclear weapons evolved in the 1960s led to a curious but in some ways reassuring conception of the developing nuclear balance. Since each superpower was acquiring large invulnerable strategic nuclear arsenals, the notion arose that these weapons served essentially a deterrent purpose. As long as each superpower possessed strategic nuclear weapons in large numbers, these held few possibilities for the acquisition or defense of values such as population, industry, or territory. The existing weapons were both too indiscriminate and too inadequate for use against the other side's strategic nuclear weapons, and mutual possession meant that the use of these weapons by one superpower on the other would prompt similarly destructive reprisals.

The reassuring aspect of the nuclear balance which evolved in the 1960s was that neither party had any clear incentive to provoke the other. By threatening interests of the other, the provoking party risked its own destruction, and no discernible advantage went to the party that struck first. This situation came to be referred to as MAD (mutual assured destruction). In spite of a great deal of discussion to the contrary, this situation continues to characterize the balance in strategic nuclear weaponry in the 1980s. Each superpower can wreak virtually unimaginable destruction on the adversary's population and industry, and neither can defend these values from the other.

The curious and less reassuring aspect of this conception lies in the vulnerability of each party to the other's weapons. The cities (people and industry) of each superpower are essentially hostages for their government's good behavior.[27] This situation was not planned; it arose as an unforeseen consequence of the weapons which began to be developed in the late 1950s. Nevertheless, once the situation was recognized in the United States, its preservation was adopted as national policy.[28] MAD was thought by many to represent a stable relationship of balance between the United States and the Soviet Union.[29] The adoption of MAD as policy was challenged by some who felt it represented an abdication of national responsibility. A government, so these critics felt, had an obligation to defend its population, not to ensure the vulnerability of its people to the adversary's weapons.[30] Critics of the MAD doctrine urged defensive efforts—ABMs (Anti-Ballistic Missiles) and civil defense activities. The major virtue of this argument lay in the fact that the programs and weapons required for deterrence and defense were clearly distinguishable. Here lay an opportunity to reduce the security dilemma faced by the superpowers.[31] If each were armed almost exclusively with ABMs (and subsequently more effective defensive weapons) and prepared in terms of civil defense, then each would signal defensive intentions clearly to the other.[32]

For better or worse, the merits of a defensive force posture never led to serious questioning of MAD within the United States, and the question of a defensive force posture was never raised in an important fashion in Soviet-American relations. What did begin to supersede MAD was a far more ominous set of developments. In the last few years the invulnerability of each superpower's strategic nuclear arsenal has come into question. The threat is not immediate, but it is coming. Highly accurate ICBMs armed with maneuverable or MIRV warheads may soon be capable of destroying hardened but stationary land-based ICBMs. And at least on the United States side vastly improved ASW (antisubmarine warfare) devices offer the possibility of locating individual submarines in the open sea. What these developments raise as an alternative to MAD is not a defensive but an offensive posture. Each side is developing counterforce weapons capable of destroying the other's strategic nuclear weapons. As these counterforce weapons begin to replace the countervalue (cities) weapons that have dominated in the past, the superpowers will move into a much more dangerous world. These new strategic nuclear weapons will have a clear offensive capability and a much less prominent deterrent value. There may be an immense premium associated with striking first, for the first strike may destroy a considerable proportion of the adversary's ability to strike back.

So in the span of a decade strategic relations between the superpowers have moved from a situation in which nuclear weapons offered some practical possibilities for a relatively secure world to a situation of competition in offensive weapons appropriate for first strikes. Under these circumstances it is hard to imagine that the Soviet Union and the United States will be as restrained toward each other as they have been in the past. Until the 1970s the United States, a relatively satisfied power that reacted only to what its leaders perceived as the threatening initiatives of others, held a strategic advantage over the Soviets. And both powers were strategically armed in a fashion that stressed deterrence of provocation to the virtual exclusion of alternative uses. Now a rough strategic parity characterizes the relations of the two powers, and this alone may lead to reduced restraint on the part of Soviet leaders who are probably less satisfied with their current position in the world than American leaders of the 1950s. Further, the offensive potential of the superpowers' strategic nuclear arsenals is growing, and this development offers increased resources for aggressive action.

The reduction of structural incentives for restraint in Soviet-American relations may have several effects. One superpower may directly challenge the other, although this course of action would still involve high risk and costs. A more plausible possibility is that a Soviet-American confrontation would grow out of the escalation of a regional security issue. Ironically, United States policy makers began to look for alternatives to MAD because of MAD's inability to manage precisely this possibility. Two broad types of regional problems appear to offer particularly likely opportunities for escalation of this kind. First, in regions in which the superpowers contest each other's influence, a conflict among regional states associated with each of the superpowers could escalate. The Middle East is the best example of such a region, but in the future portions of Africa and perhaps even other areas might offer conflicts of this nature. Second, in areas which the superpowers do not strongly influence, regional powers may initiate events that eventually generate repercussions for global security. The predicament of China or Japan as well as that of some of the outcast nations discussed in the previous section may create these conditions. By dramatically building its resources for conflict activity and/or by acting in a provocative fashion toward a regional rival, one of these nations could create a situation to which one and then the other superpower would respond.

In summary, the crucial issues for global security run roughly as follows. First, there are issues relating to the weaponry, particularly the strategic nuclear weaponry, of the superpowers. Choices about this weaponry set a context in which all other matters transpire. Ominously, these choices have for several years created more extensive resources for offensive action on the part of the superpowers. Second, there are issues relating to the actions of the superpowers in contested regions such as Europe and the Middle East as well as the actions of regional powers in areas in which the influence of the superpowers is modest. The first set of issues contributes importantly to the resources ultimately available for conflicts in these various regions, although the global naval and theater forces of the superpowers are relevant to this matter as well. Regional powers have independent interests in these conflicts, however, and they may use their resources to create strong pressures for superpower involvement in contested regions. But concerns for global security also arise from regions in which the superpowers have been less intimately involved. The attention which the superpowers devote to contested regions such as Europe and the Middle East gives some stability to local conflicts inasmuch as the U.S.S.R. and the United States have less consuming interests in these than the indigenous powers and frequently restrain them. But in areas in which the influence of the superpowers is much weaker, their restraining efforts have less effect on the regional states, which may initiate conflict episodes that will eventually draw them in as active participants.

Interaction

Soviet-United States weaponry, particularly but not exclusively strategic nuclear weaponry, appears to be a major factor determining outcomes on other global security matters. This weaponry determines in large measure the resources ultimately available for conflict activity on issues of global security. Discussions between these two powers on strategic nuclear weapons (SALT) or on theater forces (MBFR) then assume great importance. These discussions have the potential of reducing the danger of ruinous consequences arising from several conflicts of interest around the globe. Unfortunately this potential is extremely difficult to achieve. Many factors contribute to this difficulty and not all can be discussed here. However, the theoretical perspective introduced in the first section of this chapter suggests some on which this discussion will focus.

These factors are the perceived structure of the conflict of interest and the perceived utility of varying approaches for managing conflicts with this structure. The underlying structure of Soviet-American armament competition may be the Security Dilemma shown in Figure 6.3. That is, Security Dilemma may offer an accurate description of the "objective situation." Each party's interest may be best served by cooperating with the other and reducing the level of danger which the current arsenals create. It is well recognized, for example, that both the United States and the Soviet Union have become less secure through their mutual development of strategic nuclear weapons over the last thirty-five years. In an objective sense security at this point in time may be served by arms control not arms acquisition. But reasonable as this argument may appear, it has not been generally persuasive today or in previous national rivalries. In part, the practical political problems arise from domestic politics in the form of chauvinistic publics and military bureaucracies interested in weapons. But problems related to international relations plague this position as well.

While in their enthusiasm for particular weapons military bureaucracies may begin to see these weapons as objectives in themselves, for political leaders arms usually represent resources which may be useful to obtain national objectives through conflict. Thus, while a disarmed Europe might have been a safer environment for Bismarck's Prussia than an armed Europe, it would probably have been impossible to create Ger-

Figure 6.3.
Security Dilemma (Stag Hunt)

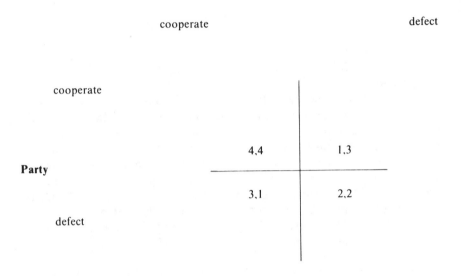

The numbers represent quantities of utility at the ordinal level of measurement.

many without superior arms. And the statesman who recognizes that he may occasionally require arms in order to secure values may reasonably wonder about the arms of his adversary. While the adversary's intentions are rarely known, it is common and to a degree prudent to be suspicious.[33] If Adversary in Figure 6.3 really prefers certain objectives to peaceful cooperation (interchange Adversary's 3 and 4), then Party's cooperation will lead to Adversary's defection. The general point here is that statesmen do sometimes value specific acquisitions more than cooperation with others. This preference is particularly common on the security issues of high politics and gives statesmen reasons for not acting on the basis of Security Dilemma as the structure underlying issues such as arms competition. The fear that others want to use their resources for conflict and will undermine cooperative agreements secretly in order to obtain advantages on issues of particular importance is bolstered by the statesman's knowledge that he himself is tempted.[34]

The Prisoner's Dilemma (Figure 6.1) offers a more realistic operational structure of arms competition. Each party continues to acquire arms because of domestic bureaucratic and popular pressures, fears of the adversary's intentions, and hopes for building resources useful for protecting or acquiring other interests. This leaves the parties in the lower right-hand corner of the matrix.

While these perceptions of conflict structure help to explain why arms control is so difficult, they are less helpful in explaining why the United States and the Soviet Union both have chosen to move away from a deterrence force posture in the direction of offensive rather than defensive weaponry. For either superpower to successfully adopt a defensive force posture would require considerably greater cooperation and mutual restraint in armaments than the underlying structure of Prisoner's Dilemma suggests is likely. But other factors are at work here as well. For one, United States leaders did not foresee all of the consequences of developing counterforce weapons. Also, the existing state of technology did not offer defensive weapons capable of effectively handling a broad range of contingencies. And some bureaucratic interests would have been damaged by a shift to a defensive posture. (An emphasis on ABMs would have shifted strategic weapons programs from the air force and the navy to the army.[35]) On the Soviet side it is unclear that deterrence (MAD) was ever accepted as a policy as opposed to a predicament in which the Soviets found themselves. And in all likelihood the Soviets were even less able technologically to manage the defensive option than was the United States.

The most obvious conflicts of interest for which Soviet-American arms competition provides resources are the regional rivalries in Europe and the Middle East. From the standpoint of superpower relations the structure of these conflicts depends in part on the importance of the immediate interests at stake and in part on the precedent which any individual conflict episode is apt to set for the future. Conflict episodes that lead to modest changes in the status quo of a region, if considered as isolated instances, are Chicken structures for both superpowers. Neither the Soviet Union nor the United States has so much to lose from slight modifications of the status quo that it will risk escalation likely to precipitate a holocaust. But actions in particular conflict episodes are watched carefully by other powers and can rarely be entirely uncoupled from general action predilections for this audience. The present adversary and perhaps other potential future adversaries as well will draw conclusions about a party's likely actions from its behavior in the current conflict.[36] So each conflict episode creates some pressures to develop an image for hard bargaining.[37] In some instances long-range concerns may be sufficiently weighty to nudge a party from Chicken to Prisoner's Dilemma preferences.[38]

From the standpoint of the regional powers the immediate issues at stake in these regional rivalries are much more likely to create Prisoner's Dilemma preferences. The Negev or the Golon Heights (or Lübeck or

Eisenach) are unimportant to the United States or the Soviet Union. Their significance arises largely from what their gain or loss might signal about the future. For Israel or Syria (or for West or East Germany) these are important matters which merit strong escalatory responses.

In such instances the problem from the standpoint of global security can be represented by the matrix in Figure 6.4.[39] Protector is an alliance rather than an adversary structure. It represents a situation in which the stronger or global ally (protector) has a dominant strategy of not supporting the option preferred by the regional or weaker ally. This option is an attack on the interests of the weaker ally's regional adversary. Instead, protector wishes to restrain its regional ally so as not to pay the price for objectives of peculiar significance to that ally. The United States applied strong restraints on Israeli policy in 1973 when Israeli zeal to destroy the Egyptian army threatened a cease-fire the United States had worked out with Soviet help.[40] And the United States was unwilling to support West German objectives in the conflict episode over the Berlin Wall in 1961. The essence of Protector is that the global ally does not perceive sufficient interest at stake in the objectives of the regional ally to support these aims

Figure 6.4.
Protector

Regional Ally

	Exercise restraint with respect to regional adversary	Attack regional adversary's interests
Global Ally — Support regional ally's attack on its adversary's interests	1,2	2,4
Restrain regional ally's attack on its adversary but defend regional ally from its adversary	4,3	3,1

The numbers represent quantities of utility at the ordinal level of measurement.

with resources. The global ally has Chicken preferences with respect to the regional ally's adversaries at least for the regional ally's most ambitious objectives. The regional ally is in some respects deficient in the resources necessary to support the interests it perceives to be at stake in the conflict, so it has to compromise these interests, accepting the stable solution in the lower left-hand corner of the matrix.

If the issues are considerably more important to the global ally or if the regional ally is more capable of independent action, a different series of structures may be relevant. This situation can be viewed as a Prisoner's Dilemma structure with protector and its regional ally collapsed to form one party and the regional ally's adversaries forming the other party. The alliance aspects of this situation may differ from Protector. One possible variation appears in the Leader matrix in Figure 6.5. The logic of this structure is that if one party leads the other follows. In this sense Leader is, like Chicken, a commitment game. But as in Protector the desired outcomes are discrete points with no intervening compromise zone. (The payoffs in the upper left-hand corner rank below those in the off-diagonal positions.) In 1973 the Israelis were extremely anxious to take advantage of an opportunity to surround and destroy a portion of the Egyptian army.

Figure 6.5.
Leader

Regional Ally

	Compromise with global ally on strategy toward adversary	Follow own preferences with respect to adversary
Compromise with regional ally on strategy toward adversary	2,2	3,4
Global Ally		
Follow own preferences with respect to adversary	4,3	1,1

The numbers represent quantities of utility at the ordinal level of measurement.

The United States wanted to keep the Soviet Union out of the military conflict, and the Israeli actions jeopardized this concern. No meaningful mutual compromise existed between these positions. The Israelis were not willing to take the risks they would face if they attempted partial destruction of the Egyptian forces, and the United States was not willing to settle for low-level Soviet military involvement. Such situations raise strong pressures within alliances. If either of the members of the alliance needs the other more than it needs the objectives sought from the adversary, an off-diagonal solution will prevail. However, if the differences between 4 and 3 are great for each party or if the two parties communicate poorly, they may fall into the lower right-hand corner of the matrix as a result of multiple attempts to lead. The disparate reactions of the Western oil-consuming nations to the OAPEC oil production showdown of 1973–1974 and the multiple reactions of the First World to Third World demands for a new international economic order represent examples of this possibility. Retrospectively, it is relatively easy to find similarities between these conflict structures and empirical examples of the recent past.[41] The problem for statesmen is to recognize these structures as they unfold and this is much more difficult.[42]

The central issue with respect to strategic nuclear weapons is whether each superpower will continue to perceive strategic nuclear war as so undesirable that the possibility of such an exchange will continue to deter any actions by it which might provoke the other. It is possible, although it does not appear particularly likely, that the development of counterforce weapons will lead to one superpower initiating a general nuclear war. Through complete surprise and extremely effective counterforce weapons, one superpower could reduce to a tolerable level the damage it would suffer as the other struck back with what it had left following a surprise attack. Or it might be possible to deter this reactive strike altogether by maintaining countervalue weapons in reserve and thereby holding the other's cities hostage. Effective counterforce weapons provide resources for action in what has been a stalemate. In a structural sense they produce a situation in which, in terms of purely military values (population, industry, and territory), it might be possible to win a strategic nuclear war through a preemptive strike. The stalemate can be viewed as a Prisoner's Dilemma structure in which the upper left-hand corner of the matrix represents nonviolent relations between the two parties. For the purposes of this scenario payoffs 1 and 2 are extremely low (highly negative) although distinctively different. Surprise and effective counterforce weapons raise the values of these two payoffs and may increase them disproportionately so as to reverse their positions in the matrix. If this reversal occurs, strategic nuclear war becomes a Chicken structure with an extraordinary premium for a preemptive strike.

These thoughts are highly speculative. It might be imprudent to ignore them, but it would be equally imprudent to casually accept that statesmen will perceive strategic nuclear war in these terms.

Much more plausible scenarios arise from conflicts among regional powers. The superpowers might get involved in these conflicts at a low level and gradually find their action escalating toward strategic nuclear war. At a low level of escalation the alliance aspects of these conflicts represent Protector structures from the standpoint of the superpowers. Neither the United States nor the Soviet Union is going to risk nuclear war over portions of the Negev or the Sinai. The major cognitive problem at this stage is apt to be one of the regional ally misperceiving the structure as Leader. The regional powers may lead under these circumstances and then find that they have to abandon their efforts with heavy costs as the British and the French did in 1956 over Suez because the global ally did not follow. In Protector the global ally has a dominant strategy of not following the regional power in the pursuit of the latter's ambitious objectives.

As the stakes increase at higher levels of escalation, however, problems may be shifted to the global ally. Whereas the United States is relatively indifferent to the status of a portion of the Negev, the existence of Israel is another matter. This latter issue is important both in terms of the immediate value attached to Israel for a variety of reasons within the American polity and in terms of the precedent which might well be set if the United States were to sit by while Israel was destroyed. These stakes raise a Prisoner's Dilemma situation between the United States and the forces that are (hypothetically) destroying Israel. And the alliance structure associated with Prisoner's Dilemma adversary relations may be Leader not Protector. By the time escalation has engaged sufficient United States interests to prompt these structures, Israel will have already led. And the United States at this point will be under strong pressure to follow—that is, to coordinate its strategy with Israel's and join the fray.

In a situation like this the increased resources for offensive action which the superpowers have recently acquired appear particularly ominous. And Israel is not the only possible example of this dynamic although it is highly relevant. The points at which one structure fades into another (Prisoner's Dilemma into Chicken and vice versa or Leader into Protector and vice versa) are vague. It is difficult for statesmen to estimate accurately the structure which specific contingencies raise in others' perceptions.

Japan and China offer examples of related although distinct problems. The related aspects are in the underlying structures, and the distinctions appear in the sequence of events through which these structures arise. As Japan and China begin to act with greater autonomy, they may gradually acquire the resources to reinforce this autonomy. If so, they will become less amenable to the pressures which the superpowers could bring to bear in the 1950s, for instance, to restrain nations such as Taiwan. Under these circumstances it would be possible for Japan or China to become engaged in a conflict that would expand to threaten the interests of the superpowers. And the options for the superpowers would be either to stand aside from ally or adversary roles and witness the destruction of these interests or to follow the lesser power's lead. Here the preliminary games of Chicken and Protector are absent because of the more autonomous relations and the increased resources of the regional actors. It might be possible for the superpowers to introduce this preliminary structure into their relations with some regional powers, but this introduction would be difficult.

For the Soviet Union the introduction would in all likelihood evoke severe challenges from the United States which would fear the growth of Soviet spheres of influence. While the United States would share this problem in some instances, in other cases the United States would essentially be revitalizing a protector relationship. Several problems characterize this possibility too, however. First, the United States would have to have the domestic will to do so. And the recent heavy costs associated with trying to act as protector for a variety of nations (some not particularly emulative of U.S. political values) have sapped this will. Second, the commitment of the United States would have to be credible to these regional powers—Japan, for instance. Japan would have to be convinced that the United States would come to its defense with nuclear weapons if necessary. Since action in this manner would probably mean that the United States would confront a nuclear adversary, it is hard to imagine that such a commitment can be made credible. Third, the United States would have to make this same commitment credible to powers that might threaten Japanese interests. This task might be easier than persuading the Japanese. It is probably easier to deter a nation from attempting to achieve objectives which carry some risk of heavy losses than it is to assure a nation faced with prospective attacks on its interests that the intentions of the deterring party are invariant regardless of the costs. Given strategic nuclear parity and the growing counterforce capabilities of the superpowers, making such a commitment credible to potential adversaries would not be easy.

Outputs

The interactions between nations on the issues discussed in the preceding section usually do not resolve the underlying problems. Particular conflict episodes may be resolved. That is, a crisis or a particularly vivid manifestation of the underlying issues may be overcome. Nevertheless, the basic questions which give rise to these crises often remain virtually untouched. The difficulties vary because the nature of the issues varies. Four characteristics will be isolated for examination here: issue complexity, divergence of perspective, degree of conflict of interest, and issue urgency.

Many global security issues may be divided into two groups on the basis of these four characteristics. One group tends to display lower levels of issue complexity, lower intranational divergence of perspective, higher conflicts of interest, and higher issue urgency than are found in the other group. Issues in the second group then have relatively higher levels of issue complexity, higher intranational divergence of perspective, lower conflicts of interest, and lower issue urgency. The problems of resolving these two different types of issues have been treated in separate literatures.[43] Briefly, theorists who deal with issues in the first group conceive of resolving these issues through bargaining. In George's terms the basic problem these issues present is developing strategies with a combination of stick (coercion) and carrot (accommodation) appropriate for resolving the conflict of interest. In contrast, issues in the second group are conceived in large measure as management problems. Here problem-oriented search and organizational learning are emphasized over coercion and accommodation. This is not to say that issues in the first group entail no search or organizational learning or that coercion and accommodation are irrelevant to issues in the second group. But analysts of these two groups of issues draw disproportionately on coercion-accommodation and management processes respectively.

Examples of global security issues falling into each of these two groups will be examined below in terms of the characteristic problems of resolving the conflict of interest. It would be reasonable to label all of the issues discussed in this essay as complex. But some are more complex than others. For example, the problem that separates the Israelis and their various Arab adversaries is basically whose authority is legitimate on what territory. The bases for the competing claims are certainly complex. But the issues are relatively straightforward. Everyone knows what they are, and the problem is what to do about them. In contrast, the issues entailed in the Soviet-American strategic weapons competition exhibit two forms of complexity that are less pronounced in the issues of the Arab–Israeli conflict. First, the arms competition issues require the application of a great deal of technological expertise. The intelligent and interested layman can understand the issues in the Arab–Israeli conflict. But important, perhaps not central, aspects of the Soviet-American arms competition require technological, military, and other expertise. This makes statesmen (who tend for these purposes to be intelligent, interested laymen) dependent on what John Kenneth Galbraith calls a technostructure for some decisions.[44] Second, Soviet-American arms control efforts regularly break new ground for which there is no expertise. That is, some of the consequences of developing particular weapons are unforeseen. Neither the United States nor the Soviet Union planned to develop a situation of mutual assured destruction. Rather this predicament arose as an unforeseen consequence of the strategic nuclear weaponry produced during the late 1950s and 1960s.

The second characteristic on which global security issues differ is the divergence of intranational perspectives. Each national party in the Arab–Israeli conflict perceives different issues. The Palestinians see the occupation of their territory by outsiders. Third-generation Israelis see their homeland attacked by outside aggressors. The Egyptians, Jordanians, and Syrians see still other facets of the central problem. By virtue of perceiving different aspects of the problem, these parties see different issues. The issue for the Israelis is long-term security. For the Palestinians the issue is acquiring a satisfactory homeland. Thus these parties often talk at rather than to each other when they interact over their problems. Certainly none of these national parties is so monolithic that no intranational differences in perspective appear. However, the political importance of intranational differences is generally modest in comparison to the international differences in perspective.

Soviet-American arms control issues also illustrate different international perceptions. For instance, the SALT I agreement was widely heralded in the United States as evidence that the Soviets accepted MAD.[45] This interpretation has since been challenged.[46] Conflicting evidence exists on this point, but it is not implausible to suggest that differences in historical experience between the United States and the Soviet Union focus the attention of Soviet leaders on defending population, industry, and territory to a degree that would make MAD considerably less palatable to Soviet leaders than it was to their American counterparts. Not only do differences in national perspectives appear in these issues, but important intranational differences appear as well. ACDA (Arms Control and Disarmament Agency) rarely sees the face of an issue that the air force sees.[47] There are numerous matters related to arms control issues on which the divergence of perspective within nations rivals the importance of the divergence between nations. Clearly, for instance, there was greater agreement between the United States and the Soviet Union on the usefulness of ABMs in 1972 than there was within the United States.

Global security issues also vary in the degree to which the interests of the parties conflict. It is not unusual for statesmen to have difficulty recognizing and seeking opportunities for integrative solutions which benefit each party.[48] But some conflicts of interest present greater difficulties for these processes than others. The Arab–Israeli conflict, for instance, is often discussed in terms that are close to constant-sum. On the one hand Israel is expected to return the territories taken in 1967 as well as make some sort of dispensation to the Palestinians. On the other hand the Arab nations and the Palestinians are expected to act peacefully toward Israel in the future. The Israeli leaders recognize all too well that the concrete benefits are all flowing one way. Once the territories are given back, they would be difficult to retake, and they serve to improve the military position of Israel's current adversaries. But promises of peace can be made and then broken quite easily.

In contrast, the SALT I agreement did not threaten either of the superpowers as thoroughly as the quid pro quo which is expected of Israel. The SALT I agreement in fact demanded very little of the superpowers. For practical purposes it allowed each superpower to keep the strategic nuclear weaponry it had, to construct more in selected areas, and to verify everything covered by the agreement through its own "agents"— that is, satellites. Neither side gave up anything other than the immediate right to construct more of certain categories of weapons. Several types of weaponry and all research and development activities were ignored entirely by the agreement. Each party got a positive payoff by learning more about the substance and process of the other's security policy, an experience that could make cooperation more frequent and thorough in the future. Finally, if either party violated the agreement in any sizable way the other could emulate this violation before it acquired any significance for national security. One of the problems which has delayed a SALT II agreement is that each nation has required more from the other in these negotiations.

A fourth characteristic on which global security issues vary is issue urgency. All of the issues discussed in this chapter are salient, although in any given instance some may be more salient than others. Some take on greater urgency than others, thus attracting the attention of national leaders, who over time may make some progress on the issues. After three crises and close to three decades of effort, for instance, the status of Berlin was resolved to the satisfaction of the superpowers and the relevant European powers. The crises over Berlin reflected, of course, Soviet concern over the German question, which was ameliorated during Willy Brandt's chancellorship. If the Soviets again grow concerned about the German question or other European issues, the Berlin situation may once again become a focus for conflict. Soviet-American arms control issues have no counterpart for these periodic regional crises.[49] Whereas the Israeli army has to be stopped immediately if its activity is about to trigger the introduction of Soviet forces into the Middle East, it is hard to persuade national leaders that a certain arms control agreement is so imperative as to require particular compromises right now. It is easy for national leaders to postpone compromises in the hope that they will not be necessary next month or next year.

The examples that have been used above to illustrate varying degrees of issue complexity, divergence of perspective, conflict of interest, and issue urgency have pictured regional crises as involving greater conflict of interest and issue urgency than Soviet-American arms control questions, and the latter have been pictured as exemplifying greater issue complexity and intranational divergence of perspective than do the issues arising from regional conflicts. Although these suggestions can be generalized, there are exceptions.[50] The important point is that several different obstacles stand in the path of resolving the global security issues discussed in this chapter. An issue may be relatively simple and so lend itself to resolution in this regard, but it may also involve a severe conflict of interest and thereby be exceedingly difficult to resolve from that perspective.

Developmental Issues

An important prerequisite for creating a system among actors on global security issues is to develop regularized procedures for interaction between the two superpowers. These procedures need to provide each superpower with expectations about the other's behavior which are generally accurate; some means for discussing unexpected, unacceptable aspects of the other's activity need to exist as well. The SALT and other forums initiated in the early 1970s under the spirit of détente were designed for this function. The results have been less promising than those envisioned, but it is probably too soon to tell whether the effort to develop accurate and acceptable mutual expectations has created an improved basis for superpower relations and thus for global security issues.

It is clear that statesmen in both the United States and the Soviet Union who have carried the banner and burdens of détente have had to deal with internal opposition. Détente challenged some concrete, powerful, and heretofore sacrosanct interests in both nations by suggesting that arms acquisition did not hold a virtual monopoly on means for obtaining security. The military bureaucracies of each nation are examples of such interests. Some aspects of détente have dealt with areas which have previously been jealously guarded national prerogatives such as national security, and a variety of publics take offense at foreign intrusion into these matters.

Beyond the central concern for mechanisms that gradually institutionalize superpower cooperation, there is a need for allowing several Western European powers as well as China and Japan improved means of participation in global security matters. The West European nations have some access to these issues through occasional consultation with the

United States. China and Japan have virtually no access. Under these circumstances Europe, China, and Japan are apt to grow increasingly autonomous on security matters that bother them, and the result will be a more decentralized set of actors. Increased decentralization will mean less opportunity for the superpowers (or any other power) to serve as a restraining influence on issues of central concern to regional powers.

Contested regions like the Middle East offer particularly difficult problems. It is in these contested regions that the incentives for competitive as opposed to cooperative action run strongest. The aftermath of the 1973 war in the Middle East, for example, offered opportunities both for resolving some aspects of the conflicting interests between Israel and its Arab neighbors and for improving the United States' position in the region. Resolving a few of the troublesome issues was a cooperative activity which required working with the Soviets on some matters. Improving the United States position was a competitive activity from the standpoint of superpower relations. Kissinger's direction of United States policy did focus on resolving some aspects of the conflicting issues, but Kissinger's attention was limited to matters which would concomitantly allow him to strengthen the United States' position in the area. When he had to choose between trying to resolve an issue that required Soviet cooperation (and thus influence) and settling for no resolution of the issue but increased United States influence, he chose the latter. This does not mean that Kissinger was particularly myopic or selfish in contrast to his colleagues in other nations. It simply illustrates the temptations for acting in a competitive rather than a cooperative fashion in contested regions.

The security fears which arise in an anarchical environment, statesmen's persistent exaggeration of the threats to their security, their imprudent actions based on fears, as well as the actual threats which some nations periodically pose for others all make the goals discussed in this section extremely difficult to achieve. A system may exist in a minimal sense that the globe has clear boundaries and that the actions of one of the actors discussed in this chapter are likely to have repercussions of some kind on the others. But if a system is to mean commonly accepted diplomatic values and practices such as those enunciated by the United Nations, then a system does not exist among these actors on matters of high politics and will be difficult to create.[51]

Projections

If the conclusions of this chapter lack originality, they are at least consistent with the work of others in a fashion that provides an increasingly secure glimpse of the future. Global security politics is beginning to become the interaction of regional security politics in several areas. That is, regional spheres of influence are developing. The greatest change is that the United States is beginning to become a regional power. Its region is large, including the Western hemisphere, Western Europe, and some areas of the Middle East. But the United States is no longer either a global policeman or troublemaker, and neither is any other power. The global role of the United States arose from changes World War II inflicted on international politics. The traditional powers were reduced dramatically in stature by that conflict. The nations of Western and Central Europe lay in defeat and/or ruins. Japan lay in both. China was in the grasp of civil war. The only competitor for the United States was the Soviet Union, and it was the perceived threat of the Soviet Union which prompted the United States to assume a global role. All of the former powers have regained some stature, and they are beginning to act on their own diplomatically, economically, and even occasionally militarily. Added to these autonomous actions are the activities of the nations created from the ashes of the European colonial empires. It is not surprising that in the face of these multiple sources of initiative, the ability and the desire of the United States to influence events on a global scale has declined.

This is clearly the direction security issues are heading. Conflicts in Asia and in some portions of Africa fall increasingly into the bailiwick of other powers. It is possible that this trend could be reversed. That is, the United States might once again mount, with the help of a few regional powers, a security system that would span much of the globe. This system would be costly in a variety of ways. There would be direct costs of money and possibly lives and indirect costs of opportunities lost in other areas as a result of putting resources into this pursuit. More importantly, the rationale for such a system would be dubious. It is clear that the United States remains a superpower on the criterion of having resources for conflict activity. And barring extensive nuclear proliferation, the only important threat to American security interests (which as a result of American resources for conflict activity are global security issues) is a confrontation with the Soviet Union growing out of a conflict among regional powers. But the ability of the United States to use its resources to resolve conflicts of interest by achieving the outcomes its statesmen desire is limited, as a decade's effort in Southeast Asia has shown.

In short, while the increasing autonomy of nations in these regions does not pose more threatening global security issues than those raised by a policy of active United States intervention in these areas, the latter policy involves the gradual attrition of United States resources with limited prospect for success. It is unclear if the United States would have difficulty working with various groups (even revolutionary groups) associated with this quest for autonomy if it chose to do so.[52] Effort might be better expended trying to draw benefits from the shifting nature of the international environment than struggling to maintain a structure of relations increasingly at odds with forces represented by the interests of others.

Notes

1. Glenn H. Snyder and Paul Diesing, *Conflict among Nations: Bargaining, Decision Making, and System Structure in International Crises* (Princeton, N.J.: Princeton University Press, 1977), p. 83.
2. See, for example, Anatol Rapoport and Albert M. Chammah, *Prisoner's Dilemma: A Study in Conflict and Cooperation* (Ann Arbor: University of Michigan Press, 1965); and Robert Axelrod, *Conflict of Interest: A Theory of Divergent Goals with Applications to Politics* (Chicago: Markham, 1970).
3. Robert Jervis, "Cooperation under the Security Dilemma," *World Politics*, 30 (January 1978), 170–71, suggests that Rousseau's Stag Hunt may be a more appropriate representation of many international conflict situations, particularly if the parties are going to play the game repeatedly. Stag Hunt may be derived from the Prisoner's Dilemma matrix in Figure 6.1 by interchanging the 3s and 4s. Stag Hunt will be discussed below and appears in Figure 6.3. Jervis's suggestion is important and holds interesting implications for international cooperation. However, Stag Hunt and Prisoner's Dilemma are invariant with respect to either party's reaction to the other's use of coercion.
4. For a lengthier discussion of Chicken see Thomas C. Schelling, *Arms and Influence* (New Haven, Conn.: Yale University Press, 1966), pp. 116–25.
5. See Snyder and Diesing, *Conflict among Nations,* chap. 2, for a discussion of several other structures.
6. Robert Jervis, *Perception and Misperception in International Politics* (Princeton, N.J.: Princeton University Press, 1976), particularly chap. 3.
7. See Ernest R. May, *"Lessons" of the Past: The Use and Misuse of History in American Foreign Policy* (New York: Oxford University Press, 1979); and Alexander L. George, "Case Studies and Theory Development: The Method of Structured, Focussed Comparison," in Paul Gorden Lauren (ed.), *Diplomatic History: New Approaches* (New York: Free Press, 1979).
8. See Schelling, *Arms and Influence.*
9. A conflict episode may break out of this structure, however. For example, the Germans eventually had no resources left with which to pursue the conflicts of interest underlying World War II.
10. There is a growing and extremely interesting literature on misperception in international relations. See Snyder and Diesing, *Conflict among Nations,* chap. 4; Jervis, *Perception and Misperception in International Politics;* idem, "Hypotheses on Misperception," *World Politics,* 20 (April 1968), 454–79; May, *"Lessons" of the Past;* Ole R. Holsti, *Crisis Escalation War* (Montreal: McGill-Queens University Press, 1972); John G. Stoessinger, *Nations in Darkness: China, Russia and America* (New York: Random House, 1975); and Ralph K. White, *Nobody Wanted War: Misperception in Vietnam and Other Wars,* rev. ed. (Garden City, N.Y.: Doubleday, 1970).

11. Robert Axelrod (ed.), *Structure of Decision: The Cognitive Maps of Political Elites* (Princeton, N.J.: Princeton University Press, 1976); and Irving L. Janis and Leon Mann, *Decision Making: A Psychological Analysis of Conflict, Choice, and Commitment* (New York: Free Press, 1977).

12. On the fungibility of power see David A. Baldwin, "Power Analysis and World Politics: New Trends versus Old Tendencies," *World Politics,* 31 (January 1979), 161–94

13. This distinction is taken from Anatol Rapoport, *Fights, Games, and Debates* (Ann Arbor, Mich.: University of Michigan Press, 1960).

14. Alexander L. George, David K. Hall, and William E. Simons, *The Limits of Coercive Diplomacy: Laos, Cuba, Vietnam* (Boston: Little, Brown, 1971), pp. 218–20.

15. Klaus Knorr, *The Power of Nations: The Political Economy of International Relations* (New York: Basic Books, 1975).

16. Hanns Maull, "Oil and Influence: The Oil Weapon Examined," *Adelphi Paper Number 117* (London: International Institute for Strategic Studies, 1975).

17. On the other hand there is a possibility that a change in the issues precipitating conflicts of interest may lead to conflict activity more moderate than that associated with the security issues of high politics in the past. See Seyom Brown, "The Changing Essence of Power," *Foreign Affairs,* 51 (January 1973), 286–99.

18. For an extensive discussion of this point see Zuhayr Mikdashi, "Collusion Could Work," and Stephen D. Krasner, "Oil Is the Exception," both in *Foreign Policy,* 14 (Spring 1974), 57–67 and 68–83 respectively; and David B. Bobrow and Robert T. Kudrle, "Theory, Policy and Resource Cartels: The Case of OPEC," *Journal of Conflict Resolution,* 20 (March 1976), 3–56.

19. The reverse is not true, however. In the recent past developing nations have endured a variety of military and economic security threats stemming from the First World nations.

20. It is not, for instance, a secure basis for reciprocity which can gradually build into a sense of community. See Stanley Hoffmann, "International Systems and International Law," in Klaus Knorr and Sidney Verba (eds.), *The International System: Theoretical Essays* (Princeton, N.J.: Princeton University Press, 1961), pp. 205–37.

21. These three crises of 1948–1949, 1958, and 1961 occurred during a period in which mutual destruction was not yet within the grasp of the superpowers although each could have done considerable damage to the other. Also, the United States had a large advantage in the number of strategic nuclear weapons it could deliver on targets in the Soviet Union during this period.

22. See Klaus Knorr, "Failures of National Intelligence Estimates: The Case of the Cuban Missiles," *World Politics,* 16 (April 1964), 455–67.

23. Alexander L. George and Richard Smoke, *Deterrence in American Foreign Policy: Theory and Practice* (New York: Columbia University Press, 1974), chaps. 6–12, discuss examples of other clashes.

24. See Bernard Kalb and Marvin Kalb, *Kissinger* (Boston: Little, Brown, 1974), chaps. 17 and 18; Mohamed Heikal, *The Road to Ramadan* (New York: Quadrangle, 1975).

25. Colin S. Gray, "Theater Nuclear Weapons: Doctrines and Postures," *World Politics,* 28 (January 1976), 300–14.
26. This phrase is taken from the title of Robert E. Osgood et al., *Retreat From Empire? The First Nixon Administration* (Baltimore: Johns Hopkins University Press, 1973).
27. See Thomas C. Schelling, *The Strategy of Conflict* (New York: Oxford University Press, 1960), p. 20.
28. This distinction between MAD as a situation and as a policy was first brought to my attention by Stanley Sienkiewicz, "The Future of SALT," a paper presented at the 1976 Conference of the Section on Military Studies of the International Studies Association, Columbus, Ohio, October 28–30, 1976.
29. Benjamin S. Lambeth, "Deterrence in the MIRV Era," *World Politics,* 24 (January 1972), 221–42.
30. See Donald G. Brennan, "Some Fundamental Problems for Arms Control and National Security," *Orbis,* 15 (Spring 1971), 218–31.
31. This term is borrowed from both Jervis, "Cooperation under the Security Dilemma," and Arnold Wolfers, *Discord and Collaboration* (Baltimore: Johns Hopkins University Press, 1962), chap. 6.
32. Such a defensive posture with respect to strategic nuclear weaponry would have problems of its own. For example, it would not serve to deter theater military struggles between the United States and the Soviet Union in contested regions as the existing force posture has. And if the superpowers relied primarily on defensive weapons, the global distribution of military power would become less bipolar. Also, the verification requirements of a defensive posture would be pretty extensive by current standards. On-site inspection would be necessary. For more on these distinctions see Jervis, "Cooperation under the Security Dilemma," pp. 206–14; and George Quester, *Offense and Defense in the International System* (New York: John Wiley, 1977).
33. Only to a degree inasmuch as suspicion can easily fade into "worst case planning" in which the analyst assumes the worst of the adversary. And this style of thinking often becomes a self-fulfilling prophecy. That is, if a benign nation is treated as an immutable adversary for long enough, it will become an immutable adversary.
34. At best this has been a cursory statement of arms control problems. For a more sophisticated version, see Joseph J. Kruzel, "The Preconditions and Consequences of Arms Control Agreements," Ph.D. dissertation, Harvard University, 1975.
35. Also see the points raised in note 32.
36. See Glenn H. Snyder, " 'Prisoner's Dilemma' and 'Chicken' Models in International Conflicts," *International Studies Quarterly,* 15 (March 1971), 66–103.
37. For some recent thoughts on the degree to which commitments may be uncoupled, see Robert Jervis, "Deterrence Theory Revisited," *World Politics,* 31 (January 1979), 314–22.
38. For example, in the Cuban crisis of 1962 Robert Kennedy voiced the opinion: "We all agreed in the end that if the Russians were ready to go to nuclear war over Cuba, they were ready to go to nuclear war, and that was that. So we

234 ISSUES IN GLOBAL POLITICS

might as well have the showdown then as six months later." Arthur M. Schlesinger, Jr., *A Thousand Days* (New York: Fawcett, 1965), p. 758.

39. See Snyder and Diesing, *Conflict among Nations*, pp. 145–52.
40. Kalb and Kalb, *Kissinger*, chap. 18.
41. These similarities, of course, have limitations. See Snyder and Diesing, *Conflict among Nations*, pp. 79–86.
42. For a summary of some of the difficulties see Steve Chan, "The Intelligency of Stupidity: Understanding Failures in Strategic Warning," *American Political Science Review*, 73 (March 1979).
43. George, Hall, and Simons, *The Limits of Coercive Diplomacy*, as well as I. William Zartman, "Reality, Image, and Detail: The Paris Negotiations, 1969–73," and I. William Zartman (ed.), *The 50% Solution* (Garden City, N.Y.: Doubleday, 1976), pp. 372–98, are examples of authors who focus on issues in the first group. And Gilbert R. Winham, "Negotiation as a Management Process," *World Politics*, 30 (October 1977), 87–114, provides an illustration of theorists who focus on issues in the second group.
44. John Kenneth Galbraith, *The New Industrial State* (Boston: Houghton Mifflin, 1971).
45. John Newhouse, *Cold Dawn: The Story of SALT* (New York: Holt, Rinehart and Winston, 1973).
46. See Colin S. Gray, "Detente, Arms Control, and Strategy: Perspectives on SALT," *American Political Science Review*, 70 (December 1976), 1242–56.
47. For an excellent discussion of these faces see Morton H. Halperin, "The Decision to Deploy ABM: Bureaucratic and Domestic Politics in the Johnson Administration," *World Politics*, 25 (October 1972), 62–95.
48. The term integrative solutions is taken from Richard E. Walton and Robert B. McKersie, *A Behavioral Theory of Labor Negotiations* (New York: McGraw-Hill, 1965), chap. 5. For examples of problems statesmen have reaching integrative solutions, see Charles Lockhart, "Conflict Actions and Outcomes: Long-Term Impacts," *Journal of Conflict Resolution*, 22 (December 1978), 565–98.
49. Except for occasional spillover from regional crises. For example, the Cuban missile crisis of 1962 was widely held to be one of the factors prompting the Limited Test Ban Treaty of 1963.
50. The Palestinian issue, for example, has grown increasingly more complex over the last thirty years, and no government (Arab or other) has ever considered this issue urgent.
51. I want to thank Professor Adda Bozeman and other members of a 1978 National Endowment for the Humanities Summer Seminar in "Diplomacy in International History," especially Matt Runci and Jim Weaver, for alerting me to varying concepts of international systems.
52. For some optimistic evidence on this point see Gerald J. Bender, "Angola, the Cubans, and American Anxieties," *Foreign Policy*, 31 (Summer 1978), 3–30.

7

Economic Issues in Global Interaction

Harold K. Jacobson

ECONOMIC ISSUES were particularly prominent in global interactions in the 1970s. They dominated the agendas of the periodic summit meetings of the heads of government of the major Western countries. They were so central to the relationship between the West and the less developed countries (LDCs) in Africa, Asia, the Caribbean, and Latin America that beyond the conflicts in Southern Africa and the Middle East they were virtually the only topics for discussion. Finally, even though arms control, human rights, and territorial issues were of overriding importance, economic issues were major factors in the interaction between communist and noncommunist countries.

What are these economic issues that loom so large in global politics? What are their sources, dimensions, and structure? How are they issues of politics rather than simply of economics? What accounts for the prom-

This chapter has benefited from the critical reading and constructive suggestions of the editors and Barbara Crane, William Domke, Miroslav Nincic, Jeffrey Rodamar, and Carolyn Somerville. I gratefully acknowledge their assistance.

inence of economic issues in global politics in the final quarter of the twentieth century? How are international decisions concerning economic issues taken? Is international decision-making concerning economic issues becoming regularized and institutionalized? How have these economic issues been resolved in international politics in the past and what are likely future developments?

These questions are the subject of this chapter. Some background discussion is essential, however, before we tackle the intricacies of such matters as floating exchange rates, trade controls and most-favored-nation tariff treatment, and the call for the creation of a new international economic order.

Theoretical Perspectives

Interactions in global politics concerning economic issues have to do with the growth and distribution of the world product, in other words with the sum of goods and services produced, and who shall enjoy these. If all states had self-contained, or autarkic, economies, economic issues would be less significant in international relations. But no state is completely autarkic, all have at least some trade with others, and many have extensive international economic relationships: their earnings from foreign trade constitute a major share of their gross national products. In addition, basic factors of production—labor, capital, and technology—tend to flow among countries without respect for political boundaries. States vary in the extent to which they seek to regulate these flows, and their actions or failure to act in this respect can cause international tensions. Economic issues in contemporary global politics, however, predominantly stem from international trade.

States trade for several purposes, the most fundamental of which is to obtain raw materials, food, and other resources not found within their own borders. With the growth and spread of industrialization, however, a more prevalent motive has been to obtain goods that can be produced more efficiently and therefore more cheaply abroad than at home. International trade permits international specialization and, through this, a greater total product. Countries can concentrate on those goods that they produce most efficiently or for which in technical terms they have a comparative advantage. Comparative advantages might be derived from such factors as natural resource endowments or special skills of labor forces. Through specializing in certain products and engaging in international trade to obtain others, countries can have larger production runs and reduce production costs by taking advantage of economies of scale.

Science and technology undergird international specialization in production and thus international trade. It is the application of science-based technology to production that has enabled the world to move beyond subsistence agriculture.[1] The development of science and the practical application of scientific findings through technology provided a powerful stimulus for states to seek resources outside their borders and made possible production on a large enough scale to call for international specialization.

From the early years of the nineteenth century, when industrialization was taking hold in Western Europe, until the onset of World War I, international trade grew at exceptionally high rates. These high rates were not attained again until after World War II, but then in the late 1950s and the 1960s international trade grew even more rapidly than it had during the nineteenth century. The result was unprecedented interdependence among the economies of the world.

Science and technology have also been responsible for raising other international issues that are commonly regarded as economic but which go beyond those commercial and monetary questions directly connected with the international exchange of goods. Technology has made possible great advances in communications and transport, but the potential of these can be realized only through international collaboration. Collaboration is essential in the use of radio frequencies to avoid harmful interference; trains and aircraft can operate internationally only if there is collaboration to insure that equipment and operating procedures are compatible. The issue of equitable sharing arises with respect to resources in limited supply. States that are not ready to use these resources immediately fear that their use by others will deplete the supply. There are also problems caused by technologies with harmful by-products. The atmospheric pollution from steel production or the water pollution from chemical and paper production sometimes cannot be confined within a state's borders, and international collaboration is essential to avoid disputes about damages and to minimize harmful environmental effects.

Economic issues are also posed by the increasingly unequal distribution of wealth among states. The regular and systematic application of technology to production began in Western Europe around the turn of the nineteenth century. The process then spread to North America, Eastern Europe, Japan, Australia, and New Zealand. It is now being extended to the rest of the world.[2] Throughout the nineteenth and the first half of the twentieth centuries the gross national products of the states that pioneered the process grew at rates that substantially exceeded those of the rest of the world. Even though the relative rates of growth were reversed in the 1960s and the gross national products of the LDCs grew more rapidly on the average than those of the developed countries, the gap between the per-capita GNP of the two groups of states continued to increase substantially. This was partly attributable to the more rapid increase in the LCDs' populations. It was also partly the simple arithmetic consequence of applying a somewhat smaller growth rate to much more substantial base in the developed countries. By 1970 the per capita GNP of the developed countries was twelve times that of the less developed states.[3] The vast disparity between the per capita GNP of the developed states and that of the less developed states raises a question that has been posed earlier in domestic politics, whether the more affluent members ought to contribute to the welfare and economic development of the less affluent either because it would be in their long-run self-interest or because it was a moral obligation.

International economic issues could be settled without governmental intervention by market forces—the law of supply and demand—as indeed they often have been. Increasingly, however, there have been calls for governmental intervention in international market forces. This too parallels what happened earlier in domestic economies.

Within countries, market forces have been found deficient for a variety of reasons, and there has been governmental intervention in economic activities to attempt to correct these deficiencies. Sometimes because of natural or historical reasons competition does not exist so governmental regulation has been necessary to prevent the abuse of a monopoly position. Regulation has also been designed to preserve competition by preventing the growth of oligopoly and monopoly situations. In addition, governments have developed programs to provide services that have not been or would not be provided by private enterprise and to promote greater economic equity than would occur if market forces operated without restraint. Since the 1930s governments in Western Europe, North America, Japan, and Oceania have adopted policies that have aimed at insuring full employment. Electorates found the high unemployment rates of the 1930s unacceptable, and the Keynesian revolution in economics suggested policies through which unemployment could be mitigated. Some economists, however, came to perceive that a tradeoff had to be made between maximizing efficiency to achieve a higher total product and maximizing equity.[4] However much they may support interference with the market, liberal economists nonetheless believe that it is the most efficient mechanism for organizing production and they never want to abandon it completely. They also believe that the means of production should generally be controlled by private enterprise: individuals or corporations seeking to enhance their own welfare by earning a profit on their investment in productive facilities.

Marxists, on the other hand, reject the market mechanism, arguing that it results in inequitable allocations; they would substitute governmental planning. They also condemn private ownership of the means of production, oppose large accumulations of private wealth, and are skeptical that the profit motive can produce beneficial results. They prefer governmental ownership of the means of production.

In such communist countries as the Soviet Union government control of economic matters has become complete; the state owns all productive facilities and the government organizes the processes of production and distribution. Other countries vary from considerable state ownership and governmental management to almost none, but in no contemporary country are production and distribution left exclusively to private enterprise and market forces. There is some governmental intervention in economic matters in all countries.

Governments seek to intervene in international economic processes for much the same reasons that they have intervened in domestic economic processes, namely, to correct perceived deficiencies in the operation of market forces: to regulate monopolies and to promote competition, to provide services that private enterprise would not, and to promote greater equity than would otherwise obtain. Governmental action internationally is also necessitated by governmental intervention in domestic economic affairs. Because of the high level of interdependence that now exists countries are increasingly discovering that they must engage in international cooperation to attempt to insure that external economic forces do not interfere with their domestic economic programs and if possible instead facilitate them.

Economic issues have gained salience in global politics because they have become increasingly important to governments. Governments are so concerned about such matters because their constituents hold them accountable for the performance of their national economies. Economic stagnation or persistently high levels of unemployment or inflation can cost incumbents reelection or even precipitate a rebellion or a coup d'état.

Economic issues have also become more prominent in international affairs because of the relative decline in the salience of security issues. Several factors have contributed to this: the nuclear standoff between the superpowers, the rough equilibrium between the forces of the North Atlantic Treaty Organization and the Warsaw Treaty Organization, the opposition of increasingly well-educated and politically mobilized populations to foreign military operations, the legal and normative injunctions that have been adopted against the use of force in international disputes, and the facilities that international governmental organizations offer for communication and for mediation. The enhanced sense of security that has resulted has permitted government officials and private individuals to turn their attention to other issues.

International economic issues are political in the sense that the outcomes are affected by actions that governments take both with respect to their internal economies and their external economic relationships. A government's action to stimulate or not to stimulate its economy can have important implications for international trade and consequently for other countries. What a state does with respect to its tariffs and other elements of commercial policy even more obviously will have repercussions for other countries. Beyond these exclusively national actions, coordinated and joint actions can result in international public policies, for instance those pursued through the World Bank that are aimed at promoting economic growth and development in LDCs.

Because they are important to governments, when conflicting interests are at stake, economic issues can be the sources of serious disputes, though few if any wars have ever been fought for strictly economic reasons. Fortunately, economic issues also have the potential for substantial mutual gains. Unlike territorial issues, where possession by one state precludes possession by others, all states can benefit from an expanding gross world product (GWP). Conflicts about the distribution of the GWP can be eased by increasing the total sum of goods and services to be divided, so that increased benefits for one state or group of states need not to be subtracted from the existing share of others. There is therefore a strong incentive toward cooperative solutions when dealing with economic issues.

The increased interdependence of states and the greater salience of economic issues have fundamentally altered the character of global political interactions.[5] It is less easy to calculate power, the capacity to achieve influence, because the base for power is now considerably more extensive than factors that contribute directly to military strength. Merely possessing a vital resource can give a state considerable influence. Statecraft is no longer the monopoly of foreign offices because bureaucracies which have domestic responsibilities need to deal with external factors to accomplish their purposes. International institutions have assumed a new importance because of the need for established frameworks for the management of interdependencies.

Analyses of economic issues in global politics of necessity draw on two disciplines, economics and political science. Although in the nineteenth century these two disciplines were closely related, in the first half of the twentieth century, particularly in Anglo-Saxon countries, they grew apart, developing exclusive concerns and distinctive methodologies. The growing role of government in economic affairs and the increasing importance of economic issues in political affairs, however, have created pressures to bring economics and political science closer together. These pressures became particularly strong in the late 1960s and continued to be prominent throughout the 1970s. There is no reason to assume that they will diminish in the future. Although our focus is on international political interactions, these cannot be understood without excursions into the economists' domain.

The Setting

The economic issues that are likely to be important in global politics in the 1980s were defined in the 1970s. These issues grew out of the historical development of the global economy prior to 1970. For this reason, 1970 provides a convenient starting point for our analysis. A description of the world economy as it existed then provides the essential setting for subsequent developments.

Between the end of World War II and 1970 the gross world product grew at an unprecedented rate. From 1950 to 1970, the GWP, measured in constant 1975 dollars, grew almost three times, reaching a total of $5,192 billion in 1970.[6] International trade grew even more rapidly. By 1970 global exports had reached $313 billion.[7] This total was more than five times what it had been in 1950.[8] The post-World War II record was extremely impressive, especially when contrasted with the frustrating performance of the world economy in the period between the two World Wars. In the 1930s the level of international trade declined and economic recession spread throughout the globe. But could the impressive achievements of the post-World War II era be maintained: could the rates of growth in the GWP and in international trade be sustained? As the 1970s developed, such queries were raised with increasing frequency and became more and more salient and worrisome. And while there was satisfaction with the rates of growth in the GWP and in international trade, there was considerable dissatisfaction in several quarters concerning the distribution of both.

Table 7.1 compares the distribution of global population and the GWP among three broad groups of countries in 1950 and 1970: developed countries with market economies; LDCs with market economies; and countries with centrally planned economies. The first group accords roughly with the states that are commonly referred to as the West. Members of the Organization for Economic Cooperation and Development (OECD) constitute the bulk of this category.[9] The LDCs with market economies are the so-called Third World, spread over Africa, Asia, and the Caribbean and Latin America. The member states of the Organization of Petroleum Exporting Countries (OPEC) are included in this group. The People's Republic of China and the Soviet Union comprise some 86 percent of the population of the countries with centrally planned economies, and other smaller communist states make up the total. As Table 7.1 shows, the Western states have gained the predominant share of the GWP; their share of the GWP has far exceeded their share of global population. Although in the period between 1950 and 1970 there was some movement in the distribution of the GWP, the increase in the share

Table 7.1

Shares of Global Population and the Gross World Product,
1950 and 1970 (percentages)

	1950		1970	
	Population	*GWP*	*Population*	*GWP*
Developed countries with market economies	20	67	18	64
Less developed countries with market economies	46	13	48	14
Centrally planned economies	34	20	34	22
Total	100	100	100	100

Source: United States of America, Department of State, Bureau of Public Affairs, Special Report 33 (May 1977, Department of State Publication 8903), "The Planetary Product in 1975 and a Preview for 1976," pp. 31, 33.

Note: In this analysis those countries having a per capita GNP of $1,600 or more are regarded as developed and those with a per capita GNP of less than $1,600 are regarded as less developed. Given this definition a small number of countries shifted categories during the twenty-year period. Given the general tentativeness of the data, the magnitude of the numbers involved, and the fact that these percentages have been rounded to the nearest whole number, the relatively small number of shifts are not of sufficient consequence to invalidate the general impression given by the percentages in this table.

of the LDCs was less than the increase in their share of the world's population.

The distribution of international trade was even more skewed in favor of the West. Table 7.2 shows the distribution of world exports by source and destination in 1970. Note that intra-Western trade accounts for more than half of world exports, and that exports from developed countries with market economies make up more than two-thirds of the world total. Because of the extent of their mutual trade, the developed countries with market economies are highly interdependent. Economic difficulties in a major Western country can cause serious repercussions in the others. Since international trade is an important mechanism that can be used to advance economic development, all countries had an interest in continuing the expansion in world trade and the LDCs became as determined to effect a major change in the distribution of international trade as they were to alter the distribution of the GWP.

Economic interactions in the 1970s therefore centered on two fundamental issues: the general desire to sustain the growth in the GWP and in international trade, and the demand of the LDCs and others to alter distribution of both. A majority of government officials and publicists thought that this could be achieved by incremental changes in the existing international system, but there was debate among these individuals about whether achieving greater equity globally would mean sacrificing efficiency, and if it would, about the extent to which growth in GWP would

Table 7.2
The Distribution of Global Exports, 1970
(percentages)

	EXPORTS TO			
EXPORTS FROM	*Developed Countries with Market Economies*	*Less Developed Countries with Market Economies*	*Countries with Centrally Planned Economies*	TOTAL
Developed countries with market economies	55	13	3	71
Less developed countries with market economies	13	4	1	18
Countries with centrally planned economies	3	2	6	11
Total	71	19	10	100

Source: United Nations, Secretariat, Department of Economic and Social Affairs, *Statistical Yearbook, 1976* (New York: United Nations, 1977), p. 434.

be slowed. In contrast, others—especially Marxists and neo-Marxists—argued that meaningful change could be achieved only through a radical restructuring of the system.[10] They maintained that Western corporations and governments would use their dominant position in the world market economy to advance their own interests while exploiting the poorer countries, and that such countries should withdraw from the world market economy and develop through self-reliance.

Principal Actors

In the preceding section the world economy was divided into three major groups of states: the developed countries with market economies, the LDCs with market economies, and the countries with centrally planned economies. Now it is appropriate to examine these three major groups in detail, to identify the principal actors within them, and to describe their characteristics.

Developed countries with market economies are the dominant force in the contemporary world economy. In the period since the end of World War II, even though these countries comprised only a fifth or less of the world population, they produced and consumed roughly two-thirds of the GWP. Within this group of countries, seven are of particular importance. In 1970 they accounted for 84 percent of the group's share of the GWP.[11] These seven countries and their percentage of the broad category's share of GWP in 1970 are: United States of America, 41 percent; Canada, 4 percent; Federal Republic of Germany, 11 percent; France, 8 percent; United Kingdom, 5 percent; Italy, 4 percent; and Japan, 11 percent.

After the United Kingdom's entry in 1973, all four of the European states were members of the European Economic Community. Formed in 1958 by Belgium, the Federal Republic of Germany, France, Italy, Luxembourg, and the Netherlands, the European Economic Community committed its member states to eliminating barriers to the free movement of goods and the factors of production (people and capital) within the community and to establish a common external tariff with respect to trade with nonmember countries. These objectives were to be attained according to a fixed time schedule, and actual progress occurred more rapidly than the treaty required. The treaty also specified other objectives toward the creation of a full economic union among the participating states but it did not provide a time schedule for their attainment. Nevertheless, the EEC's Common Agricultural Policy was achieved simultaneously with the customs union and rapid progress was made in formulating and implementing an antitrust policy. By the mid-1960s the member countries of the EEC were operating as a single unit in negotiations about foreign trade. Efforts were made toward the formulation of common policies in transport and other areas, and toward cooperation with respect to monetary policy, but progress proved more elusive in these fields. When the United Kingdom joined the EEC in 1973, Denmark and Ireland also became members. In the early 1970s, the nine countries that were members of the EEC accounted for about a third of the share of the GWP that accrued to developed countries with market economies.

Among the several motivations for creation of the European Economic Community, the desire to establish an economic unit large enough to compete effectively with the continental economies of the United States and the U.S.S.R. was certainly important. The member states of the EEC viewed their national markets as being too small to permit taking full advantage of economies of scale in production, and they worried that relatively small national units would be unable to afford the research and development costs associated with modern technology. In short, one factor in the creation of EEC was a desire to improve the competitive position of the member countries within the world economy and among the developed countries with market economies.

The United States supported the creation of the EEC, seeing it as an instrument for strengthening the Western states against communism and as an insurance against a renewal of conflict in Western Europe which twice in the twentieth century had provoked catastrophic world wars. The United States also saw economic benefits to be gained from the European Economic Community. It thought that the creation of the Community would stimulate economic growth among its members, thereby increasing opportunities for U.S. trade and investment. In the decade of the 1960s the expectations of both the member states of the EEC and the United States proved correct. Between 1960 and 1970 the combined Gross Domestic Products of the original six members of the European Economic Community grew by some 67 percent while that of the United States grew by only 50 percent and that of the United Kingdom by only 32 percent.[12] United States trade with the EEC members trebled between 1960 and 1970, while in the previous decade it had only doubled.[13] During both decades U.S. exports to the EEC grew more rapidly than did total U.S. exports.

Because of the successful functioning of the European Economic Community and the relatively small size of Canada's economy, for some purposes it is possible to think of the core of the group of developed countries with market economies as consisting of three large units, the United States, the European Economic Community, and Japan. When issues are limited to trade, these three units are sufficient, but when problems go beyond trade and include matters with salient implications for domestic economic policies, then the core unit must be thought of in terms of the seven separate countries.

The United States, the European Economic Community, and Japan accounted for respectively 26 percent, 21 percent, and 7 percent of the GWP in 1970.[14] They had in common the important characteristics of being developed states with market economies, but beyond this there were important differences among them.

The member states of the European Economic Community and Japan were more heavily dependent on foreign trade than the United States. In 1970 exports to other states equaled 12 percent of Japan's gross domestic product, and 11 percent of the EEC's (or 22 percent if intracommunity exports are included), but only 5 percent of that of the United States.

The composition of the external trade of the three units differed also. Japan and the member states of the European Economic Community were more reliant on imports of food and raw materials than was the United States, and manufactured goods constituted a larger portion of their exports. In contrast, food and raw materials were important components of the exports of the United States but not of the other two units.

Finally, the per capita GNP in the United States was considerably above that of both the EEC and Japan. In the early 1970s Japan's per capita GNP was only 42 percent of that of the United States and the per capita GNP of the nine members of EEC was only slightly larger, about half of that of the United States. Of course, there was considerable variance among the EEC members. In the early 1970s, Denmark's per capita GNP, the highest in the EEC, was more than twice that of Ireland, which was the lowest. Five member states (Denmark, France, the Federal Republic of Germany, Belgium, and Luxembourg) had per capita GNPs of more than $3,000, two (the Netherlands and the United Kingdom) had per capita GNPs that were somewhat less than $3,000, and two (Italy and Ireland) had per capita GNPs of less than $2,000.

Countries with centrally planned economies constitute a second major category of actors in global economic interactions. In 1970 the U.S.S.R. accounted for 59 percent of this group's share of the gross world product, and the People's Republic of China, 17 percent.[15] The economies of several other communist states, including most of those in Eastern Europe were linked with that of the U.S.S.R. through the Council for Mutual Economic Assistance (CMEA).[16] The economy of the U.S.S.R., however, was so large that it dwarfed those of the other nine members of CMEA. In the early 1970s, the gross national products of the Democratic Republic of Germany and Czechoslovakia were about a tenth of the size of that of the U.S.S.R. and Poland's was about a seventh. Because of the overwhelming importance of the U.S.S.R. and the People's Republic of China among the states with centrally planned economies our attention can be focused on them.

In the U.S.S.R., China, and other communist countries, the state owns the productive facilities, and the government directs the processes of production. Prices and quantities to be produced are determined by administrative decisions rather than by the forces of supply and demand as they are determined at least in theory within the market economies. There is a state monopoly for foreign trade which controls all external transactions. Thus the extent of foreign trade is also determined by administrative decision rather than market forces. Tariffs in market economies tend to affect the quantity that individuals will decide to import by affecting the prices of the goods. Since how much will be imported by a communist country is an administrative decision, tariffs do not have the same function in centrally planned economies. Consequently lowering tariff barriers may not have the same likelihood of increasing trade with centrally planned economies as it does for market economies.

In quantitative terms, foreign trade was not very important for either the U.S.S.R. or the People's Republic of China. In 1970 exports constituted less than 2 percent of the U.S.S.R.'s gross domestic product and less than .1 percent of China's.[17] Because of the limited extent of their foreign trade, neither the U.S.S.R. nor China played a role in global economic interactions that was in any way commensurate with its broader role in world politics.

The vast physical size of the U.S.S.R. and of China partly explains the relative insignificance of external trade for their economies. Both countries had most of the resources that they needed within their own borders and, as the third most populous and the most populous countries respectively in the world, both had internal markets of sufficient size to allow for specialization and taking advantage of the economies of scale.

In addition, central planning tends to push countries that practice it in the direction of autarky; planners exhibit an understandable tendency to prefer production that is under their own control rather than outside of their administrative jurisdiction. Finally, the U.S.S.R. and China both rejected extensive participation in the world market economy on ideological grounds.

There are two important differences between the U.S.S.R. and China. The population of the former is only about one third of that of the latter, and there is a great gap between the U.S.S.R.'s per capita gross national product and that of the People's Republic of China. In the early 1970s the U.S.S.R.'s per capita GNP was nine times as large as that of China. The U.S.S.R.'s per capita GNP ranked it with the poorer members of the EEC, while that of China ranked it among the poorest in the world. Thus when the countries of the world are divided into simply two categories, developed and less developed, the U.S.S.R. must be included in the former and China in the latter.

The final category of states in global economic interactions are the LDCs with market economies. This designation should not obscure the fact that there is extensive governmental intervention in the economies of many of these countries and that the regimes of many of them have a self-professed socialist character. Nor should it obscure the fact that there are several income levels among the countries. The outlying cases, small states such as Kuwait and Qatar where oil income has produced enormously high per capita GNPs, are well-known. What is not as well-known is that there are substantial differences among LDCs simply on a continental basis. In the early 1970s the per capita gross product of the countries of Central and South America was almost three times larger than that of the countries in Africa, which in turn was about one and a half times that of the Asian countries. The some 800 million individuals who lived in absolute poverty were concentrated in Asia and sub-Saharan Africa.

Despite these differences in income level, the LDCs shared a common desire to raise the level of their per capita GNPs. Although they differed in the extent to which they expressed resentment about the existing distribution of the GWP, they were united in their determination to obtain a greater share. This unity was given formal expression in the formation in 1964 of the Group of 77. The occasion for this step was the first United Nations Conference on Trade and Development (UNCTAD). The LDCs decided that they would improve the chances of advancing their economic goals if they acted as a unit and voted together during the conference. The caucus that they formed became known as the Group of 77 because it originally included 77 states. Although the caucus was originally created for the UNCTAD meeting, it has become permanent and pervasive. Group of 77 caucuses are now a regular feature of all universal-membership international governmental organizations (IGOs). They have enabled LDCs to advance their positions on many economic issues in several international fora. As of 1979 there were 119 states in the Group of 77, and it included states with centrally planned economies such as Cuba and Yugoslavia, as well as those with market economies. In addition, even though it did not participate in their caucuses, the People's Republic of China regularly voted with the Group of 77. The Group of 77 has become the principal instrument for the aggregation and articulation of the interests of the poorer states in the world.

Beyond the common characteristics of being relatively poor (in relation to the advanced industrial states of the West and to the communist states of Eastern Europe) and being determined to improve their economic status, there were many differences among the states that compromise the Group of 77. Now we must examine the other differences beyond those involving levels of per capita GNP.

Seven of the 113 had populations in the early 1970s of 50 million or more. The seven states and their populations in millions are: India, 563; Indonesia, 122; Brazil, 98; Bangladesh, 72; Pakistan, 67; Nigeria, 61; and Mexico, 54. The remaining 105 states had populations of less than 40 million, and of these only about a dozen had populations more than 20 million. For some purposes the Group of 77 should be divided into two groups, the more populous and the less populous states.

The more populous members of the Group of 77, and particularly the seven most populous states, were in a different position in the world economy than the others. Their territories were relatively extensive, and as a consequence most of them contained a variety of resources. Because of the size of their populations their GNPs were relatively large, even if on a per capita basis they were relatively low. The size of their GNPs made it possible to mobilize substantial resources for investment and other purposes. Their internal markets were of sufficient size to allow specialization and the taking advantage of economies of scale and to attract the commercial interest of developed countries. Finally, because of their relatively large populations, their earnings from exports were a smaller percentage of their gross national products than was the case with the less populous members of the Group of 77. In 1970 only for Indonesia and Nigeria did export earnings constitute more than 8 percent of GNP.

The less populous less developed states were in a different position. Their export earnings were in many cases more than 30 percent of their gross domestic products, and for some they were even more than 50 percent. Moreover, their exports were often heavily concentrated, comprising principally one or two basic commodities, which were frequently sold primarily to a single state. France and the United Kingdom were usually the principal purchasers of the exports of the primary products from their former colonies in Africa and Asia, and the United States was often the principal purchaser of such products from Central and South America. Because of the importance of export earnings to their GNPs and because of the concentration of their exports with respect to composition and destination, these countries were highly vulnerable to changes in limited markets.

This vulnerability caused LDCs to attempt to form various groups designed to protect their position as commodity exporters. By far the most well-known of these is the Organization of Petroleum Exporting Countries (OPEC), and it is also the one that has had the most substantial effect on the world economy. Formed in 1960, in the wake of a sharp decline in the price of petroleum, OPEC is in effect a cartel among the petroleum producing countries, an instrument for achieving agreement on the amount of petroleum that they will produce and the price that they will charge. In the late 1970s OPEC included thirteen members.[18] The consequences of the organization were not very visible until the 1970s, but they became glaringly obvious in 1973 when the members of OPEC decided to quadruple the price that they would charge. This action and the threat of further price increases provided strong material backing for the rhetorical demands of the Group of 77. Because of the importance of petroleum to the world economy and the success of the cartel, the OPEC countries need to be considered a separate and important group within the LDCs.

The 1973 OPEC price increase had substantial effects on the world economy, which we will examine in detail later. We need to mention one of these effects, however, now. Since the price increase was global, it affected less developed as well as developed countries. Forty-five LDCs were identified those the Most Seriously Affected (MSAs) by the increase in the price of oil and the global inflation and recession. They were all countries that were not themselves oil-producers, that imported substantial quantities of oil, and that could not immediately significantly increase their export earnings. Twenty-four of these states were also among the twenty-nine identified by various international institutions as the least developed in the world.[19] All of the least developed countries (LLDCs) had per capita GNPs of less than $200, limited capital resources, and few or no natural resources that could be a source of export earnings. In the mid-1970s the twenty-four most seriously affected countries, which were also among the least developed, faced the greatest immediate economic difficulties, and their long-run prospects for economic development were bleak. This group particularly, and the MSAs and LLDCs more generally, constituted additional categories within the Group of 77 that were a special focus of international concern.

These then are the principal actors in global economic interactions: (1) among the developed states with market economies: the United States, Canada, Japan, and the EEC; and within the EEC, France, the

Federal Republic of Germany, Italy, and the United Kingdom; (2) among the states with centrally planned economies: the U.S.S.R. and the People's Republic of China; and (3) among the less developed states: The Group of 77, comprising mainly states with market economies but including also some with centrally planned economies; and within the Group of 77, Central and South American, African, and Asian states; more populous and less populous states as another broad subdivision; and the members of OPEC, the MSAs and the LLDCs as special subcategories. How do these principal actors interact?

Institutions

By the 1970s, the web of international governmental organizations (IGOs) in which interactions concerning economic issues could occur was both dense and elaborate. The basic institutional framework evolved in the closing days of World War II and in the years immediately following the war. The United Nations and the key U.N. agencies were created then. The crucial IGOs with limited memberships such as OECD and CMEA also date from that period. This basic institutional framework was elaborated in the 1950s and 1960s, and a few additional IGOs were created in the 1970s.

The United Nations was the site of the most inclusive and most general discussions of economic issues in the 1970s. Since the seating of the People's Republic of China in 1971 and the admission of the two German states, the Federal Republic and the Democratic Republic, in 1973, the United Nations had achieved a truly universal character. With 151 member states in 1978 the United Nations included virtually all of the independent states in the global political system. Its mandate permitted discussion of all economic issues. But although the United Nations included all relevant actors and could take up virtually any economic subject, since its powers were limited, its principal function came to be the adoption of normative resolutions on general economic issues.

More focused discussions of particular issues occurred in the U.N. agencies. These agencies and the number of their member states as of early 1979 were:

International Labor Organization (ILO)	138
Food and Agricultural Organization (FAO)	144
United Nations Educational, Scientific and Cultural Organization (UNESCO)	146
World Health Organization (WHO)	150
International Civil Aviation Organization (ICAO)	143
Universal Postal Union (UPU)	159
International Telecommunication Union (ITU)	154

World Meteorological Organization (WMO)   149
Intergovernmental Maritime Consultative
    Organization (IMCO)   107
World Intellectual Property Organization (WIPO)   83
International Atomic Energy Agency (IAEA)   110

The functional areas covered by these organizations are apparent in their titles. Beyond being fora for detailed discussions of specific policy issues they were often used for the negotiation of conventions that would be legally binding on the states that ratified them. Like the United Nations, these agencies operated on the principle of sovereign equality so that each member state had one vote, and resolutions could be adopted on the basis of a simple or qualified majority vote. All of these organizations were open to all states. However, the U.S.S.R. did not belong to the FAO and China did not belong to the ILO, the WIPO, or the IAEA.

In addition to these eleven, there were five U.N. agencies that in principle were open to all states but that concentrated mainly on the economic problems of the market economies: the International Bank for Reconstruction and Development (IBRD or World Bank) and its off-shoots, the International Finance Corporation (IFC) and the International Development Association (IDA); the International Monetary Fund (IMF); and the General Agreement on Tariffs and Trade (GATT). The Soviet Union did not belong to any of these organizations. Some smaller East European states with communist governments, however, belonged to some of them. Czechoslovakia, Hungary, Poland, Romania, and Yugoslavia were members of GATT. Yugoslavia belonged to all of the international financial institutions and Romania belonged to IMF. In 1980 the PRC joined IMF and the World Bank.

The World Bank and the International Monetary Fund were created at the Bretton Woods Conference in 1944. The purpose of the Monetary Fund is to promote exchange stability and exchange liberalization, that is, to facilitate countries' efforts to keep the value of their currencies relatively constant and make them freely convertible into other currencies. Member states provided the IMF with funds that could be used for loans to other members when these states needed assistance to support the value of their currencies. In 1969 the International Monetary Fund in effect created a new international reserve asset by establishing a special drawing account to which member states were given special drawing rights (SDRs). Members of IMF participating in the scheme are obliged to accept SDRs up to specified amounts in settlement of another participating country's debts. IMF has a system of weighted voting, and a state's voting strength is proportional to its contribution, which in turn is proportional to its participation in international trade. Under this system the Western states hold dominant power in IMF, and the concurrence of the United States and the member states of the EEC is an essential condition of the Fund's taking important decisions. Since the value of their currency is set by administrative decisions and since all of their foreign exchange transactions are controlled by agencies of the central government, the International Monetary Fund has little relevance for the Soviet Union and other communist countries. This is probably the principal explanation for the fact that they are not members. In addition, given the voting system and its limited role in international trade, the U.S.S.R. would not have the power in IMF that it has in such organizations as the United Nations, where it is included among the five states given permanent membership and the right of veto in the Security Council.

Membership in the International Bank for Reconstruction and Development is open only to members of IMF, the obvious reason being that an international lending institution would like its borrowers to maintain stable currencies and to pursue sound fiscal policies. The purpose of the World Bank is to make long-term loans to cover basic development needs rather than temporary balance of payments deficits, which are supposed to be met by IMF loans. IBRD raises money on normal capital markets to loan to its members, using the subscriptions of member states as a guarantee for these loans. The International Finance Corporation operates like the World Bank in borrowing on capital markets and it provides equity and loan capital for private enterprises. It also holds shares in national and regional development finance corporations.

The International Development Association, which was established in 1960, is the "soft money" window of the World Bank. IDA relies on contributions by its richer member states for its funds, which are used to make loans on exceptionally favorable terms for less developed member states. Typically its loans are for a period of fifty years, with a ten-year initial grace period, and no interest charge, only a service charge of three-quarters of 1 percent per year.

The General Agreement on Tariffs and Trade is the final organization with broad membership that concentrates on the problems of the market economies. Its mandate is commercial policy, and it has been a major instrument in achieving trade liberalization. GATT was a by-product of the abortive attempt to create a comprehensive International Trade Organization (ITO). GATT was originally seen as a limited instrument for lowering tariffs and other barriers to trade, but when ITO failed to come into being because of the unwillingness of the U.S. Congress to accept the treaty, GATT became the only forum for the consideration of commercial policy. GATT's greatest contribution has been to sharply reduce tariffs on trade in manufactured goods. This has been done through a series of tariff-cutting conferences in which bilateral agreements to reduce tariffs—either on particular goods or on whole schedules of items—are extended to all contracting parties to GATT under the most-favored-nation principle. According to this principle, each contracting party is entitled to receive identical treatment with that of the most-favored-nation, in other words it is a rule of nondiscrimination.

Even though they were technically not autonomous agencies but were subordinate organs of the United Nations, three additional organizations created in the 1960s merit special attention. All were designed to promote economic development in the Third World. One, the United Nations Conference on Trade and Development, has been mentioned already. A principal reason for the creation of UNCTAD was the desire of the LDCs to establish an alternative forum to GATT for the discussion of commercial policy. While the basic principle of GATT is nondiscrimination in trade, the LDCs wanted to create a trade regime that would be frankly discriminatory in their favor. International trade, they argued, should be skewed so that it would accelerate the development of LDCs. Another difference between UNCTAD and GATT is that, even though each member state is accorded one vote in each organization, since the ability to grant trade concessions is the principal basis for influence in GATT, the Western industrialized states are much more influential in it than they are in UNCTAD.

The United Nations Development Program (UNDP) and the United Nations Industrial Development Organization (UNIDO) were created with a similar development orientation. The UNDP was an amalgamation of the United Nations Expanded Program of Technical Assistance and the United Nations Special Fund, programs which resulted from U.S. initiatives in the 1940s and 1950s. UNDP's purpose is to provide technical assistance in the form of experts and training and pre-investment assistance. It is funded by voluntary contributions. UNIDO was established to fill a gap that the LDCs perceived in the array of U.N. agencies; its mission is to promote industrialization within the LDCs.

Limited-membership IGOs must be added to this already dense web of IGO networks with universal or near-universal membership. Three important limited membership IGOs have already been mentioned: CMEA, which brings together several states with centrally planned economies; OECD, which links the industrial states of the West; and the EEC, which tightly connects the economies of nine of OECD's twenty-four member states. Seven other members of OECD have eliminated tariffs on trade among themselves through their membership in the European Free Trade Association.[20] These seven states also have free trade in industrial products with the members of EEC through an association agreement.

The less developed countries have also engaged in several attempts to achieve regional economic integration, but none of these has been as successful as the EEC. Regional integration could be a way of promoting self-reliance among developing countries. Unfortunately, in terms of this objective the economic relationships of the member countries of the schemes with the developed states of the West tend to be much more important than their economic relationships with their partners in the regional schemes, and consequently intraregional trade has only a marginal impact on their economic development. Some of the more prominent regional economic integration attempts among LDCs and their membership as of 1978 were:

1. *The Andean Group;* formed in 1969, comprising Bolivia, Columbia, Ecuador, Peru, and Venezuela.
2. *The Association of South East Asian Nations;* formed in 1967 comprising Indonesia, Malaysia, the Philippines, Singapore, and Thailand.
3. *Caribbean Community and Common Market;* formed in 1973 to replace the Caribbean Free Trade Association which had been established in 1968, at present comprising Antigua, Barbados, Belize, Dominica, Grenada, Guyana, Jamaica, Montserrat, St. Christopher-Nevis-Anguilla, St. Lucia, St. Vincent, and Trinidad and Tobago.
4. *Central American Common Market;* formed in 1960, comprising Costa Rica, El Salvador, Guatemala, Honduras, and Nicaragua. Honduras discontinued participation in 1969.
5. *Central African Customs and Economic Union;* formed in 1964 but with a history of collaboration dating to the colonial period, comprising Cameroon, Central African Republic, Congo, and Gabon.
6. *Regional Cooperation for Development;* formed in 1964, comprising Iran, Pakistan, and Turkey.
7. *West African Economic Community;* formed in 1973 but with a history of collaboration dating to the colonial period, comprising Ivory Coast, Mali, Mauritania, Niger, Senegal, and Upper Volta.
8. *The Economic Community of West African States;* formed in 1975, comprising Benin, Cape Verde, Gambia, Ghana, Guinea, Guinea-Bissau, Ivory Coast, Liberia, Mali, Mauritania, Niger, Nigeria, Senegal, Sierra Leone, Togo, and Upper Volta.

The broad purpose of these groupings is to promote the economic development of the member states by increasing the size of their markets and increasing the weight of the members in international economic bargaining. Cartels of producer states were another means toward the same objective, and the success of OPEC has already been mentioned.

Finally, several regional development banks were created. The most heavily capitalized, the Inter-American Development Bank and the Asian Development Bank, included both developed and less developed states, but many, such as the African Development Bank, limited their membership to LDCs.

This web of IGO networks binds all of the states in the global political system together, and several of them are deeply enmeshed in parts of the web. Through their memberships in the IGO networks that comprised the web, all states are committed to achieving cooperative solutions to economic problems, and the IGO networks provide fora where such cooperative solutions can be fashioned through discussion and the harmonization and coordination of policies, through the negotiation of conventions, and through the conduct of operational activities. Regimes created by decisions in these networks have made possible the unprecedented growth in international trade and the world product.

This positive and optimistic picture, however, needs to be qualified in various respects. In the final analysis all of the IGOs depended on the voluntary collaboration of their member states.

This was most evident in the case of the United Nations Development Program, which obtained the funds that it dispersed through voluntary contributions, which donor states were free to discontinue should they choose. None of the major donor states have discontinued their contributions, but some have occasionally reduced theirs. The United States contribution for 1974 was more than 22 percent less than what it had been in the previous year.

States can always withdraw from the international governmental organizations to which they belong, and they would suffer little sanction other than loss of the privileges of membership. IGOs generally seek to make the benefits of membership outweigh the costs, but this strategy has not always been successful. For instance, in 1977 the East African Community, the regional economic integration scheme that joined Kenya, Tanzania, and Uganda, collapsed despite the fact that at one time intracommunity trade among EAC members was higher than among any regional economic integration effort among LDCs. The member states simply proved unwilling to take the actions reqired to coordinate their policies so as to be able to continue to gain the benefits of this trade. In 1977 the United States withdrew from the International Labor Organization. The official explanation was that the organization was being diverted from its proper functions by the introduction of extraneous political disputes into its affairs. It rejoined in 1980.

The broad point is that although there are a large number of international governmental organizations that provide comprehensive coverage for economic issues, there is no guarantee that this system will continue. States can always withdraw from IGOs and attempt to pursue their policies in isolation. Although the probabilities of this occurring on a large scale appear to be low, after the economic difficulties and crises of the 1970s they seem higher than they ever have been.

Another problem is that the probability of achieving constructive solutions for economic problems could be lowered because of inability to resolve doctrinal and other conflicts within and among various IGOs. The most powerful Western states generally favor an international economic regime oriented toward market principles; they seek to have trade conducted on a nondiscriminatory basis. Many of the LDCs, however, argue that the existing international economic order works to their disadvantage; they seek a system that would actively discriminate in their favor. Thus there has been a continuing conflict within the IGOs that include both Western and less developed countries.

In such organizations as the United Nations, UNCTAD, and UNIDO, where each state has one vote and decisions require only a numerically qualified majority, the positions of the LDCs have carried, though often only after a sharp dispute. These organizations consequently are inclined to favor active governmental intervention with market forces in international economic affairs to promote the economic development of the LDCs. The most powerful and important broad-membership IGOs—those that have the greatest resources and the decisions of which have the most substantial consequences—IMF, the World Bank, and GATT —where Western influence is greater, are strongly oriented toward the operating principles of the open market, toward free competition. Because of this basic difference in orientation the programs advocated by the two sets of organizations are not always harmonious.

Regional economic integration schemes, such as the EEC, involve treating the member states more favorably than nonmembers, an exception that according to GATT rules is permissible under certain circumstances, and as has been noted the LDCs have sought to emulate EEC's example. But even though the discrimination against nonmembers involved in customs unions was regarded as legitimate, there were nevertheless sharp controversies with nonmembers about the extent of the discrimination. The United States had been willing to accept discrimination against its exports to the member countries of EEC in the 1950s and 1960s, because strengthening the economies of the Western European states was a vital element of its strategy of containing communism. In the 1970s, however, when the Western European economies were considerably stronger than they had been, the United States became less amenable to this discrimination.

A final problem is that different IGOs have different constituencies within states. Agricultural ministries look to the Food and Agriculture Organization and health ministries look to the World Health Organization as the IGOs where the problems with which they are primarily concerned could be solved. They guide the policies of their countries in these institutions and they resist attempts to have policies with respect to "their problems" considered in other fora. To a certain extent states are linked sectorially more closely than they are with respect to issues of general policy. OECD comes the closest to dealing with the general economic policies of its member states, but even OECD has had to be supplanted by periodic ad hoc summit meetings of the heads of government of the seven most important Western countries. Thus the institutional development with respect to issues of central economic policy has been weaker than with respect to sectorial policy.

Inputs

The dominant theme of global interactions in the various IGO fora is, as Helmut Schmidt, the Chancellor of the Federal Republic of Germany, so aptly put it, "the struggle for the world product."[21] The most fundamental division, of course, is between the LDCs, which want their share of the GWP to be rapidly increased, and the developed countries, those with both market economies and centrally planned economies, the governments of which are under constant pressure to provide a steadily increasing standard of living for their citizens. But there are also other divisions. Among the LDCs there are divisions between those states that produce petroleum and those that do not, between those that are landlocked and those that have access to the sea and between other groups. Among the developed states there are divisions between those with centrally planned and those with market economies, and among the United States, the members of the European Economic Community, and Japan. A decision on almost any subject would affect all these subgroups differently. In making any decision all of the participating states seek to protect and promote their own economic interests.

An expanding GWP could render all of the conflicts less acute because it would allow the argument to focus on how increments to the GWP should be divided and avoid the zero-sum character of debates about how a fixed sum should be allocated. In an expanding world economy the relatively rich states need not see improving the lot of the poorer states as inevitably leading to an absolute decline in their own standard of living. Thus all states have an interest in the continued expansion of the GWP.

Western states had been primarily responsible in the 1940s and 1950s for the creation of the web of IGO networks and the regime that governed international trade. Since they were basically satisfied with this regime and felt that it served their interests well, in the 1970s the Western states were defenders of the status quo. They wanted to insure the continued smooth functioning of the system. The LDCs, on the other hand, wanted change, and in the seventies they were the ones that seized the initiative and sought to promote change. The states with centrally planned economies, because of their overwhelming preoccupation with their internal processes of development and the limited role that international trade had in their economies, played only a small role in the debate. The U.S.S.R. and the Eastern European communist countries usually gave rhetorical support to the demands of the LCDs. Perhaps because of this, even though the LDCs often indicated that they regarded these states as developed, they made few demands on them. The minimal quality of the demands may also have reflected the fact that the experience of the 1950s and 1960s had accustomed the LDCs to expect little material support from the U.S.S.R. and the other Eastern European communist states.

There have been other debates, but none as strident or pervasive as that between the less developed and developed countries. The United States, the EEC, Japan, and other Western states have all sought to defend and advance their own economic interests, as they defined them, and these definitions have sometimes been conflictual, but this debate has been restrained by the many interdependencies among these countries and the substantial common interests that they have had in preserving the smooth functioning of the global economic system.

The LDCs have raised their demands for change and tabled their proposals in the universal-membership agencies of the United Nations family. Within these agencies the Group of 77 caucus is the instrument for aggregating the interests of the LDCs, and frequently the Group of 77 speaks with a unified voice through a designated spokesperson. In the 1970s, as long as the Group of 77 consensus included the members of OPEC, there was a threat of potential economic coercion to back up the demands of the 77.

OECD has provided a framework for discussions among the developed countries with market economies of their responses to LDC demands. The range of views among the OECD countries, however, is wide. Some states, particularly the United States, the Federal Republic of Germany, and Japan, are firmly committed to operating the international economy on the basis of market principles. Furthermore, they see the LDC demands as involving substantial costs that they would have to bear and for which there is little sympathy among their electorates. Consequently they are resistant to making concessions. There is another group of Western states consisting of such states as the Netherlands, Norway, and Sweden, however, that have had considerable sympathy for the position of the LDCs and have urged concessions.

The U.S.S.R. and the Eastern European communist states also caucus, and their voting is more homogeneous than either that of the members of the Group of 77 or of OECD. They generally back the LDC demands with their votes but provide little material support.

Issues

The issues in contention in global economic interactions may be grouped into three broad categories. The first category involves economic relationships between developed and less developed countries. The discussion of these issues is known as the North–South dialogue. The second category involves economic relationships between states with market economies and those with centrally planned economies. Because of the crucial role of the United States and the U.S.S.R., this discussion is known as the East–West debate. The final category consists of issues of particular concern to the advanced industrial states with market economies. This debate can be termed the Western internal discussion. Before outlining the separate issues in the three categories, I should emphasize that even though it is possible to separate the issues and the broad categories for purposes of analysis, there are important links among them. We will deal with these links later in the chapter.

THE NORTH–SOUTH DIALOGUE

Issues between the less developed and the developed countries have been analyzed and debated in international institutions since the late 1940s, but the debate gained a new prominence in the mid-1970s after the dramatic decision of the Arab members of OPEC to embargo petroleum and then OPEC's decision to quadruple the price of petroleum. Previously the advanced industrial states had been concerned about the economic development of LDCs. One motivation was to preserve or gain political influence.[22] Another was perceived long-run self-interest; the higher the level of economic development, the greater the possibility of mutually beneficial trade. Charity, in the sense of a felt solidarity with humankind and a desire to help those who were in misery or less fortunately placed, was also a factor. But the petroleum embargo and price increase threatened the economic stability of the advanced industrial states, and for some it even threatened their continued economic viability. Thus the OPEC actions dramatically illustrated how important LDCs could be in terms of the developed countries' own narrowly defined self-interest.

The LDCs promptly moved to take advantage of the situation. Backed by OPEC's power, the Group of 77 formulated new demands and pressed those that had been introduced previously with new vigor. The Group of 77 called for the creation of a New International Economic Order (NIEO). The new order they sought, however, was mainly a modification of that in existence, not the radical departure called for by Marxists and neo-Marxists. Withdrawal from the world market economy was not a realistic option even for the seven largest LDCs, much less those that were smaller. To accelerate their development the LDCs badly needed the capital, technical skills, and markets of the West.

A sharp confrontation occurred in the Sixth Special Session of the U.N. General Assembly in March 1974. Later that fall in the Assembly's regular session the Group of 77 took advantage of their voting strength and despite the strenuous objections of the United States and other Western countries forced adoption of the Charter of the Economic Rights and Duties of States.[23] The Charter embodied many of the NIEO proposals.

The LDCs sought preferential access to the markets of the developed countries. The demand for a generalized system of preferences for LDCs had first been raised formally at the initial session of UNCTAD in 1964. A generalized system of preferences, giving exports from the LDCs a competitive advantage in relation to exports from already industrialized countries, was seen as a way of stimulating industrialization in the LDCs. This was particularly important to the middle income LDCs such as Brazil, Mexico, Korea, Taiwan, and Singapore. At a conference of the UNIDO in 1974, after noting that only 7 percent of global industrial production occurred in LDCs, the Group of 77 pushed through a target of making the proportion 25 percent by the end of the twentieth century.

An additional LDC demand was for commodity agreements. The LDCs argued that the terms of trade were continually shifting to their disadvantage and that the price of the manufactured goods that they imported steadily increased relative to the price of the raw materials that they exported. They also objected to the sharp fluctuations in the prices that they received for their raw material exports and demanded mechanisms that would stabilize these prices. Copper exporters such as Zaïre and Zambia, cocoa exporters like Ghana, and coffee exporters like Colombia particularly suffered from these fluctuations.

The LDCs implored the advanced industrial states to transfer greater resources to them in the form of loans and grants and they argued that a larger portion of these should be provided through multilateral institutions rather than bilateral programs. Targets for such transfers had been set in the United Nations in the late 1960s and early 1970s. According to these targets the net transfer of resources from developed to less developed countries should equal at least 1 percent of the GNPs of the former, and official development assistance (ODA)—government resources transferred either through multilateral institutions or bilateral programs— should equal .7 percent of the developed countries' GNPs. Concessional aid was particularly important to the MSAs and the LLDCs.

There were ancillary demands to this general pressure for greater economic assistance. The LDCs sought to make the transfer of resources automatic rather than subject to voluntary decisions by individual developed countries and asked to have a transfer of resources built into the new reserve asset, the Special Drawing Rights (SDRs) that the International Monetary Fund had created. They also sought to increase the technical assistance programs of U.N. agencies that were financed by the regular budgets of these agencies rather than by voluntary contributions to the United Nations Development Program. The LDCs called as well for relief from the debts that they had amassed and were continuing to amass. Further, the LDCs sought greater power in international financial institutions, particularly the World Bank and the International Monetary Fund.

Further LDC demands were for larger transfers of technology. They recognized technology as the main source of the industrialized countries' economic strength and they sought to place themselves in a more favorable position in this respect. While other LDC requests had a reasonably clear focus, this one was more diffuse. To the extent that it referred to existing technology, it related to systems of patents and conditions for licensing. But to the extent that it referred to the capacity for technological innovation it related to higher-level training and the creation of research and development infrastructures.

The LDCs were concerned about transnational corporations (TNCs) and they sought greater control over their activities. They perceived that TNCs controlled the modern technology essential to economic growth. Highly publicized incidents of TNC involvement in the internal political affairs of LDCs created a general apprehension among LDC governments. These governments wanted to prevent TNCs from exercising political influence and wished to insure that the economic activities of TNCs would promote national development goals rather than the private economic interests of the firms or the economic position of the TNC's home countries. The LDCs wanted to be able to control TNCs without fear of intervention by the home countries and they asserted the right to nationalize foreign properties within their borders and to set the level of compensation using procedures based solely on national rather than international law.

As it became apparent that outer space and the deep ocean bed could have economically productive uses, the LDCs feared that the developed countries would use their advanced technology to monopolize the benefits of these new environments and sought to put them under international control. The concept was developed, particularly in connection with the deep sea bed, that the resources of these environments were the common heritage of humankind, the clear implication being that their benefits should be shared among humankind on a global basis.

These were the most prominent of the LDC demands. The list of issues in global economic interactions between less developed and developed countries, however, included two other items of crucial importance: food and population. Because of the introduction of public health measures in the developing countries, infant mortality had dropped sharply in the period following World War II. Since fertility did not decline as rapidly, the LDCs experienced unprecedented population growth. In fact, population growth was so great that it was difficult for the production of food to be increased rapidly enough to meet minimal nutritional needs in some areas, much less to improve the quality of diets. In Africa the production of food actually declined on a per capita basis during the late 1960s and early 1970s. There was consensus first among specialists in the West and then extending more broadly to other areas of the world that checking population growth and increasing the supply of food were basic economic issues that must be dealt with at the international as well as the national level.

It also became apparent that the capacity of the earth to sustain economic growth was not unlimited, that uncontrolled economic activity could so despoil the human environment as to render it useless for further economic activity or even uninhabitable. The problem was most salient in the advanced industrialized countries, where the level of economic activity was highest, and it was these countries that first called for action to protect the environment. Environmental protection, however, soon became a global issue. Environmental degradation could occur anywhere, and this degradation could have effects that would extend far beyond the local area. Although the LDC governments recognized this and were concerned about the quality of their immediate environment, they were determined that measures to protect the environment should not block or constitute serious obstacles to their efforts to achieve economic development. Environmental protection thus became linked with the broad list of development issues.

THE EAST–WEST DEBATE

The issues at stake in the debate between states with centrally planned economies and developed states with market economies were far less numerous than those involved in the North–South dialogue. Trade was the central question. Given the vast geographic territories and populations of the U.S.S.R. and the People's Republic of China, private entrepreneurs in Western countries saw these states as enormous potential markets. Several of the smaller Eastern European countries were also viewed as potentially important markets because of their historic ties with the West and their relatively high level of economic development. The communist countries, on the other hand, wanted access to Western technology and frequently needed to import agricultural commodities to make up for production shortfalls.

Because communist countries conduct their foreign transactions through state monopolies, their international trade is subject to political control. It is also subject to political control on the Western side. During the Cold War period Western governments inaugurated controls on trade with communist countries. Wishing to avoid contributing to communist military strength, they established licensing systems to block the export of items that they judged to have military significance. Most-favored-nation treatment was generally not extended by the United States to imports from communist countries. The communist countries, especially the U.S.S.R. and some of the Eastern European states with relatively high per capita GNPs, sought to trade with the Western states on a non-discriminatory basis. At the same time, as the 1970s wore on, these countries increasingly had to ask for credit to finance their purchases from the West, because their receipts from exports were inadequate to pay for the goods that they desired to import.

Trade with communist countries has been the subject of lively debate in the Western countries.[24] Some officials and commentators have warned against allowing this trade to become a substantial portion of the total trade of Western countries. They have argued that since communist countries exercise centralized control over their foreign trade, this trade could be manipulated for political purposes and the Western countries ought to guard against becoming vulnerable to such manipulation. Other officials and commentators have expressed concern about the U.S.S.R.'s increasing economic and military strength and have argued that the West should not allow its technology to be used to increase this strength still further. Finally, other officials and commentators have maintained that since communist countries want to gain access to Western technology through trade, by permitting and facilitating this trade or by blocking it, the West could induce communist countries to give greater attention to human rights and to pursue more liberal internal policies. Counterbalancing these arguments has been the attraction of increased exports and the general proposition that increasing trade would increase interdependence and thereby strengthen the self-interest of countries in continued cooperation rather than conflict.

The Western Internal Discussion

Among the developed countries with market economies, the economic issues are more technical and specific. There is broad agreement that private enterprise should play a major role in the organization of production and that market forces should generally guide the direction of international trade. The disagreements that exist involve issues of detail within this broad consensus and often are debates about which instrumentalities would be appropriate or most effective. In addition, in the 1970s the advanced industrial countries with market economies faced unfamiliar economic problems for which there have been no proposed solutions of demonstrated effectiveness or that evoked wide confidence. The central problem for the Western states is how to insure the continued growth of their economies without provoking ruinous inflation.[25] This problem existed before the OPEC quadrupling of petroleum prices, but OPEC's economic shock exacerbated the problem and added new dimensions to it. The governments of the developed countries with market economies need further economic growth so that they can respond to the demands of their constituents for better conditions of life. Continued economic growth is also an essential condition for the developed countries with market economies adopting more generous policies toward the LDCs: a more generous stance would not be feasible politically if it required a reduction in living standards within the developed countries.

From the end of World War II until the 1970s the developed countries with market economies had seen increasing their international trade as an important instrument for economic growth and they had been able to stimulate their international trade through measures that were relatively easy for them to take. The key measures were reducing obstacles to trade by lowering tariffs on manufactured items and insuring that currencies were freely convertible and retained a relatively stable value. The liberal trading structure created through these measures made possible an enormous expansion in international trade.

As Western governmental leaders projected continued growth for the economies of their states, increasing international trade continued to be an important instrument in their plans. However, it is an instrument that was more difficult to use than had been the case in the 1950s and 1960s. By the mid-1970s tariffs were at such a relatively low level that it became clear that nontariff barriers (for instance, health and sanitary regulations, customs procedures, and government purchasing regulations) as well as tariffs would have to be tackled if there were to be further trade liberalization. Inevitably, the remaining obstacles involved sensitive domestic interests. Eliminating them would be controversial and success in attaining further trade liberalization would require strong political efforts. Whether or not these efforts would be forthcoming was in doubt.

In addition, serious problems arose in the monetary area. Through 1971 the monetary regime established at the Bretton Woods Conference and implemented through the International Monetary Fund had worked reasonably well. By the late 1950s the currencies of the major Western countries and thus of the states that played the major role in world trade were all freely convertible. Most currencies had a fixed value that was generally denominated in terms of the dollar, and the dollar was in principle convertible into gold.

During the 1960s the United States persistently spent more abroad than it earned. The causes of this imbalance were disputed. The U.S. government maintained that because the dollar was overvalued in relation to other major currencies U.S. exports were so expensive that they were not competitive in terms of foreign currencies in foreign markets and imports to the United States were unrealistically inexpensive. Critics in the United States and abroad argued, sharply in contrast, that the true causes of the U.S. deficit were excessive military expenditures abroad and excessive direct foreign investment by U.S. transnational corporations. While this debate went on, U.S. deficits were covered by foreigners accepting dollars in payment, and some of these dollars were simply held by private sources and others were added to official reserves.

Soon the supply of dollars abroad became ominously large, and it became quite unrealistic to expect that the United States would or could allow these dollars to be converted into gold. The U.S. government argued that the countries that earned more abroad than they spent, such as the Federal Republic of Germany and Japan, should appreciate the value of their currencies so that their exports to the United States would be more expensive and U.S. exports more competitive. Because of the dollar's status as the major reserve currency, it would have been impractical for the United States to attempt to achieve the same objective by devaluing the dollar. Other governments countered by suggesting that the United States should alter its military and investment policies and thereby lessen its expenditures abroad. The debate continued without resolution until August 1971 when President Richard M. Nixon suspended the convertibility of the dollar into gold. The crisis that this action provoked launched a search for a new monetary regime.

To sustain and expand international trade the Western countries wanted to retain currency convertibility and to insure that the relative values of currencies would not fluctuate too much. If entrepreneurs could not have relatively stable expectations about the prices of foreign goods and services they would avoid foreign transactions and they would be reluctant to make foreign investments. Unfortunately, it proved difficult to create a new monetary regime that would insure currency convertibility and stability and also be widely acceptable. New issues compounded those already in contention in the 1960s. The increased price of petroleum exacerbated the United States' difficulty in balancing its foreign expenditures and earnings from abroad, and other countries which previously had been able to balance their foreign expenditures and earnings fell into deficit. Because the Western countries had different internal economic and political structures and accorded different weight to the importance of controlling inflation, they pursued different domestic economic policies.[26]

The Western European countries that include substantial numbers of foreign workers in their labor force, such as the Federal Republic of Germany, could respond to economic slowdowns by sending some of these workers back to their own countries. Even if the foreign workers lost their jobs but remained in the host country, since they are not enfranchised they were a less potent political force than unemployed citizens would be. At the same time, because of the ruinous inflation that Germany suffered in the 1920s, the public and the political leaders in the Federal Republic are extremely desirous of preventing and controlling inflation. The provision in Germany's constitution requiring that federal government income and expenditures be balanced symbolizes the long-run character and the intensity of this concern.[27] Japan, which like the Federal Republic of Germany in the 1970s persistently earned more than it spent abroad, had depended throughout the 1950s and 1960s on exports to spur the growth of its economy. Furthermore, for many reasons the Japanese market has been relatively difficult for foreign entrepreneurs to penetrate. Because of the Japanese lifetime employment system, Japanese firms are much less inclined than those in the United States to lay off workers. There is a propensity in the Japanese system to react to economic downturns by efforts to increase exports. Since United States firms do lay off workers, and since these workers are overwhelmingly U.S. citizens, the U.S. political system is very sensitive to unemployment. Increases in the level of unemployment in the United States will quickly result in the government adopting expansionary economic policies.

The discordant economic policies of the Western countries further fueled trade disequilibria in the 1970s. U.S. efforts to counter unemployment were inflationary, stimulating the demand for imported goods and making U.S. exports more expensive, thereby increasing the size of the U.S. deficit. Suggestions by the United States that the Federal Republic of Germany should stimulate its economy so that more would be imported from the United States provoked fears of inflation there and tended to be ignored. The Japanese did not welcome U.S. proposals that it should limit its exports and increase its imports.

The seeming inability of the Western countries to resolve the issues that divided them in their internal discussions provoked fears that the liberal trading structure that had been so carefully constructed in the years after World War II and that had resulted in such an increase in international trade might be in jeopardy. In any case, there was widespread fear that further progress toward trade expansion was problematic as protectionist forces became increasingly vocal in most of the Western countries.

Interaction

The agendas of most international governmental organizations with mandates to deal with economic issues include virtually all of the issues that have been outlined above. There is some division of labor in that different aspects of issues are treated in different IGOs, but there is also considerable duplication. The same arguments are repeated time after time, both in the same and in different institutions.

In part this repetition is caused by the fact that the problems are broad and interrelated and the mandates of international governmental organizations are often only vaguely defined. One cannot realistically discuss the economic problems of the LDCs without reference to the economic condition of the developed countries. The ILO, UNIDO, WIPO, UNDP, the World Bank, and other IGOs are all involved in the transfer of technology. But the desire of the various sides to have issues discussed in fora where the probabilities of their point of view prevailing are greater is perhaps a more basic explanation for the repetition.

The LDCs generally prefer the United Nations and its affiliated bodies in which each member state has one vote. Their voting power, mobilized through the Group of 77 caucus, is one of the principal strengths of the LDC coalition and thus they want to have matters discussed where maximum use can be made of this strength. The LDCs therefore want discussions to occur in such bodies as the General Assembly of the United Nations, UNCTAD, and UNIDO. These institutions, however, have neither control over significant resources nor the authority to take decisions that would be legally binding on member states. Their output is therefore generally confined to hortatory resolutions, urging the actions that the LDCs sought.

Such hortatory resolutions seldom go beyond broad general expressions of sentiment, and more often than not they have the character of an undifferentiated list of desirable goals rather than a detailed and sequential plan of action. The Group of 77 is a large coalition, bringing together states with very diverse characteristics. To try to do more than aggregate their separate interests would risk the fragile unity of the Group: it could tolerate little effort at setting priorities.

The developed states with market economies have sought to blunt the voting power of the Group of 77 by having the economic issues that were in contention discussed in the World Bank, the Asian and Inter-American Development Banks, the International Monetary Fund, and the General Agreement on Tariffs and Trade. Their weighted voting systems have insured that the Western states have had a determining influence in any decisions that might be taken in the international financial institutions. Although GATT does not have a system of weighted voting, the system of reciprocally negotiating tariff reductions guarantees that the interests of the major trading countries will not be ignored and that these countries will be major factors in decision-making. Since the international financial institutions have control of important resources and since the GATT negotiations can have a major impact on trading patterns, the LDCs have little choice but to participate in these meetings.

Another tactic of the Western states has been to attempt to shift the discussion to smaller bodies. In the mid-1970s when the discussions of the creation of a new international economic order were intense, the Western states succeeded in having issues discussed for more than a year in the Conference on International Economic Cooperation (CIEC), an ad hoc body that consisted of twenty-seven states, eight developed countries and nineteen LDCs. However, since the nineteen LDC representatives acted as a subordinate body of the Group of 77 and took instructions from that group, in the final analysis the nineteen were no more flexible in CIEC than their parent coalition was in the U.N. General Assembly.

In the North–South dialogue the other important element of strength of the LDCs beyond their voting power is OPEC and the threat it can pose to the economies of the developed states. The Western states have sought to minimize this factor by the creation within OECD of the International Energy Agency (IEA). The purpose of IEA is to serve as a forum for coordinated action by the consumer countries to lessen their vulnerability to OPEC. The participating states in IEA have agreed on schemes for sharing available supplies in the event of future shortages and have formulated strategies for conservation and the development of alternative sources of energy.

Both the less developed and the developed countries have sought to highlight the economic problems that they considered to be important by proposing that the United Nations sponsor special conferences devoted to the discussion of these issues. In the 1970s the United Nations sponsored conferences on the environment, food, and population, issues that the developed states considered to be crucial, and on science and technology for development, water, housing, and technical cooperation among developing countries, issues that the less developed states stressed. The conferences were devices for calling public attention to problems. They were also attempts to form transnational coalitions of national officials with similar responsibilities and similar interests. The developed states wanted the LDCs to slow their population growth and increase their food production. They thought that these goals could be advanced by discussing the issues with individuals in LDC governments who had operational responsibilities in these fields rather than discussing them with the diplomats who usually represented their countries in U.N. bodies. The LDCs similarly believed that they could advance their interests by involving individuals from the developed countries who could be expected to be sympathetic to their interests.

More generally, both the LDCs and the developed countries sought to establish links with sympathetic elements in the opposing camp and to use these links to bring about changes in the position of the entire group.

The states with centrally planned economies can usually be counted on to vote with the LDCs. LDC complaints against the industrialized states of the West often fit with communist ideological interpretations, and the communist states can gain tactical advantages from siding with the LDCs against the West. Since the bulk of LDC economic interactions are with Western states and since as a consequence most LDC demands are aimed at the West, the communist countries can often support LDC positions with little worry about having to back their verbal support with actions that would have material consequences.

Western European states are generally more sympathetic at least rhetorically to the position of the LDCs than the United States. There are several reasons for this. Western European states are more dependent upon the natural resources of LDCs, particularly petroleum, and international trade constitutes a larger share of the GNPs of the Western European states. The Western European states have historic ties with the LDCs in Africa and Asia that have been their colonies, and these historic ties make them more sympathetic to the African and Asian demands. Finally, several of the Western European states are more accustomed to a larger governmental role in economic affairs and hence do not have the same aversion as the United States does to LDC positions that call for governmental action in international economic transactions. Among the Western European states the Scandinavian countries and the Netherlands are the most sympathetic to the LDC positions. France, with its own tradition of planning, finds it easy to contemplate planning on international levels. The position of the Federal Republic of Germany, on the other hand, is closer to that of the United States, and the United Kingdom too is frequently aligned with the United States. Because of the differences among the developed countries with market economies, the Western European states have often initiated concessions to the LDCs, and then the United States has followed suit.

During the 1970s, however, the U.S. economy became more closely connected with those of LDCs, and the U.S. position in the dialogue has shifted. By 1977 LDCs bought 35 percent of U.S. exports and 45 percent of U.S. imports came from LDCs. Twenty percent of U.S. private foreign direct investment was in LDCs, and 47 percent of U.S. earnings from private direct foreign investment came from LDCs.[28] These changes have been paralleled by a more forthcoming U.S. posture in the North–South dialogue, yet there have been definite limits to the concessions that the U.S. government has been willing to make.[29] U.S. government officials have felt that some of the LDC proposals, particularly those relating to commodities, would seriously inhibit efficiency in the global economy, and that others would force the United States to transfer more funds than it wished to LDCs and, from the U.S. point of view, to the wrong recipients.

The discussions between the states with centrally planned and market economies and among the states with developed market economies have inevitably become intertwined with the North–South dialogue. The issues are not completely separable. The concessions that the developed countries can make to the LDCs are dependent, among other factors, on the state of their economies. And energy is a major problem for all countries whatever their level of development or their type of economic system. Some problems, however, can be relatively isolated, and they have been discussed in smaller bodies. The members of the EEC have formulated a common policy for their trade with communist countries, and export controls with respect to trade with communist countries have been discussed within the North Atlantic Treaty Organization. The Western states have held discussions to coordinate their economic policies within the Organization for Economic Cooperation and Development. Finally, the heads of government of the seven industrially most important states in the mid-1970s began to hold periodic summit meetings.

Debates on all of the issues often appear inconclusive. A fundamental reason for this is that in the present global political system the ability to act, to mobilize resources, rests predominantly with nation states. International governmental organizations can only spend money that is provided to them by national governments. Tariff and nontariff barriers to trade are put into effect by national governments. The EEC is the principal exception. It can raise money in its own right and it controls the commercial relations of its member states with other countries. Even in the EEC, however, national governments are primarily responsible for policies with respect to population growth, food production, and levels of economic activity generally, as well as for environmental protection and general economic policies such as those involved in efforts to insure full employment and combat inflation.

The debates in international governmental organizations, however, have clarified issues, and this in turn has an impact on national actions. As the debates have continued, all sides have increasingly understood that the economic condition of the developed states with market economies is of concern to all because of the crucial role of these states in the global economic system. If these economies are not functioning well, progress in the economies of all other states is difficult. The debate has also clarified the abiding and increasing interest of the Western economies in those of the LDCs. The Western economies are dependent upon the natural resources of the LDCs, and those countries offer important opportunities for further expansion of the trade of the developed countries.

Finally, links among the world's economies are becoming increasingly clear. This was dramatically illustrated in the 1970s when food shortages in any part of the world immediately led to higher food prices in other areas because of the tightness of the global supply.

Outputs

The outputs of the global economic interactions in the 1970s can also be analyzed in terms of the three broad debates: the North–South dialogue; the East–West debate; and the Western internal discussion.

One consequence of the economic debates of the mid-1970s already mentioned, the heightened awareness of the importance of the health of the economies of the industrially developed states with market economies to the health of the global economy, has sufficient general importance that the point merits amplification. This increased appreciation was not gained from Western rhetoric alone; instead, the rhetoric merely served to underscore developments in the world. In 1974 the developed states with market economies struggled to adjust to the increased price of petroleum. By the winter of 1974–1975 these economies were in the midst of a major recession. Their gross domestic product (GDP) grew by only .2 percent in 1974 and decreased by 1.2 percent the following year.[30] Because of the importance of these economies for the exports of all other areas, the growth of the gross domestic product of the other two major groups of states, the LDCs and the countries with centrally planned economies slumped also. The LDCs were particularly hard hit, the growth rate of their GDPs fell from 7.1 percent in 1973 to 5.8 percent in 1974 and to 3.6 percent in 1975. The experience demonstrated the interdependence among national economies throughout the world and it underscored the importance of the economies of the developed countries with market economies to the global economy. These facts could not be ignored. However much one might seek a different distribution of the gross world product, to be effective strategies would have to take interdependence and the crucial role of the Western economies into account.

OUTPUTS RELATED TO THE NORTH–SOUTH DEBATE

OPEC's cartellike actions and the threat of further such actions have provided coercive power to back up the negotiating position of the Group of 77. The sharp increase in the price of petroleum has also had a significant and immediate impact on the distribution of trade and income among the major groups of states. Table 7.3 compares the distribution of exports according to the three principal groups of states in 1970 and 1975. In only half a decade the value of the exports of the LDCs with market economies as a share of world exports jumped from 18 percent to 24 percent. The value of the exports of developed countries with market economies declined relatively, and Western exports were redirected from developed to

Table 7.3
The Distribution of Global Exports, 1970 and 1975
(percentages)

	EXPORTS TO							
	Developed Countries with Market Economies		*Less Developed Countries with Market Economies*		*Countries with Centrally Planned Economies*		TOTAL	
EXPORTS FROM	1970	1975	1970	1975	1970	1975	1970	1975
Developed countries with market economies	55	46	13	16	3	4	71	66
Less developed countries with market economies	13	17	4	6	1	1	18	24
Countries with centrally planned economies	3	3	2	2	6	5	11	10
Total	71	66	19	24	10	10	100	100

Source: United Nations, Secretariat, Department of Economic and Social Affairs, *Statistical Yearbook, 1976* (New York: United Nations, 1977), p. 434.

LDCs with market economies. The developed countries had to export more to the petroleum producing countries to meet their higher petroleum bills. Table 7.3 also shows an increase in Western exports to communist countries, which will be discussed in the next section.

These shifts in the direction of trade had an impact on the distribution of the GWP. Table 7.4 shows the shares of the global population and the GWP that the three groups of states accounted for in 1970 and 1975. The process of change was sharply accelerated in the 1970s: in contrast to the experience of the 1950s and 1960s, the share of the GWP accruing to the LDCs with market economies increased dramatically. To a certain extent this change belied the pessimistic assessments of those who argued that the position of the LDCs could be achieved only through a radical restructuring of the international economic system. The fact that the change did not occur until economic coercion had been employed, however, cast doubt on the optimistic liberal view that satisfactory progress could be gained through evolutionary change.

The increased shares of world exports and of the GWP were overwhelmingly gained by the OPEC countries, but even if the benefits were not broadly shared among LDCs, at least a group of them had their situation improved dramatically. The demonstrated economic strength of the OPEC countries and the solidarity between these countries and the others in the Group of 77 also undoubtedly contributed to a new climate in which the developed countries were more willing to make concessions to the LDCs. OPEC's actions and the threat of further price increases, however, were not the only factors. Some such concessions had been made long before OPEC demonstrated its strength in 1973. Furthermore, it remains open to question whether or not the concessions made after 1973 are more significant than those made prior to that date. Nor is it

Table 7.4

Shares of Global Population and the Gross World Product,
1970 and 1975 (percentages)

	1970		1975	
	Population	*GWP*	*Population*	*GWP*
Developed countries with market economies	18	64	18	61
Less developed countries with market economies	48	14	48	17
Countries with centrally planned economies	34	22	34	22

Source: United States of America, Department of State, Bureau of Public Affairs, Special Report 33 (May 1977, Department of State Publication 8903), "The Planetary Product in 1975 and a Preview for 1976," pp. 31, 33.

clear whether or not the ensemble of concessions will have a significant impact on narrowing the gap between the per capita GNPs of the developed and the less developed countries.

As early as 1964 the contracting parties to GATT added Part IV to the agreement dealing with trade and development. Part IV spelled out efforts to see that trade promoted development and among other provisions specified that the developed countries would not seek reciprocity when granting trade concessions to LDCs. In 1971 the EEC adopted a generalized system of preferences for LDCs. Under EEC's system manufactured products from LDCs are admitted duty-free; however, a ceiling in terms of monetary value is fixed annually for each product. These ceilings may not be lowered, and they have been progressively raised. The United States followed suit and in 1974 adopted a generalized preference system that went into effect in 1976. The U.S. system also provided for duty-free entry for specified manufactured goods but, unlike the EEC's system, no ceilings were established.

The actions of the EEC and the United States in granting generalized preferences, a demand that the LDCs first raised in UNCTAD in 1964, did not settle the issue. The LDCs wanted the preferences extended and wanted to have them made permanent. The United States particularly insisted that they should be temporary, that they were a unilateral concession given by the developed countries to facilitate the growth of the LDCs. The U.S. Congressional Act stipulated that the U.S. preferences should be reviewed after a decade, the implication being that eventually LDC industries ought to be able to compete equally with those of the developed countries.

From the outset, the EEC had insisted that the expansion of imports of manufactured items from LDCs should be controlled. The EEC feared that unemployment in low-skill manufacturing industries would be caused within the community if this expansion were too rapid. Although the United States took a more liberal position rhetorically, in practice it too had similar concerns. During the 1970s more and more imports of manufactured goods came to be subject to so-called orderly marketing agreements. These were agreements negotiated between importing and exporting countries specifying quantities that would be imported and limiting the increases. The practice first developed with respect to textiles, and in 1973 GATT adopted a system that sanctioned the practice, but it made it subject to certain conditions and established a mechanism for monitoring behavior in this area. Other voluntary and involuntary restraints on imports were also adopted.

The flow of resources to LDCs increased significantly during the 1970s, even though the magnitude of the flow largely remained subject to the voluntary decisions of the developed countries. In 1970 the net flow of resources to LDCs was $17.1 billion and by 1975 it was $46.7 billion.

Even allowing for inflation, this was a substantial increase. It is important though to analyze the way in which this increase was achieved. Table 7.5 shows the net transfer to LDCs in 1970 and 1975 by major groups of donor countries. The members of OECD's Development Assistance Committee (DAC) are: Australia, Austria, Belgium, Canada, Denmark, Finland, France, Federal Republic of Germany, Italy, Japan, the Netherlands, New Zealand, Norway, Sweden, Switzerland, the United Kingdom, and the United States. Several features of the table are worthy of note. First, the transfer of resources from countries with centrally planned economies—the Soviet Union, the Eastern European communist countries, and the People's Republic of China—declined slightly. Second, the largest component of the increase, 60 percent, was private funds from DAC countries. These funds trebled, while official development assistance from DAC countries only doubled. Finally, by 1975 the transfer of resources from OPEC countries had come to constitute a substantial proportion of the total.

In 1975 the transfer of resources from the member countries of DAC to LDCs was 1.05 percent of their gross national products. This was the first time that the broadly proclaimed and generally accepted 1 percent target had been met, but it was met only because of the substantial increase in the flow of private funds. The Official Development Assistance of the DAC countries was .33 percent of their gross national products in 1975, an insignificant increase from the 1970 figure of .31 percent. Some DAC member countries substantially increased their ODA during the 1970s. Sweden's ODA exceeded .7 percent of its gross national product in 1974 and the Netherlands' exceeded .7 percent of its GNP the following year.[31] Norway achieved .7 percent in 1976. U.S. Official Development

Table 7.5
The Net Transfer of Resources to Less Developed Countries
(in billions of dollars)

	YEAR	
CATEGORY OF DONOR COUNTRIES	*1970*	*1975*
Members of the Development Assistance Committee of OECD	$15.7	$40.4
(of which ODA)	($6.8)	($13.6)
Members of OPEC	$.4	$5.5
Countries with centrally planned economies	$1	$.8
Total	$17.1	$46.7

Source: Organization for Economic Cooperation and Development, *Development Cooperation: Efforts and Policies of the Members of the Development Assistance Committee, 1972 Review* (Paris: OECD, 1972), and *1977 Review* (Paris: OECD, 1977).

Assistance fell from .31 percent of its GNP in 1970 to .25 percent in 1975 and .22 percent in 1977. The Federal Republic of Germany's ODA was only .27 percent of its GNP in 1977, and Japan's was only .21 percent.[32] Perhaps because the overall amount of Official Development Assistance was so far from the target, the increase in the total net transfer of funds to the LDCs did not quell their demand for increased assistance.

Largely because of the increased importance in the mid-1970s of private funds in the net transfer of resources to LDCs, the terms on which these resources were transferred hardened considerably. Concessional grants were a smaller proportion of the funds. A larger proportion of the funds had to be repaid, interest rates on loans were higher, and the period for repayment was shorter.

Total LDC debt grew from $17.9 billion in 1960 to $72.9 billion in 1970 and $172.9 billion in 1975.[33] Starting in 1973 LDC debt grew at an annual rate of 20 percent or more. Prior to 1973 the annual rate of increase in LDC debt never reached 20 percent. One reason for the substantial increase of LDC debt in the 1970s was that, like the developed countries, LDCs had to pay increased prices for the petroleum that they imported. To some extent the LDCs covered these increased costs by borrowing from private banks in the Western developed countries. Ironically, these banks were eager to lend funds because their assets were swelled by deposits made by OPEC countries from their increased earnings from petroleum exports. In addition, the recession in the Western countries lessened the demand for funds there.

The sharp increase in LDC debt alarmed many national and international officials. It undoubtedly contributed to LDC pressures for debt relief, and in 1977 Sweden, Canada, Switzerland, and the Netherlands agreed to write off debts owed to them by LLDCs. In 1978 the United Kingdom decided to convert loans to most of the LLDCs as well as to several South Asian countries into grants on the ground that it did not make sense to continue collecting debt service payments from countries to which new aid was being given on a grant basis. Other Western donors were moving toward similar measures in the context of their aid programs. None of the donor countries, however, could liquidate debts owed to private parties. Meanwhile, efforts were made to increase the lending authority of the international financial institutions, and an agreement was reached on rescheduling the debts of individual LDCs. Between 1970 and 1975 the annual capital subscription disbursements of DAC member countries to multilateral financial institutions jumped from $.5 billion to $1.7 billion, and their contributions to all multilateral agencies rose from $1.1 billion to $3.8 billion.[34] The international financial institutions, and particularly the International Monetary Fund, came to play a leading role in rescheduling the debts of individual LDCs. Private banks followed the IMF's lead.

Although the developed countries came to see that they had an important interest in gaining assured access to the natural resources of LDCs and in eliminating excessive fluctuations in the prices that they paid for these resources, little progress was made in the negotiation of commodity agreements. Between World War II and the early 1970s commodity agreements had been negotiated for coffee, olive oil, sugar, tin, cocoa, and wheat. Discussions of the problems of commodities were intensified in the mid- and late 1970s, but it appeared that few new agreements would be concluded, even though the developed countries had agreed in principle to accept the LDC proposal to create a common fund to finance commodity agreements.

However, when the agreement of association between the EEC and states in Africa, the Caribbean, and the Pacific (ACP countries—largely former dependent territories of the EEC members) was renegotiated in the early 1970s, the ACP countries were successful in their attempts to write into the agreement some provisions relating to commodities. The Lome Convention of 1973 contains provisions aimed at stabilizing the income that the ACP countries receive from their export of commodities. The STABEX system provides for compensation payments when an ACP country's income from exports of specified commodities falls below a certain level if these receipts constitute a specified portion of the country's total export earnings. These payments may have to be repaid if the price for the exports increases; otherwise they are forgiven. It is conceivable that the Lome agreement could be a prelude to a broader agreement on commodities, just as the EEC generalized system of preferences was a prelude to the U.S. adoption of a similar system.

Real progress was made in the 1970s with respect to slowing population growth and increasing food production. The resources devoted to population programs increased from about $80 million in 1970 to over $300 million in 1976. The World Population Conference which the United Nations convened in 1974 encouraged countries to adopt population policies and to consider setting targets for slowing population growth. More important, the global rate of population growth actually started to decline in the early and mid-1970s.[35]

The United Nations also convened a World Food Conference in 1974. It led to the establishment of the World Food Council to monitor changes in the supply of and demand for food. Even though the U.S.S.R. was not a member of the Food and Agriculture Organization, it became a member of the World Food Council. The World Food Conference also led to the creation of an International Fund for Agricultural Development (IFAD). This fund was an important innovation in international institutions. Its purpose was to support projects that would contribute to increased agricultural productivity in LDCs. The funding of IFAD was shared equally between members of OPEC and OECD. Voting strength was divided into thirds: one third was given to the members of OECD, another third to members of OPEC, and the final third to LDCs that were not members of OPEC. In other words, states that had traditionally been referred to as LDCs would control two-thirds of the voting power within IFAD. This was the first institution to have such a system.

In general, however, little change was made in the decision-making structures of existing IGOs. The voting power of the OPEC states was increased in the International Monetary Fund and the World Bank in accordance with their increased role in world trade, but the formula of basing a member's voting strength on its financial contribution was not abandoned.

Progress has been made with respect to what had come to be known as the "global commons," outer space and the deep sea bed. Satellite communications offered the LDCs ways of quickly increasing their capacity for communicating with one another and with other areas of the world. Although it was the developed countries that created and managed the technology for satellite communications, they could use this technology to communicate with other areas of the world only if these areas gave their consent to the establishment of ground stations. The International Telecommunication Satellite Organization, created in 1964, is in effect a global public utility. For the first several years it operated under temporary arrangements, but when the permanent arrangements were negotiated in the early 1970s the LDCs were able to use their voting strength and control over access to their territories to increase their role in the management and operation of the organization. Assignment of radio frequencies for the operation of communication satellites was the responsibility of the International Telecommunication Union (ITU), and the LDCs used their voting strength in ITU to insure that their intersts would be protected.

Comprehensive negotiations on the law of the sea began in 1973 and were still in progress in 1980. It seemed likely, however, that an international authority would be created that would have power to license mining on the deep sea bed and to collect fees from this licensing. It also seemed likely that an enterprise would be established that would be collectively owned by the global community. This enterprise would be able to mine the sea bed and to sell the materials obtained for a profit. Thus both through the licensing of the authority and the operations of the enterprise, the international community would have a significant source of income to be used for development purposes that would not depend upon government contributions.

Finally, progress has been made with respect to the protection of the environment. The U.N. Conference on the Human Environment, held in Stockholm in 1972, aroused world-wide concern for the degradation of the environment. As a consequence of the conference, the United Nations Environment Program (UNEP) was established and a voluntary fund was created that UNEP could use to finance projects that would have a catalytic effect in increasing global environmental protection activities. Steps were taken toward the creation of global monitoring systems. National governments began to act to protect the environment within their own territories. By 1976, 95 of the United Nations' member states had established administrative machinery within their own governments to perform environmental protection functions.[36] In various places throughout the world atmospheric and water pollution began to be lessened.

OUTPUTS RELATED TO THE EAST–WEST DEBATE

The other two major categories of economic issues in global interaction can be handled more briefly. Trade between the developed countries with market economies and those with centrally planned economies expanded briskly from the mid-1960s through the mid-1970s. In the half decade from 1970 to 1975 this trade, measured in terms of absolute monetary value, more than trebled. The rapid increase in trade was related to the general relaxation of East–West tension. Each side was more eager to trade with the other as the Cold War atmosphere was replaced with that of détente. In addition, with the development of the communist economies, their needs for access to advanced Western technology grew, and, as other markets seemed to reach saturation points, the attractiveness of the communist countries, which contained a third of the world's population, increased for Western exporters.

As the 1970s wore on, however, the expansion in trade, particularly between the West and the U.S.S.R. and the communist countries of Eastern Europe, began to slow. The most basic general reason was that the communist countries have not been expanding their exports to the West as rapidly as they have expanded their imports from the West. The resulting deficits have been financed by the communist countries borrowing in the West. By 1976 their indebtedness to the West was about $40 billion.[37] It seems probable that in the short run the only way in which the communist countries can continue to expand their imports would be by increasing their debt, and their willingness to incur debt and Western willingness to lend are limiting factors to the expansion of trade. For the communist countries to expand their debt further would probably require their acceptance of lenders scrutinizing and monitoring their economies. The International Monetary Fund does this routinely when it lends substantial amounts to its member states, and Western private financial institutions are often willing to accept the IMF's surveillance as a basis for their own lending. Romania was the only communist state that was a member of IMF. However, in 1979 there were indications that Poland would accept Western private institutions exercising financial surveillance comparable to that exercised by IMF.

There have also been political obstacles to the expansion of this trade. The U.S.S.R. and some Eastern European communist states have been unwilling to recognize the EEC and have insisted that East–West trade issues should be settled individually with the community's member states. The Community, on the other hand, although it has invited the Council of Mutual Economic Assistance to conduct trade negotiations, has doubted that CMEA has the authority to represent its member states. Desultory negotiations have been conducted between the European communities and CMEA, but without substantial results. Bilateral agreements, however, have been concluded between the community and some Eastern European countries.

Even more serious obstacles have existed in the case of the United States. In October 1972 the United States signed a trade agreement with the U.S.S.R. granting most-favored-nation treatment to Soviet goods in return for various Soviet commitments including a declaration of intent to place large orders for U.S. agricultural and industrial goods, provisions for third-country commercial arbitration, and improved facilities for U.S. businesses in Moscow. Authorizing legislation was required to bring this agreement into effect. The necessary authority was included in the 1974 U.S. trade act, but under the so-called Jackson-Vanik amendment (named after its sponsors, Senator Henry M. Jackson and Representative Charles A. Vanik) the legislation specified that the United States may not conclude a commercial agreement to grant most-favored-nation treatment or offer U.S. government credits to any communist country that denied freedom of emigration. To grant MFN treatment or access to such credit facilities as the Export-Import Bank and the Commodity Credit Corporation, the U.S. president was required to certify that he had received assurances that the country concerned was permitting the emigration of its citizens. The purpose of the Jackson-Vanik amendment was to use the prospect of trade as a lever to induce the Soviet Union to ease its restrictions on the emigration of Jews. The U.S.S.R. responded to the Jackson-Vanik amendment by informing the United States that it could not accept a trading relationship established on what it viewed as a discriminatory basis. In response to Soviet and Soviet-backed military interventions in Africa and Afghanistan, the United States took a more restrictive stance than earlier toward granting licenses for American manufacturers to export high-technology goods to the Soviet Union.[38] Although Jewish emigration from the U.S.S.R. in 1978 totaled about 30,000 and although there were various discussions about how trade between the United States and the Soviet Union might be increased, concrete steps toward this goal, such as repeal of the Jackson-Vanik amendment, still had to be taken.

Developments with respect to trade between the United States and Eastern Europe have been somewhat more favorable. The United States granted Poland most-favored-nation treatment in 1960, and Poland was exempted from the Jackson-Vanik amendment. Most-favored-nation treatment was extended to Rumania in 1975 and to Hungary in 1978 on the basis of a presidential certification. The Jackson-Vanik amendment did not apply to Yugoslavia.

Western trade with the People's Republic of China expanded more slowly in the mid-1970s than Western trade with the U.S.S.R. and Eastern Europe, and a consequence China did not amass as large a debt in the West as did the other communist countries. China protected its credit by emphasizing the technique of obtaining equipment from Western suppliers and repaying them with goods produced by the equipment. The People's Republic of China negotiated a trade agreement with the EEC in early 1978. The five-year agreement granted each side most-favored-nation status and committed both parties to several steps to increase trade. Following U.S. recognition of the People's Republic, the United States granted China most-favored-nation treatment. China and Japan meanwhile negotiated an agreement that granted China access to massive Japanese credit. Thus, even though Western trade with the People's Republic of China had initially grown more slowly than that with the U.S.S.R., the prospects for its further expansion in the 1980s appeared bright. Access to Western technology would be essential for the realization of the ambitious modernization goals that China adopted in the late 1970s, and there seemed to be fewer political obstacles to trade between the West and China than there were between the West and the U.S.S.R. The People's Republic of China abandoned its traditional hostility toward dealing with the West and hostility toward China lessened, especially in the United States.

OUTPUTS RELATED TO THE INTERNAL WESTERN DISCUSSIONS

Among the developed countries with market economies, economic issues have been generally resolved within the framework of existing institutional mechanisms. Perhaps the most remarkable accomplishment has been the ability of these countries to cope with the sharp increase in the price of petroleum products with only minimal disruptions. The price increase and the recession in 1974 and 1975 did not fundamentally disrupt the trade liberalization that these states had accomplished since World War II. The cycle of escalating tariffs and other barriers to trade and competitive currency devaluations that had plagued the world economy in the 1930s were avoided. In 1974 the members of OECD adopted a pledge not to take unilateral action to restrict imports, and this pledge has been renewed in subsequent years. In 1973, at a meeting in Tokyo, GATT inaugurated a multilateral trade negotiation to reduce obstacles to trade still further, and the following year the U.S. Congress gave the president legislative authority to participate in these negotiations, including the authorization to cut existing tariffs by 60 percent and to eliminate entirely those that were under 5 percent. Slow progress was made in the multilateral trade negotiations, but eventually they moved forward to a successful conclusion in 1979, continuing the process of lowering obstacles to trade.

The developed countries have also managed to preserve currency convertibility. From August 1971 when President Nixon suspended the convertibility of dollars into gold, and the system which had been established under the International Monetary Fund in which currencies were pegged to the value of the dollar and the dollar was convertible into gold collapsed, the value of the currencies of the major trading states has fluctuated according to the market forces of supply and demand.

In the ensuing negotiations to establish a new monetary regime, the United States favored continuing a system of fluctuating exchange rates. The United States wanted to be free to manage its internal economy without being constrained by the necessity of maintaining the value of the dollar. Other Western countries, for which international trade constituted a much greater proportion of their gross national products, however, placed a much higher value on exchange-rate stability. France, particularly, argued the necessity of returning to a system of fixed exchange rates.

The U.S. position prevailed, and the system of fluctuating exchange rates was finally given legitimacy through amendments to the IMF Articles of Agreement that went into effect in 1978. Under the new system governments may establish fixed values for their currencies or may allow them to fluctuate, but they pledge to take action to maintain a relatively stable value for their currencies, and the IMF can monitor developments and make recommendations which, if ignored by the country concerned, might close its access to IMF credit.

In December 1978, eight members of the EEC—all except the United Kingdom—moved to attempt to insure that at least their own currencies would remain in a relatively stable relationship by creating the European Monetary System. They agreed to stop their currencies from fluctuating against each other by more than a prescribed margin, intervening when necessary on the market with money borrowed from a newly created European Monetary Fund. The European Monetary Fund was formed by the members pooling 20 percent of their gold and dollar reserves. Credits drawn from this account are expressed in terms of European Currency Units, the value of which is based on a basket of the members' currencies. German Chancellor Helmut Schmidt originally proposed the creation of the new system. He was convinced that the currency fluctuations within Europe had slowed economic growth in the European community in the 1970s by deterring trade and investment. French President Valéry Giscard d'Estaing backed his proposal. Although the creation of the European Monetary System was clearly a reaction to the sharp currency fluctuations induced by the decline in the value of the dollar and was designed to reduce the significance of the dollar in global trading arrangements, Chancellor Schmidt and other Europeans argued that greater currency stability in Europe would be beneficial to the dollar and to the United States. The United States ultimately accepted this interpretation, and the establishment of the European Monetary System gained the full backing of President Carter and his administration.

Steps have also been taken toward regulating the activities of transnational corporations (TNCs). In 1976 OECD adopted a Declaration on International Investment and Multinational Enterprises. The declaration contained provisions aimed at making TNCs responsible to host governments and subject to the same rules of behavior as national firms. Other provisions sought to insure that transnational corporations would receive the same treatment by governments as national firms. OECD established a Committee on International Investment and Multinational Enterprises to monitor the consequences of the Declaration. OECD's action, however, did not forestall pressure within the United Nations to adopt a code of conduct for TNCs.

At the same time that progress has been made on the solution of a variety of issues, others have remained virtually untouched. Little of any significance has been done to coordinate the domestic economic policies of the principal Western countries, despite the statements of good intentions emanating from their economic summits of the mid-1970s. The most troublesome consequence of this has been that the rates of inflation among them have varied considerably, increasing the difficulties of keeping their currencies in stable relationships. The United States has continued to spend more abroad than it earned. In 1978 its imports exceeded the value of its exports by $28.5 billion. As a consequence of the U.S. deficits the quantities of dollars held by foreigners have grown to mammoth proportions. Many of these dollars have come to constitute so-called Eurodollars, a vast supply of American currency held in Europe, not subject to the control of any national monetary authority. As of 1978 Eurodollar deposits exceeded $500 billion. These Eurodollars have been used as the basis for the creation of global credit, and they financed the deficits that many states faced because of the increased price of petroleum imports. The fact that this expansion of credit is uncontrolled, however, has been a major source of concern. Although Eurodollars helped to ease the petroleum crises, they could also be put to other less benign purposes.

There were signs in 1978, however, that the major Western countries might be moving toward coordination of their domestic economic policies. As unemployment began to affect German as well as foreign workers, the government of the Federal Republic of Germany became more inclined to adopt expansionary policies despite their possible inflationary impact. And in the United States, almost in counterpoint, concern about inflation mounted. The dramatic decline in the value of the dollar in 1978 also convinced the Carter administration that currency fluctuations were not totally benign. In the thirteen months from October 1977 through October 1978 the dollar fell by 38 percent against the Swiss franc, 34 percent against the Japanese yen and 26 percent against the German deutschmark. The Carter administration became convinced that the decline of the value of the dollar was contributing to domestic inflation. Together with the Federal Republic of Germany, Switzerland, and Japan, the United States launched a closely coordinated foreign exchange intervention effort to protect the value of the dollar. Thus by the end of the 1970s there was greater consensus among the principal Western countries concerning economic issues than there had been earlier, and this was a hopeful sign.

Developmental Issues

Although substantial progress has been made in solving international economic issues in the 1970s, basic problems remained. Dealing with these problems will rank among the major issues of the remaining years of the twentieth century. The crucial ones can be subsumed under three broad rubrics: (1) narrowing the gap between the per capita GNPs of the developed and the less developed countries; (2) managing the policies of the developed states so that there could be continued growth without destructive inflation; and (3) improving international institutions.

In a division of the world into two broad categories of developed and less developed countries and including both states with market economies and states with centrally planned economies in each category, in 1970 the gap between the gross national product of the developed countries and that of the less developed countries was 12 to 1.[39] Even if the relatively favorable progress of the LDCs that occurred in the 1960s were continued and even if the targets that the United Nations set for the Second Development Decade (the decade of the 1970s) had been met (6 percent annual growth for gross product, 3.5 percent growth for gross product per capita, assuming an average 2.5 percent annual population growth) this gap would only begin to narrow around the year 2000. However, if more favorable but feasible policies toward the LDCs were pursued, by 2000 the gap could be narrowed to 7 to 1.[40] Can the world tolerate a continuation of the 12 to 1 gap? Could the policies be adopted that would be required to narrow the gap to 7 to 1? These were crucial issues that clearly will be answered one way or another in the remaining years of the twentieth century. How they are settled will determine whether those advocating equity through reform or those demanding radical restructuring of the international economy were correct.

The second set of issues concerns the ability of the developed states to manage their economies so as to insure continued growth without destructive inflation. Their record in the late 1970s was encouraging but did not offer conclusive proof that it would be possible. The continued large deficits in the U.S. balance of payments are a major source of concern, as is the U.S. rate of inflation. And the economic difficulties of all of the developed countries with market economies have created a climate that is ripe for the growth of protectionism. A new wave of protectionism could destroy the liberal trading structure that has been so carefully constructed since World War II and that had been responsible for the enormous growth in world trade that occurred during this period. A new wave of protectionism would also frustrate the hopes of the LDCs to expand their exports of manufactured goods to the developed countries. Thus hopes for improving the position of the LDCs depend substantially on the maintenance and expansion of the open Western trading system. They also depend on the West's being prosperous enough to continue and to expand its concessional assistance to the LLDCs.

Along with these substantive issues, there are questions about whether or not the international institutional structure is adequate. The LDCs criticize the international financial institutions because of the dominant weight of the developed countries in their decision-making structures, while the developed countries criticize the one-state, one-vote formula of the United Nations and its related agencies as unrealistic. No system of representation for IGOs has been found that would command the same broad legitimacy as the one-person, one-vote formula does within national politics. To give states with populations of vastly different sizes equal power in decision-making does not intuitively seem to be fair while giving individuals equal power does seem to be fair. On the other hand, wealth has long been abandoned as a criterion for allocating power within domestic political systems. The world badly needs a formula for allocating power in IGOs that is different from the two systems that are used predominantly now.

An even more fundamental problem is how to make IGOs responsible to popular opinion in the same way that national governments are. A government in a democratic country must face periodic elections, and its continuance in office will depend upon its obtaining the support of a majority of voters. Even in nondemocratic countries, governments must be concerned about popular support. Governments can be removed from office by rebellions and coups as well as by elections. But IGOs generally do not include among their organs individuals who are directly responsible to popular opinion. IGO secretariats are bureaucracies, and the policy organs of IGOs—assemblies and councils—are generally comprised of delegates or representatives from national bureaucracies. To the extent that member states assign significant power to IGOs, there is a risk of transferring important elements of public policy from popular to bureaucratic control. If more power is to be given to international organizations, this problem will loom increasingly large. The only IGO to have significant power to act independently, the European Community, has put into effect a system of direct elections for the members of its parliament.

In the meantime, global economic interactions are handled through an extensive web of IGO networks, and although each individual organization can be viewed as inadequate, the ensemble of institutions can minimize the inadequacies of particular ones. UNCTAD may be too strident in taking the side of the poor. but UNCTAD's pressures may contribute to organizations dominated by the rich countries, such as GATT and IMF, pursuing more generous policies. Popular control is preserved by national governments generally retaining control over the instruments of action.

An institution providing central guidance for the global economic system is lacking, but to a certain extent ad hoc arrangements—particularly the periodic economic summit meetings of the heads of government of the seven most important states with market economies—have been crafted to fill in this gap. The Conference on International Economic Cooperation was an attempt to set up a body that would bring developed and less developed states with market economies together and be small enough to facilitate detailed negotiations. Despite the lack of results, this was an experiment that could be repeated. The major communist states now have only limited connections with the world market economy, but as these connections increase, the need for more institutional links will increasingly be felt. The membership of the Soviet Union in the World Food Council is surely a forerunner of other institutional developments.

Projections

To attempt to forecast the future course of the world economy would obviously be foolhardy. Yet the record of the years since the end of World War II gives considerable grounds for optimism. Compared to what had happened in the 1930s, when efforts at international collaborative solutions to economic problems proved fruitless and states sought to solve their economic problems through autarkic techniques, the record of the years after World War II has been one of remarkable achievements. A wide variety of international institutions has been created, and national officials have learned to use these institutions to forge cooperative solutions that benefited all states by making possible enormous increases in the gross world product. There is general awareness of global economic interdependence. This record of more than thirty years of successful collaboration provides a basis for believing that this collaboration will be continued. National and international officials seem to have learned how to surmount the obstacles that had plagued earlier efforts. They seem to be learning how to cope with interdependence.

Another ground for optimism is the significant progress that has been made in understanding the operation of the world economy. Plausible and useful models of the world economy have been developed. Because of their existence, it has become possible to analyze the consequences of the continued pursuit of existing policies as well as the probable consequences of different policy choices. The intellectual tools for managing the global economy are at hand.

What does not exist, either for national economies or for the global economy, is a realistic understanding of the interaction between political and economic variables. It can be determined that with economically feasible policies the gap between the GNP of developed and less developed states could be narrowed from 12 to 1 to 7 to 1 by the end of the twentieth century. But what would the political consequences of such policies be? To what extent would it be politically feasible for the developed countries to accept increased imports of manufactured goods from the LDCs?

Although political scientists have begun to study economic issues and economists have begun to worry about political factors, much more needs to be done in the way of creating a true science of political economy. Thus far neither the liberal nor the neo-Marxist version of political economy has provided a wholly satisfactory explanation of the forces at work in global economic interactions or an adequate guide to policy. Developing a discipline of political economy may be crucial to the successful resolution of the major political-economic problems that the world faces now and will face in the remaining years of the twentieth century.

Notes

1. The process is described in Simon Kuznet's classic study, *Modern Economic Growth: Rate, Structure and Spread* (New Haven, Conn.: Yale University Press, 1966).
2. For a succinct and stimulating analysis of this historical process, see

W. Arthur Lewis, *The Evolution of the International Economic Order* (Princeton, N.J.: Princeton University Press, 1978). N.J.: Princeton University Press, 1978).

3. Wassily Leontief et al., *The Future of the World Economy* (New York: Oxford University Press, 1977), p. 3.

4. See, for instance, Arthur M. Okun, *Equality and Efficiency: The Big Tradeoff* (Washington, D.C.: Brookings Institution, 1975).

5. For a detailed analysis of this, see Robert O. Keohane and Joseph S. Nye, *Power and Interdependence: World Politics in Transition* (Boston: Little, Brown, 1977).

6. United States of America, Department of State, Bureau of Public Affairs, Special Report 33 (May 1977), "The Planetary Product in 1975 and a Preview for 1976," p. 31. The methods by which this figure was computed are explained in the pamphlet. The most significant assumption built into the computation is that since so much of the economic activity in very poor countries consists of subsistence agriculture, based as they are on monetary transactions GNP data understate the true level of income of these countries. For this reason, countries with per capital GNPs of less than $400 per year have been given a supplement of 60 percent, countries with per capita GNPs of from $400 to $800, a supplement of 30 percent, and countries with per capita GNPs of from $800 to $1,600 a supplement of 10 percent.

7. United Nations, Secretariat, Department of Economic and Social Affairs, *Statistical Yearbook, 1976* (New York: United Nations, 1977), p. 425.

8. United Nations, Department of Economic and Social Affairs, *Statistical Yearbook, 1953* (New York: United Nations, 1954), p. 369.

9. The members of OECD are: Australia, Austria, Belgium, Canada, Denmark, Finland, France, the Federal Republic of Germany, Greece, Iceland, Ireland, Italy, Japan, Luxembourg, the Netherlands, New Zealand, Norway, Portugal, Spain, Sweden, Switzerland, Turkey, the United Kingdom, and the United States. Yugoslavia has special status with OECD.

10. For an intellectually elegant version of the argument that the existing international economic system worked against and exploited the underdeveloped countries see: Arghiri Emmanuel, *Unequal Exchange: A Study of the Imperialism of Trade* (New York: Monthly Review Press, 1972).

11. United States of America, "The Planetary Product in 1975 and a Preview for 1976," p. 31.

12. International Bank for Reconstruction and Development, *World Tables, 1976* (Baltimore: Johns Hopkins University Press, 1976).

13. United Nations, Secretariat, Department of Economic and Social Affairs, *Statistical Yearbook, 1962* (New York: United Nations, 1963) and *Statistical Yearbook, 1976*.

14. International Bank for Reconstruction and Development, *World Tables, 1976*.

15. United States of America, "The Planetary Product in 1975 and a Preview for 1976," p. 31.

16. In 1978 the member states of CMEA were: Bulgaria, Cuba, Czechoslovakia, Democratic Republic of Germany, Hungary, Mongolia, Poland, Rumania, the U.S.S.R., and Vietnam. In addition, Yugoslavia was an associate member.

17. United Nations, *Statistical Yearbook, 1976.*
18. Algeria, Ecuador, Gabon, Indonesia, Iran, Iraq, Kuwait, Libya, Nigeria, Qatar, Saudi Arabia, United Arab Emirates, Venezuela made up OPEC.
19. The most seriously affected LLDCs include Afghanistan, Bangladesh, Benin, Burundi, Central African Republic, Chad, Ethiopia, Gambia, Guinea, Haiti, Laos, Lesotho, Mali, Nepal, Niger, Rwanda, Somalia, Sudan, Tanzania, Uganda, Upper Volta, Western Samoa, Yemen, and Democratic Yemen. The other LLDCs are: Bhutan, Botswana, Malawi, Maldives, and Sikkim.
20. These countries are Austria, Finland, Iceland, Norway, Portugal, Sweden, and Switzerland.
21. See Helmut Schmidt, "The Struggle for the World Product," *Foreign Affairs,* 70 (April 1974), 437–51.
22. The several motives for Western aid programs are discussed in David Wall, *The Charity of Nations: The Political Economy of Foreign Aid* (New York: Basic Books, 1973).
23. U.N. General Assembly Resolution 3281 (XXIX).
24. For a sample of this debate see the articles by Samuel P. Huntington, Franklyn Holzman and Richard Portes, John Kiser, Maurice J. Mountain, and Robert E. Klitgaard, "Trade, Technology and Leverage," *Foreign Policy,* 32 (Fall 1978), 63–106.
25. For an economic analysis of this problem, see Organization for Economic Cooperation and Development, *Towards Full Employment and Price Stability: A Report to the OECD by a Group of Independent Experts* (Paris: OECD, 1977). The independent experts were Paul McCracken, chairman (USA); Guido Carli (Italy); Herbert Giersch (Federal Republic of Germany); Attila Karaosmanoglu (Turkey); Ryutaro Komiya (Japan); Assar Lindbeck (Sweden); Robert Marjolin (France); Robin Matthews (United Kingdom).
26. For a good analysis of some of these differences, see the special issue of *International Organization* edited by Peter J. Katzenstein, "Between Power and Plenty: Foreign Economic Policies of Advanced Industrial States," *International Organization,* 31 (Autumn 1977), 587–920.
27. Paragraph 2, Article 110, The Basic Law of the Federal Republic of Germany. A copy of this constitution may be found in Randolph L. Braham (ed.), *Documents on Major European Governments* (New York: Alfred A. Knopf, 1966), pp. 106–52.
28. United States of America, Department of State, Bureau of Public Affairs, GIST, "U.S. Prosperity and the Developing Countries," August 1978.
29. See the article that Richard N. Cooper wrote before he became Under Secretary of State for Economic Affairs in the Carter administration, "A New International Economic Order for Mutual Gain," *Foreign Policy,* 26 (Spring 1977), 66–120.
30. U.N. Document E/5995, "World Economic Survey, 1976: Current Trends in the World Economy," p. 55.
31. Organization for Economic Cooperation and Development, *Development Cooperation: Efforts and Policies of the Members of the Development Assistance Committee, 1972 Review* (Paris: OECD, 1972), and idem, *1977 Review* (Paris: OECD, 1977).
32. Organization for Economic Cooperation and Development, "Development

Aid: Another Year of Disappointing Results," *OECD Observer,* No. 93 (July 1978), pp. 19–22.

33. Organization for Economic Cooperation and Development, *1977 Review,* p. 211.
34. Ibid., p. 188.
35. See Lester R. Brown, "World Population Trends: Signs of Hope, Signs of Stress," *Worldwatch Paper 8* (Washington D.C.: Worldwatch Institute, 1976).
36. United Nations Environment Program, *The State of the Environment, 1976* (United Nations: Geneva, 1976), p. 18.
37. United States of America, President, *International Economic Report of the President, Transmitted to the Congress January 1977* (Washington, D.C.: Government Printing Office, 1977), p. 65.
38. United States of America, Congress, Joint Economic Committee, *Notes from the Joint Economic Committee,* vol. V, no. 2 (26 January 1979), p. 3.
39. Leontief et al., *The Future of the World Economy,* p. 3.
40. Ibid.

8

Global Interaction on Political Issues

Timothy M. Shaw

THE POLITICS OF INTERNATIONAL RELATIONS represents one salient element in the world system and reflects central aspects of underlying structural conditions and changes; global interactions on political issues constitute one part of the international superstructure that consists of processes and institutions related to the world substructure. The range and ranking of these political issues continually change, particularly in the contemporary period when international communications are so frequent and familiar, although underlying substructural features evolve more slowly.

At the level of politics, two dominant and divergent trends can be identified in current and future global interactions, namely, movements toward both interdependence and dependence. The former, essentially a First World perspective, is optimistic about the possibilities of greater cooperation and decentralization whereas the latter, mainly a Third World perspective, is pessimistic about continued conflict and concentration. The interdependence approach is based on the assumption that the

Table 8.1

Alternative Approaches to Present and Future World Politics

	OPTIMISTIC-COOPERATIVE	PESSIMISTIC-CONFLICTUAL
Present structure	Interdependence	Dependence
Present content	Interrelatedness	Inequalities
Present trend	Diffusion	Concentration
Present policy	Coordination	Disengagement
Future structure	Equilibrium	Instability
Future content	Contract	Confrontation
Future trend	Reformation	Transformation
Future policy	Integration	Isolationism

Table 8.2

Alternative Perspectives on Present and Future World Politics

	GROWTH-COMPLEXITY	DEVELOPMENT-CONTRADICTION
Present structure	Cross-cutting coalitions	Bipolarity
Present content	Sufficiency	Shortages
Present trend	Transition	Crisis
Present policy	Trilateralism	Self-reliance
Future structure	Overdevelopment	Underdevelopment
Future content	Redistribution	Exploitation
Future trend	Participation	Authoritarianism
Future policy	Internationalism	Isolationism

world substructure is moving toward both growth and complexity whereas the dependence approach is based on the premise of substructural underdevelopment and contradiction. These very different modes of analysis and response are represented in Tables 8.1 and 8.2 and symbolize alternative, perhaps incompatible, views of international politics. The ideological and intellectual tension between the interdependence and dependence, optimistic and pessimistic perspectives is reflective, then, of diplomatic differences among global actors and of diverse trends within the world system itself.

Theoretical Perspectives

Global politics has changed dramatically in recent decades and is likely to continue doing so at least until the end of the century as world structures evolve. International affairs—the production and distribution of values on a global scale—have become more complex and controversial for a variety of reasons related to changes in substructure.[1] First, the dominant powers—the United States and the Soviet Union—are not, for the first time in international history, European states. Second, the continuing process of decolonization has produced a rapid multiplication in the number of state actors. Third, the related processes of modernization and integration have generated a rich range of nonstate actors: intergovernmental, transgovernmental, and transnational institutions at both regional and global levels. Fourth, the rise of such actors has led to new coalitions and axes which cut across established East–West or socialist-capitalist divisions. Fifth, the range of issues in international affairs has multiplied beyond tradition concerns of war and peace, diplomacy and trade, as new actors and axes have generated novel issues such as development, pollution, race, debt, and the oceans. And finally, given the first five structural characteristics, world politics has become dominated by two simultaneous and contradictory trends.

The first of these trends is toward concentration of power and affluence; the second is toward decentralization of opportunity and development. The political tensions generated by these incompatible trends are concentrated in the familiar designation of North–South issues. But as we hope to show in this chapter, the so-called North–South question is more complicated and profound than merely a debate or conflict over international trade and technology. Rather it reflects or represents a fundamental dilemma and disjuncture in the global structure that is increasingly apparent in the past, present, and future politics of world affairs.[2]

Global politics has become more complex, then, as the range of actors, issues, and coalitions has multiplied: changes in substructure generate changes in superstructure. The production and distribution of values is no longer the function of interactions among one type of actor alone, namely the nation-state. Rather, politics occurs among a wide variety of actors and at several levels—global, continental, regional, national, and transnational. These new complexities have begun to produce a novel international political culture in which consensus and power are elusive. The prospects for international dominance are considerably reduced as no one actor has sufficient resources to be influential at all levels over all issues and among all other actors all of the time.

Nevertheless global dominance is becoming more problematic in the contemporary world order, and international inequalities continue to increase rather than to decrease. The differences among states and other actors have been exacerbated by the related impacts of industrialization and modernization, by colonialism and underdevelopment. The majority of new actors are poor, weak, and small states who are highly vulnerable to external pressures and constraints. However, because of the tenuousness of their individual independence and viability together they have begun to demand a fundamental transformation in global politics. They are intensely dissatisfied with their characteristic inheritance of poverty and underdevelopment and have come both to blame the world system and to demand a change in global politics as prerequisites for greater development and opportunity in the future. They consider the present nature of world politics to operate ineluctably against themselves and their interests. So they seek to force a decentralization and reorientation of world affairs, power, and prospects against one of the prevailing trends, namely, toward concentration and inequalities. The dissatisfied demand a basic transformation in the pattern and criterion of the distribution of values in the international system, a fundamental change in the world substructure.[3]

The preferences and responses of the rich are symbolized by the emergence and activities of the Trilateral Commission with its emphasis on the possibilities of interdependence. By contrast, the reaction and pressure of the poor are indicated by the notion of dependence and the policy options that stem from it. These twin concepts or approaches are suggestive, as already indicated above, of the divergent perceptions and options of First and Third Worlds. Interdependence is an essentially complacent or incremental approach that prescribes more trade, aid, and other international interactions to realize global development and order. In contradistinction, dependence is a critical and fundamental response to underdevelopment and subordination, proposing some form of disengagement from external affairs and self-reliance as the prerequisite of development. Whereas interdependence advocates seek integration into an increasingly transnational world as the sine qua non of both modernity and prosperity, *dependentistas* see disengagement as the prerequisite of development. The interdependence perspective proposes as a cure for inequalities the very international interactions that from a dependence perspective are seen as the cause of underdevelopment. In the latter approach, given an unhelpful inheritance of subordination, self-reliance and not integration is proposed as the sine qua non of development.

In brief, the non-aligned countries argued that the development of the rich capitalist countries is intimately related to the colonial and neo-colonial exploitation of the periphery. Underdevelopment is an historical phenomenon which can only be understood in the context of the integration of the periphery into the international capitalist system. While the integration of the periphery into the international capitalist system has created the potential for stable development, its realization is always blocked by an international division of labor which compels the periphery to constantly adapt to the needs of the center. The Third World functions as a reservoir of raw materials and cheap labor power contributing to the development of the center while indigenous social systems are disrupted and Third

World societies are less able to satisfy their own basic needs than they were before the colonial period. Any "development" that occurs is distorted and uneven, involving only a small part of the population and confining itself to sectoral and regional enclaves. Underdevelopment is thus the other side of the coin of capitalist development. Once this basic relationship of dominance and dependence is established, its forms may change, but the substance remains the same.[4]

Advocates of the dependence and interdependence approaches have their own institutional affiliations and concerns which are quite revealing of their interests and ideologies. The dependence perspective was closely associated initially with the Economic Commission for Latin America (ECLA); it has now become the new orthodoxy in Third World-related organizations such as UNCTAD and the Third World Forum. By contrast, the interdependence school is closely linked with the Council on Foreign Relations as well as the Trilateral Commission, which together have been influential in both the U.S. State Department and the Carter White House. Any sociological investigation of structures of knowledge and influence can easily slip into a conspiratorial analysis that overlooks important differences and debates within as well as between schools. However, it is quite clear, as noted below, that certain individuals and institutions have played crucial roles in orchestrating the debates over NIEO and future world systems, from the Club of Rome to the Dag Hammarskjold Foundation. And if Algerian influence has been inportant in the nonaligned-UNCTAD nexus, then American actors have been the *animateurs* in the Trilateral-OECD arena (as reflected in the pages of the increasingly unradical and establishment journal *Foreign Policy*).[5]

Attempts to bring these distinctive viewpoints together as in the Paris dialogue, the Commonwealth Experts' Group, and Willy Brandt's Independent Commission on International Development Issues have not been, and perhaps cannot be, too successful because of widely divergent assumptions, perceptions and prescriptions. The two viewpoints may be not only different but also antithetical and contradictory, although possible forms of compatibility are considered below. Advocates of NIEO, when informed by *dependencia,* seek to *transform* established global structures by instituting new forms of international exchange and interaction in which redistribution for equity is the major criterion. By contrast, those concerned with interdependence seek to *reform* present institutions not so much to reduce inequality but to ensure relative tranquillity, based on the ethic of reciprocity rather than redistribution. They seek to divert and manage the demands of nationalist *dependentistas* without substantial change or "concessions."

This threat from the Third World has led the Council and Trilateral Commission to stress heavily the themes of interdependence, mutuality of interests, and cooperation between the rich northern part of the world and the poorer southern section. . . . [t]he "world order bargain" would involve trading access to supplies for access to markets, technology, and capital.[6]

The charmed circle of *interdependencia* may be somewhat widened beyond current Trilateral Commission and OECD members to include a few Newly Industrialized Countries, say, Brazil, Saudi Arabia, or South Korea. But the overall result is intended to keep the world safe not so much for democracy as for exchange; communism is less of a threat than protectionism. Shoup and Minter contend that, as expressed through its 1980s Project,

> the Council's present plans for the Third World involve no real changes in the global distribution of wealth and power. . . . Developing nations are still viewed primarily as sources of raw materials and export markets for the Trilateral world. An international division of labor would be maintained which would give the Third World little chance to develop the manufacturing which produces wealth. The overall aim of Council planning efforts for a new world economy is, thus, to preserve, as much as possible, the existing structure of Western power and predominance. Council plans include, as a prime goal, increasing integration of the world capitalist system, a structure which perpetuates underdevelopment in the Third World and, because of its individualistic and private profit orientation, cannot provide the ideological or organizational basis for mass development projects.[7]

Although the interdependence perspective may possess some utility for explaining the complexities and ambiguities of myriad actors in the First World, it entails essentially negative connotations in relation to North–South links. As Hedley Bull comments, "the term "interdependence" has become a cant word that serves to rationalize relations between a dominant power and its dependencies, in which the sensitivity is more one-sided than it is mutual.[8]

The Setting

Hitherto the world system has been organized to maximize efficiency and output; world politics has been less concerned with the distributive aspect of interaction. The combination of new actors, issues, and coalitions has come to challenge such established criteria. Instead, this cluster of contemporary phenomena tends to push in the direction of a transition toward the acceptance and implementation of a new set of values based on a greater equity of distribution. This concern for justice rather than production is by no means limited to the economic sphere but rather pervades all issue areas of the global system, with implications for the world substructure. Development is no longer defined as merely economic growth but includes also the maximization of human potential, psychological happiness, and cultural distinctiveness, in short, the realization of basic human needs which include habitat and food but which also incorporate social development and autonomy. In issue areas such as communications, culture, housing, and well-being, as well as in economics, the new world is insisting on fundamental changes in old world structures.

In addition to pleas for participation leading to new forms of world politics, there is another cluster of issues that reinforces skepticism about the continued desirability of a quest for maximum output and efficiency. This centers on the interrelated problems of pollution and scarcity in the global environment. Continued industrialization, at least in the northern hemisphere, is threatened by ecological deterioration on the one hand and the diminution of essential, nonrenewable resources on the other.[9] Growth alone is no longer assumed to be a panacea, and even various forms of the welfare state are under serious attack. Keynesian economics cannot readily overcome impending structural and ecological difficulties; the advent of a stable and satisfying postindustrial society remains problematic. The combined impact of underdevelopment in the South and overdevelopment in the North has been severely to challenge established values and relationships throughout the world system. It has also disturbed established modes of inquiry.

In particular, the new salience of economic and environmental questions has served to revive the tradition of political economy as a relevant mode of analysis of world affairs. The post-Vietnam era has produced a new skepticism of behavioralism and positivism and a criticism of ahistoric and noneconomic forms of explanation. These, combined with the Third World emphasis on development and the post-OPEC concentration on the price and supply of resources, have drawn attention once more to the genre of work associated with political economy.[10] "High politics" have increasingly come to be defined in economic rather than strategic terms; their salience is being increased not only by energy crises and "stagflation" but also by the rise of the multinational corporation as an influential type of actor in world affairs. The impending end of *Pax Americana* merely reinforces the analytic and behavioral revolution away from traditional and toward essentially economic concerns.[11] As Oran Young, and Richard Mansbach, Yale Ferguson, and Donald Lampert have suggested, we need (1) to transcend a monomial, state-centric focus for a mixed-actor one and (2) to overcome conservatism in our mode of analysis.[12]

Given the rise of new complexities and inequalities in the world system as well as the appearance of new issues and coalitions, an appropriate approach and motive for analysis increasingly would seem to be that of

international political economy. Such a mode focuses on the politics of
who gets what, when, how, and why in the global system. It is based on
the premises that politics and economics are both ubiquitous and interrelated in the contemporary world order. It transcends the interdepen-
dence-dependence dichotomy, recognizes the need to go beyond the
nation-state, and reflects the interrelationship of world sub- and super-
structures. Harry Targ summarizes the limits of both in his own critique
of the field by noting

> the challenge that theories of dominance and dependency have offered to
> state-centric frameworks for the analysis of international politics. These
> challenges suggest an emerging global system that is *wholistic, central-
> ized, stratified, system dependent* (not actor dependent), *culturally ho-
> mogeneous and technocratic.* The substance of traditional descriptions of
> international politics has been *atomistic, decentralized, symmetrical,
> actor dependent, culturally pluralistic, and political or ideological.*[13]

However, as noted at the outset, there are tensions between centralization and participation, concentration and fragmentation. These contradictions are reflected in the present state of the global hierarchy.

Although power capabilities and affluence are distributed in an increasingly unequal manner internationally, and although the North–South
issue suggests a dominant global dialectic, together they have produced a
rather complex global hierarchy. The several statuses of state, let alone
nonstate, actors reinforce the trend toward complexity in the world political system. However, perhaps the central feature of the contemporary
distribution of power is the rise of a group of middle powers in both North
and South, East and West, who moderate and mitigate any tendency
toward a simple polarization at the global level.

The middle world consists of a group of states with particular strategic, administrative, or economic potentials or a variety of each. It includes Canada and Cuba from the First and Second Worlds respectively
and several leading Third World countries—Brazil, Mexico, Nigeria, and
Saudi Arabia. These all tend to have an enhanced, politico-economic
potential compared to the very poor Fourth World and seem to be advancing toward some form of partial industrialization. They also often
achieve a form of regional hegemony—economic, political and/or infra-
structural—akin to the dominance of the great powers at the global level.
Moreover, they tend to be quite closely associated with one or other of
the world powers but are by no means mere puppets. At times they may
act as surrogates and serve in wars by proxy. But they retain a potential
for independent action as well and may in certain circumstances even
drag their mentors into their own battles and schemes.

In the First and Second Worlds, middle powers may provide a degree
of flexibility and choice for both great and minor powers: the superpowers

prefer Canada and Cuba, France and East Germany, to do things that they themselves cannot afford to do. However, the role of such powers in the Third World is perhaps even more significant and structural. New middle powers have a place in the semi-periphery and have greater prospects for growth and attention than those Fourth World countries at the real periphery. Not only can they enjoy the benefits of semi-industrialization; they may also revive or reinforce faith in orthodox development strategies and goals. The semi-periphery is better able to bargain effectively with foreign countries and corporations while retaining its belief in established patterns of economic growth and political order. Its leaders are able to participate as privileged members of the transnational global elite and to benefit themselves from cooptation. Such association merely reinforces their borrowed lifestyles and belief systems. It also increases their ambivalence about confrontation with and disengagement from the North.

The presence of this intermediary layer of middle powers, then, both mitigates and complicates any tendency toward a global dialectic.[14] New "middle-class" states play an ambiguous role which reduces the level of political conflict between North and South and offers the prospect of considerable cohesion, at least between First, Second, and Third Worlds. The excluded Fourth World of the periphery becomes dependent not only on the great powers but also on one or more middle power. Its relative deprivation in terms of both status and power is reinforced by the emergence of "subimperialism."[15]

Principal Actors

The major actors in global politics, then, are no longer just states or even the superpowers. Rather the state-centric model is being replaced increasingly by a mixed-actor approach which more accurately represents current practice. There is a growing controversy in the literature about the role of transnational actors, particularly the multinational corporation, reflecting earlier debates over the impact of intergovernmental organizations at both global and regional levels, and over transnational and transgovernmental institutions.[16] This range of recognized actors allows for a wide variety of relationships among similar and dissimilar actors— state/state, state/nonstate and nonstate/nonstate. It also generates several host-home state relationships involving nonstate institutions and significantly alters the foreign policy-making process. This new pluralism of actors and relations has proceeded furthest in the case of the Atlantic Community, as well as Japan, in other words, among those states and institutions that identify most closely with the world view of the Trilateral Commission and its correspondents.

By contrast, the new nationalism of the Third World has tended to exclude transnational and transgovernmental links and to be only somewhat more tolerant of intergovernmental organizations, especially if they are predominantly Third World in composition and orientation. In general most such new forces are seen to be neocolonial in the Third World because of their continuing association with dominant northern states and interests. Interdependence for some may imply dependence for others. As Edward Morse suggests, "the upshot of the modernization process on contemporary international society has been a series of paradoxes and incompatibilities whose resolution is problematic." [17]

This uncertainty of response compounds any simple prediction about the future distribution of power in world politics, although, as we have already noted, the rise of a somewhat disparate group of middle powers would appear to be quite likely and reflective of structural evolution. In any case, the range of issues and actors does tend to erode the possibility of another singular global hegemony. Reflecting on the implications of such complexity and pluralism, Steven Spiegel comments that

> pressures within the global system are likely to pull in many directions during the next several years—between a consolidation of superpower primacy and the reemergence of various secondary powers; between the competing superpowers themselves; between the power suppliers and power consumers; between a nineteenth century imperial politics and a new technologically and economically oriented politics; between the frustration and inefficiency of technology and the achievement it promises. [18]

The ineluctable trend toward complexities and inequalities in world politics has been compounded by the emergence of new issues as well as new actors and coalitions. There are now two rather distinctive global agendas, one reflecting northern interests and the other representing southern imperatives. Both, however, are very different from earlier debates over, say, the creation of the United Nations or the World Bank. The North is presently preoccupied with problems of inflation, recession, pollution, energy, and social decay, as well as the continuing issues of détente, proliferation, and disarmament. By contrast, the South is still preoccupied with how to satisfy basic human needs, that is, with internal and international development, particularly with the problems of commodities, debt, population, technology, and food. There is also a growing set of issues that transcends the North–South divide and constitutes a cluster of common problems—oceans, space, arms races, and international institutions—which may serve as the impetus for, and basis of, a new global contract.

In general, the processing of these issues has led to coalition-formation largely along the lines of established East–West–South divisions. However, on particular issues, such as the Law of the Sea or debt relief, coalitions may cut across these lines to reflect the interest of, say, the landlocked states or most indebted countries. And in more detailed and protracted negotiations, large coalitions tend to break down and to reflect more closely diverse national interests. In any event, development and the environment rather than war and peace are now the new high politics for most actors, at least on the global agenda. The list of international issues can perhaps usefully be gauged by reviewing recent world conferences held within the U.N. system: on the environment (Stockholm, 1972), population (Bucharest, 1974), food (Rome, 1974), women (Mexico City, 1975), industrialization (Lima, 1975), habitat (Vancouver, 1976), water (Argentina, 1977), nuclear energy (Salzburg, 1977), and desert problems (Nairobi, 1978). Also Special General Assemblies have been held on development (1974 and 1975), disarmament (1976), economic cooperation among developing states (1978), racism (1978), science and technology for development (1979), and international development (1980). In addition, there is a continual series of regular and special meetings of the Nonaligned, OECD, OPEC, Commonwealth, World Bank, etcetera.

Although the agendas of these and other institutions are now quite well-set, there may be some shift of emphasis as particular problems arise, such as a Sahel drought or near-bankruptcy in one or two countries. However, the processing of this wide range of interrelated issues remains difficult and consensus is elusive. Indeed, any expectation that this series of conferences will lead to a new, singular world order is probably misplaced. Rather they serve the purpose of continually raising concerns and consciousness which may eventually come to inform more limited and bilateral negotiations.

> The pace and progress of negotiations is likely to be much slower than some initially expected. A "New International Economic Order" will not be created overnight to be ratified by some glorious international gathering reminiscent of the Congress of Vienna. Rather, it will be hammered out in a multiplicity of forums encompassing many different countries negotiating on what may often seem to be unrelated issues. This fact alone will make the management and monitoring of the negotiations very difficult both for governments and for nongovernmental observers.[19]

Inputs

The debate over a New International Economic Order—the dominant attempt to forge a new basis for global politics—perhaps may be usefully likened to the process of making international law. Even if a consensus is elusive and not all interests are fully satisfied, the continuing debate itself provides an environmental constraint within which incremental decisions are made and implemented on particular issues between particular actors. The NIEO motif itself limits the propensity of state and nonstate actors to violate its norms, at least at the level of rhetoric. So even if NIEO provides merely an alternative network of global contacts and conferences reflective of current and emerging issues, it certainly encourages further international socialization and awareness, and it may well result in substantive as well as procedural change, with substructural as well as superstructural reforms.

The continuing contemporary debate may also provide visibility and legitimacy for particular actors and proposals that might otherwise be ignored. The weak and the poor now have ready forums in which to embarrass, if no longer to frighten, the strong and the rich. Such conditions provide a conducive environment in which to turn dependence to good advantage. Moreover, in other situations, such as default or declaring *force majeure,* the poor may be able to upset the global system to the detriment of the powerful: hence the continuing readiness of the rich to reschedule debts and help maintain the flow of trade, especially of raw materials. Such responses are more reflective of the resilience of Trilateralism than of any transition to a new global polity.

Nevertheless, the NIEO debate and related issues raise a foreign policy imponderable over how to respond to a world of complexities and inequalities, especially given the inability of any one actor to determine outcomes. The interrelatedness of factors and issues makes any simple or unilateral decision inappropriate, but attempting to respond appropriately in a situation characterized by complexity may lead to inertia or ineffectiveness. This difficulty is exacerbated, according to Morse, because of the gap between reality and perception, between identifying and resolving a problem. He cites this type of paradox as one of "the quixotic qualities of foreign policy in the contemporary international arena."

> Foreign policy today . . . tends to reflect an almost inevitable gap between perceptions of what the world is and the actual structures of international relationships. Reality changes so quickly that the reflexes for action typical of governments tend always to lag behind. This disjunction between reality and perceptions of it is, of course, endemic in policy; policy tends to be based upon past experiences rather than guided by some notion of what the future may hold. . . . In a world in which change has become the norm, it is especially inevitable that this gap will widen.[20]

However, others see the NIEO debate in particular as producing more immediate policy results because of the salience of the new high politics and the imperative of trying to meet basic human needs. Mahbub ul Haq reflects this recent awareness by commenting that

> the debate on a new international economic order has begun only recently. . . . But I remain convinced that the revolution in thinking which

has swept the world in the last five years on the issues of national development strategies is already on its way and will change our perceptions on the international economic order quite dramatically in the next few years.[21]

He goes on to suggest that a positive response by the rich, although delayed, is inevitable given the increase of interdependencies and the growing if grudging awareness of Third World power. For Haq, "it becomes obvious that the Third World *is* the future international order and that the developed countries have to start thinking today in terms of fashioning policies to come to some reasonable accommodation with this future order." [22] Given both the nature of the new majority and the intensity of North–South relations, the politics of coalition-formation and -maintenance become particularly salient.

The initial new-state response to an inheritance of defenselessness during the Cold War era was to adopt the strategic policy of nonalignment. However, the advent of détente and the elusiveness of development combined to produce a redefinition toward an economic claim: nonalignment is now less reactive and less defensive and more an assertion of the demands and rights of the poor. It seeks a redistribution of opportunity, wealth, and influence in favor of the small and weak countries: it has been transformed into an alignment of poor against rich, of periphery against the center. The Third World recognizes, indeed encourages, certain images and attributes associated with an international "class war" in the new world order debate. The crucial unity of the new nonalignment movement which seeks substantial structural change is maintained by shared ideology and common perception of relative deprivation. Despite its considerable heterogeneity, the Third World has maintained its stature as a Trade Union of the Poor because its solidarity is essential to its success. Unity within the Group of 77 is crucial, so debate is kept at a level of generality, difficult choices are avoided, and consensus becomes the procedural norm of the group.

> Compromising conflicting interests would be difficult under any circumstances, but it is especially difficult for poor countries that cannot afford to sacrifice present gains for future benefits. Consequently, no one has been asked to sacrifice anything; negotiating proposals simply add together everybody's demands, or promise losers that they somehow will be compensated. Such proposals make meaningful bargaining difficult, for any compromise threatens to unravel the whole package unless all gain something; but this is surely unlikely in a bargaining universe in which only some demands can be met, and in which almost nothing benefits all the developing countries. This is an issue which the Third World has not yet faced, preferring to maintain the fiction of unity.[23]

Overt attempts by the West to expose and undermine the tenuousness of Third World cohesion probably would be counterproductive. Nevertheless through the impact of dependence, transnational links, and bilateral negotiations the North has begun to moderate or complicate Third World positions. Notwithstanding the attrition brought about by northern tactics, the myths of unity are likely to be perpetuated given the essential fragility of Third World political power.

The new majority has been particularly successful in scoring a series of somewhat pyrrhic victories in the field of international organization. Along with demands for redistribution of economic and strategic goods, the Third World has insisted on greater openness and participation in world institutions. These claims continue to be made, particularly for the restructuring of the U.N. system to reflect the new primacy of developmental issues over those of strategic concerns. The U.N. system has begun to respond by establishing new organs and institutions, such as UNCTAD and the Director-General for Development and International Cooperation, and by changing representation in its secretariats and consultants. Such moves have exacerbated the problems of coordination and compatibility. Nevertheless, there is a continual insistence on democratization in world affairs to reflect changes in membership and issues.

International organizations can now be divided into those still dominated by OECD states (for instance, IMF and IBRD) and those increasingly influenced by the nonaligned (UNCTAD and the General Assembly). The North–South debate is reflected in the diverse and distinctive policies of these different types of agency as well as in the tone of their resolutions. The proliferation of universal organizations more amenable to Third World interests has been matched at the continental and regional levels through myriad functional, political, and social institutions. Together these add up to a considerable organizational response to an inheritance of northern dominance.

Many U.N. as well as subuniversal institutions now "act" to reinforce the claims of the Nonaligned for redistribution and participation, providing an aura of legitimacy for them. These institutions serve not only as forums for the debate but also as catalysts for new coalitions. Yet whereas the arenas and style of world politics have undergone a profound change during the last decade, the actual distribution of power and affluence at the level of substructure remains rather resistant to alteration. Nevertheless, the growing sophistication of Third World interest-aggregation and -articulation is suggestive of continual challenge to and eventual response by the less numerous, and hitherto less organized, OECD membership. The politics of coalition-building on NIEO issues is likely to be a significant feature of global politics for the foreseeable future. As Geoffrey Barraclough notes, "the issues are fundamentally political, not economic, and will not be solved by economists' blueprints, however plausible. This is the reality of the current international situation, little as we may like it." [24]

Coalitions may also develop on other issues, such as pollution and proliferation, the law of the sea and the law of warfare. Some of these cut across even the rhetoric of the North–South divide and lead to the possibility of cross-cutting ties. Because of their very diversity and complexity, these may, perhaps paradoxically, result in a form of cohesion and order in global affairs. Seyom Brown summarizes one widespread view of the implications of complexity for world order.

> Such a complex system of world politics, involving many cross-cutting coalitions between and within countries and lacking a dominant worldwide axis of conflict, might appear to be much safer than either the cold war system organized around two hostile blocs or previous balance-of-power systems. Its very complexity and lack of coherence might appear to be the best guarantee of stability, since without salient focuses for systemwide polarization, local wars could not easily draw in all major powers. In this respect global society would begin to resemble the most developed domestic societies where elaborate patterns of interlinked individual and group interest restrain militants who would polarize the society.[25]

Such global pluralism—involving a rich range of actors, coalitions, and issues—raises a fundamental question about the organization of international society, namely the possible obsolescence of the nation-state, hitherto the dominant type of international actor. Daniel Bell has suggested that it "has become too small for the big problems in life and too big for the small problems."[26] Yet new nationalism in the Third World and sub-nationalism in the First and Second Worlds seem to work against the reduction of this apparent paradox.

> Whether one looks at the security of the world as a whole, the growth in the global economy, the spread of ecological and environmental problems, the requirements of government for resources and technology, or general social problems, national autonomy is everywhere on the decline and the need to rely on actions taken by others virtually universal. Yet the nation-state remains the major form of legitimate political organization capable of allocating resources within societies and of providing international order. It has been reaffirmed by the process of decolonization after World War II, by the growth of nationalism, and, certainly not least of all, by the emergence of nuclear deterrence. Here we find a basic paradox which seems to be at the heart of contemporary international politics, where, at a time when the nation-state has appeared to be functionally obsolete, it has been reaffirmed by the same processes which would call for its transcendence.[27]

Issues

Coalition-formation is both a response to new and interrelated issues as well as a factor in the further complication of global politics; it may serve to perpetuate the existence of the state in world politics but it also encourages its relative relegation to the status of "other" actors along with intergovernmental, transgovernmental, and transnational institutions. This phenomenon combined with growing national-international linkages means that politics at the world level is increasingly broad in scope and heterogenous in content. Moreover, issues are increasingly internationalized and politicized because of the obsolescence of the internal-external distinction and the rise of new forms of high politics such as development and environment. Therefore, coalition builders have a vast range of actors from which to seek support and with which to bargain. And, as multiple issues are always being processed simultaneously, coalition-formation encourages tradeoffs and generates crosscutting ties, many of which cut across orthodox East–West and North–South axes. Coalition politics reflect, therefore, the interrelatedness of current and future global problems.[28]

Coalition politics both is informed by and influences structural inequalities. In the new global hierarchy, the power of the strong and the powerlessness of the weak both are moderated as different criteria of influence are recognized in addition to economic or strategic attributes. If power is elusive for the strong, new forms of influence are available to the weak because of the politics of coalition-formation in which each actor is formally equal.

In particular, coalition politics serves to reinforce the salient role of middle powers who often have considerable national attributes and bargaining skills. Their influence is enhanced not only because of their capacity for serving as intermediaries but also because rich and poor increasingly recognize their unique status in world affairs. The middle powers are able, then, to recruit from North and South for particular coalitions because of their in-between position and so to reinforce images of themselves as influential catalysts and mediators.

Changes in perceptions and issues at times may give a rather transitory quality to contemporary world politics; the dominant theme seems to change from, say, population to drought to food to technology and back again. And different actors would appear to have a different role and capability depending on the major issue of the time. Such shifts in emphasis may in part reflect the activities of *animateurs* seeking to establish broadly based coalitions as well as the communications revolution that enables interconnections, comparisons, and evaluations to be made very quickly at the global level. In reality, shifts in influence and status may occur more slowly, reflective of evolving world structures, although quite rapid rises and falls in the price of oil and gas, coffee and copper exert a considerable toll. Again, however, the middle powers tend to come through relatively unscathed either because they have a range of resources and capabilities or because they are able to borrow when difficulties arise, given their new centrality in world politics and order.

In general, shifts in the politics of price and supply in the distribution of values work against poor states and peoples and toward a further concentration of resources and influence. Nevertheless there continue to be demands for redistribution and decentralization, and the ideology of NIEO is supportive of such claims. Moreover, the global hierarchy is never static, and the possibility, however distant, of upward-mobility still serves as a mechanism of social control. Therefore, cooperation as well as conflict continues to characterize contemporary world affairs. As Barraclough notes, the continued ability of the North, particularly the EEC, to divide and rule puts the South on the defensive.

> It is therefore pretty obvious that some poor countries will be left out in the cold, or will finish up at best in a client status, if they happen to have a place in the political or strategic calculations of one or other of the great powers. In any case, it will be a very unequal world, with some developing countries pulling ahead and other lagging behind.[29]

Interaction

Change in the world system, particularly at the substructural level, tends to be slow, uneven, and ambiguous; it rarely leads to discernible results for all actors. Given the high level of interconnectedness, any particular event or change may take a considerable time before all its repercussions are recognized or incorporated. Moreover, the ability of any one actor to either precipitate a major change or calculate its likely results on other actors or the world system is severely limited. Complexity compounds the problems of reliable prediction or easy cost-benefit analysis. This is particularly so for larger and more plural states in which widespread debates over foreign policy occur; for in these cases the problematic calculations of external effect influence internal decisions.

Yet despite the slowness, unevenness, and uncertainty of change in global politics, the early 1970s may come to be seen as a period of considerable global readjustment reflective of structural change. The ending of the era of decolonization and a new skepticism about the possibility of development combined to produce a new thrust to nonalignment and demands for new global relationships. At the same time, the postwar period of almost continuous growth began to sour among the advanced industrialized states. Interest in a new world order is not limited, then, to any one group of actors. The 1960s were in many ways a decade of optimism associated with decolonization and détente, a period of economic "miracles" and apparently successful welfare states. But the difficulties and ambiguities posed during the United Nation's first "Development Decade" escalated into major issues in the second "underdevelopment" decade. And at the beginning of the Third Development Decade there is even less optimism that structural changes are feasible or that they would have a noticeable impact on growing inequalities.

So the prevailing mood of pessimism about the inequities of inherited international structures at the end of the sixties was transformed into crisis and confrontation with the advent of global recession and shortages in the early seventies. Yet despite intense misgivings the global dialectic between North and South has been hard to sustain given the pervasiveness of interdependence and the characteristic complexities and discontinuities of the modern order. Further, despite the apparent intransigence of certain actors, the very complexity of issues and the delicacy of structures gradually has produced a growing awareness that any NIEO would take considerable time, effort, and risk to design, debate, and implement. This awareness has, in turn, served to moderate demands and enhance awareness of the unpredictability of too rapid change. Instead, there is a new willingness to think through the effects of proposed courses of action and to consider planning rather than confrontation as the best way to proceed. So forms of cooperation continue even though basic interests may diverge. Coalition politics itself, of course, involves a co-existence of cooperation on the one hand and conflict on the other. And the fragility of coalition cohesion reinforces the need for care and caution to maintain the widest possible range of support.

Cooperation across "worlds" has been facilitated by the role of middle powers on the one hand and by transnational elite ties on the other. The boundary between First and Third Worlds has become less clear-cut because of the emergence of several upwardly mobile middle powers who are increasingly ambivalent about their status. This has led them to prefer collaboration to confrontation, counterdependence to disengagement. Several have been able to develop by the "invitation" of the rich states and corporations whose interests they are prepared to serve without neglecting their own. However, their advance from the periphery to the semi-periphery serves to intensify the relative deprivation and dependence of the majority of states and peoples in the Fourth World.

The inheritance of international inequality and the difficulties of transcending it except for the middling-rich were demonstrated by the global impact of the oil crisis and the associated recession. The high price of oil made a few OPEC states either rich or able to grow. Two other groups of states were able to weather the shocks: the industrialized states "passed on" the increases in price by charging more for their capital exports, and other intermediate states of the Third World were able to borrow while readjusting their external trade. The hardest hit were the least developed states or the Fourth World; they had to pay a high price for oil and fertilizers, the cost of other imports—manufactures and food—went up, and income from their own commodity exports declined. Some were simultaneously suffering from drought and few were able to borrow enough to cover their large balance-of-payments deficits. The increasing distinctions between Third and Fourth World states have implications for the tenuous unity between Africa, Asia, and Latin America and for the uneven distribution of wealth and opportunity among them, with Africa and Asia having the least promising prospects.[30]

Inequalities within the ranks of the Nonaligned have already affected the politics of leadership and negotiation over NIEO. The mood can change depending not only on the issue and the situation but also on the implications for particular states. For instance, the metamorphosis of U.N. debates from deadlock to dialogue in the eighteen months between the Sixth and Seventh Special U.N. Sessions can be explained in terms of the emergence of a more moderate, representative, and sensitive leadership, which was concerned with unity as well as victory. The content of the NIEO proposed in the Seventh Special Assembly tended to favor the Third rather than the Fourth World.

> Benefits would accrue largely to the middle-income developing countries, many of which are rich in raw materials and on the verge of industrialization. There are few provisions that would bring practical benefit to the emerging sub-group of developing countries, the Fourth World. . . . Thus, while solidarity among developing countries permitted radical leadership in 1974, the more explicit divergence of views among these countries in 1975 resulted in more moderate leadership, which reflected the balance of interests within the Group of 77.[31]

Aside from leadership and location, the other salient factor affecting North–South relations is transnational linkage between leaders.

Transnational elite relations also serve to erode the boundaries between worlds; given their pervasiveness these relations tend to blur the edges of the rich–poor debate and so offer the prospect of compromise and incrementalism. Close links and mutual interests among elites are especially prevalent between center and semi-periphery. The bargain between them has changed over time as the balance of power has evolved. The new elites are no longer merely dependent "compradors" but have successfully engaged in the politics of counterpenetration, opting for collaborative arrangements in which ownership and management are increasingly shared. Such common lifestyles and values are not possible, however, for the very poor in the real periphery. Given their relative lack of resources, their choice remains the starker one between dependence and disengagement; they are unlikely to secure reasonable terms for cooperative ventures as their bargaining chips are so thin and scarce.

If counterpenetration encourages cooperation rather than confrontation because of transnational elite ties, then counterculture may potentially encourage confrontation by aggregating support for alternative world orders. We return to this question of counterelites in the penultimate section of this chapter.

Outputs

Despite the growing complexity of world politics and the redefinition of high politics from strategic to economic issues, two forms of interaction and understanding may be ripe for revival. Together they reflect changes in the values of and output from the global polity. These are a "new realism" associated with the earlier genre of power politics and a "new functionalism" associated with the earlier genre of international integration. The former consists of a revival and revision of Morgenthau, the latter of Mitrany.[32]

Third World scholars such as Mahbub ul Haq and Ali A. Mazrui reflect the former perspective by asserting that the new salience of resources and shortages advance the power and demands of the poor. Mazrui argues, for instance, that resource power no longer leads to dependence but rather serves to support Third World claims for redistribution and counterpenetration. He suggests that the nouveaux riches have more to gain than to lose by further association with and integration into the world system.[33] Haq echoes this point by arguing that a dramatic shift in the world balance of power is indicated by the growing proportion of population, production, and destruction possessed by the Third World. As the industrialized countries become a smaller minority (of both states and peoples), so their influence and affluence will be increasingly questioned and undermined.

Haq also argues that as the Third World recaptures control over its own resources, production, and potential—and gains its own intellectual as well as political and economic liberation—so the rich will come to realize that accommodation with it is an imperative. He suggests in addition that redistribution internationally is similar to that internally; redistribution at both levels is essential for reasons of justice and peace. For Haq, inherited global institutions and relations need to be redefined to overcome such inequalities and instabilities.

> The reasons for this inequality in relationships must be sought in international economic structures and mechanisms which put the Third World at a considerable disadvantage and which require thorough-going institutional reform. It is not that the rich deliberately exploited the poor. It is merely that this pattern was based on concepts of feudalism, not democracy; in unequal relationships, not equality of opportunity. As such, it was inherently unstable.[34]

The appeal of "realism" and power politics as both theory and policy may be particularly strong for the nouveaux riches middle powers of the Third World. They already appreciate that national income by itself is no guarantee of international influence and have attempted to diversify their capabilities. This effort to secure an impressive mix of resources—strategic, diplomatic, educational, and cultural as well as economic—has gone furthest in the cases of Brazil and Saudi Arabia but other semi-peripheral powers display a similar awareness of the imperative to diversify sources of power, for example, Mexico and Nigeria. Paradoxically, the redefinition of high politics toward economic and ecological issues may yet lead to a remilitarization of international affairs as regional powers accelerate the arms trade with the Third World and engage in local wars by proxy. So the current economic definition of power may yet prove to be transitional as new wealth is gradually transformed into coercive potential.

In contrast to the new nationalism and assertiveness of the Third World leading to the possible revival of realism, a significant First World response to emerging world issues is to advocate a revival of functionalism. Mitrany's thesis on peace was intended to reduce the possibility of another world war between industrial states; current treatises on equity and justice are intended to reduce the possibility of conflict between rich and poor. Although few scholars make the connection, the contemporary advocacy of new institutions to respond to emerging world order issues such as pollution and scarcities constitutes, in essence, a revival of functionalism—developmental cooperation will ensure order.

Stanley Hoffman, for instance, has argued that for a moderate international system to be created, a new consensus and novel forms of cooperation need to be devised among more equal and interdependent states. He suggests that a rich hierarchy along with complex patterns of heterogeneity, regional decentralization, and continuing transnationalism would produce lower levels of violence and new varieties of functional cooperation. A combination of complexity and functionalism will, according to Hoffman, reinforce the moderation and diversification of the order.[35]

John White has also advocated a revival of functionalism, although like Hoffman he fails to mention Mitrany and his original school. Moreover, his case for proliferation of agencies is related to the desirability of function determining scope of membership or activity. White rejects the idea that all agencies should be either universal or associated with the U.N. system. Rather he advocates new particularistic institutions in response to common interests in specific sectors and issues; he indicates that a more independent grouping of Third World states would support such collective organization.[36] White proposes the fragmentation of large, universal U.N. agencies into specific, intermediate institutions serving regional or producer groups. These could mobilize resources and advise on behalf of a more select membership and so advance its development through appropriate capital and technology flows. Oran Young also supports a similar scheme of specific, decentralized, and flexible interstate institutions rather than the standard solution of adding more to the UN system.[37]

Respect for Third World power potential and support for new forms of functional interaction are now reinforced by a network of nongovernmental institutions concentrated in the rich states. Organizations such as the Overseas Development Council in Washington, the Institute of Development Studies at Sussex, the Dag Hammarskjold Foundation in Sweden, the Reshaping the International Order Foundation in Rotterdam, and the North–South Institute in Ottawa all help to create a positive environment within which the NIEO debate can occur, decisions can be made, and positive policies can be proposed, adopted, and coordinated.[38] We turn next to an analysis of the politics of alternative futures; these are inseparable from the NIEO debate and from the projections of underlying structural trends.

Developmental Issues

The contradictory pressures toward concentration and participation, dependence and interdependence have led to a proliferation of international forums and institutions designed to reconcile and overcome them. These tend to be divided in origin, procedure, and orientation along North–South lines, although given the growing awareness of the interrelationship between underdevelopment and overdevelopment there are increasing attempts being made to transcend this particular divide, represented in the institutions mentioned above. As already noted, the premises of the dependence and interdependence literature lead to markedly different policy prescriptions, namely to disengagement or integration, self-reliance or collaboration respectively.

However, the Third World is increasingly skeptical about the development model or path offered by the advanced industrialized states of either East or West. Rather some parts of it have begun to try to overcome underdevelopment without thereby falling victim to the problems of overdevelopment. Despite historical and continuing transnational links, the South is beginning to show signs of growing ambivalence toward and distance from the North.

> It should not be assumed that developing countries would wish to conform uniformly or closely to the economic and social patterns that now obtain in industrial societies. In spite of the pervasive nature of international culture contact, we expect that each developing country will wish to follow its own path, conditioned by its own circumstances and aspirations.

It is our hope that in so doing the developing countries can avoid some of the costs, inequities and strains that have historically been associated with the development of the developed countries of today.[39]

This new tendency to reject orthodox models in favor of distinctively indigenous solutions is also reflected in Haq's portrayal of Third World interests: "The Third World is not anxious to join the rich or to share the values of the West. It is not even seeking an equity of income. But the Third World *is* seeking the opportunity to meet human needs. They want equity of opportunity soon, not equity of income which they realize cannot be achieved in the near future."[40]

The third Club of Rome Report (RIO) is even more explicit about the definition of development not being conceived in terms of present Western living standards: "The poor countries should reject the aim of imitating Western patterns of life. Development is not a linear process, and the aim of development *is not to 'catch up.'* . . . Many aspects of Western life have become wasteful and senseless and do not contribute to peoples' real happiness."[41]

The possibility of some sort of convergence toward a mature, steady state and away from both underdevelopment and overdevelopment has recently been raised, given the interrelated issues of, say, poverty and pollution. Any reduction of inequalities and progress toward greater equity requires change both within and between states, particularly in salient areas such as economic development and social progress. The imperatives of underdevelopment and scarcities demand a response of less consumption in the rich states and rapid development in the poor—a redistribution of resources internally and globally.

Current projections for crucial substructural issues on the northern as well as southern agendas (resource depletion, energy shortfalls, pollution increases, and climatic variability, as well as population pressures, food insufficiencies, and the growing rich–poor gap) all point to fundamental political as well as existential difficulties in the future, notwithstanding new technologies, reserves, and processes. These cautionary forecasts derive from sectoral reports as well as global models, from nongovernmental and intergovernmental agencies as well as from national governments.[42] Together they add up to a serious warning about the need to reconsider lifestyles and goals at individual, institutional, national, and global levels.

These projections about structural difficulties constitute fundamental challenges to the established assumptions, norms, and processes of the world poliltical system, involving shifts in the near future in terms of structural change, power distribution, regional and global arms races and control, new forms of conflict, and a possible spread of authoritarian regimes. On the other hand, the projections also serve to reiterate the imperative of cooperation and planning if breakdown and catastrophe are to be avoided. They add a further dimension to the transformation of global politics: the contemporary co-existence of affluence and poverty cannot continue for reasons of both ethics and equilibrium.

The environmental and developmental substructural and superstructural challenges identified in the literature on the world's future may combine, then, to produce an emerging, if tenuous, global consensus on the need to reduce consumption in the First World and to promote development in the Third World through redistribution: "The new political sensibilities of Northern elites and the new egalitarianism of Southern power holders share the objective of changing present international economic norms and rules in order to effect major transfers of income and economic opportunity to the South." [43] However, this consensus is fragile and exists among an enlightened, "alternative" transnational elite rather than among all rulers. A critical transnational perspective should make us cautious about the modesty and disinterest of most members of the ruling classes.

The acceptance of so-called alternative lifestyles within the rich states —self-regulation or -discipline—can be seen as an integral part of any new world order. [44] Simultaneously, the adoption of strategies of self-reliance within the Third World would help to restructure and redefine North–South relations. Sufficiency would be the criterium rather than affluence, elimination of poverty rather than the maximization of the consumption of the few. These twin thrusts are supported on the one hand by the Club of Rome and on the other by the Group of 77. They combine the ascetic lifestyle of subcultures in the industrialized economies with the examples of China and Tanzania from the poor states.

Indeed, such convergence may be an imperative if development for the poor is to be realized simultaneously with achievement of a steady state for the rich. Given the world's finite resources and the responsibility of the rich states for rapid resource depletion, a Third World interest in modest, egalitarian forms of development would constitute a significant contribution to global conservation.

There are no major new frontiers left in the global system; world society has to readjust to the continuing constraints of the environment. The First World is at present held to be largely responsible for international dependence and resource depletion; therefore, limitations on its consumption are essential for redistribution and the creation of a new world order: "if developed nations actually translate their affirmation of interdependence into support for more egalitarian structures in the international economy, there should be no fundamental conflict between self-reliant development and increased international economic cooperation." [45]

A plea for the early recognition of ecological and existential scarcity has recently been made by Herman Daly. He has argued that "sufficient wealth efficiently maintained and allocated, and equitably distributed—not maximum production—is the proper economic aim."[46] This new maxim could also be applied to global politics as well as to economics. Further, Daly argues that the Third World cannot, even it is wished, ever catch up with the rich as resources would be rapidly and finally exhausted: "We need to recognize another impossibility theorem in political economy: specifically, that a U.S.-style high-mass consumption, growth-dominated economy for a world of 4 billion people is impossible. Even more impossible is the prospect of an ever growing standard of per-capita consumption for an ever growing world population."[47]

There is not only a conceptual, ideological, or existential compatibility between alternative lifestyles and collective self-reliance, but political coalitions and associations among the advocates of each may advance the implementation of such a new world order. "New coalitions" which link groups within both First and Third Worlds provide a constituency for ideas about change that may overcome the resistance of governments and established interests.[48] Relations between consumer organizations in rich states and exporters of cheap manufactured goods in the poor, or linkages beteen North American wheat farmers and the starving in the Sahel, or between Arab oil producers and insulation contractors in the North are all examples of links or interdependencies between apparently disparate groups in different "worlds." However, their influence may as yet be only marginal when decision makers attempt to assert national interests or priorities.

The development of a transnational constituency over world order issues based on common needs or mutual support has been seen as one way to increase awareness and access, to influence the constellation of bargaining situations, and to make interdependence a more progressive and viable concept. A transnational constituency may both publicize and provide support for a global welfare state. A "Trade Union of the Third World" would be strengthened by association with trade unions in the rich states and would constitute a potential international proletariat in any global class war with established ruling groups.

Whereas such "interest alignments" which cut across groupings of states may advance Third World claims, their impact remains rather unpredictable because they gain most support within the industrialized world by offering goods at lower prices, that is, by satisfying, not by challenging, consumerism.[49] Moreover, the demand for cheaper food, clothes, and radios is not infinite even in the rich states. Further, these imports at present are very vulnerable to the imposition of nontariff barriers which threaten long-term access. Nevertheless it is important to recognize that the internal constituency within industrialized states that might identify with certain poor state demands is wider than just human-

itarian institutions. Given increased international inequalities, philan-
thropic and aid agencies will tend to support the Fourth World[50];
multinationals and consumer institutions have more in common with intermediate, Third World states.[51]

Projections

Given the prevailing and contradictory political trends toward concentration and decentralization, dependence and interdependence, projections and speculations about the future of world politics, if not about all
of the substructural factors such as population, proliferation, and pollution, remain hazardous. Nevertheless two broad schools of prediction are
emerging, the optimists and the pessimists, the internationalists and the
isolationists. The former constitute one strand within the convergence
school in which complexity is assumed to be inevitable and desirable,
whereas the latter represent a nationalistic response of both North and
South to global recession and competition, one attempt to cope with
structural contradictions.

The enlightened internationalist perspective marries the concern for
economic disparities of the *dependentistas* with the ecological concerns
of the functionalists; it attempts to transcend the growth-development
and complexity-contradiction dichotomies. Such an approach tends to
express sympathy for the imperatives of self-reliance while recognizing
the ineluctable trend toward transnationalism; it would serve to support
progress toward redistribution while also insisting on a global response to
the problems of pollution and proliferation.

Such enlightened internationalism is expressed in the analysis and
action of the RIO Foundation, which blends economic and ecological
imperatives.[52] Essentially it advocates an attack on world problems in
which self-reliance by the poor and self-restraint by the rich together
produce a redistribution of wealth and an associated reduction in waste,
so that both economic inequalities and environmental deterioration are
overcome. Enlightened internationalism is based on the premise that "interdependencies are not symmetrical; in the aggregate some countries are
much more vulnerable to nonmilitary actions of foreign states than others."[53] It also treats the threat from the South seriously. According to
Tony Smith, the "liberal" response "assumes that Southern power is real
and that since some, although certainly not all, of the demands for a New
International Economic Order are not inimical to Northern interests, and
others may be turned to advantage, they sould be satisfied."[54]

However, if enlightened internationalism takes NIEO seriously and
attempts to reform global structures and relations, then the revival of
neomercantilism constitutes a threat to revert to previous structures and

relations, to the status quo ante. The neomercantilist urge is a northern, particularly American, reaction to the difficulties of both dependence and interdependence and is essentially compatible with neo-isolationism. One of its major proponents is Robert Gilpin.

Gilpin has suggested three alternative models of the future based on present trends and values in global politics, focusing particularly on the interaction between state and nonstate actors, notably the multinational corporation. His alternative approaches tend to transcend the rich–poor gap assumed in the interdependence–dependence dichotomy because of his concern with the erosion of power in the North brought about by the rise and spread of the multinational corporation. He anticipates that corporation–state tensions within the industrialized countries themselves will generate nationalist sentiment in the North in the future as it has done already in the South.

Gilpin presents "three models of the future drawn from current writings on international political economy: liberalism, Marxism and economic nationalism"[55]; these constitute a further development of the political economy approach proposed earlier in this chapter. He labels the first model "sovereignty-at-bay": "according to this view, increasing economic interdependence and technological advances in communication and transportation are making the nation-state an anachronism."[56] This liberal perspective, which is largely compatible with the interdependence school, welcomes economic integration through transnational corporate and financial structures: "In this liberal version of the future the multinational corporation, freed from the nation state, is the critical transmission belt of capital, ideas and growth."[57] Growth and complexity are envisaged and favored.

Gilpin's second model is that of *dependencia,* which derives from more radical, new-state approaches to hierarchy and exploitation; it is most compatible with the development–contradiction approach to global politics.

> The sovereignty-at-bay model envisages a relatively benevolent system in which growth and wealth spread from the developed core to the lesser-developed periphery. In the dependencia modes, on the other hand, the flow of wealth and benefits is seen as moving—via the same mechanisms —from the global, underdeveloped periphery to the centers of industrial financial power and decision. It is an exploitative system that produces affluent development for some and dependent underdevelopment for the majority of mankind. In effect, what is termed transnationalism by the sovereignty-at-bay advocates is considered imperialism by the Marxist proponents of the dependencia model.[58]

Further, if the sovereignty-at-bay perspective is most appropriate for dealing with rich-rich relations, then *dependencia* bears most resemblance to contemporary rich-poor linkages; the former is compatible with an orthodox theory of "development" whereas the latter adopts a more critical view of "underdevelopment."

Finally, Gilpin introduces a model that focuses on the nation-state rather than on transnational society despite current trends and preoccupations as reflected in the dichotomy contained in Table 8.2: "In opposition to both these (previous) models, therefore, the third model of the future—the mercantilist model—views the nation state and the interplay of national interests (as distinct from corporate interests) as the primary determinants of the future role of the world economy."[59] Such neomercantilism is based on the premise that as American power is in decline so the favorable environment for multinational corporate activities will come to an end. Instead, this alternative projection is based on the assumption of a new period of economic competition between the major powers in which national economic objectives will further supplant considerations of global economic efficiency or equity. According to such neomercantilists, "the world has reached the limits of interdependence and loss of national self-sufficiency."[60]

Gilpin tends to come down himself in favor of a neomercantilist position because of the perceived decline of U.S. power in the global system and the general salience of the nationalist response. But corporate activities are ubiquitous and increasingly geocentric; they are no longer dependent on *Pax Americana*. Moreover, despite Gilpin's reservations, the related trend toward regionalism may serve to reinforce rather than to constrain corporate influence.

> In a world economy composed of regional blocs and centers of power, economic bargaining and competition would predominate. Through the exercise of economic power and various trade-offs each center of the world economy would seek to shift the costs and benefits of economic interdependence to its own advantage. . . . The question of how these benefits and costs will be distributed is at the heart of the increasingly mercantilist policies of nation states in the contemporary world.[61]

This final, neomercantilist perspective, however, may be quite compatible with the earlier emphasis above on the crucial place of the semi-periphery in any emergent order. For it is the middle powers with their intermediate role and interests that are most likely to combine a judicious mixture of nationalism and transnationalism—a strategy characterized as counterpenetration by Mazrui—to enhance their own growth and influence. Given their control over significant resources and regions, the middle powers' bargaining strength may be enhanced although their need for collaboration will continue. So the balance of power may continue to shift somewhat in their favor in the near future without involving a fundamental restructuring of the world system, that is, constituting an outcome not incompatible with *interdependencia*. Elsewhere Gilpin may have overdramatized this marginal shift in favor of the new middle powers, one that *dependentistas* would consider to be inadequate as a response to uneven development, arguing that "a capitalist international economy plants the seeds of its own destruction in that it diffuses economic growth, industry and technology, and thereby undermines the distribution of power upon which that liberal, interdependent economy has rested."[62] However, the incorporation of the nouveaux riches into the semi-periphery involves only a partial diffusion of technology and production in which the essential skills, decisions, and profits may still be retained by the center. This constitutes a reform of the system for some and a rationalization of it for others; these are largely compatible with a Trilateral perspective and prescription.

Such counterpenetration as an intermediate strategy, involving an expansion not an abandonment of OECD, is very different from the enlightened internationalism of RIO and others because it is less critical and consistent, a new form of *realpolitik* rather than a step toward a defined and planned new order. This new interdependence is essentially a revised form of integration which employs conflict as well as cooperation but is not necessarily incompatible with an outward-looking growth strategy. It is based on a continuing confidence in trickle-down and orthodox development policies.

In contrast to this optimistic, liberal preview, Thomas Weisskopf represents the new orthodoxy in which underdevelopment and inequality are expected to be perpetuated and intensified because of the nature of the international capitalist system. According to Weisskopf, the prevailing substructural trend for the foreseeable future is toward subordination, inadequate growth, and dependence.[63] He also suggests that elites in both First and Third Worlds share an interest in maintaining such inequalities and indeed that the former have helped maintain "order" in the latter. However, he indicates that in the future the center may tire of providing coercive support to Third World elites battling against internal opposition to the status quo.

> In the long-run such policies will prove too costly to the elites in the rich countries, whose stake in most of the underdeveloped world is less immediate than that of the elites in the poor countries. Weakened by a selective and gradual withdrawal of support from their stronger allies, the elites in the poor countries will become increasingly vulnerable to pressures from below and will ultimately give way to revolutionary movements.[64]

Bruce Russett also suggests that without a new global order conflict will increasingly be centered *within* the poor states, whose elites will become the targets of frustration and resentment. However, Russett is cautious about the potential impact of a yawning absolute gap for international politics: "Thus in the world of 2000 AD, perhaps even more so than now, the poor half of the world will not be able to challenge the rich fifth for control—but it will have the ability to harass the rich and bring the entire system into chaos."[65]

In the final analysis, it may be this prospect of anarchy—another image of the future—which informs the alternatives of dependence and interdependence, enlightened nationalism and neomercantilism. The potential for serious conflict within and between states, particularly between rich and poor and within the poor countries, posed by internal and international inequalities is substantial, but it is reduced somewhat by the prospect of the inevitable reaction to the specter of anarchy: an authoritarian response.

The salient characteristics of the present transition from "old" to "new" global structures and politics are now beginning to be recognized: "the disintegration of geopolitical and ideological bipolarity, the rise of nonmilitary issues, and the diversification of coalition and adversary relationships seem to be the dominant tendencies in international politics."[66] As already noted, the emergence of multiple actors, issues, and coalitions create the possibility of cross-cutting ties which undermine both East–West and North–South bipolarities. Whereas they may offer enhanced prospects for peace and justice, they also contribute to the problems of collective negotiation. Multiple coalitions may also increase the influence of the South if, as noted above, they can be used as means to attract support within the industrialized states themselves.[67] Yet images of cross-cutting ties should not be allowed to divert attention from the potential of a conflictual structural dialectic of rich and poor, reflected in political conflict within and between states.

I conclude with three cautionary notes about future global politics on the interrelated issues of convergence, complexity, and response. First, the fifth report of the Club of Rome points to the need for a new approach to inequalities as a prerequisite for world order.

Alternative strategies include greater concern with the quality of life than with quantitative material-economic growth in the rich world; more attention to appropriate modes of development in the poor world; and a better-functioning international economic order to assist in creating a more equitable pattern of development. Such strategies call for the conservation of finite sources and stocks of energy and other national resources, for developing safe and economical alternatives, and not being seduced into Faustian bargains with dangerous technologies. Alternative strategies require more efficient food production, storage, and distribution systems, and replacing reliance on arms for national security with reliance on trustworthy international institutions. The legitimate expectations of the world's people could be fulfilled through such alternative strategies, but not through a blind pursuit of traditional methods.[68]

Second, given complexities as well as inequalities, management of the world system may become increasingly problematic. Rufus Miles, for instance, suggests that there are managerial as well as physical limits to growth.

> There are limits to the human capacity to design and manage, by the political process, huge, complex, interdependent human and ecological systems . . . scientists and engineers may offer technical solutions to all sorts of problems, but politicians and the bodies politic are the ultimate deciders as to how the largest human systems will be designed and managed. That the current level of complexity is putting a heavy strain on man's political capacity is self-evident.[69]

Third, the debate over redistribution and convergence may already be *passé* and a historical era may be ending for the global system. Gregory Schmid, for example, sees the several interconnected crises of the early 1970s as indicative of the end of the first postwar era, namely that of interdependence. So rather than foreseeing a new world order of greater equity and justice, he, like Gilpin, points to the emergence of new forms of nationalism and intervention against continuing transnational integration; he predicts that a new period of mercantilism will follow that of dependence and interdependence.

> In the long term sweep of history, the postwar era from 1945 to approximately 1970 will stand out as a unique period in which special circumstances were operating which permitted the growth of a relatively free market for international transactions. . . . From some future perspective, the period of the 1980s and 1990s may even be seen as an era of a new mercantilism.[70]

The inability of international actors to achieve a new and more equitable world order would likely ensure an escalation to a higher level of political confrontation as well as the unfulfillment of many basic human needs in the foreseeable future. This would constitute a continuation of the structural trends toward concentration and inequality instead of the beginning of the process of realizing redistribution and equity, with profound implications for global politics.

Notes

1. For a reasoned overview of the contemporary world system, see Oran Young, "On the Performance of the International Polity," *British Journal of International Studies* 4 (October 1978), 191–208.
2. For a provocative review of current world affairs, see Geoffrey Barraclough, "Waiting for the New Order" and "Struggle for the Third World," *New York Review of Books*, 25 (26 October and 9 November 1978).

3. See Timothy M. Shaw, "The Elusiveness of Development and Welfare: Inequalities in the Third World" in Ronald St. John MacDonald, Douglas M. Johnston, and Gerald L. Morris (eds.), *The International Law and Policy of Human Welfare* (Sijthoff, 1978), pp. 81–109.

4. Orlando Letelier and Michael Moffitt, *The International Economic Order* (Washington: Transnational Institute, 1977), p. 34.

5. See, for example, C. Fred Bergsten, "The Threat from the Third World," *Foreign Policy* 11 (Summer 1973), 102–104, and "The Response to the Third World," *Foreign Policy* 17, (Winter 1974–75), 3–34; Richard N. Cooper, "A New International Economic Order for Mutual Gain," *Foreign Policy* 26 (Spring 1977), 65–120; and Joseph S. Nye, "Independence and Interdependence," *Foreign Policy* 22 (Spring 1976), 129–61.

6. Lawrence Shoup and William Minter, *Imperial Brain Trust: The Council on Foreign Relations and United States Foreign Policy* (New York: Monthly Review, 1977) p. 272.

7. Ibid., p. 273.

8. Hedley Bull, *The Anarchical Society: A Study of Order in World Politics* (London: Macmillan, 1977), p. 280.

9. For an introduction to current and projected world problems at the level of both structure and relations, see Malcolm J. Grieve, Tom Keating, Don Munton, and Timothy M. Shaw, "Global Problems for Canadians: Forecasts and Speculations," *Behind the Headlines* (forthcoming).

10. See, for instance, two non-Marxist introductions to the contemporary global political economy: David H. Blake and Robert S. Walters, *The Politics of Global Economic Relations* (Englewood Cliffs, N.J.: Prentice-Hall, 1976), and Joan Edelman Spero, *The Politics of International Economic Relations* (New York: St. Martins Press, 1977).

11. See Robert Gilpin, *U.S. Power and the Multinational Corporation: The Political Economy of Foreign Direct Investment* (New York: Basic Books, 1975).

12. See Oran Young, "The Actors in World Politics" in James N. Rosenau, Vincent Davis, and Maurice East (eds.), *The Analysis of International Politics* (New York: Free Press, 1979), pp. 125–44; and Richard W. Mansbach, Yale H. Ferguson, and Donald E. Lampert, *The Web of World Politics: Non-State Actors in the Global System* (Englewood Cliffs, N.J.: Prentice-Hall, 1976), pp. 1–6.

13. Harry R. Targ, "Global Dominance and Dependence, Post-Industrialism and International Relations Theory: A Review." *International Studies Quarterly* 20 (September 1976), 473. Emphasis in original.

14. See Timothy M. Shaw, "From Dependence to (Inter)dependence: Issues of the New International (Economic) Order," *International Political Science Association,* Moscow, August 1979.

15. See Timothy M. Shaw, "Inequalities and Interdependence in Africa and Latin America: Sub-Imperialism and Semi-Industrialization in the Semi-Periphery," *Cultures et Développement* 10 (1978), 231–63; and Johan Galtung, "Conflict on a Global Scale, Social Imperialism and Sub-Imperialism: Continuities in the Structural Theory of Imperialism," *World Development* 4 (March 1976), 153–65.

16. See, in particular, Robert O. Keohane and Joseph S. Nye, *Power and Interdependence: World Politics in Transition* (Boston: Little, Brown, 1977) and

the fine review article on different approaches to analysis, particularly the dependence and interdependence "schools" examined here, by Kal J. Holsti, "A New International Politics? Diplomacy in Complex Interdependence," *International Organization* 32 (Spring 1978), 513–30.

17. Edward L. Morse, *Modernization and the Transformation of International Relations* (New York: Free Press, 1976), p. 20.

18. Steven L. Spiegel, *Dominance and Diversity: The International Hierarchy* (Boston: Little, Brown, 1972), p. 259.

19. John W. Sewell (ed.), *The United States and World Development: Agenda 1977* (New York: Praeger, for Overseas Development Council, 1977), pp. 14–15.

20. Morse, *Modernization and the Transformation of International Relations*, pp. 179–80.

21. Mahbub ul Haq, *The Poverty Curtain: Choices for the Third World* (New York: Columbia University Press, 1976), p. 152.

22. Ibid., p. 170. Emphasis in original.

23. Robert Rothstein, "Foreign Policy and Development Policy: From nonalignment to International Class War," *International Affairs* 52 (October 1976), 616.

24. Barraclough, "Waiting for the New Order."

25. Seyom Brown, *New Forces in World Politics* (Washington: Brookings Institution, 1974), p. 189.

26. Daniel Bell, "The Future World Disorder," *Foreign Policy* 27 (Summer 1977), 132.

27. Morse, *Modernization and the Transformation of International Relations*, pp. 178–79.

28. See Grieve et al., "Global Problems for Canadians."

29. Barraclough, "The Struggle for the Third World."

30. See Timothy M. Shaw and Malcolm J. Grieve, "The Political Economy of Resources: Africa's Future in the Global Environment," *Journal of Modern African Studies* 16 (March 1978), 1–32.

31. David Wright, "UN's Seventh Special Session: Turning Point in Dialogue with Developing Countries," *International Perspectives* (January/February 1976), 24.

32. Compare analogous discussions by Robert O. Matthews over whether the "power politics" or "dependence" perspective is most appropriate and by I. William Zartman over the relative merits of the "decolonization" and "dependence" approaches; see Robert O. Matthews, "The Third World: Powerful or Powerless?" in Alkis Kontos (ed.), *Domination* (Toronto: University of Toronto Press, 1975), pp. 69–87; and I. William Zartman, "Europe and Africa: Decolonization or Dependence?" *Foreign Affairs* 54 (January 1976), 325–43.

33. See Ali A. Mazrui, *A World Federation of Cultures: An African Perspective* (New York: Free Press, 1976).

34. Haq, *The Poverty Curtain*, pp. 157 and 163.

35. See Stanley Hoffman, "Regulating the New International System" in Martin Kilson (ed.), *New States in the Modern World* (Cambridge, Mass.: Harvard University Press, 1975) pp. 171–99.

36. See John White, "International Agencies: The Case for Proliferation" in

G. K. Helleiner (ed.), *A World Divided: The Less Developed Countries in the International Economy* (Cambridge: At the University Press, 1976), pp. 275–93.

37. See Young, "On the Performance of the International Polity."

38. See *NIO Register: Register of Institutes and Organizations Active in Areas Related to the New International Order (NIO)* (Rotterdam: RIO Foundation, October 1978).

39. *Towards a New International Economic Order: A Final Report of a Commonwealth Experts' Group* (London: Commonwealth Secretariat, 1977), p. 18.

40. Mahbub ul Haq, in *Scanning our Future: A Report from the NGO Forum on the World Economic Order* (New York: Carnegie Endowment, 1975).

41. Jan Tinbergen et al., *RIO—Reshaping the International Order: A Report to the Club of Rome* (New York: Dutton, 1976), p. 71. Emphasis added.

42. For an overview of these forecasts and speculations see Grieve et al., "Global Problems for Canadians."

43. Roger D. Hansen, "The 'Crisis of Interdependence': Where Do We Go from Here?" in his collection of *The U.S. and World Development: Agenda for Action, 1976* (New York: Praeger, for Overseas Development Council, 1976), p. 55.

44. See Johan Galtung, "Alternative Lifestyles in Rich Countries," *Development Dialogue* 1 (1976), 83–96.

45. Samuel L. Parmar, "Self-Reliant Development in an Interdependent World" in Guy F. Erb and Valeriana Kallab (eds.), *Beyond Dependency: The Developing World Speaks Out* (Washington: Overseas Development Council, 1975), p. 5.

46. Herman E. Daly, *Steady State Economics: The Economics of Bio-Physical Equilibrium and Moral Growth* (San Francisco: Freeman, 1977), p. 177.

47. Ibid., 6. On the intellectual impact and implications of a "steady state" system and "no growth" society, see Anthony J. Wiener, "Some Functions of Attitudes Towards Economic Growth," Ian Wilson, "The Changing Metabolism of Growth," and E. J. Mishan, "Extending the Growth Debate" in Kenneth D. Wilson (ed.), *Prospects for Growth: Changing Expectations for the Future* (New York: Praeger, 1977), pp. 53–70, 143–60 and 283–92.

48. See Tinbergen, *Reshaping the International Order,* pp. 106–107.

49. See Paul Streeten, "The Dynamics of the New Poor Power" in Helleiner (ed.), *A World Divided,* pp. 87–88.

50. See, for instance, Gerald K. Helleiner, "The Least Developed in the New International Economic Order: Devil Take the Hindmost?," *Cooperation Canada* 25 (1976), 3–13.

51. See, for example, Richard L. Sklar, "Post-Imperialism: A Class Analysis of Multinational Corporate Expansion," *Comparative Politics* 9 (October 1976), 75–92.

52. See Tinbergen, *Reshaping the International Order.*

53. Hansen, "The 'Crisis of Interdependence'," 63.

54. Tony Smith, "Changing Configurations of Power in North–South Relations since 1945" *International Organization* 31 (Winter 1977), 18–19.

55. Robert Gilpin, "Three Models of the Future" in C. Fred Bergsten and Law-

rence B. Krause (eds.), *World Politics and International Economics* (Washington: Brookings Institution, 1975), p. 38.

56. Ibid., p. 39.

57. Ibid., p. 42.

58. Ibid., p. 43.

59. Ibid., p. 45.

60. Ibid., p. 48.

61. Ibid., p. 60.

62. Gilpin, *U.S. Power and the Multinational Corporation,* p. 260.

63. Thomas E. Weisskopf, "Capitalism, Underdevelopment and the Future of the Poor Countries" in Jagdish Bhagwati (ed.), *Economics and World Order: From the 1970s to the 1990s* (New York: Macmillan, 1972), pp. 42–77.

64. Ibid., p. 66; compare the critique of external, systemic forces in the *dependencia* approach in Tony Smith, "The Underdevelopment of Development Literature: The Case of Dependency Theory," *World Politics* 31 (January 1979), 247–88.

65. Bruce M. Russett, "The Rich Fifth and the Poor Half: Some Speculations about International Politics in 2000 AD" in his *Power and Community in World Politics* (San Francisco: Freeman, 1974), p. 166.

66. Brown, *New Forces in World Politics,* p. 118; compare a suggestive article on the revival of power and economics in the world system by David A. Baldwin, "Power Analysis and World Politics: New Trends versus Old Tendencies," *World Politics* 31 (January 1979), 161–94.

67. Brown, *New Forces in World Politics,* pp. 109–119.

68. Ervin Laszlo et al., *Goals for Mankind: A Report to the Club of Rome on the New Horizons of Global Community* (New York: Dutton, 1977), pp. 365–66.

69. Rufus E. Miles, *Awakening from the American Dream: the Social and Political Limits to Growth* (New York: Universe, 1976), p. 223.

70. Gregory Schmid, "Interdependence Has Its Limits," *Foreign Policy* 21 (Winter 1975–76), 196–97.

9

Building Global Institutions

Charles Pentland

IN INTERNATIONAL as in national politics, institutions reflect the deeper character of society. If there is considerable doubt as to their capacity, especially at the international level, also to shape that society in the direction of a more just, cohesive and stable order, most observers will agree that what international organizations do, what authority they have, how they are working, and the debates they provoke, are all useful indicators of where the international system at large is going. This chapter will thus explore the relationship between international intergovernmental organizations and broader patterns of world order on the assumption that whatever their intrinsic interest and whatever their impact on states, these institutions and the issues surrounding them can serve as a measure of the degree and quality of political development in the global system.

Theoretical Perspectives

There are at least five readily identifiable theoretical positions on the relationship between international institutions and global political order.

Sharing a minimalist position on this question (although at variance on many other points) are the *political realists*[1] and the *dependency theorists,*[2] whether of the Marxist or the structuralist persuasion. From these perspectives, international institutions are by and large marginal to the major questions of world order. The realists view international organizations as an arena for the conflict of national interests, serving at best to facilitate the working of traditional diplomatic practices. If dominated by one state or a coalition of like-minded states, an organization becomes simply another instrument for the imposition of national policies on the rest of the world, whose global impact depends on the power of the states controlling it.

Dependency theorists take a similar view. Just as nation-states reflect in their structures and policies the interests of the dominant classes or groups, so international organizations reflect the interests of their major member-states. Indeed, they are often viewed as extranational extensions of the dominant classes in their member-states to impose their interests on other societies. Of course, this tendency of international organizations to project the interests of one group of states can be countered by the creation of organizations binding together states which feel threatened by domination and penetration. If, for example, the economic development policies of the World Bank are perceived as reflecting the priorities of the principal capitalist donor states (especially the United States), then one response is to create indigenous organizations for Third World solidarity such as the Latin American Economic System (SELA).

Viewed from the minimalist position of the political realists and the dependency theorists, international organizations have no independent resources or authority, no potential for development, and are indeed of little interest in themselves. International politics is taken to be a struggle for power and wealth, in which the central actors are, and will probably remain, national governments. If there are any forces at work beyond or across national boundaries which are likely to erode states' power, it is not conventional international institutions but multinational corporations, international trade unions, and various transnational structures of class and ethnic solidarity. But the expectation is that short of a cataclysmic nuclear or revolutionary end to the state system (in which international organizations would be equally irrelevant) the primacy of states as executors of national or class interests is likely to continue.

The *pluralist* or *liberal nationalist* also posits the persistence of the nation-state system in most of its essentials but gives a considerable role to international institutions in transforming interstate relationships to a more pacific, structured character.[3] As the logic of national self-determination works its long course from the revolutions of nineteenth-century Europe through the decolonization (and balkanization) movements of the mid-to-late twentieth century and as the nation-states continue to develop their capacities, economic, social and technological interdependence is expected to increase among them. The role of international institutions is not to challenge state sovereignty but to manage this growing interdependence, to help reduce blockages in the free flow of goods, people, and ideas between states, and to provide a forum for discussion and negotiation. The pluralist, then, argues that the nation-state is here to stay, that it "develops" through the liberation and modernization of its component states and through intensification of communication among them,[4] and that international organizations are essential facilitators of these processes.[5]

At the same time, international organizations are accorded little true autonomy as actors nor are they expected to be decisive in the process of global political development. In fostering independence and modernization and in managing and nurturing the liberalization of international exchanges, institutions such as the United Nations and the General Agreement on Tariffs and Trade (GATT) can only reflect the consensus of their membership. Moreover, that membership can be expected to preserve traditional intergovernmental forms and practices—voting by unanimity on important questions, reaffirming principles of nonintervention, requiring ratification before international agreements become part of national law. There is no expectation, in short, that international organizations will acquire supranational authority. Insofar as they are backed by a working consensus of their members, they can have a real impact on the international system, but the transformations they effect are not expected to challenge the very foundations of that system. Like international law, international organizations are seen by the pluralists as embodying and perfecting the "logic of Westphalia," not attacking it.[6]

Global *functionalism*, on the other hand, begins from the premise that this logic is obsolete and dangerous.[7] The nation-state, argue the functionalists, is too small to cope effectively with problems of physical security and economic welfare, as it has traditionally done, for its citizens. Modern communications technology and a growing sense of earth's ecological fragility have underlined the obsolescence of national boundaries, while at the same time nation-states remain the focus of man's most atavistic, destructive emotions. In the functionalist view, then, international cooperation is a means not only to make organizational forms more congruent with the transnational scale of most problems, but also to wean humanity away from its fixation on nationalism. As the vehicles of this cooperation, international organizations are expected not simply to do their assigned tasks efficiently, but also, in so doing, to attract the loyalty of the population they serve.

The organizations that are so central to functionalism are of a special kind—narrow, technical, and focused less on the government of men than on the administration of things. The strategy of change is to discern specific areas where a few governments at least can agree that it makes sense to work together. An organization is created, vested by the governments with real authority within that sector, its precise design, powers, and membership determined by the function it is to serve. To the extent that such organizations succeed in their tasks, other governments will seek to join in. More important, the lessons of cooperation learned by elites and public alike are transferred to more and more sectors of economic and social life. Functionalists thus envisage international organizations accumulating organically, spreading into most areas of international life, gradually divesting nation-states of their tasks and their sovereignty. At some point, states will not only have become unable and unwilling to go to war; they will have been so undermined and overlaid by the network of international institutions that the term "international system" will have passed into archaic usage.

It is obvious that functionalists place their hopes and expectations on technical, noncontroversial organizations along the model of many United Nations Specialized Agencies (although many of these are too broad in scope to be effective). Organizations focused directly on military and diplomatic ("high politics") questions cannot successfully challenge national sovereignty and are doomed to sterility in a world where sovereignty prevails. Regional organizations, too, pose problems, since they presuppose the overriding importance of territoriality and may simply lead to new rounds of regional supranational state-building which threaten world order. Organizational form, therefore, must follow functional need if global security and welfare are to be maximized.

Neofunctional theories of international organization start from many of the same premises and look to many of the same mechanisms of change as functionalism.[8] But they add to the dynamics of technical self-determination a consideration of the process of negotiation among governments, transnational interest groups, and the officials of international organizations, which serves to reassert the primacy of political variables. Neofunctionalists are less hesitant than functionalists to view the process of system-change as one of state-building, or at least a gradual transition from low-level economic and social cooperation to a fully supranational political order. Whereas neofunctionalists, to the dismay of functionalist critics, have so far shown more interest in integration processes on the regional than on the global levels, certain types of global organization in the social, economic, and technical fields are perceived as appropriate vehicles for change along neofunctionalist lines.[9]

In this perspective, international institutions are a true reality in the global system, not just as constraints on what national actors do but also as emergent actors in their own right. They are created initially because their member-states wish to manage jointly what they can no longer manage separately or manage only by fragile and often fleeting processes of simple cooperation. Once such a regime is established, the neofunctionalists argue, a number of other things change. First, political forces begin to reorganize and coalesce so as to influence the new authority directly rather than through their respective national governments. Second, the officials of the organization itself come to develop their own sense of identity and collective mission; they begin to deploy their technical expertise, diplomatic skills, and legal mandate to increase their organization's scope and level of authority. This growth takes place not through the sort of natural, organic "spillover" process posited by functionalists, but through a bargaining process in which the organization as an actor with its own interests in growth and claiming as well to speak for the collective interests of the member-states, acts as an initiator, broker, and executor of the decision. Every success in this role is expected to add to the organization's independent authority, and the shared perception by states of their growing interdependence (and thus the need for common institutions) tends to stack the cards very much in favor of such an outcome.

Of the four theoretical approaches to global organization set out so far, functionalism and neofunctionalism clearly give the most significant role to international institutions and expect the most radical change in the global system. Functionalism does, however, have in common with pluralism the notion that however modified by the presence of institutions, the nation-state system might nevertheless persist. The institutions, under those circumstances, would remain, in the juridical sense at least, international. Neofunctionalism, on the other hand, looks to the eventual demise of the nation-state and the transfer of sovereignty to new levels, at which point the international organization would itself have become a state. International organizations, therefore, are essential agents in the transformation of global society to a form which logically and juridically makes them obsolete.

If the culmination of that process of change is seen by neofunctionalists as a distant prospect, it poses more immediate questions for the global *federalists*.[10] On the one hand, federalists place great emphasis on all forms of international cooperation and organization—global and regional institutions, cooperation on matters of security, economic welfare, technology, and culture. Common institutions are to be granted greater and greater authority, financial independence, and coercive power in order to manage the affairs of states. And yet clearly the preference of federalists has always been to do away with the state system as quickly as possible, substituting for it (preferably on a global scale, although regional federalism as a stepping-stone or pilot project is not ruled out) a federal system in which states have transferred to the central authority a monopoly of coercive power as well as the power to legislate in policy areas that transcend state borders.

A global organization like the United Nations, then, is viewed either as second-best—an arrangement to be sustained because at the moment world government is not possible—or as a framework in which the federal system will be built. Schemes, therefore, come forward for weighted voting in the General Assembly ("representation by population" being more appropriate for a government than "one-state, one-vote"), for independent financial resources (taxation of seabed mining and the like to free the organization from direct dependence on national assessments), for a standing army or peacekeeping force, and for extension of the compulsory jurisdiction of the International Court of Justice. To the extent that they were all realized, such projects would spell the end, strictly speaking, of the international organizations in which they came to fruition. Much more dramatic than neofunctionalism, but with the same ends in mind, global federalism treats international institutions as the essential instrument for putting an end to international politics as we know it and for ushering in the era of world politics.

Each of these five theoretical positions purports to explain the present functioning (or malfunctioning) of international institutions as well as to suggest how they might develop in the future. Although their interpretations and predictions are by no means always mutually exclusive, there are nevertheless dramatic differences among them, not the least of which is plausibility. But to arrive at a clearer sense of how our broad theories and expectations might fit the evolution of global politics, we now turn to a closer examination of contemporary institutional patterns and trends.

The Global Pattern of Institutions

In broad historical perspective the emergence of formal intergovernmental institutions has been part of the general growth in the scale and complexity of world politics over the last hundred years. This period, which saw the population of these international organizations increase from fewer than ten (in 1870) to more than 270 (in 1977), also witnessed a rapid, if not always smooth, rise in many other indices of international interdependence.[11] World trade and transnational investment, for instance, grew at a faster rate than the world's economic product, especially after World War II. The number of international nongovernmental organizations (NGOs) increased from about sixty in 1880 to about 2,400 in 1977.[12] Not least, the same period saw the globalization of international relations, beginning with the last phase of colonialism in the late nineteenth century and culminating in the dismantling of Europe's overseas empires in the mid-twentieth. The number of states in the international system grew from 63 in 1914 to over 150 in the late 1970s.

If states, nongovernmental organizations (both subnational and transnational) and international organizations were all proliferating over this period, so too were the tasks they were expected to perform. It is customary to date the beginning of the modern welfare state from the social policy of Bismarck's Germany in the 1870s. By the time this trend had come to fruition along with the post-1945 "Keynesian revolution" and the rise of authoritarian states in the socialist and less developed world, it was not unusual for even the most fervently liberal capitalist governments to be taxing and spending 30 to 40 percent of their economies' gross product and regulating most aspects of their citizens' lives. Similarly, international organizations began with the modest and uninspiring functionalism of such "public international unions" as the Universal Postal Union (1874) and the International Telegraphic Union (1865), and moved slowly into the legal and political dimensions of peace and security with the establishment of the Permanent Court of International Justice (1920). In the post-1945 era, international organizations too reflected the Keynesian revolution in the creation of the International Monetary Fund, the World Bank, the GATT, and other rudimentary instruments of international economic management. If their impact on international society is considerably less than that of governments on their national societies (only the European Community among international organizations spends even close to 1 percent of its members' total GNP), nevertheless international organizations today have responsibilities covering practically every sphere of human existence.

Some will view it as paradoxical that the era of international organizations seems to have coincided with, rather than succeeded, the era of national self-determination and state-building, but of course it is in great measure the increased number of states (and consequently of interstate interactions) and the increased range of their activities that have produced the need for international regulation. To some extent, the growth of international organizations is a response simply to a "traffic" problem, that is, to the clogging and complexity of erstwhile adequate channels of communication, quite apart from the substance of issues. But there is also the fact that even as states have taken on new economic, technological, and scientific functions, these functions have been assuming an increasingly transnational character and have challenged the capacity of any one state to deal with them in isolation.

The contemporary pattern of international organizations is a fluid, heterogeneous one on which a great many analytic frameworks or simple classificatory schemes seem artificial and skewed. We can, however, at least arrive at some sense of how that pattern has emerged and also how it might be going by considering, first, the membership, and second, the activities of the 270-odd intergovernmental organizations. It would be useful then to examine some of the new institutional or quasi-institutional forms which have arisen in recent years as a complement or possibly a challenge to this network of organizations.

In classifying international organizations by membership, it is important to consider both size and criteria of participation. In principle, of course, the membership of international organizations can range from being co-extensive with the number of sovereign states in the system at one extreme, to simple bilateralism at the other. In practice, there are few examples at either extreme, the United Nations coming closest to universality (significant absentees being Switzerland and the two Koreas)[13] and bilateral relationships tending on the whole to be handled informally or irregularly (relations between Canada and the United States, arguably the world's most intense bilateral ties, involve few institutions apart from the International Joint Commission). Most international organizations in fact involve between a half-dozen and twenty states. There is some logic in this, perhaps, since bilateral relationships cannot easily be kept isolated, tending to ramify into multilateral forms (GATT and the European Coal and Steel Community are good instances of this), while organizations with huge, cumbersome memberships (like the United Nations and the Organization of African Unity) tend to fragment into factions or regional and subregional groupings.[14]

As far as criteria of participation are concerned, obviously organizations open to any state with generally recognized sovereign status will tend to be larger than those insisting on functional capacity, special interest, or geographical or cultural criteria, or those simply evolving out of traditional linkages. Nevertheless, as the examples of the Intergovernmental Maritime Consultative Organization (seventy members), the OAU (forty-five members), and the Commonwealth (thirty-six members) demonstrate, even noninclusive organizations can become large and often unwieldy. In the present array of institutions only the United Nations and most of its specialized agencies are open to membership by virtually any sovereign state (subject of course to its ability to carry out the obligations of membership and to general acceptance of its "peace-loving" character). About one-third of today's international organizations have their membership determined by a relatively narrow functional capacity or special interest (for example, the International Atomic Energy Agency, Intelsat, the International Whaling Commission, OPEC, and other commodity organizations or cartels). A handful of organizations like the Commonwealth and the associations of francophone countries have membership inherited from past imperial relationships.[15] The remainder, over 60 percent of all international organizations, have membership based on geographic (regional) criteria, whether explicit or implicit. Overall, it is the noninclusive forms of organization which have seen the fastest growth since World War II. In the 1970s especially, whereas the number of universal organizations has not grown, that of functional and special-interest organizations has grown about 25 percent, while regional organizations have increased about 15 percent.[16]

What do these organizations do? Again, there are at least two ways to answer that question. One is to identify the substantive policy sectors of international life in which international organizations play a part. The other is to examine the different political, legal, and administrative roles played by the institutions in these various sectors.

The major policy sectors are as follows, with examples of corresponding organizations:

1. the development and administration of international law (International Court of Justice, International Law Commission, European Commission for Human Rights);
2. maintenance of peace and security (United Nations central organs, Organization of American States, Arab League, NATO, Warsaw Pact, Organization of African Unity (OAU), Western European Union);
3. political cooperation and consultation (Association of Southeast Asian Nations (ASEAN), United Nations, OAU, Arab League);
4. general economic cooperation and management (GATT, International Monetary Fund, OECD, ASEAN, European Community);
5. resource and commodity management (OPEC and other cartels; International Energy Agency; buyer–seller commodity agreements—past and present—such as for cocoa, coffee, wheat; the proposed Common Fund);
6. economic integration (European Community, Andean Common Market, Caribbean Common Market, Economic Community of West African States);
7. economic development (World Bank, U.N. Development Program, U.N. Industrial Development Organization, UNCTAD, Latin American Economic System, the regional development banks as well as the Third World integration schemes mentioned under 6);
8. environmental management (U.S. Environmental Program, European river commissions for Rhine and Danube, U.S.–Canada International Joint Commission, African organizations for locust control);
9. technical cooperation (UPU, ITU, International Civil Aviation Organization, Intelsat, Euratom, Central Office for International Railroad Transport);
10. social welfare (International Labor Organization, World Health Organization, Intergovernmental Commission for European Migration);
11. cultural and scientific cooperation (UNESCO, Commonwealth, Francophone Association, Council of Europe, International Bureau of Weights and Measures, International Oceanographic Commission).

In the sectors toward the top of this list are found the institutions most prominent in the public eye as well as in the publications of political scientists, historians, and lawyers interested in problems of world order. But whatever their significance, these organizations are few and their numbers remarkably stable. In the middle of the list (4 through 7) are found institutions that have begun to receive more attention as the world's agenda has filled with economic issues. Their numbers grew steadily in the postwar era, especially in the 1960s and early 1970s. Like the political organizations, these economic organizations are often broad enough to cover two or more sectors. The institutions in the last four categories are by far the most numerous and the least known. Although they constitute more than two-thirds of all international organizations their tasks are so narrow, technical, and obscure, their direct political impact so minimal, that their work is unknown to all but a few specialists.

The functions that international organizations perform in these policy sectors can be grouped, according to one observer, into four categories: (1) service; (2) norm creation and allocation; (3) rule observance and settlement of disputes; and (4) operation.[17] Another formulation distinguishes seven types of decision taken by international institutions: (1) representational; (2) symbolic; (3) boundary; (4) programmatic; (5) rule-creating; (6) rule-supervisory; and (7) operations.[18] Given that such decisions would occur in different combinations in the performance of the four functions, it would not be difficult to merge these two schemata. But a more elaborate and sophisticated way of looking at what "international regimes" do, incorporating and improving on the above concepts, has been developed by J. G. Ruggie, who distinguishes between purposes, instrumentalities, and functions.[19] *Purposes* may be (1) acquisition of new capabilities (collaboration on research and development); (2) making more effective use of existing capabilities (pooling of national resources); and (3) coping with the consequences of their use (protection of "the commons"). *Instrumentalities* can provide (1) simply a common framework for national behavior, with no attempt at ordering or control; (2) a joint facility, which aims to harmonize, standardize, and coordinate national behavior; (3) a common policy, which integrates national behavior; and (4) a common policy substituted for national behavior and eliminating national automony. *Functions,* finally, may be (1) informational; (2) managerial (making allocative choices); or (3) executive (effecting a division of labor among its members according to a normative order).

It would take us well beyond the scope and purpose of this paper to try and fit the universe of international organizations systematically into the three-dimensional matrix (36 cells) created by this scheme. But it should be noted that both the instrumentalities and the functions dimensions indicate a higher and a lower order of organization and imply a developmental direction. At present, most international organizations clearly fit under the "joint facility" category of instrumentality, with a few under common policy (integrative), and perform informational and, to a lesser extent, managerial functions. Movement, if any, toward higher levels of organization is glacial. As far as the purposes dimension is concerned, contemporary organizations seem to distribute themselves in all three categories, with most probably making more effective use of existing capabilities.

This, then, in very cursory fashion, is the pattern of international organization in the global system of the 1980s. It is not difficult to discern in that complex pattern the shape of the major institutional issues that confront the international community and that will be discussed later in this chapter. Suffice it to add here that the pattern of intergovernmental institutions is further complicated, and the issues further bedeviled, by the presence of transnational actors such as nongovernmental organizations and multinational corporations, by the quasi-institutionalization of summitry (especially in the Western or "trilateral" world), by the growing importance of official and semi-official elite networks among states, and by the emergence, especially striking in the 1970s, of multilateral, broad-theme conference diplomacy. Some of this clearly represents a groping toward new and more flexible organizational forms by governments ever more incapable of coping alone and yet increasingly unhappy with the working of traditional intergovernmental institutions.

Support for Global Institutions

Like other institutions, international organizations need the political support of their constituents—in this case governments—if they are to survive to grow. Few states, of course, will deny their adherence to the general idea that the international system needs a well-developed set of institutions. More significant, however, is their support for specific organizations and their policies; that support may be manifest in declaratory policy and elite attitudes, levels of activity, and the willingness to implement decisions made by the organization. Aside from the orientation of major states, support also refers to the general climate or prevalent political culture in the international system. To what extent is there a shared notion, across the system, as to the appropriate types, functions, and powers of international institutions? I shall look briefly at this latter question before turning to the attitudes of the major nation-states toward global institutions.

In one sense it could be argued that there is a single international political culture which shares a positive attitude and many common perceptions about the role of international organizations. Embodying and sustaining this culture are the diplomatic elites of most nation-states. State Departments, Ministries of Foreign Affairs and their equivalents, as well as political and bureaucratic elites who are involved in the more generalized or legally oriented aspects of foreign policy are likely to be more disposed toward institutional collaboration than are the specialist departments grounded more in particular domestic interests. The support of these latter groups for international organizations is likely to be linked much more to specific issues and interests, and much less stable. For precisely these reasons, this diplomatic elite culture, however uniformly internationalist in its views, is unlikely to prevail over the various spokesmen for national and international interests in specific situations. The most that can be said is that it provides a constant, diffuse level of support, acting as a sort of quiet, passive "conscience" to governments often inclined toward narrow self-interest or unilateral action.

But beneath this rather fragile skein of the diplomatic elite culture and the superficialities of ceremonial and legal form, there are some significant political-cultural cleavages in the contemporary global system which often cast doubt on the legitimacy of many global institutions. International organizations have their historical roots in a diplomatic system which was initially European and remained essentially so as late as World War II. The postwar globalization of the system saw the participation in such institutions of states which did not always share the values and priorities of that earlier European system or of the contemporary Western world descended from it.

Differences in ideology, inasmuch as these imply divergent views of the state (and related concepts of sovereignty and nonintervention), of law (international law in particular), and of the future, certainly explain some of the variations in the support for international organizations among states. Here it is probably useful to uphold the conventional distinction between the three "worlds" of (1) the Western (or westernized) developed market economies of the OECD countries; (2) the Soviet Union and its allies; and (3) the less developed countries. With respect to the first group, of course, we have to make some allowance for differences between Anglo-Saxon and continental European ideas of law, as well as for Japanese traditions. And the Third World category covers a multitude of variations, including the heavily legalistic Latin American perspective on international organization and the rich traditions of Chinese and African law. In attempts to codify international law as well as in the composition of the International Court of Justice itself, such cleavages are a hard reality, and it would be surprising if they were not equally significant in relation to support for international institutions.

It is important, however, not to make too much of political culture in this respect. Support for global institutions in general and for certain organizations in particular will also be determined by whether a major state or group of states is: (1) generally satisfied with the condition of the world and the distribution of major values in it (that is, is it a status quo or a revisionist state?); (2) generally in a majority or a minority in any or all global institutions; and (3) more oriented toward its immediate neighborhood than to global issues (that is, does it seek to play an isolationist, regionalist, or global role?). A satisfied or status quo state or group of states (such as the United States and all of the OECD countries) will place a high premium on global institutions as long as these are identified with "law and order" notions of peace and security and the management of the established economic order. Dissatisfied or revisionist states can be expected to demand radical institutional reform and, failing that, to attempt to capture or create counterinstitutions on the global or regional level, as the Third World countries attempted through UNCTAD.

Majority states—those who are consistently able to master the votes to win decisions on issues that matter to them—will obviously find it easier to support international institutions with considerable enthusiasm and treasure, as the Americans demonstrated in the United Nations until the early 1970s. Chronic minority groups, such as the Soviet Union and its allies during the United Nations' first two decades, can be expected (assuming they even wish to remain members) to take refuge in the veto and in the "letter of the law" in order to hinder development of the organization as a more effective instrument of the majority. Such actions will naturally be viewed (and proclaimed) by the majority as lack of support for the organization. The Americans, who used to make this argument, now unhappily find themselves in the minority with great regularity. Growing use of the Security Council veto, the cutback of the United States' U.N. budgetary contribution to 25 percent, the recent withdrawal from the International Labor Organization—these are all indicators of a major debate in the United States and abroad about America's continued commitment to global organizations.

Support for such institutions will also be conditioned by the geographic reach of states' foreign policy interests. The effects on the League of Nations of American interwar isolationism are probably the best-known example, the United States viewing its priorities as domestic and hemispheric and, while engaging in much informal collaboration with the League, denying it the major substantive and symbolic support of full membership. With the emergence of regional blocs in the Third World and the retreat of France and Britain into a primarily European orientation, global institutions in the 1970s may be suffering from a more generalized absence of global thinking, especially on economic issues. The search for regional solutions to trade, monetary, and development problems may be undermining the legitimacy of many of the multilateral institutions created in the 1940s.

From these general considerations let us turn now to the attitudes of the major states toward global institutions. If there has been any one power that has constantly championed global organizations from World War II on, it is of course the United States. The whole panoply of organizations—the central U.N. system for peace and security, the specialized agencies including the World Bank system, the GATT (and its failed predecessor, the International Trade Organization)—from the outset bore an American imprint. It is not unreasonable to see in this the reflection of military and economic hegemony, and to attribute American enthusiasm for such institutions to the visible evidence that they were acting at least as helpful adjuncts to, and occasionally as direct instruments of, that domination. This is not to deny the genuine force of idealism and altruism in American support for global institutions, or the fact that this support produced a "public good" of security and economic order from which much of the world profited over two decades. Nevertheless Americans seem more prone than most peoples to present their support for international organizations in the language of idealism and humanism and to remain seemingly unaware of how well the institutions have served their narrower national interests or of how closely their designs for "one world" reflect culturally bound concepts of political and economic order.

The United States has found itself, since the late 1960s, increasingly in the minority in most global fora. It can no longer expect the votes of Western Europe and the other OECD states, of Latin America and of a handful of African and Asian friends, to carry the day for it, as was so often the case in the 1950s. If its voting power has diminished in the face of the Third World's presence, however, the United States remains, along with its economic partners, the major provisioner of United Nations programs (especially in development), a country with the world's preeminent economy (without whose agreement no multilateral trade or monetary arrangements can work), and one of two global military superpowers with a veto in the Security Council. If the United Nations and other global institutions no longer work *for* the United States in the same way, they cannot work *without* it or *against* it. It must be said, however, that American administrations and public opinion do not seem to have found much comfort in these new circumstances. Third World resolutions, cheerfully backed by the Soviets, on the Middle East or southern Africa, often embarrassingly, have to be vetoed. Massive General Assembly majorities for resolutions on development, the remnants of colonialism, or other North–South issues often have to be labeled irresponsible and denied the resources to make them stick. Those resources continue to be channeled through global fora controlled by the donors, such as the World Bank. Much American institutional enthusiasm seems quite understandably to have passed to these bodies and to narrower groupings of the like-minded, such as OECD. Trilateralism may be the best illustration of this tendency away from the American tradition of globalism.[20]

The Soviet Union's early attitude to global institutions was conditioned by its newly acquired superpower status, its minority position, its residual revisionist outlook on world order, and the confinement of its policy interests to its immediate peripheries, especially Europe. That the Soviets would be discussing a successor to the League only a few years after their expulsion from that body is explained largely by the alignments and fortunes of the war. Their postwar status called for participation, at least on security matters, even if the Charter of the United Nations reflected Soviet concerns in only a few places. Economic and functional organizations seemed to offer more dangers than advantages and were largely eschewed.

Soviet globalism, then, was selective, amounting to maintaining a presence and conducting a defensive strategy in the United Nations—a strategy that could be advanced as supporting the "original" conception of the United Nations against those who would would override national sovereignty and use the United Nations to impose their own vision of world order. Only on colonial issues was any sort of activism at all in evidence. As for economic and many functional activities, nonparticipation and nonsupport for financial and security reasons could be justified again as resistance to illegitimate extensions of the organization into the management and expansion of the capitalist world.[21]

Like any state, the Soviet Union was well able to put aside such arguments when circumstances changed. Strictures on the illegality of the "Uniting for Peace Resolution" were forgotten in 1956 when that resolution could be deployed against Britain and France in Egypt. And as the Third World's numbers grew and attacks on colonialism and the capitalist world's economic dominance began to be the main force of U.N. debates (and to color the activities of the Specialized Agencies), Soviet support and activity began to become broader, even if the position it took on North–South issues seemed suspiciously to combine a maximum of condemnation of the North with a minimum of generosity to the South.

For most of the postwar period, China was in no sense a global actor. The Republic, a member of the League of Nations, reappeared in the United Nations as a much less significant actor, confined by 1949 to Taiwan although retaining, largely at American insistence, the right to represent all of China and to sit as a permanent member of the Security Council. The People's Republic, on the other hand, claimed for two decades the exclusive right to speak for all of China in the United Nations —a position most other states were prepared to accept. At the same time, China considered itself a target of the organization, dominated as it was by a United States which could push through such resolutions as the one condemning China's "aggression" in Korea in 1950. In the early 1960s, its dispute with the other superpower now out in the open, China even proposed an alternative international organization to embrace those Afro-Asian states like itself who wished to resist Western and Soviet domination. Within ten years, however, Peking was in the United Nations and Taiwan was out. Since entering, China has continued attempts to align itself with the Third World and to deny any superpower pretensions. It has used the veto to protect what it sees as vital interests, but generally it has been scrupulous in acting as the quiet, good citizen. It belongs to many specialized agencies but plays little role in them or in other international organizations.[22]

Japan, as a defeated power in World War II, was not able to join the

United Nations until 1956. Since that time it has played a modest role both in the central organization and in the specialized agencies. Indeed, Japan's performance in international organizations generally has been more than discreet, especially given its rise to the status of a global economic superpower. On peace-keeping matters it has been understandably reticent about offering forces or undertaking mediatory action[23]; its role has been limited to verbal support. On economic matters its role has of course been more significant, although Third World countries remain critical about Japan's relative lack of interest in governmental, multilateral as opposed to private, bilateral forms of development assistance. Should it prove possible some day to recognize Japan's new status by means of a permanent Security Council seat (an idea mooted by President Carter) and should recent trends in its military development continue, Japan may come to have a much more significant impact on global organizations than at present.

The major Western European states have a rather mixed record of support for global institutions, particularly for the United Nations itself. West Germany, of course, has been a member only since 1973, and it did not experience the events of the United Nations' first decade which raised serious British and French doubts about the organization. Of the latter two countries Britain has been on the whole a stronger supporter of the United Nations and of global economic and functional agencies than has France.[24] The early years were, however, uncomfortable for both. Pressures for decolonization came from a coalition of the United States, the Soviet Union, and the Third World, formed out of different but convergent interests. Over Suez it seemed to be the same countries ganging up again against France and Britain. Not only did the United Nations seem a hostile place, but also each of these powers had what they perceived to be institutional alternatives to turn to: for Britain, the Commonwealth, an organization with members all over the globe, and for France, Europe, black Africa, and the francophone world. But once decolonization had largely run its course (with the United Nations serving frequently as a dumping ground for problems met en route, especially by Britain) and once their remaining global aspirations (and presence) had diminished, Britain and France began to take a more active, positive role in United Nations business. For both, there remain institutional alternatives to attract attention, money, and political energies, but one of these, Europe, has in fact become a vehicle for the concentration of nine states' policies (including those of Britain, France, and West Germany) in several international bodies, not least the United Nations itself.[25] The foreign ministers confer regularly and frequently, as do their ambassadors abroad (including in New York). On most economic issues they have in fact passed on much of their responsibility for foreign policy to the organs of the European Community. The general trend toward coordination of

Western European foreign policies may in time produce less distinctive individual positions in global institutions. At the same time, however, these European middle and small powers may collectively provide a valuable new source of support, especially for U.N. security activity.

If the capabilities of the great powers are vital for the effective functioning of global organizations, however, in the end most observers recognize that it is the small powers who need these organizations for their security and prosperity and who are their most fervent supporters. The idea that small powers have a special place as beneficiaries and supporters of international organizations can be traced through the League of Nations era. It was especially visible in debates about the status of the great powers at San Francisco in 1945, and it has been nurtured by all the Secretaries-General of the United Nations. For the small developed states such as the Scandinavian countries, highly dependent on exports, the success of global economic organizations fostering freer trade and stable monetary relations is vital. Peace-keeping or "preventive diplomacy," meanwhile, provides the means for limiting the potential of great powers to bring on mass destruction and maximizes the opportunity for multilateral intervention in which small powers can play a positive role.

For less developed states, on the other hand, the security functions of global organizations, while significant from time to time, are generally perceived as secondary to the state-building and economic development functions. Global economic and technical organizations are valued and supported to the extent that they aid in the redistribution not only of wealth but of the real power to govern, from the rich center to the Third World states. There is among these states an understandable inclination to give greater support to global institutions where the Third World's members make a difference (the General Assembly, UNCTAD, for example), to try to reform others which, while valued, do not as yet reflect this majority (for instance, expansion of the Economic and Social Council's membership and the whole restructuring debate in the United Nations[26]), and to criticize institutions like the Security Council, the World Bank, and the IMF which remain dominated by the donors (whether of security or finance).

Here emerges one of the classic dilemmas of international organization. The effectiveness of global institutions clearly depends on the support and full participation of the major powers—or at least most of them —who alone have the military, technological, and economic capabilities to invest in whatever common action is required. For these states, the minimum return expected on the investment is some responsiveness of the organization to their particular policy interests and some form of final say on its actions. The small states, on the other hand, need effective institutions more than do the great powers. Yet they recognize the dangers in the capture of those organizations by the dominant power (or powers) and find the "final say" concept offensive to their "one-state, one-vote" egalitarianism. On these grounds, small states may tend to prefer bodies where the majority rule prevails. To these bodies, however, great powers are reluctant to give over resources.

It would seem that this lack of congruence between majority support and effectiveness, or between votes and resources, is a growing threat to the legitimacy of international institutions. Those organizations that command the greatest economic and military resources tend to have limited support beyond the participating great powers. Organizations with mass support among states, however, tend to be denied the resources to succeed in their declared aims. The more political these aims, that is, dealing directly with matters of security, sovereignty, and the distribution of power in the international system, the more debilitating this lack of congruence will be. The saving grace of the functional, technical, and welfare institutions may simply be their lower profile.

Issues of Global Institutional Development

The first section of this chapter set out some of the main theoretical perspectives on the nature, purposes, and prospects of international institutions. There followed a survey of the contemporary international landscape which attempted to discern the distribution and growth trends of different types of organization, distinguished principally by patterns of membership and by activities. A third section then examined the attitudes and participation of states in relation to global institutions, in an attempt to assess the quality of support these institutions have acquired. From this broad overview of the context of global institutional development, I shall turn now to the major issues to which it gives rise. The principal aim is of course to gain some understanding of current and emergent issues of institutional development. But none of these issues is novel or peculiar to the 1970s. Some sense of how issues emerged during the brief history of international organizations, how and why states were divided by them and tried to handle them, and how they were resolved, can help us get a clearer idea of prospects for the 1980s.

ISSUES OF TASK

Nations have always disagreed as to what international organizations should and should not be doing. Not surprisingly, however, the two periods in which pressures to expand the functions of international institutions were greatest—the mid-1940s and the 1970s—also saw the most vigorous debate about the proper sphere of their activity.

Before World War II such questions were rarely raised. Two criteria can be said to have determined the functions of the handful of institutions founded between 1860 and 1939. In the case of "public international unions" (the Universal Postal Union, the International Telegraphic Union, the European River Commissions) the tasks were technical, specific, and largely uncontroversial, arising largely from increases in the routine exchanges across borders brought about through technological change. Such tasks seemed inherently, self-evidently translatable to international jurisdiction.[27] As far as peace and security questions were concerned, too, the Hague Conferences (1899 and 1907) and the Versailles Conference (1919) produced legal and political institutions reflecting a widespread rejection of the balance of power and the use of force to settle disputes. The consensus, however fleeting, was that the Permanent Court of Arbitration, the Permanent Court of International Justice, and the League of Nations were necessary responses, in the form of impartial, legalistic, quasi-automatic mechanisms, to the manifest inadequacy of the old methods of self-help and alliance in dealing with problems of peace and security. It was not necessary to believe in the ultimate demise of the nation-state. It was simply a matter of having collective mechanisms available to curb those states inclined toward aggression. The League's creators had a deceptively clear notion of what it would do and in what circumstances. Attempts in the 1920s to improve the League's capacity to meet aggression aimed not only to make its response more sure but also to make its mandate still more precise.[28]

In the 1940s, when the postwar institutional design was discussed, there was really no question that the League would have to have a successor, performing essentially the same functions of deterring or repelling threats to the peace but possessing improved means of detection, engagement, decision, and execution. Nor was it seriously doubted that the public international unions would continue, many of them revamped and brought into the U.N. system as specialized agencies. Transnational technological, social, and cultural needs suggested the creation of several new agencies—FAO (1944), UNESCO (1945), WHO (1946), ICAO (1947) and WMO (1950), later joined by IMCO (1958) and, under slightly different arrangement, IAEA (1957). Many of these organizations, to be sure, were broader of mandate and membership than the early public international unions, and their founding was not free of controversy. But on the need for collaboration in these areas there was little disagreement. (Even Soviet unwillingness to participate in many of them reflected not a denial of the need but a fear of intervention and domination by the West).

The major issues of task in the 1940s concerned whether international institutions should concern themselves with (1) the management and development of the international economy; or (2) the dismantling of empires and the nurturing of national self-determination. The interwar experience of the ILO and the findings of the Bruce Report, the self-destructive character of international economic relationships in the 1930s, the Western (especially American) interest in a stable, expanding global economic system, and the new expanded sense (expressed by Keynes, Beveridge, and others) of what government could and should do all represented pressures leading toward a quantum leap in the mandate of international organizations. There was of course disagreement about how, and in what measure, these new tasks of economic management should be assumed by international institutions (as evidenced for example in the British-American debate at Bretton Woods over the role of the IMF).[29] But on *whether* the global economy required collective management there was general consensus. The exceptions again were the Soviet Union and its allies, who chose understandably to stand aside from institutions like the World Bank, IMF, and GATT which they saw as sustaining international capitalism and extending American economic dominion.

Concerning international supervision of colonies and their progress toward independence, there was again a majority favoring an expanded mandate for the United Nations. Over the initial objections of the minority—this time not the Soviets but the European colonial powers—a Trusteeship system was created with greater supervisory power than the League's Mandate system, and a built-in presumption toward eventual independence for all colonies. In this lie the beginnings of the state-creating task or the "developmental functionalism" of the United Nations, so prominent from the 1960s onward.[30] On an overlapping concern, namely for international oversight of states' treatment of their citizens, there was greater consensus, born of course out of the experience of the war.[31]

The 1950s saw not so much further expansion but rather reinterpretation of the tasks of international organizations. In 1956 the United Nations began definitely to abandon the illusions of collective security (temporarily sustained by Korea) in favor of preventive diplomacy, a notion of peace-keeping more appropriate to a loose bipolar world. In the longer run, of course, in requiring of the United Nations more developed capacities for detection, mediation, and military interposition, the new doctrine also implied an expanded definition of the peace-keeping function, well beyond the relatively simple, legalistic notions of collective security. Initially, at least, there was a broad consensus supporting such a development.

In economic fields, too, reinterpretations of the role of global institutions began, setting the stage for later expansion of tasks. The recovery of Europe and the beginning of the landslide of decolonization turned the World Bank from the "reconstruction" to the "development" part of its official title. The Bank accordingly added two more flexible lending instruments to its system, the International Finance Corporation (1956) and the International Development Association (1960). But the real harbinger of change was the growing demand of the poor countries for a Special United Nations Fund for Economic Development (SUNFED) controlled not by the minority of donors (as was the World Bank) but by the majority of recipients.[32] Henceforth the main debates about the United Nations' tasks would see the Third World states calling for increased U.N. resources and powers, to be managed not by the great-power oligarchy but by the General Assembly. The rich Western countries would be found on the defensive, the Soviets and their allies on the sidelines (unless advantage could be gained by running with the majority).

By the end of the 1960s, expectations about the expansion of global peace-keeping capabilities had been severely dampened. The Congo experience was taken as showing the dangers of overextension. The financial and diplomatic legacy of the United Nations' operation, whatever the judgment about its success, made the chances of similar actions in the future seem remote. Although the Cyprus and West Irian operations—on a more modest scale—were working well, the traumas of the Congo and the expulsion of UNEF from Egypt in 1967 combined to produce a sober reappraisal of the limits of U.N. peace-keeping as a growth area; instead, a General Assembly special committee in 1965 began a long examination of peace-keeping whose outcome was likely to be routinization at a fairly low level.

By contrast, pressures for task expansion continued to build in the areas of prime concern to the Third World. Proclamation of the 1960s as the U.N. Development Decade implied increasing multilateralization of development assistance, requiring greater roles for the specialized agencies, the World Bank System, and the United National Development Program (formed in 1965). Several new agencies long called-for by the Third World came into being, notably the U.N. Conference on Trade and Development (UNCTAD) (1964), the U.N. Industrial Development Organization (UNIDO) (1966), and the U.N. Capital Development Fund (1966). Creating the institutions and staking out new and broad mandates for them proved, however, easier than persuading the rich countries to devote sufficient resources to them, let alone make them the centerpiece of global development strategy. The second UNCTAD conference at Delhi in 1968 and the third at Santiago in 1972 witnessed the anger and frustration of many Third World states at Western, particularly American, reluctance to move in this direction.[33]

By the early 1970s a number of trends converged to create a new era of significant if disorderly expansion in the tasks of international institutions. Unlike the quantum leap of the 1940s, however, which was based on a broad consensus, the growth process of the 1970s has been marked by debates fought out in a variety of institutional settings, involving different mixes of actors on different sides. For once, the classic peace and security issues are not especially controversial—indeed, U.N. peace-keeping has made a modest and quite effective return after a period of retrenchment.[34] On the other hand, major institutional questions have been forced onto the global agenda by the decline of American economic hegemony (symbolized by the measures of August 1971 and the subsequent end of the Bretton Woods monetary system), by the avowed failure of the Development Decade and the inauguration of a second (in effect the decade of the New International Economic Order), by the leap in the price of petroleum (and the discovery of "commodity power" more generally), and by the emergence of new forms of conference diplomacy.

An immediate effect of America's relative economic subsidence in the face of competitive states and economic blocs has been a decline in the central monetary management role of the IMF (in favor of floating rates and regional arrangements) and in the effectiveness of the GATT. This in turn has raised questions about the continuing relevance of their traditional tasks. The other factors, however, all seem to push in the direction of new institutions and expanded tasks for existing ones. Thus the Stockholm Conference (1972) gave birth to the U.N. Environmental Program while the Rome Conference on Food (1974) produced a World Food Council (under the General Assembly) in uneasy co-existence with FAO.[35] Similar sessions on population (Bucharest, 1974), human settlements (Vancouver, 1976), water (Mar de Plata, 1977) and desertification (Nairobi, 1977), have spawned programs that place new demands on existing institutions. The Third Conference on the Law of the Sea, in progress since 1974, will probably have similar effects, including the creation of an International Seabed Authority (what powers this regime will have is still at issue).[36]

As in the 1960s and 1970s the broad tendency in the development issue area and in the many areas of conference diplomacy into which calls for the New International Economic Order have penetrated, is for the Third World to demand, and the Western states to resist, expansion of the mandate of global institutions (especially those controlled by General Assembly-style bodies). The Western response has frequently been to deny resources to such bodies and to turn to narrower regional or specialist organizations (OECD, IEA), a strategy that leaves globalism to the dispossessed and risks greater confrontation in the future.

ISSUES OF SCOPE

Defined most broadly, issues of scope concern the breadth and criteria of participation in international institutions. To put it slightly differently, what is the appropriate "community" of states upon which to construct an organization to deal with a given problem? The classic form of this issue is the debate between regionalism and universalism. Perhaps more important today, however, is the contest between advocates of functional specialization or special interest, on the one hand, and partisans of universalism or the general interest, on the other.

Because of the relative paucity of international organizations and the de facto Eurocentrism of the pre-World War II international system, these issues were of little significance for the League of Nations (even pan-American regionalism, already established in the late nineteenth century, cast a weak shadow on what then passed for universalism). In the founding of the post-1945 institutional order, however, the debate over regionalism became central, involving principally the Latin Americans, the Arab states (their League was formed in 1945), and the British Commonwealth as advocates of some measure of decentralization in the new United Nations. The Charter's ambiguity—and flexibility—on the division of labor with respect to peace and security problems as between the Security Council and "regional arrangements or agencies" (article 52) reflects the strength of those forces at the San Francisco Conference vis-à-vis the defenders of U.N. supremacy.

In this outcome a shift in the American position from the traditional Wilsonian universalism to recognition of the advantages of regional institutions (especially in the Western hemisphere) was decisive. The ensuing cold war, undermining the great power consensus required for global collective security, hastened the process of regionalization under great power sponsorship in Western and Eastern Europe, Latin America, the Middle East, and parts of Asia. If the priorities were collective defense and regional peace-keeping, the need for economic organizations was also recognized—if only to complement and underpin the political-military ones. This whole process, visible in the creation of the OAS (1948), NATO (1949), OEEC (1948), Comecon (1949), the defense pacts of the 1950s, and the early institutions of Western European integration, was accompanied by remarkably little debate of the sort seen in 1945. There were, to be sure, worries—especially among lesser powers—about the apparent demise of global collective security and the return to regional defense pacts, in a haunting parallel to the era of Locarno. Between the two superpowers, however, rhetorical attacks on each other's blocs came to be accompanied by tacit acceptance of the bloc system itself.

More contentious, especially in the 1950s and 1960s, were the claims of regionalism with respect not to extraregional defense but to intraregional peace and security (the extent to which the two were separable in practice also became an issue). The cases of Guatemala (1954), the Dominican Republic (1965), and Czechoslovakia (1968) suggested that claims of exclusive regional jursidiction would most likely be made in the backyards of the major powers, who had the means to keep such issues off the United Nations' agenda and within more congenial regional bodies. But even small-power disputes, such as the Algeria-Morocco border conflict (1963) saw the protagonists maneuvering to place the matter before the most favorable tribunal (namely, OAU, Arab League, or United Nations). This is a useful reminder that high-minded debates about principles of regionalism and universalism are usually rooted in immediate interests.[37]

If the universalism of the United Nations in the security field was challenged early by regional alliances and political institutions, the economic universalism of GATT and the Bretton Woods system seemed without major challenge (Soviet abstentions apart) until the 1960s. The economic recovery of Western Europe and its early attempts at integration, supported by the United States, were judged to fit in the customs union provisions of GATT and did not, in the 1950s, pose any threat to the gold and dollar-based IMF system. By the late fifties, however, some observers were pointing to the inherent stresses of a dual-centered capitalist world while others, particularly the more open Atlantic trading nations, put forward schemes for broader trading systems to subsume an increasingly protectionist and hence divisive EEC.

By the late 1960s the debate over economic regionalism had not only supplemented that over political-military regionalism, but had also translated itself into a broader argument about the appropriate institutional framework for managing the global economy. The European-American debate was fought out in the Dillon and Kennedy rounds of GATT, over EEC preferential trade with Third World associates, over the EEC's Common Agricultural Policy, and in discussions of the dollar problem.[38] At the same time, a new challenge to globalism was being raised by the Third World. A major catalyst here was the United Nations itself working through its regional Economic Commissions for Latin America, Asia and the Far East, and Africa. Influenced by Raul Prebisch and the indigenous *dependencia* school of economists, the Commission for Latin America (ECLA) was active in urging Latin American governments toward greater regional cooperation and developmental autonomy. Underdevelopment, it was argued, stemmed from the integration of less developed countries into the liberalized, American-dominated global economy, not from their inherent qualities.[39]

As developmental economic regionalism began to manifest itself in Latin America and to a lesser extent in Africa, Western states began to cock a wary eye. Simple free-trade areas, leading to wider markets but not discriminating against outside suppliers (for instance by a high common tariff) and not setting up regimes for foreign investment, were accepted, and even quietly sponsored (for example, the United States and the Latin American Free Trade Association, France and a variety of integration schemes in central and West Africa). Organizations proposing tougher measures to counter dependence as they saw it, such as the

Central American Common Market in its early years, or the Andean Pact with its Decision 24, met a formidable combination of counterpressures from the metropole.[40]

By the 1970s it became clear that globalist (and especially American) fears about a "world of regions" had been a little exaggerated. Political organizations like the OAU, the Arab League, and ASEAN demonstrated a continuing lack of local resources for conflict management, while another such body long favored by the Americans, the OAS, underwent a major reorientation which reduced its security functions in favor of social and economic ones. Meanwhile developmental regionalism seemed to be foundering as well, struggling against internal tensions or external hostility. Thus LAFTA, CACM, and the Andean Pact in Latin America, and the East African Community and the francophone African common markets were either stagnant or near collapse. New regional institutions did make their appearance, but their future seemed less than assured.[41] Only the European Community survived the seventies with enough strength to mount a continued challenge to American trade policy and a growing challenge to the dollar-based monetary system.

Issues of scope have lately taken on a different guise. From an era of regionalism the international system may be shifting to one of special-interest organizations, posing new problems for global institutions. Special-interest organizations bring together like-minded states in an effort to pursue specific goals in a rather narrow sector of international economic and social life. OPEC is in many respects the prototype. Indeed, the movement toward a New International Economic Order, which it was instrumental in triggering, has been the main stimulus for such organizations. In the first place, OPEC's striking success encouraged emulation in the form of producer cartels for such commodities as copper, bauxite, iron ore, and bananas.[42] In the case of commodities like tin, sugar, and coffee, regulated by producer-consumer institutions, the new stress on producer solidarity threatened to break the agreements wide open. Second, the industrialized countries—in most cases the principal consumers—have created new institutions to concert their interests in this confrontation. Some of these countries, however—notably France —have refused to accept that it is a confrontation; these sharp differences were displayed openly in the 1974 transatlantic debate over the creation of the International Energy Agency.[43] There remains in the philosophy of trilateralism, too, a strong motif that the developed countries first have to band together and then to deal with the rest of the world.

Like the Third World, then, the industrialized world seems to have abandoned many of the globalist, "partnership in development" themes of the sixties. This is a product principally of the frustrations of the development decades, the influence of the Group of 77 in UNCTAD and the example of OPEC (especially between 1970 and 1974). Of course, globalism is alive and well in the World Bank and UNDP, but the emblems of the 1970s are likely to be the confrontations of UNCTAD III and IV and the inconclusive dialogue between North and South at the Conference on International Economic Cooperation (CIEC).[44]

The CIEC, however, also serves to remind us of a seeming countertrend to this particularism, namely the phenomenon of global conference diplomacy referred to earlier in this chapter. Such conferences as Stockholm, on the environment, begin from the premise that functional issues can be aggregated into wholes for which only a global forum and set of instruments will be appropriate. Ironically, given the fashion for special-interest organizations, it is usually the Third World countries who have articulated the general, global interests (to be manifested in universal participation and majoritarian decisions) whereas the developed states attempt to defend the old functionalist principle by which only states with a capacity to act effectively or with a particular interest in a field should be involved in regulating it (in the broader interest, to be sure). It is this rather than the ancient regionalism debate that is likely to be the important issue of scope in coming years.

ISSUES OF AUTHORITY

The authority of an international organization is best seen as a compound of several elements, including the legal status of its organs and their decisions vis-à-vis the laws and institutions of its members, the financial, coercive, and other assets of power it controls, and the legitimacy and autonomy it is accorded by member-states and their populations. In large measure, "organizational development" refers to the growth of authority in this sense[45]; the distinctions drawn at the beginning of this chapter between schools of thought on global institutions reflect different perceptions and expectations about such development. Not surprisingly, states too have found the question of authority vexing.

Early international institutions, it is true, were hardly calculated to raise such questions. If the intellectual climate in which world order was discussed tended toward utopianism, the political climate recognized the hard realities of national sovereignty in the design of the League of Nations and the public international unions. The latter were accepted as extranational delegations of narrowly focused functional authority, no threat to any government's freedom of action. Only the ILO, under its vigorous, probing Director Albert Thomas, seemed potentially to pose such a threat, but in practice its modus operandi was limited to research, nonbinding conventions, and moral suasion.[46] The League, with its unanimity rule for voting in Council and Assembly alike, with its discreet, bureaucratic Secretaries-General, its weak Covenant provisions on the use of force, and its steadily declining legitimacy, became a less and less likely repository of supranational authority.

A dominant theme in discussions of the institutional order to follow World War II was how to remedy this lack of international authority, so costly in the 1930s, in relation not only to peace and security but also to economic management. In the eyes of the Western states and of most small powers, the United Nations needed to free itself somewhat from strict devotion to the forms of national sovereignty. The Charter reflects this conclusion in several ways: (1) the Security Council can take, by qualified majority (with only the five permanent members having the veto) decisions binding on all member-states; (2) General Assembly resolutions require only a two-thirds majority, although they are not binding (to what extent they have the force of law has, however, been an issue); (3) the Secretary-General is given certain powers of initiative, especially under Article 99; (4) the obligations of member-states and the collective means of the organization to react to threats to the peace are stronger and less ambiguous than in the League Covenant. While all states favored a more effective United Nations, of course, these specific provisions toward that end were debated vigorously before, during, and after the San Francisco Conference. In some instances it was the Soviets attempting to maximize the scope of their veto in an organization they expected to be Western-dominated. In others, it was the small powers resisting the vestiges of great-power privilege such as that same veto. Generally speaking, the weaker the state, the stronger a United Nations it desired, for obvious reasons.

A debate over authority also ran through the series of meetings setting up (or restoring) the specialized agencies and the World Bank system. With respect to the specialized agencies, the strongest state or coalition of states in each functional sector (usually the United States) tended to argue for a minimal reporting or "traffic control" function, on the nineteenth-century model, whereas states less able to dominate or even to compete (many of them major Western states) demanded stronger regulatory powers to permit the agencies to ensure an equitable distribution of whatever value—markets, air routes, cultural products, radio frequencies—was at stake.[47] On monetary and economic matters, too, the British (now clearly in the second rank) argued for an IMF with extensive regulatory powers, large reserves, and a new global currency—in effect a global central bank. The much more modest American concept, however, prevailed. Far from a central bank, this system made the IMF, via the link between gold and the dollar, the mechanism through which the United States effectively financed world trade. The flaws of this system did not become generally visible until the late 1960s.[48]

The 1950s were in many ways the high point of independent authority for many international institutions. Three developments—all of them controversial—were especially significant for the United Nations in peace and security matters. First, the passing of the U.S.-sponsored "Uniting for Peace" Resolution in 1950, over Soviet protests, increased the possibilities for the General Assembly majority to take up a security problem even if one or more permanent members of the Security Council were opposed to U.N. action. Second, thinking about the means of U.N. intervention shifted from traditional notions (inherited from the League) about deterrent or punitive "collective security" to the new concept of intermediary "preventive diplomacy." The five years from late 1956 were a period of innovation, task expansion, high legitimacy, and, above all, optimism about the future of U.N. peace-keeping in its bureaucratic and military dimensions. Third, the expanding political role of the Secretary-General was seized upon by many observers—whether friendly or hostile to the trend—as the best indicator of the United Nations' growing authority. Dag Hammarskjold skillfully deployed the assets accruing to the head of an international bureaucracy, to an increasingly indispensable mediator, and to the personification of the international community, into unprecedented political influence. In this he had the backing of most of the smaller member-states and, in most cases, the United States. Initial Soviet complacency, however, soon turned to the hostility manifested in the "troika" proposals of 1961, aiming at a fundamental and debilitating transformation of the Secretary-Generalship.[49]

The identification of growing authority with the expanded power of the international bureaucracy and of its executive head is evident as well with respect to the specialized agencies, although the controversies surrounding the various Directors-General have been narrower in their implications than those in the United Nations.[50] On the regional level, especially in Western Europe, supranationalism—again closely identified with the emergence of an independent, authoritative, international bureaucracy—proceeded apace, especially after the Treaty of Rome was signed in 1957 creating the European Economic Community. It appeared, as one observer put it, that despite vestigial French objections, the nation-state was in "full retreat" in Europe.[51] While some suggested that a trend toward regional supranationalism could damage efforts at global integration, others looked to the European community method for guidance at the global level.[52]

Retrenchment, however, was not long in following. The expansion of the United Nations' and especially the Secretary-General's authority suffered a series of setbacks from the politically costly Congo operation, through the ensuing financial crisis to the withdrawal of UNEF from Egypt in 1967. On the regional level, too, the supposedly smooth progress of the EEC toward federal union was rudely broken by a series of French actions from 1960 to 1966, and this could not but undermine easy assumptions about the inevitability of economic and technological pressures toward integration. Significantly, the regional organizations founded in the 1960s, such as the OAU or even the OECD, embodied in rigorous form the traditional principles of intergovernmentalism and nonintervention, whereas older organizations like the OAS resisted pressures for greater authority (as manifested in a standing peace force) and indeed moved some distance the other way. In the OAS as in the United Nations and several other cases, the crisis of authority stemmed in great measure from the close association, in many minds, of growing supranationalism with the exercise of American domination in the organization. The connection may not have been logically necessary, but in the 1950s it had seemed empirically undeniable.

In the past decade the issue of authority has shifted both in its major venue and in the alignments it has witnessed among states. The focus is now less on the central United Nations and more on the specialized agencies, the economic development agencies, and certain other, related global institutions, while the protagonists tend to be the majority of the Third World, pushing for supranational authority with the industrialized states resisting.

One reflection of this pattern is in the Third World claim that General Assembly resolutions, while only recommendations, can acquire, through repetition and accumulation over the years, the force of customary international law—a position challenged by most Western governments and legal scholars.[53] For obvious reasons it suits the majority to consider the General Assembly as having true legislative functions. Another reflection of this pattern emerges if one compares global organizations and programs where some increased international authority is favored by the Third World, with those where it is favored by the industrialized states. The latter tend to stress relatively minor agencies like UNEP, highly technical ones where expertise monopolized by developed states tends to count heavily (INTELSAT), or ones where a pre-established voting pattern is weighted in favor of major contributors (World Bank, IMF). Third World states, by contrast, want to vest with greater authority bodies such as the proposed International Seabed Authority, which they wish to exercise redistributive powers on the basis of General Assembly-style majority voting.

The power and authority of international institutions to make rules in respect to their member-states thus remains a central issue of world order. In the 1980s, as in the 1950s, the theme of supranationality still divides states, even if the cleavages have changed. The difference is that the current debate is not about authority that institutions are visibly gaining, but only about claims being made for the future.

ISSUES OF CONTROL

As the power-oriented analysts (the realists and the dependency theorists) continually remind us, competition among nations for influence and control is as central to the working of international organizations as to any other area of international relations. To some degree, all states view international organizations as extensions or instruments of their national policies and attempt to deploy their assets in order to shape the outcome of institutional decision-making, whether by influencing other members directly or by determining the very agenda of decision. The question of "who governs?" is thus as pertinent to international institutions as to any other political setting. This question, in turn, has its counterpart in the international institutional debate: Who *should* govern? By what criteria should the management of global institutions be determined?

The liberal "harmony-of-interest" assumptions of the early advocates of international organization, as well as the cooperative experience of the public international unions, had the effect of putting such questions aside in the early part of this century. The designers of the League of Nations, it is true, built into their conception of the Council the nineteenth-century notion of a great-power concert with special duties and obligations regarding international order. But there was little question raised about the propriety of such an arrangement or the extent of privilege it implied. Such great-power status was generally assumed to be in the natural order of things.

The United Nations continued this tradition, according permanent membership and the veto right in the Security Council to the five victorious states considered great powers in 1945—the United States, the Soviet Union, Britain, France, and China. Against resistance put up by the small powers—notably Australia—in San Francisco, it was argued that this special status merely reflected what every clear-headed observer already knew: the United Nations could not function without the backing of the major powers, and to permit the organization to act against the wishes of one of these would only be self-destructive. In practice it was soon recognized that only two of these powers really counted, but that their approaches to control of the United Nations necessarily differed. Taking the offensive, the United States naturally appealed to the majority view, invoked the common interests of mankind as represented in the General Assembly, and sought "flexibility" in adapting the Charter to those needs. On the defensive, the Soviet Union stuck to the letter and the legalities of the Charter, and used the veto whenever necessary. The irresistible force of informal dominance ran up against the immovable object of a minority superpower.

In other global agencies similar issues arose, although not with the same force. In the economic institutions—IMF and the World Bank—voting power would have to be proportional to economic power and financial contribution. In the functional agencies there was some debate about according privileged status to states with a special expertise or stake in the organization's work, as was done, for instance, in the ILO's Governing Body, or later in IMCO. In most cases, however, decision-making organs were constituted on an egalitarian basis. This, of course, is the formal level; informally, the major powers and particularly the United States (usually major functional powers as well) tended to get their way.

With American dominance at its highest in the 1950s it is not surprising to find the issue of control being fought out on several fronts in global institutions. Debates about the United Nations' development were in large measure a reflection of this deeper struggle for influence. Soviet use of the veto and Western attacks on the practice were an obvious instance of this struggle, as was the largely successful American effort to give the General Assembly a more significant role, especially in peace and security matters. The great membership question of the early 1950s, too, was in essence an aspect of the same issue. Each superpower would block the membership applications of the other's alleged clients, in part for propaganda purposes (although this tended to be increasingly counterproductive) but largely to prevent the opponent's bloc of reliable votes from growing. When this duel ended in 1955 it was through a "package deal" admitting equal numbers from each side and a few neutrals, effectively preserving the existing pattern of influence.

The 1960s were characterized by a shift in both the *dramatis personae* and the focus of the issues of control. A vestige of the East–West struggle could be seen in the U.N. debate over the Secretary-General (the troika proposal) and, to some degree, in the financial crisis (although the latter also involved some alienated Western powers). But it was now largely the Third World members who initiated contests for control. Initially their focus was on the composition of the major organs, which they argued should better reflect the new majority in the General Assembly. The outcome was an expansion of the Security Council from eleven to fifteen members and of the Economic and Social Council from eighteen to twenty-seven (both effective in 1965). Prior to this the Third World states had tended to look to the General Assembly and related agencies such as UNCTAD to oversee programs that mattered to them, ECOSOC being perceived as dominated by the developed states. (For similar reasons, Third World countries pushed major decolonization questions out of the Trusteeship Council and into the General Assembly's Special Committee of Twenty-Four.) Once the ECOSOC's composition had been amended, it was expected to become a more important center of Third World diplomacy, although questions continued to be raised about its capacity to control the steady proliferation of economic and social programs.

From the mid-sixties on, the central issues of control in the United Nations have been fought between the Western, developed states and the Third World. The Western, particularly American, strategy has been two-fold: first, to place renewed emphasis on the Security Council and, like the Soviet Union in the forties and fifties, to use the veto if necessary to protect its minority position[54]; second, to ignore or attack where possible the "automatic majorities" of the General Assembly and concentrate on the exercise of its still considerably informal influence. There seems, however, general resignation that the United States and the other developed states are engaged in a continuing defensive political struggle in the central U.N. organs. It must be waged, if only to make possible the future use of these instruments in critical situations arising in Namibia, Indochina, Lebanon, or elsewhere. But for getting things of an economic or functional character done, these states turn to organizations that can be more easily controlled (such as regional or special-interest bodies) or that show greater correspondence between voting power and real economic and technical capability.

The issue of who governs international institutions and according to what principles has arguably never been posed so forcefully as at present across the whole range of global structures. Three principles of control compete and co-exist uneasily. The first, majoritarianism, is advanced by the weak and poor states whose numbers continue to swell. Their argument is that effective control of an organization's policies and programs as well as determination of its priorities should rest with those organs (like the General Assembly) that decide on a one-state, one-vote basis. When this is not the case, programs should be removed and placed in different, often new, institutions which better represent the whole global community. The second principle is based on the ascriptive right of great powers to manage the global system, especially where peace and security are concerned. The application of this principle has run into some difficulties of late, however, given the decline of two Permanent Members of the Security Council (Britain and France) and the rise of credible candidates for that status in Japan, West Germany, India, and possibly Brazil. The third principle is the functionalist one that special expertise or interest in a field carries with it a claim to special status or influence—hence the weighted voting in the World Bank and IMF (according to subscriptions), the privileged position of the major shipping nations in IMCO. Like the second principle, however, the third tends in practice to support the control of the developed states right across the range of global institutions and programs.

ISSUES OF STRUCTURE

Issues of structure are concerned with the search for the institutional design best suited for the effective functioning of an international organization. Effectiveness, of course, is not easily measured or agreed upon; frequently one state will demand structural reforms that would make an organization more effective in its eyes but less so in the eyes of others. Concerns about structure, in fact, are sometimes hard to differentiate from concerns about authority or contról. We are dealing here, therefore, with effectiveness not as a neutral, technocratic concept but as one which is politically charged. Structural issues, clearly, are raised only partly for reasons of impartial concern for efficiency in decision-making and execution. Nevertheless such concerns are often expressed, by almost all states and by international civil servants, and are likely to become more prominent as the numbers and the fields of operation of international institutions continue to expand.

Issues of structure have tended to center on, first, the efficacy of particular decision-making organs or processes in translating perceived needs into policies and actions and, second, the problem of coordinating the activities of different organizations and programs. Broadly speaking, the concern for coordination became serious only in the 1960s, to be aggravated by the politics of the New International Economic Order in the 1970s. When global institutions were fewer in number and simpler in their responsibilities, the question of their efficacy naturally assumed a greater prominence compared to the problem of coordination.

Prior to World War II the only issue of this kind to cause much worry and debate concerned whether the League had been designed adequately to meet threats to the peace. From the outset there was discussion of the loopholes in the Covenant which seemed to permit a variety of uses of force while at the same time obliging members to impose sanctions on aggressors only in very specific circumstances. In the 1920s several unsuccessful efforts, such as the Geneva Protocol of 1924, were undertaken to close such gaps. Even had the Covenant thus been revised, however, there was still the question of getting effective decisions out of a Council or an Assembly which required unanimity. Attempts at reform of the League's security system tended to fall victim to differences among the leading powers, France and Britain, whose confidence in collective security had been undermined in different ways by the absence of the United States.[55]

In the formative period of the United Nations the central structural issues were once more concerned with the effectiveness of the organs, individually and in relation to each other, in acting upon threats to the peace. Although, as we have seen, the veto caused considerable controversy, first among the great powers and then between these and the small powers, it was in the end generally accepted as the price of a workable Security Council. Qualified majority voting, it was generally agreed, was an improvement over the League's unanimity rule in making possible more rapid responses to crises. Relations between the Security Council and the General Assembly were subject to some debate, the product of which was a somewhat sharper delineation of responsibilities in the peace and security field than had existed under the League, the Council's primacy being more clearly asserted. As far as coordination was concerned, it seemed appropriate to give the General Assembly the functions of overall review and the new Economic and Social Council the role of coordinating the Specialized Agencies.

Although ECOSOC in fact soon proved incapable of asserting effective control over many of these agencies, the crucial structural questions until the mid-1960s remained focused on the respective powers of the Security Council, the General Assembly and, later on, the Secretary-General. Much of their debate took the form of an East–West dispute (the smaller powers principally siding with the West) over interpretation and development of the Charter. In broad terms the Soviets and their supporters argued that the Charter was a treaty, to be changed only through unanimous consent of the signatories, while the West, led by the United States, took the view that each organ of the United Nations would naturally interpret the Charter and develop its capacities as it saw fit. Hence the acquisition of new capacities by the Assembly in the peace and security field and the growth of the Secretary-General's political powers could be justified by the intentions, if not the words, of the founders in San Francisco. In the 1950s this position, reflecting a consensus of the West and the Third World states (for different reasons), won out.

As that coalition has gradually fragmented over the past two decades, however, the structural issues have become more confused and multidimensional. It is now the Third World (often joined by China) that is likely in any instance to adopt a dynamic, expansionist, even supranationalist, view of the Charter's evolution, especially with respect to the General Assembly's role and the capacity of the Secretariat. The West, by contrast, has moved closer to the constitutional conservatism of the Soviet Union. At the same time, however, the debate about the Council and the Assembly has come to be overshadowed by a broader concern with Charter reform or restructuring which takes its prime inspiration from the economic and functional spheres.

As the restructuring issue has developed into the 1970s several distinct constituencies of interest have emerged. Most of the Third World countries view structural change as an opportunity to tailor the U.N. institutions and programs more to fit effective policies of economic redistribution. The developed countries see it as a chance to establish better controls over spending and the proliferation of elaborate new programs as well as to curb the politicization of many U.N. economic activities. The various agencies themselves also maneuver for primacy or sometimes just for survival.[56] These different sets of interests converged on an agenda for reform which, as it emerged in 1975, embraced almost every aspect of the U.N. system and even reached beyond it.

In almost every area of reform there are interesting differences between the views of the developed and the less developed countries, although these differences often seem highly nuanced and the unified positions of the two main blocs in fact conceal important differences within them (as between the United States and Europe). Whereas, for example, the Third World states prefer the General Assembly as the centerpiece of a reformed system, in which the major functions of policy-making, negotiation, and supervision should be invested, the Western states tend to place more stress on the revitalization of ECOSOC. The Third World has also wished to extend the Assembly's oversight into organizations like GATT, the IMF, and the World Bank (where Western priorities have tended to prevail) and to constitute "their" organization, UNCTAD, as the controlling body for trade questions. The Western states, on the other hand, have tended to underline the need for coordination and nationalization of programs, and above all for more effective planning, programming, budgeting, and evaluation of U.N. operations.[57]

These differences notwithstanding, the United Nations members have managed to agree on a great many items on the "restructuring" agenda, at least insofar as that consensus is expressed in general terms. But like all structural issues, those of the 1970s and 1980s are closely linked to substantive concerns, in this case those expressed in demands for a New International Economic Order. As long as there is only glacial progress on the latter, structural issues will be kept alive as part of the broader conflict.

Conclusions

The five types of issues set out in this chapter recur in various guises throughout the history of international institutions. A sense of their history, as well as a close analysis of the patterns these issues assumed in the 1970s, helps to make clearer the possible lines of future institutional development at the global level.

First, it is clear that while these issues may be analytically distinct, two or more of them often become closely linked in the political processes within or surrounding international institutions. Actors frequently find themselves playing simultaneously on several, perhaps all, of these chessboards. Unlike simultaneous chess, however, the politics of international institutions finds the actors perceiving the pattern on one board in light of the pattern on another. Thus the position a state takes on structural reform is heavily influenced by whether the prevailing ethos of control allows it an effective share in running the organization and by the degree of supranational authority the organization has.

A second, related point is that while these issues all center on general principles of international order and organization, and are usually argued in such terms, the states' positions are rooted in the familiar concerns for national advantage. It would be surprising to find a state advocating a principle of organization that, if implemented, would damage its own security, economic well-being, or status. In this sense at least, the Realists' expectations are borne out. But this observation, like so many from that school of thought, is a healthy reminder rather than a startling insight.

Thirdly, an exploration of international institutions by means of the issues they raise reinforces the suspicion that all of the theoretical schools mentioned at the outset are of limited range, dealing only with certain preoccupations at the expense of many other dimensions of organization. Realists and dependency theorists, for example, are obsessed with the issue of control, functionalists and neofunctionalists with task and authority, world federalists with scope and authority. Such obsessions can be theoretically damaging—neofunctionalism, for instance, has clearly paid too little attention to issues of control (de Gaulle's lesson in Europe) —and can limit the explanatory power of any emergent theory.

Fourthly, the examination of these issues clearly shows no ascending curve of institutional development at the global level nor, if institutional forms can be said to reflect it, any striking evidence of "political development" on the global level. The tasks of global institutions, it is true, have known two major periods of expansion (roughly 1943–1948 and 1973–present).[58] In scope, however, there seems a trend toward fragmentation and particularization, although it is perhaps functional and "special interest" communities of states rather than regional ones which now pose the challenge to globalism. This may not, of course, be a bad thing, but it is probably not global institutional development. The authority of international institutions, and the support and legitimacy that underlie it, have not grown markedly since World War II; indeed, it may have declined from a peak in the late 1950s and early 1960s (both globally and regionally).

As for control, the issue becomes more and more difficult as it becomes less clear who governs, or can govern, the international system. Of the three principles at war here—majoritarianism, functional interest or expertise, and great power oligarchy (or hegemony)—the third has clearly lost much of its legitimacy while neither of the others has gained primacy. The consequence is alienated or diffident great powers and possible organizational paralysis and frustration. This fear is reinforced, finally, if we look at issues of structure, for here the success of major efforts to increase effectiveness and interagency coordination is contingent on what happens in substantive fields, especially those relating to the New International Economic Order.

In endowing itself with this proliferation of international institutions, the world has acquired a new level and style of politics superimposed over and interpenetrated with, the national level. It has even acquired what may fairly be called the rudiments of government, certainly no cruder than what passes for government in many states. But it is quite another thing to claim that we are therefore en route toward the world federalist or neofunctionalist end. Little in the way that nations handle their differences on institutional issues or in the character of those issues themselves suggests that. To the extent, however, that issues of security and economics become perceived as, or translated into, institutional issues, we may be witnessing a slow process of socialization at the global level.[59] This may not be political development but it is arguably better than what we had before.

Notes

1. Examples of the realist approach to international organizations are in H. J. Morgenthau's two chapters (27 and 28) on international government in *Politics among Nations,* 5th ed. (New York: Knopf, 1973).
2. As examples of dependency theory applied to international institutions, see T. Hayter, *Aid as Imperialism* (Harmondsworth: Penguin, 1971) and J. Galtung, *The European Community: A Superpower in the Making* (London: Allen & Unwin, 1973).
3. I. L. Claude's classic treatise, *Swords into Plowshares,* 4th ed. (New York: Random House, 1971) expresses this position forcefully. See especially chaps. 1 and 19.
4. See K. W. Deutsch, *Political Community and the North Atlantic Area* (Princeton, N.J.: Princeton University Press, 1957). The "elite networks" explanation of European Community policy-making is in many respects a descendent of Deutsch's pluralist approach. See D. J. Puchala and P. Busch, "Interests, Influence and Integration: Political Structure in the European Communities," *Comparative Political Studies* 9 (October 1976), 235–54.
5. For example, through the U.N.-sponsored process of state-building described by Claude as "developmental functionalism." *Swords into Plowshares,* pp. 405–406.
6. On this concept, see L. Gross, "The Peace of Westphalia, 1648–1948," *American Journal of International Law* 42 (January 1948), 20–41. See also E. Morse, *Modernization and the Transformation of the International System,* (New York: Free Press, 1976), chap. 2.
7. The functionalist classics include L. S. Woolf, *International Government* (London: Allen & Unwin, 1916); and D. Mitrany, *A Working Peace System* (Chicago: Quadrangle, 1966). A recent application is in J. P. Sewell, *Functionalism and World Politics* (Princeton, N.J.: Princeton University Press, 1966).

8. Neofunctionalism has its origin in studies of European regional organization by E. B. Haas, notably his *The Uniting of Europe* (Stanford, Calif.: Stanford University Press, 1958).

9. For a rare attempt to apply neofunctional analysis to a global organization, see E. B. Haas, *Beyond the Nation-State* (Stanford: Stanford University Press, 1964).

10. A well-developed world-federalist model is presented in G. Clark and L. B. Sohn, *World Peace through World Law* (Cambridge, Mass.: Harvard University Press, 1958).

11. Two especially useful contributions to the debate about trends in interdependence are P. J. Katzenstein, "International Interdependence: Some Long-term and Recent Changes," *International Organization* 29 (Autumn 1975), 1021–34, and R. Rosecrance et al., "Whither Interdependence?," *International Organization* 31 (Summer 1977), 425–71.

12. For trends in NGO's to about 1970, see Kjell Skjelsbaek, "The Growth of International Nongovernmental Organization in the Twentieth Century," *International Organization* 25 (Summer 1971), 420–42. More recent data are in the *Yearbook of International Organizations,* 16th ed. (Brussels: Union of International Associations, 1977).

13. Switzerland now appears to be taking the first steps toward joining the United Nations. See *New York Times,* April 1, 1979. See also M. M. Gunter, "Switzerland and the United Nations," *International Organization* 30 (Winter 1976), 129–52.

14. Note, for instance, the growing importance of the United Nations' regional Economic Commissions and the regionalization of the administration of World Health Organization and other specialized agency programs. On subregional tendencies in Africa, see T. M. Shaw, "Cooperation and Conflict in Africa," *International Journal* 30, (Autumn 1975), 671–88.

15. Good surveys of these organizations are M. Doxey, "The Commonwealth in the 1970's," *The Year Book of World Affairs* (London: Stevens, 1973), pp. 90–109; and B. Weinstein, "Francophonie: A Language-based Movement in World Politics," *International Organization* 30 (Summer 1976), 485–507.

16. Calculations are based on data from the *Yearbook of International Organizations.*

17. E. B. Skolnikoff, *The International Imperatives of Technology* (Berkeley, Calif.: University of California, Institute of International Studies Research Series, no. 16, 1972), chap. 7.

18. See R. W. Cox, H. K. Jacobson, et al., *The Anatomy of Influence* (New Haven, Conn.: Yale University Press, 1973), pp. 8–11.

19. J. G. Ruggie, "International Responses to Technology: Concepts and Trends," *International Organization* 29 (Summer 1975), pp. 557–83.

20. On American attitudes toward the United Nations, see H. W. Barber, "The United States vs. the United Nations," *International Organization* 27 (Spring 1973), 139–63; S. M. Finger, "United States Policy Toward International Institutions," *International Organization* 30 (Spring 1976), 347–60; S. Weintraub, "What do We Want from the United Nations?," *International Organization* 30 (Autumn 1976), pp. 688–95; and R. E. Riggs, "The United States

and the Diffusion of Power in the Security Council," *International Studies Quarterly* 22 (December 1978), 513–44.

21. For an analysis of Soviet policies in the United Nations, see J. G. Stoessinger, *The United Nations and the Superpowers,* 4th ed. (New York: Random House, 1977).

22. An early and still sound analysis of Chinese policy is S. Kim, "The People's Republic of China in the United Nations," *World Politics* 26 (April 1974), 299–330.

23. A recent sign of possible increased Japanese activism in this area is the attempt to mediate in the China-Vietnam war. See *New York Times,* March 11, 1979.

24. For France, a major exception is UNESCO. See J. P. Sewell, *UNESCO and World Politics* (Princeton, N.J.: Princeton University Press, 1975; and W. R. Pendergast, "UNESCO and French Cultural Relations," *International Organization* 30 (Summer 1976), 453–83.

25. The European Community has had observer status at the United Nations since 1974. On its foreign relations generally, see W. Feld, *The European Community in World Affairs* (Port Washington, N.Y.: Alfred, 1976).

26. An excellent survey of United Nations institutional reform is in R. I. Meltzer, "Restructuring the United Nations System: Institutional Reform Efforts in the Context of North–South Relations," *International Organization* 32 (Autumn 1978), 993–1018.

27. For an early study, see P. S. Reinsch, *Public International Unions* (Boston: Ginn, 1911).

28. On the League, the authoritative history remains F. P. Walters, *A History of the League of Nations* (London: Oxford University Press, 1952).

29. See R. N. Gardner, *Sterling-Dollar Diplomacy: The Origins and Prospects of Our International Economic Order* (New York: McGraw-Hill, 1969).

30. See J. N. Murray, Jr., *The United Nations Trusteeship System* (Urbana, Ill.: University of Illinois Press, 1957); and D. W. Wainhouse, *Remnants of Empire: The United Nations and the End of Colonialism* (New York: Harper & Row, 1964).

31. See M. S. McDougal and G. Bebr, "Human Rights in the United Nations," *American Journal of International Law* 58 (July 1964), 603–41.

32. A good discussion of expansive pressures on the World Bank system in the 1950s and 1960s is in Sewell, *UNESCO and World Politics.* See also E. S. Mason and R. E. Asher, *The World Bank since Bretton Woods* (Washington: Brookings, 1973).

33. ON UNCTAD, see B. Gosovic, *UNCTAD: Conflict and Compromise* (Leiden: Sijthoff, 1972); and J. S. Nye, Jr., "UNCTAD: Poor Nations' Pressure Group" in Cox, Jacobson, et al., *The Anatomy of Influence,* pp. 334–70.

34. For a survey of recent developments here, see L. L. Fabian, "Toward a Peacekeeping Renaissance," *International Organization* 30 (Winter 1976), 153–61.

35. On the Stockholm Conference, see L. G. Engfeldt, "United Nations and the Human Environment: Some Experiences," *International Organization* 27 (Summer 1973), 393–412. On food and the aftermath of Rome, see the special

issue of *International Organization* 32 (Summer 1978), edited by D. J. Puchala and R. F. Hopkins.

36. See E. Miles (ed.), *Restructuring Ocean Regimes: Implications of the Third United Nations Conference on the Law of the Sea,* a special issue of *International Organization* 31 (Spring 1977).

37. On problems of intraregional collective security, see J. S. Nye, Jr., *Peace in Parts* (Boston: Little, Brown, 1971).

38. The European-American debate is analyzed in R. N. Cooper, *The Economics of Interdependence* (New York: McGraw-Hill, 1968); D. P. Calleo and B. M. Rowland, *America and the World Political Economy* (Bloomington, Ind.: Indiana University Press, 1973); and A. Shonfield, *International Economic Relations of the Western World 1959–1971,* Vol. 1 (London: Oxford University Press, 1976).

39. On recent directions in the dependency literature, see R. D. Walleri, "The Political Economy Literature on North–South Relations: Alternative Approaches and Empirical Evidence," *International Studies Quarterly* 22 (December 1978), 587–624; and J. A. Caporaso (ed.), *Dependence and Dependency in the Global System,* a special issue of *International Organization* 32 (Winter 1978).

40. On different strategies of developmental regionalism, see W. A. Axline, "Underdevelopment, Dependence and Integration: The Politics of Regionalism in the Third World," *International Organization* 31 (Winter 1977), 83–105.

41. For a study of Latin America's evolution toward a new form of developmental regionalism, see R. D. Bond, "Regionalism in Latin America: Prospects for the Latin American Economic System (SELA)," *International Organization* 32 (Spring 1978), 401–23.

42. A good summary of these cartels is in J. E. Spero, *The Politics of International Economic Relations* (New York: St. Martin's Press, 1977), chap 9. See also K. A. Mingst, "Cooperation or Illusion: An Examination of the Intergovernmental Council of Copper Exporting Countries," *International Organization* 30 (Spring 1976), 263–87.

43. See R. D. Keohane, "The International Energy Agency: State Influence and Transgovernmental Politics," *International Organization* 32 (Autumn 1978), 929–51.

44. For an early assessment of the CIEC, see J. Amuzegar, "A Requiem for the North–South Conference," *Foreign Affairs* 56 (October 1977), 136–59.

48. P. C. Schmitter, "The Organizational Development of International Organizations," *International Organization* 25 (Autumn 1971), 917–37.

46. On the ILO, see Haas, *Beyond the Nation-State,* part II.

47. See, for example, the Anglo-American debate over postwar aviation at the founding conference of ICAO: US Department of State, *Proceedings of the International Civil Aviation Conference, Chicago, Illinois, Nov. 1–Dec. 7, 1944* (Washington: U.S. Government Printing Office, 1948).

48. On the IMF in the 1970s, see P. M. Boarman and D. G. Tuerck (eds.), *World Monetary Disorder: National Policies vs. International Imperatives* (New York: Praeger, 1976).

49. See B. Urquhart, *Hammarskjold* (New York: Knopf, 1972).

50. R. W. Cox, "The Executive Head: An Essay on Leadership in International Organization," *International Organization* 23 (Spring 1969), 205–30.

51. E. B. Haas, "International Integration: The European and the Universal Process" in *International Political Communities: An Anthology* (New York: Doubleday, 1966), p. 93.

52. This was especially the case with neofunctionalists like Haas. See his *Beyond the Nation-State,* part I.

53. On the issue of the legal status of General Assembly resolutions see M. Sørensen (ed.), *Manual of Public International Law* (New York: St. Martin's Press, 1968), pp. 160–62; and L. Gross, "The United Nations and the Role of Law," *International Organization* 19 (Summer 1965), 191–94.

54. The United States did not use the veto until 1970. Since then it has used it more than twenty times. In recent discussions of Charter reform not surprisingly the veto's chief defenders are the United States, the Soviet Union, and the Western powers. See Riggs, "The United States and the Diffusion of Power in the Security Council," p. 529.

55. On this period, see Walters, *A History of the League of Nations,* chaps. 22 and 24.

56. On the bureaucratic interests, see Meltzer, "Restructuring the United Nations System," 1014–15.

57. Ibid., 1000–1009. Meltzer gives a good summary of the main issues, positions, and developments in the negotiations.

58. Compare C. F. Bergsten, "Interdependence and the Reform of International Institutions," *International Organization* 30 (Spring 1976), 361. Bergsten mentions three phases of development, but his second, in the early sixties, was mostly regional in focus (integration in Europe and Latin America).

59. On this, see R. N. Rosecrance, "The Political Socialization of Nations," *International Studies Quarterly* 20 (September 1976), 441–60.

10

Global Issues in Theoretical Perspective

Gavin Boyd

NUMEROUS THEORETICAL CONCERNS are raised by discussions of issues in the foreign policies of the global actors as well as by discussion of questions in contest between them. There are significant differences between the attributes of these states, the ways in which they are involved in global politics, the contexts in which their foreign policy choices are posed, the substantive matters that are the subjects of those choices, and the ways in which such issues are recognized, defined, considered, decided, and managed. The issues on which there is interaction between the principal members of the global system, moreover, lead to outcomes that reflect contrasts in the policy orientations, bargaining strengths, and international behavior of these actors.

The most fundamental common feature of the foreign policies of the global actors is that each is an authoritative quest for the realization of external values through international and transnational activity and that each has multiple functional links with each administration's authoritative domestic allocations of values. The various foreign policies, however, differ in coherence and functional qualities. The external and related internal values, moreover, differ considerably. The liberal-democratic but self-interested political outlooks of the Western actors and Japan contrast with the revolutionary political philosophies of the U.S.S.R. and China. The differences are made evident in largely opposed forms of foreign policy behavior and especially in the use of international communications, although there is considerable economic cooperation across the ideological lines of division.

Several patterns of interaction result from the quests for external values. Security issues are in contest primarily between the superpowers and secondarily between all the industrialized democratic global actors and the U.S.S.R., and between the Soviet Union and China. Economic issues are contested mainly between the United States, the European Community, and Japan, and the outcomes are the main factors that shape the evolution of the international economy. Political issues, mainly problems of equity, order, participation, institutional development, and overall growth in the global system, are subject to interaction mainly between the economically dominant actors, and between them and the developing countries, all of which—with the exception of China—are regional actors.

Attribute Contrasts

Within the group of industrialized democratic global actors there are significant structural, functional, normative, and societal differences. These differences are associated with contrasting degrees of coherence and effectiveness in international behavior and in the management of domestic policies. The variations are especially significant because these advanced open states have to realize their external values in conditions of *complex interdependence,* which set demanding requirements for foreign policy issue management.

The large Western states and Japan differ in their degrees of hierarchy, levels of institutional development, patterns of political participation, degrees of executive effectiveness, and overall forms of individual, group, and organizational rationality. Japan is relatively a more hierarchical polity than the United States, its governmental and nongovernmental institutions are more effective in aggregating interests and demands, and it is less affected by pluralistic stagnation and by societal pressures for allocations in excess of government resources. Underlying these differences are contrasts between the intense individualism of the American political culture and the strong group and community orientation of the Japanese political culture.

In comparative perspective, then, the lack of coherence in U.S. foreign economic policy, which is discussed in Chapter 2, has much signifi- cance. This lack of coherence results from difficulties in the critical relationship between forms of political participation and levels of institu- tional development, a relationship that is especially important for the aggregation of inputs in the foreign policy process.[1] Generalizing from the U.S. experience, one can say that in a polyarchy the aggregation of socie- tal, interest-group, bureaucratic, and legislative demands on issues relat- ing to the attainment of external values requires a high level of institutional development, within and outside the government structures, if foreign policy behavior is to be coherent and functional. Yet even with such institutional development, the coherent and functional management of foreign policy issues will require appropriate orientations of the politi- cal psychology of members of the primary and secondary elites in the foreign affairs structures, which will exclude the deficiencies of "cyber- netic" decision-making, as will be discussed below.

Many of the contrasts and similarities between the attribute mixes of the industrialized democratic global actors have significant effects on the political psychology of their elites. In general, their autonomous and dif- fuse agents of socialization produce elites with open personalities, ac- customed to cognitive complexity and disposed to undertake trustful cooperative activity, for shared benefits. Because of the capacities of these elites to resolve differences between their policy preferences through persuasion and bargaining, their polities can be characterized as reconciliation systems. But open personalities can be highly self- interested political actors, setting personal goals above organizational goals and national interests; they can also be quite ideosyncratic. More- over, their political skills and the qualities of their task orientations may vary greatly. Fairly uniform international outlooks, grounded in collective experience, with self-critical restraints on idiosyncratic factors, are likely to be evident in the leaderships of highly developed national political parties, such as those of West Germany and Britain, and such parties can foster relatively strong commitments to community rather than sectoral interests. Weak political parties, such as those in France and the United States, in effect challenge their leaders to cultivate the most productive forms of self-interested rationality and can impose little discipline on their idiosyncrasies. The consequences for foreign policy management are likely to depend on structural factors that determine executive account- ability. In the United States high accountability limits the administration's capacity to express idiosyncrasies in foreign policy behavior, but this is not the case in France.[2]

The very different attribute mixes of the large communist states affect foreign policy issue management, first, by setting requirements for system maintenance, second, by influencing the processing of information, and, third, by sustaining elite value commitments that call for symbolic and substantive expression in external behavior. System maintenance for the U.S.S.R. and China requires much closure to and rejection of foreign influences, despite each regime's need for large infusions of Western and Japanese technology. An important aspect of the system maintenance requirement is that it involves preserving the basic features of the primary elite's psychological environment through communication flows that re-iterate the content of that environment. The processing of information about the outside world serves that purpose, because the reporting offi-cials are under strict political discipline. The results are misinterpreta-tions of happenings in the outside world and slow adaptation to new issues. Yet in so far as elite values are maintained there are compulsive expressions of these in communications to external audiences, using po-litical idioms keyed to the national political culture. In the Soviet case, however, some deradicalization permits more sophistication than is fea-sible in Chinese efforts to influence foreign societies, as the latter articu-late the qualities of a more revolutionary political culture.[3]

Over time, the confidence of revolutionary elites in the effectiveness of their external communications tends to decline, and this process can be hastened by deradicalization and by failures to transmit the values of the political culture to client states and movements. The Soviet experi-ence suggests that with such a decline there is likely to be an increasing reliance on military capabilities in the service of foreign policy objectives, with emphasis on the projection and use of armed strength.[4] Yet moves that may precipitate crises in the central balance are likely to be avoided, as contrary to Leninist operational codes, because of an awareness of decisional problems that would be encountered in crisis situations. Such decisional problems would tend to be posed because of the increased overload resulting from extreme centralization of authority and because of the difficulties of accelerating interactions between the primary and secondary elites, given the apparent tendencies of the ruling groups to push task responsibilities on to their immediate subordinates. The basic theoretical consideration relevant here is that a ruling revolutionary group's disposition to engage in policy issues tends to be affected by status and legitimacy considerations associated with its claimed role as the source of prescriptions for "correct" statecraft, because there are incentives to formulate such prescriptions in general terms, so as to evade informal accountability.

Sources of Foreign Policy Issues

For each global actor, the sources of foreign policy issues are domes-tic and external, and these are connected by multiple linkages. For deci-sion makers, the domestic sources are usually more prominent, more familiar, more understandable, easier to take up, and more pressing; externally posed issues are generally more difficult to manage.

The domestically posed foreign policy issues are incompatibilities between internal inputs into the policy process or between such inputs and external factors. The patterns vary with respect to the levels of the diverging and conflicting inputs, the extent of the incompatibilities, their complexities, and the degrees to which they can be managed. In the industrialized democracies the principal domestic sources of issues affecting foreign economic policy are industrial, trading, banking, and farming interests; their demands, especially on commercial questions and investment matters, are usually difficult to reconcile and are at variance with the preferences of bureaucratic agencies and legislative groups. Overall, the degree of coherence is likely to be determined by levels of institutional development in the political aggregating structures and by the extent to which there is consensus about the main directions of economic policy, based on relative satisfaction with executive performance. Such satisfaction is high in West Germany and Japan, and in those cases there is also highly effective interest aggregation relating to questions of foreign economic policy.[5] The degrees of *pressure* with which foreign policy demands are made, especially in the large trade and investment issue areas, are determined mainly by the size of the interest groups, legislative coalitions, and other bodies seeking to influence policy. In relation to the individuals and associations making such demands the strength of the executive's position will, of course, vary according to its authority structure and its influence relationships. The position of the French executive is normally very strong, but for structural reasons rather than its influence relationships, whereas the position of the West German executive is also strong on account of very active influence relationships as well as because of structural factors.[6] These differences provide a context for some generalizations based on the configuration of domestic sources of foreign policy issues in the United States. In a very polyarchic industrialized democracy with weak aggregating structures there is likely to be extensive and highly diversified interest articulation on foreign policy questions, especially concerning trade and investment; the resultant pressures on the executive will be strong and difficult to accommodate. To cope with these, the executive will have to rely heavily on influence relationships because its polyarchic authority structure entails high accountability.

In the revolutionary global actors the domestic sources of foreign policy issues make up quite different patterns. Questions about external behavior are posed mainly by intra-elite differences over ideological, nationalist, and organizational imperatives relating to foreign policy. Views and preferences have to be expressed in terms of the ideology, however, which conceal latent meanings, and while debate is thus limited and indirect, high-level engagement with the sources of diverging foreign policy demands tends to be authoritative and severe. Secondary domestic sources of foreign policy issues that do not invite drastic authoritative resolution are inputs from the working levels which indicate needs for adaptation to changing external situations. Such sources appear to have more significance in the Soviet foreign policy process than in China's, because the U.S.S.R.'s level of institutional development is higher, and the pressures for political conformity on officials are less exacting and more predictable.[7]

Abstracting from the available information about domestic sources of issues in Soviet and Chinese foreign policy, one can say that intra-elite differences, as the primary domestic sources of problems about international behavior, tend to assume great prominence for all members of the ruling group in a mobilization system because the authority of the dominant faction or collective leadership is critically dependent on its capacity to impose or generate consensus and because perceived competitors and adversaries in the policy process must be deprived of legitimacy through ideological denunciations. While deradicalization, attributable to the diverse effects of modernization, tends to promote some degrees of sophistication and tolerance in the management of intra-elite differences, and in the use of inputs from the working levels, its relativization of ideological principles can open the way for factionalism and thus for narrowly partisan attitudes to foreign policy questions. As factions tend to be unstable, preoccupations with maintaining them and with problems of consensus formation tend to affect the quality of engagement in external tasks. In the U.S.S.R., the maintenance of Brezhnev's dominant faction, together with the cult of his personality, evidently limits opportunities for inputs into the foreign policy process from Prime Minister Kosygin and the Council of Ministers, while ensuring active but not necessarily expert involvement in external affairs by the Politburo, and there are evidently strong tendencies to persist in external endeavors that Brezhnev's group has favored even if officials in the Ministry of Foreign Affairs may be aware of a need for change. This evidently helps to explain the persistent ineptness of Soviet behavior toward Japan. Yet Brezhnev's faction is likely to exhibit increasing instability as the magnitude of the succession problem in the Politburo increases.[8]

Soviet experience since the early 1960s suggests that a significant level of institutional development and some pragmatic revisions of ideology can facilitate the resolution of intra-elite differences. Chinese experience, however, indicates that in a mobilization system whose leaders wish to maintain revolutionary fervor this concern will itself be destabilizing, because it will be unequally shared and will give rise to highly intolerant personal and group orientations. Generalizing further, one can say that a basic source of high-level policy differences in a revolutionary as distinct from a deradicalized mobilization system is likely to the tension between attempts to preserve cognitive simplicity in the ideology so as to prevent losses of emotional fervor, on the one hand, and concerns to promote greater instrumental rationality in domestic and foreign affairs at the cost of accepting cognitive complexity and, tacitly, the need to learn from other societies, on the other.

The external sources of foreign policy issues are relational and situational. Received foreign policy behavior, of course, varies in its operational significance for any national administration's external endeavors; while the degree of compatibility may be high or low, the accompanying pressures and inducements may also be high or low, and the opportunities for engagement to secure modifications of that behavior may be either substantial or minor. Meanwhile, the context or situation is normally constraining because of the high or low levels or interdependence which link each actor with the others, strong or weak affinities, the volume of communication flows, and the attitudes associated with established patterns of interaction.

For industrialized democracies, most of the behavior received from similar states is diffuse, extensive, complex, and relatively lacking in coordination, because of the significant degrees of autonomy enjoyed by government agencies involved in the management of foreign relations, and the high levels of autonomy with which transnational enterprises participate informally and semi-officially in the implementation of policy as well as in its formulation. The patterns of received behavior, as sources of foreign policy issues, show varying degrees of coherence and thus indicate desirable choices with greater or lesser degrees of clarity. Here one can refer again to the contrasts between Japan's highly coherent foreign economic policy behavior and the much less coherent economic statecraft of the United States.[9]

The relative coherence of received foreign policy behavior, the leverage associated with it, and the magnitude of the values affected are clearly very significant in the cognitive mapping of externally posed foreign policy choices by national executives and staffs. Critical influences on this mapping are domestic political concerns about benefits to be given to sectoral or organizational interests and broader public policy concerns about national interests. Executives unsupported by strong nongovernmental organizations, being preoccupied with constant problems of securing cooperation through patronage, are understandably restricted in their grasp of and interest in foreign policy choices affecting the community as a whole. To the extent that such limitations can be overcome, through leadership or organization building, to facilitate concentration on the implications of foreign policy choices for national interests, received foreign policy behavior becomes significant insofar as it invites equitable joint decision-making. Expectations of that kind are, of course, discouraged by unstable and disconnected statecraft, which generally evokes cautious and defensive responses, and by inflexible and forceful bargaining, which generally provokes counterpressures to obstruct the coercive diplomacy.

Foreign policy behavior ranking high in substantive content, complexity, and openness to joint decision-making is evident in the attempts of the United States and the European Community to manage issues in their complex interdependencies. Substantively, each side's behavior poses questions for the other across the issue areas and especially in trade, investment, and monetary affairs, as well as in security matters. All the questions raised concern external values of high salience. The behavior originating on each side comes from numerous governmental agencies, legislative groups, and organizations informally involved in statecraft. Coherent bargaining positions are often not made evident, and the complexity is increased by linkages, especially on the U.S. side, as executives strive to spread the use of their bargaining power with maximum effect. Motivations to engage in joint decision-making are strong, but this is seen as a competitive rather than an integrative process, for situational factors, including geographic separation and senses of regional identity, preclude the development of an Atlantic "community." Relatively high levels of mutual understanding as well as imperatives to manage interdependencies sustain the positive orientations toward issue resolution through negotiation, which on the whole becomes a fairly symmetrical striving toward joint realization of external values.[10]

Situational sources of foreign policy issues for executives in industrialized democracies are the slowly changing patterns of societal affinities and antagonisms, the shifting economic and military power levels, the regime characteristics, and the interdependencies that set the limitations to foreign policy options. Of these situational factors, those of immediate concern are the interdependencies that undergo change mainly because of the activities of transnational enterprises. Regulating these activities tends to be the principal method of coping with situational sources of economic foreign policy issues, and such regulation requires the cooperation of other industrialized democratic states.

The most important propositions that can be formulated concerning the relational and situational sources of foreign policy issues for industrialized democracies have to do with the expansion of their interdependencies and their problems of governance and of foreign policy performance. The politically more coherent and more actively mercantilist states pose issues for and encounter issues posed by the more polyarchic and less actively mercantilist states, while the interdependencies of all these actors continue to increase asymmetrically. Executives in the more polyarchic states tend to be more cybernetic than holistically rational decision makers, and this affects the ways in which they present and respond to foreign policy issues.[11] Bargaining power, largely a function of economic size, may offset or increase the negotiating strength and transnational capabilities of the politically more coherent and more actively mercantilist states. A large polyarchic industrialized democracy is likely to be more protectionist than liberal, and more competitive than integrative, in its foreign policy behavior and thus will pose issues for other industrialized democracies, but it will have difficulty making coherent use of its bargaining power. Medium-sized but more hierarchical industrialized democracies may be protectionist but can afford to be liberal in foreign economic policy and may be significantly integrative in their behavior in response to situational factors and neofunctional logic. West Germany's acceptance of the need for a European Monetary Union, seen to be required because of the weaknesses of the U.S. dollar as an international currency, reflected integrative motivations deriving from a sense of West European regional identity and an awareness of high interdependencies with other Community members.

Alliance issues posed for industrialized democracies by their mutual behavior in relation to threatening states tend to be linked with the management of economic interdependencies if the hostile states show a credible if ambivalent interest in co-existence. In such contexts questions of burden-sharing are likely to surface, as the leading democratic power sees its protection undervalued by its allies. Yet for strategic reasons that power will have strong incentives to maximize its control of the alliance's offensive potential, especially to ensure that it will not be drawn into an unnecessary conflict by an ally's militancy over secondary issues. The imperative to maximize control over offensive resources will tend to be compelling because this will be essential for crisis management in a time in which advances in weapons technology can give potentially decisive advantages to the side that resorts to swift preemption.[12] Smaller democratic allies, however, can demand participation in alliance management and yet may endeavor to shift risks and costs to the leading democratic power.

Revolutionary states, as sources of security issues for industrialized democracies, can pose threats explicitly or ambiguously. Explicit threats, for purposes of coercive diplomacy, require capabilities for crisis management and hence may be avoided if a revolutionary leadership lacks confidence in its capacity for such management and does not wish to rouse firm opposition in the industrialized democracies. Gains at the expense of such democracies may thus be sought through client states and movements in the developing areas, if those countries can be induced to accept such gains as small costs for preserving the overall status quo. Ambiguous threats are posed by offensive deployments and hostile ideological communications if these are accompanied by cooperative behavior. Cooperative activity, within limits, provides opportunities to influence the political processes of industrialized democracies by stirring hopes for détente. It may entail acceptance of some cultural penetration by such democracies, but this may be seen as an incidental disadvantage, outweighed by successes in inducing acceptance of revolutionary advances in the developing areas. Apart from strategic considerations, cooperative behavior directed at industrialized democracies is likely to be motivated by needs for technology because of lags in research and development, which appear to be inevitable in command economies.[13]

Behavior received *from* the industrialized democracies is the principal external source of foreign policy issues for the large revolutionary states. This behavior is interpreted largely in accordance with ideological beliefs and with little sensitivity to the critical assessments of international happenings in Western and Japanese research literature and journals of opinion.

For the Soviet and Chinese leaderships, behavior received from the industrialized democracies is significant in strategic, ideological, and economic contexts. In both communist regimes, and especially in China, ideology is the basic source from which the meaning of external happenings is derived, but it is restrictive in terms of concepts, logic, and language. New events, then, evidently tend to be understood partly or even largely on the basis of past experience, from which meanings can be drawn with little risk of ideological controversy. Alternatively, there may be innovative development of the ideology to define the significance of such events, but, as the Soviet case suggests, this will not be easy for a collective leadership or for a dominant faction whose talents are primarily bureaucratic. Fundamentally, Soviet and Chinese versions of Marxism-Leninism require that the foreign policy behavior of industrialized democracies be understood as expressions of their class structures, but this presents difficulties with respect to their interests in co-existence. Strategically, the behavior of those democracies is a source of issues insofar as they are prepared to use force against Soviet- or Chinese-supported states and revolutionary movements, and are seen to be preparing aggression against the Soviet Union or China. In these respects there are no cognitive problems relating to the ideology, except to the extent that deterrence rather than war-fighting doctrines are seen in the policies of the adversaries.[14] The economic diplomacy of the industrialized open states is a source of opportunities, not altogether in line with Marxism-Leninism; these invite the acceptance of interdependencies, but long established autarkic orientations remain strong influences on both Soviet and Chinese policies.

As sources of foreign policy issues, the international economic activities of the industrialized democracies are open to engagement by the large revolutionary states; the opportunities they present are used, and this raises questions about the influence of functional logic on ruling elites in revolutionary states. The authoritarian personalities who make up those elites show little sensitivity to functional logic, and, generalizing from this, one can say that such elites, because of their basic concerns with the legitimizing functions of their ideologies, are strongly motivated to maintain doctrinal hostility to the political cultures of the industrialized democracies, while recognizing the utility of the technology which those countries are willing to transfer.

Issue Processing

Foreign policy issue processing in industrialized democracies is normally a diffuse, competitive, and disjointedly incremental conversion of diverging and conflicting inputs into decisions by government agencies and informally associated transnational actors. The degree and quality of executive direction in this processing vary, and there are contrasts with respect to the involvement of secondary elites and middle echelons and with respect to the evaluation of information about policy choices.

The identification, definition, discussion, and resolution of foreign policy questions by executives in advanced open polities involve complex interactions within authority and influence relationships, and these interactions entail diverse forms of socialization, while being affected by more general forms of socialization outside the government structures. The pluralism, combined with the complex patterns of exchange in which transmissions of meaning are mixed with forms of bargaining and with exercises of authority and the use of influence, results in extensive formal and informal accountability. Consciousness of this, in turn, inclines executives and staffs toward disaggregated and incremental solutions.[15] If the executive can impose strong direction on the processing of issues, more substantial and holistic decision-making will be possible but may not occur unless other necessary conditions are satisfied. These other conditions include strong executive task orientation, adequate information processing, and significant openness to engagement among the relational sources of foreign policy issues.

Foreign policy issues may have varying degrees of prominence in the overall policy process, may activate large or small numbers of participants among the legislators, bureaucrats, and interest-group figures, may precipitate complex and protracted or simple and short debates, and may present differing problems with respect to the political interests of the executive and its concerns with overall foreign policy performance. The degrees of pluralism and the range and duration of debate may be limited by structural factors that facilitate strong executive direction of foreign relations, as in France, or may be greatly extended by the effects of high accountability on a structurally weak executive, as in the United States. The character of the issues, moreover, may arouse extensive or limited interest; monetary questions, for example, normally arouse much less concern among interest groups than issues relating to the expansion or restriction of trade, while security questions, except insofar as they involve major risks or heavy allocations of resources, tend to evoke only modest public and small-scale legislative participation.

The processing of foreign policy issues is, first, a matter of intelligence, requiring the organization and analysis of information. In large industrialized democracies this is primarily a bureaucratic function, and as such it is affected by common problems—the influence of established departmental views and interests, the displacement of organizational goals by personal ambitions, inertia associated with standard procedures, as well as general tendencies to disaggregate policy implications and to view these not in holistic and broadly functional terms but with reference to executive political interests.[16] The degrees to which all these distorting factors are offset by communications transmitting knowledge from nongovernmental sources, including journals of opinion and research institutes, depends mainly on the extent of public and elite interest in the issues. Highly pluralistic information processing, of course, does not necessarily make for greater objectivity in the treatment of foreign policy issues, but a low level of public discussion and legislative interest does increase executive reliance on bureaucratic evaluations of the available choices and enables the executive to be very selective in its consideration of both problems and opportunities in foreign policy. This adds to the significance of Charles F. Hermann's observations on agenda setting, which are mentioned in Chapter 2.

Because the ranges and complexities of foreign policy issues are increasing for industrialized democracies with the growth of their interdependencies, the difficulties of information processing in their bureaucratic structures and the problems associated with executive selectivity in agenda setting are becoming more serious. At the same time, executive inclinations toward incrementalism are becoming more pronounced because of the growing complexities of foreign policy issues. Meanwhile, the dispositions of these administrations to favor sectoral interests in deciding such issues may well tend to become stronger in view of growing competitiveness within the political elites for control of the expanding resources of public office. This is a difficult problem of political development at the advanced level—a problem of governability—and it provides a context for the formulation of more observations about issue processing.

The processing of foreign policy issues in an industrialized democracy under conditions of complex interdependence is a matter of aggregating internal demands, functionally and in terms of executive political interests, and of coping with externally posed problems and opportunities, again functionally and in terms of executive needs for domestic support.

Critical factors, then, are the relationships between participation and institutional development in this processing, and between the kinds of commitment and forms of rationality that are activated. As external interdependencies grow, participants in the very large economic issue area become more numerous and make more complex demands, with increasing pressure; hence, if the level of institutional development is low in the aggregating structures, the danger of policy incoherence will tend to increase. Executive commitment to sectoral interests, meanwhile, if increasing at the expense of concern with broad community interests, can intensify competition among the societal participants in the foreign policy process, while of course imparting bias to the rationality applied in decision-making. Further, executive commitment of an idiosyncratic character, if able to find expression in the competitive instrumental political culture, may affect rationality in decision-making, especially in areas where scope for administrative initiative is provided, that is, in areas of external relations where societal demands are relatively manageable. Hence, in external security matters the executive of an industrialized democracy can be rather unconstrained in the application of idiosyncratic considerations and may thus be impelled to seek foreign policy achievements that would be difficult to attain in foreign economic policy because of its high input complexity and the impossibility of presenting sectoral rewards as national gains.

Primary and secondary elite commitments and forms of rationality are outcomes of elite socialization and recruitment processes, and these are largely determined by levels and types of institutional development, which are also of vital significance for the processing of foreign policy inputs. High institutional development in the major political parties tends to give coherence and stability to elite value and policy orientations while moderating idiosyncratic aspects of these orientations; it also tends to incline leaderships toward broad national concerns rather than sectoral interests. Institutional development in the foreign affairs structures of the administration, which is a matter of improving functional qualities in the service of broad national purposes, as Hermann's work has indicated, is dependent on political and bureaucratic leadership, but it can contribute significantly to the socialization of political elites, as has long been evident in Britain.

High-order value integrations, necessary for the management of issues of interdependence in line with broad community interests, require the subordination of individual, group, and organizational objectives to those larger concerns. This is what is implied in the concept of institutional development; it is difficult to achieve in a wholly instrumental political culture, where there is a lack of what David Apter calls consummatory values that are capable of drawing commitments beyond self-interested rationality to community concerns.[17] There is no basis for expecting that free competition in the articulation of foreign policy demands, in an instrumental political culture, will result in foreign policy issue management that will be functional for the national political economy. That can be ruled out not only because of the highly uneven distribution of bargaining power among participants in the foreign policy process, but also because an executive that is responsive only to sectoral interests will tend to maximize its political benefits from foreign as well as from domestic policy by selectivity that is largely unrelated to questions of national benefit.

Whereas sectoral bias tends to affect foreign policy issue processing by administrations in industrialized democracies and has an effect on decision-making that is disaggregated and incremental, more holistic approaches to foreign policy questions are evident in the large revolutionary states. These approaches are made possible by high degrees of executive control over the policy process and are motivated by consummatory value commitments. Nevertheless, the holistic quality of policy-making is strongly affected by each ruling group's determination to maintain its virtually absolute power, and to guide if not dominate the affinitive revolutionary states that accept its inspiration and support.

Information processing, as has been seen, is hindered in revolutionary states by the cognitively restrictive roles of the belief systems and by the strict political discipline imposed on officials. The evaluation of new events is slow and distorted, and the ruling groups tend to remain in psychological environments characterized by excessive optimism about ongoing external activities and by remote rather than close task orientation, which in effect shifts responsibilities to the secondary elites.[18]

The resolution of intra-elite differences on foreign policy issues is difficult in revolutionary states because of the strong interest of each dominant group in restricting communications that might undermine its control. Diverging views thus have to be expressed indirectly, obliquely, and esoterically, with little debate. The dominant group, especially in China, tends to set exacting requirements for political conformity by individuals under its influence, and these individuals are inhibited also by uncertainties about the retroactive requirements that may be set by future ruling groups.

The difficulties of functional interplay between the leadership and members of the secondary elite in the foreign affairs structures—to some extent an interplay between authority and expertise—affect the processing of externally posed foreign policy issues. The leadership's inadequate grasp of realities in the outside world may prevent it from recognizing negative feedback from established external activities, and accordingly these may continue with little adaptation. In Asia, Soviet efforts to establish an anti-China collective security pact have continued for a decade despite the indifference and coolness of all the states to which this proposal has been addressed.[19] In Western Europe, China has been encouraging political integration on the basis of apparently fixed beliefs that this is the rational choice for contiguous states threatened by the U.S.S.R., and China has not been able to develop rapport with major European Community states on political and security issues because of the strongly ideological quality of the communications used.

Externally posed issues of foreign *economic* policy appear to be the most manageable for revolutionary elites. The principal trading partners —the major industrialized democracies—have incentives to provide the technology that is sought, and their competitiveness inclines them to make credits available, as the revolutionary states tend to experience chronic trade deficits. The principal issues for the revolutionary states are the degrees to which dependence on technology transfers should be accepted and the extent to which manifestations of political hostility should be restrained in order to secure technology of potential military significance. The main proposition to be advanced here is that an advanced revolutionary state will have a strong compulsion to seek technology from the industrialized democracies because of strong conservative tendencies and inertia in its bureaucracy, which slow indigenous research and development.[20]

The externally posed security and political issues are clearly difficult to process. In the Soviet case the current balance between cooperation and conflictual activity is intended to ensure that the regime's security will be enhanced by forms of revolutionary change in the West and in the Third World, but increased endeavors to promote such change may disturb the accommodating attitudes encouraged in the West by Soviet cooperative activity, including trade expansion. The question of whether there should be increased projections of military power to promote and support desirable forms of political change, moreover, evidently cannot be separated from the question of the military establishment's role in Soviet society, which appears to be a source of tension between the army and the party.[21] In China the prime task of external security policy is protection against the Soviet threat, but despite awareness of the regime's military weaknesses there is reluctance to seek adequate military understandings with the West or even to evolve forms of communication that could have a significant influence on Western strategic thinking.

For large revolutionary states, the externally posed political and security issues may represent opportunities and problems in the spread of drastic social change and for the acquisition of influence over affinitive regimes. For elites in these revolutionary states, external behavior must have a large conflictual component, despite the need for co-existence relationships that facilitate technology imports, because the desired forms of revolutionary change are not considered to be possible by peaceful means but require struggles at the national and international levels, and because relaxed co-existence as distinct from ideologically hostile co-existence would undermine each revolutionary state's internal controls. Deradicalization appears to be an inevitable form of political change in revolutionary states, but while it is occurring the compulsions of the ruling elites to promote radical change abroad by conflictual methods and to maintain significant levels of tension in relations with nonrevolutionary states are likely to remain strong and may even intensify because of the need to overcome domestic pressures for liberalization. Very active conflictual external activity, moreover, may be undertaken for increased legitimacy by a successor ruling group that is seeking to establish its authority in a revolutionary state.

Altogether, the orientations of the large industrialized democracies and the major revolutionary states sustain forms of issue processing that have two major patterns of effects. Expanding interdependencies between the industrialized democracies are being managed incrementally, disjointedly, and with varying degrees of equity and order. Lower-level interdependencies between those democracies and the revolutionary states are being managed in a very asymmetric fashion, while the direct and indirect conflictual activity of the revolutionary states contributes to radical change in developing countries which are to a significant degree dependencies of the industrialized democracies. These two patterns are outcomes of diverse forms of interaction.

Issues in Interaction

Issues in what may be called the trilateral pattern of interaction between North America, Western Europe, and Japan are managed with high levels of sensitivity to common interests, extensive intergovernmental and transnational exchanges, and multilevel communication flows that facilitate relatively comprehensive mutual understandings. There are major contrasts in the distribution of bargaining power, in the coherence with which interaction is directed, in bargaining strategies, and, of course, in incentives. Overall, there are significant differences between the relative degrees of integrative and competitive negotiation of issues in this pattern, as well as in the extent to which incrementalism prevails rather than joint or collectively holistic management of interdependencies.

The industrialized democracies in the trilateral pattern are first of all *open,* in varying degrees, to mutual penetration transnationally, intergovernmentally, and at the government-to-government level. This openness results mainly from cultural factors and from sustained experiences of productive interaction. In Japan unique cultural characteristics hold down the degree of receptivity to communications penetrating the national polity, but in the United States such receptivity is high, although principally with respect to the major West European states and particularly Britain, primarily for cultural reasons.[22]

The degree of openness to governmental, intergovernmental, and transnational communications varies also with structural factors. Strong administrative direction of industrial, banking, and commercial firms and a weak legislature limit transnational penetration of the French polity, in which cultural nationalism is also responsible for low overall receptivity to intergovernmental and governmental communications, especially from the United States.[23] Whereas cultural factors may make for significant openness to foreign political influences, the higher the degree of executive direction of the policy process, the weaker will be the effects of those influences. The greater the competitiveness and assertiveness of the participants in the policy process, however, the greater will be the scope for external penetration, subject to cultural factors.

Openness to external penetration tends to tighten links between domestic and external sources of foreign policy issues. Some domestic participants in the policy process can share interests with external sources of problems in statecraft, as has been evident for the U.S. administration in the cases of the major oil companies. High interdependencies, however, remain the basic factors responsible for tight links between the domestic and external sources of foreign policy issues for industrialized democracies. Such links mainly determine relative levels of sensitivity to national and common interests in bargaining, but it must be stressed that these are affected by cultural affinities and antipathies. Thus U.S. management of relations with Japan has been less considerate than have been its dealings with Britain, although the levels of interdependence are higher in the U.S.-Japan relationship, and the development of a strong economic partnership with Japan is of great importance for the U.S. role in the international economy.[24]

The distribution of bargaining power in an interactive context affects issue management. Strong bargaining power based on economic size is the principal explanation for the United States' success in maintaining higher levels of effective protection for its manufactured products than those imposed by the European Community. To increase their bargaining power, the members of the Community have strong incentives to become more cohesive, because for the present the bargaining strength of the United States can be used against each of them individually.

The effective use of bargaining strength, however, requires organizational and policy coherence. In these respects the United States tends to be weaker than West Germany, Japan, and France, because its system is strongly polyarchic. As for relative integrative or competitive intent, this is a matter of executive unity as well as orientation, and those factors are also related to dispositions toward incrementalism in the negotiation of issues. The weighing of inferences from these observations is difficult, but some major points can be made, chiefly with reference to U.S.-West European relations.

In industrialized democracies, administrations with strong control over foreign policy making that are implementing active mercantilist external economic policies will have incentives to further their objectives mainly through informally associated transnational enterprises, deferring or avoiding issues raised by foreign administrations because of the successes of those enterprises, as long as the international political economy remains sufficiently liberal. When foreign administrations become demanding and begin to exert bargaining leverage in order to reduce trade and payment deficits, efforts are likely to be made to gain greater access to other markets and to secure accommodations with the aggrieved trading partners by relaxing explicit import restrictions while nevertheless limiting imports with the collaboration of the informally associated transnational enterprises.

Polyarchic administrations that are less capable of developing coherent foreign economic policies tend to confront actively mercantilist states with forms of protectionism. Such protectionism is feasible if the national economy is large and highly diversified and relatively less dependent on foreign trade. Retaliatory protectionism by the more mercantilist states, however, can activate domestic pressures against polyarchic administrations for a more liberal approach, and these pressures, even if not fully effective, can hinder coherent use of such an administration's bargaining power. Transnational enterprises based in a polyarchic system can have strong incentives to press for a liberal foreign economic policy in order to ensure that other governments will not be provoked to adopt restrictive measures. The pressures thus exerted may be sufficient not only to prevent shifts away from liberalism by a polyarchic administration but also to hinder all its efforts to evolve a more unified and functional external economic policy.

Spreading frustrations within major interest groups over failures in foreign economic policy can periodically activate a polyarchic administration to make large, coherent, and forceful demands against more actively mercantilist rivals. Over time, however, political coalitions formed in support of those demands tend to weaken and, in the absence of strong political structures like those through which the West German and Japanese administrations can operate, bargaining in support of those demands cannot be sustained. Polyarchic executives normally manage issues incrementally, it must be stressed, with little high-order value integration and tend to operate in this fashion unless challenged by dramatic increases in societal and interest group demands on questions of foreign economic policy.

The problems of the polyarchic administrations in relation to the stronger executives implementing actively mercantilist policies can be aggravated by difficulties in securing fuels and raw materials. The relatively more hierarchical industrialized democracies can cope more effectively with such difficulties and thus can gain further advantages over their politically less unified trading rivals. Whereas internal adjustments and restructuring can be undertaken by the stronger executives, they can also bargain more firmly with primary exporting states in the Third World and, while exploiting competition between them, can offer some of them privileged trading partnerships. Further, these stronger executives can be more effective in managing trade with the command economies; indeed, coherent use of the opportunities for commerce with those economies can be quite difficult for polyarchic governments.[25]

Shifting to a developmental perspective, one needs to take note that a more holistic management of issues in the complex interdependencies between industrialized democracies will require the emergence of stronger executives in the more polyarchic states, and greater coherence in their aggregating structures. Elementary logic rules out any solutions based on weakening the authority structures of the democracies with stronger executives, as this would simply mean more pervasive disjointedly incremental cybernetic decision-making, less productive interaction, and a general lowering of performance levels in foreign and domestic economic policies. There is a need, then, for institutional development in the more polyarchic industrialized democracies, and this will have to be considered further after some discussion of other areas of issue management in the Trilateral grouping.

Interaction on security issues between the industrialized democracies is largely a restricted elitist interplay with some economic linkages. These states form a moderately cohesive security community in which unresolved issues of alliance control motivate several of them to shift burdens to their strongest member, whose incentives to lead and sustain the coalition obligate acceptance of those burdens. In its role as protector, as Chapter 6 suggests, the United States seeks to ensure the security of its allies with a primary concern for its own interest, whatever their failures as members of the security community. The protector or leading alliance member may threaten to reduce commitments in order to secure increased economic or military cooperation from allies, but this type of pressure will lack credibility. On the other hand, if the protector moves toward tentative settlements with the main adversary, members of the security community will tend to shift more burdens to the protector and may seek to open the way for accommodative options of their own with that adversary.

Between the industrialized democracies and the large revolutionary states, interaction on economic and security issues tends to be linked, with differing strategies on each side. For the revolutionary states, there are opportunities to exploit the ambitions of capitalist enterprises for profitable sales of technology, and the ambivalence of imperialist governments regarding such sales and the questions of responding to revolutionary gains in the Third World and to shifts in the central balance. For the Trilateral states, the perceived issues are questions of relative emphasis on strategies of interdependence and of opposition to revolutionary advances, and these questions are complicated by others raised by the hostility between the large revolutionary states.

A large industrialized revolutionary state has major advantages, because of its strongly hierarchical character, in dealing with industrialized democracies on economic and security issues. In the more polyarchic industrialized states, competition between transnational enterprises and the influence of these on the national administrations can be used to secure advantageous trade if a credible political commitment to co-existence is evidenced. Such a commitment, moreover, can introduce much uncertainty and ambiguity into security questions that are raised for industrialized democracies by a revolutionary state's gains in military strength. At the same time, the gravity of those questions will tend to increase as advances on the frontiers of weapons technology promise great advantages to the side that takes the offensive. Deterrence logic, the natural basis for military doctrine in the Trilateral grouping, is in effect made weaker by those inevitable advances in weaponry, whereas preemptive logic, which strongly influences revolutionary strategic thought, is made stronger.[26]

A developing revolutionary state threatened by an advanced revolutionary state may look to industrialized democracies for support. Yugoslavia's choice has been repeated by China's. What can be generalized from this, however, is that the choice is likely to be made with reservations if there is a strong resolve to preserve ideological fervor and maintain a heavy concentration of power in the primary elite. Evidence of such reservations, meanwhile, will influence responses from the industrialized democracies, and they may also be affected by social distances, which can hold down levels of understanding and cooperation.

Interaction between the industrialized democracies and the developing countries mainly concerns trade, investment, and development issues. These justifiably raise strong normative as well as theoretical concerns, and they relate not only to matters of equity between the advanced states and the new nations but also to problems of political development and social reform in the new nations.

The relatively more coherent advanced open states with strong executives are well-placed to accommodate Third World demands for a New International Economic Order, but they are also well-placed to continue their successful forms of mercantilism and to exploit conflicts of interest between the developing countries. Their policies largely reflect the profit-seeking values and nationalist orientations of their political and corporate elites. France, however, is more sympathetic than West Germany to Third World aspirations. The more polyarchic advanced open states, subjected to strong domestic protectionist pressures, tend to be relatively unsympathetic to proposals from the developing countries.

What can be envisaged, on present trends, is continuing expansion of the selective exploitation of resources and market opportunities in the less developed countries by Western and Japanese transnational enterprises, with increasing manipulation of the administrations in those countries, and a narrowing of the already limited scope for their indigenous enterprises. The international activities of the transnational enterprises are likely to remain oriented toward profit maximization, to the virtual exclusion of political and normative considerations and subject to minimal regulation by the home governments.

The problems of limited economic sovereignty and weak bargaining power faced by the "soft states" of the Third World call for what Robert O. Keohane has entitled "normatively infused organizational strategies" for the development of international structures and elite networks, and, more fundamentally, for the normative outlook formulated by Robert L. Rothstein concerning issues of equity and growth in the global system.[27] Questions of international political design thus come into view, and they have several dimensions—institutional, participatory, functional, and cultural.

To move national elites in advanced states toward higher levels of normative motivation and to more holistic forms of rationality will require potent new processes of socialization. Those necessary for resolution of the problems of equity and growth in the North–South relationship cannot be expected to develop on the basis of any satisfactory experiences of cooperation with developing states. Narrow nationalism associated with the competitiveness of internal power rivalries will continue to incline administrations in the industrialized democracies toward exploitation of the major differences in bargaining strength in their dealings with new states. The emergence of leaderships with superior vision and motivation, however, may be encouraged by the activities of highly motivated citizens, with the support of internationally oriented research institutes. Some impressive efforts to promote such forms of citizen participation are being undertaken in the United States, especially by associations for the study of foreign affairs.

Global Institutional Development

The interactions between industrialized democracies and between them and the developing states, which result in the principal negotiated allocations of values in the international political economy, have thus far been institutionalized in ways favorable to the large advanced open polities and their transnational enterprises. Demands from the Third World countries, supported to some extent by the OPEC states, are gradually eliciting concessions from the industrialized democracies, but these permit little progress toward the development of institutions that would be capable of engaging with problems of global order, equity, and growth.

The industrialized democracies manage their complex interdependencies through relatively exclusive structures and ad hoc arrangements identified mainly with their own grouping. In these, and particularly in the IMF and the World Bank system, strong roles are assumed by the large members. Outside the multilateral pattern there is considerable bilateralism, managed by the large states, whose administrations seek to preserve wide freedom for action and are thus reluctant to support further institutional development for multilateral interaction. There is a potential for such development, which could facilitate more comprehensive and possible more equitable management of the very extensive interdependencies in the Trilateral context, but the West Europeans show reluctance to develop close working relations with the United States and Japan, and the United States' interest in maintaining a broad scope for bilateral activities within and outside the pattern is very strong. Inadequacies in the multilateral management of interdependencies, attributable to the pervasive disjointed incrementalism and cybernetic decision-making of national administrations and to weak senses of obligation to and confidence in the grouping, are aggravating problems of domestic economic management for numerous governments, especially the more polyarchic ones, while permitting expansion of the largely unregulated activities of transnational enterprises and thus of their nonauthoritative allocations of values across national boundaries.[28]

The ties, incentives, and problems of the Trilateral pattern overshadow the interactions of the industrialized democracies with the developing states, and the institutionalization of these interactions is restricted by the attempts of the former to prevent their relative bargaining strengths from being reduced by concessions to Third World demands for greater participation in the shaping of the international economy. On their side, the new states lack the cohesion that would be necessary to maximize their bargaining strengths as suppliers of raw materials and importers of technology and consumer goods. Substantive interactions occur in the organizations dominated by the industrialized democracies, such as the IMF and the World Bank, and these are influenced by encounters in the United Nations General Assembly and the UNCTAD meetings, which the advanced states do not wish to transform into collective decision-making mechanisms. At such encounters, Third World demands for a

New International Economic Order assume significance mainly to the extent that they are backed by the OPEC states, and the degree to which such support is given appears to be sufficient to secure gradual concessions by the industrialized democracies in the substantive interactions in which they remain protected against the voting power of the new states in the U.N. context. There has been a progressive liberalization of World Bank financing for development in the Third World, and the principle of establishing a common fund for financing primary commodity buffer stocks has been accepted.[29] At a later stage, there may well be some weakening of Trilateral domination of the IMF and the World Bank system to permit more Third World representation. Over the long term North–South interactions may be institutionalized in ways that will significantly fulfill Third World aspirations for participation and for equitable treatment of aid, investment, and trade issues. If this occurs, however, it is likely to be a gradual and disjointed process, deriving impetus mainly from Third World pressures, to the extent that they can be concerted.

Some of the hopes of developing states, meanwhile, may be realized in regional economic orders. This possibility is suggested by the relative success of the African, Caribbean, and Pacific countries in negotiating the first and second Lome agreements. Under those agreements the European Community members accepted trade, aid, and investment obligations designed to assist economic growth in the associated states. Although these states have been disappointed by the Community's observance of the agreements, the relationship does provide a basis for institutional development that may to a certain extent meet the expectations of the associated states for equitable economic cooperation and less unequal bargaining.[30] That, in turn, could activate moves by the United States to build up a new regional economic order with Latin America, and by Japan to work for a similar objective in East Asia.

The significant institutionalization of Trilateral interactions and the limited institutionalization of North–South relations, globally and regionally, support no substantive multilateral engagement with global security issues. The most important of these issues, the problem of stable restraint in the central balance, is a matter of exclusive superpower interaction wich involves little accountability to other states or to the U.N. system. Superpower interaction on contested matters in the Third World, morever, is open to only limited involvement by interested states and is managed largely outside the U.N. context. Both states of affairs accord with superpower preferences and reflect the tendencies of the industrialized democratic middle powers to rely on U.S. military protection and to cultivate optimism about the prospects for enduring co-existence.

Altogether, the very prismatic international system exhibits an uneven, fragmented, and relatively unproductive assortment of interactions.

They are evidence of a distribution of bargaining power that favors the industrialized democracies and of pervasive influences that orient their policy makers toward sectoral rather than national values, and national rather than global interests, in the competitive management of complex interdependencies. The chief beneficiaries, from the actions and inactions of these policy makers, are the transnational enterprises, whose large unregulated penetrations of foreign economies are steadily expanding. Explanations of this broad pattern have to be sought, basically, in processes of political socialization that are distinctly national; as has been seen, these produce mainly competitive, manipulative, and instrumental attitudes to interaction with other states. Although increasingly extensive cooperation has to be obtained from such states for the reasonably comprehensive management of interdependencies with them, inclinations toward integrative bargaining and negotiation generally fail to develop because elite attentions remain focused on personal, organizational, and sectoral interests, and on the day-to-day requirements of disaggregated and incremental decision-making to further those interests.

It must be affirmed, then, that innovative forms of political socialization in the industrialized democracies would seem to be required in political designs for world order, justice, and development. What has been called a world order movement has begun among small groups of scholars, industrialists, and statesmen in the West and in Japan, and this movement now has an enormous educative task. If this task is undertaken, some of the prescriptions and designs formulated within the movement will not be premature.

Notes

1. See Stephen D. Krasner, "US Commercial and Monetary Policy: Unraveling the paradox of external strength and internal weakness," *International Organization,* 31 (Autumn 1977), 635–72.
2. See Anthony King, "Executives" in Fred I. Greenstein and Nelson W. Polsby (eds.), *Handbook of Political Science* (Reading, Mass: Addison-Wesley, 1975), vol. 5, pp. 173–256. See also Edward L. Morse, "France" in Wilfrid L. Kohl (ed.), *Economic Foreign Policies of Industrial States* (Lexington, Mass.: D. C. Heath, 1977), pp. 69–104; and Marie Claude Smouts, "French Foreign Policy: The Domestic Debate," *International Affairs,* 53 (January 1977), 36–50.
3. For basic discussions of information processing problems in "overmanaged" systems, see E. Feit, "Political Groups under Severe Pressure: A Comparative Study Based on the Communication Control Model," *General Systems Yearbook,* 1964, pp. 265–282; and Amitai Etzioni, *The Active Society* (New York: The Free Press, 1968), pp. 135–312.

4. See Lawrence L. Whetton (ed.), *The Political Implications of Soviet Military Power* (New York: Crane, Russak & Co., 1977); Richard Pipes (ed.), *Soviet Strategy in Europe* (Crane, Russak & Co., 1976); and Stephen White, "Communist Systems and the 'Iron Law of Pluralism'," *British Journal of Political Science,* 8 (January 1978), 101–118.

5. See Michael Kreile, "West Germany: The Dynamics of Expansion," and T. J. Pempel, "Japanese Foreign Economic Policy: The Domestic Bases for International Behavior," *International Organization,* 31 (Autumn 1977), 723–774, 775–808.

6. See Kreile, "West Germany," and John Zysman, "The French State in the International Economy," *International Organization,* 31 (Autumn 1977), 839–78.

7. See T. H. Rigby, "The Soviet Government since Khrushchev," *Politics,* 12 (May 1977), 5–22; and George P. Jan, "The Ministry of Foreign Affairs in China since the Cultural Revolution," *Asian Survey,* 17 (June 1977), 513–29.

8. See Grey Hodnett, "Succession Contingencies in the Soviet Union," *Problems of Communism,* 24 (March–April 1975), 1–21.

9. See Pempel, "Japanese Foreign Economic Policy"; and Krasner, "US Commercial and Monetary Policy."

10. For discussions of Atlantic relations, see William Wallace, "Issue-Linkage among Atlantic Governments," *International Affairs,* 52 (April 1976), 163–79; and Michael Smith, "From the 'Year of Europe' to a Year of Carter: Continuing Patterns and Problems in European-American Relations," *Journal of Common Market Studies,* 17 (September 1978), 26–44.

11. See comments in Leon N. Lindberg, "Energy Policy and the Politics of Economic Development," *Comparative Political Studies,* 10 (October 1977), 355–82.

12. To place these observations in the broader context of U.S. strategic problems, see John D. Steinbruner, "National Security and the Concept of Strategic Stability," *The Journal of Conflict Resolution,* 22, (September 1978), 411–28.

13. See Joseph S. Berliner, *The Innovative Decision in Soviet Industry* (Cambridge, Mass.: M.I.T. Press, 1976).

14. Soviet theory does not acknowledge that deterrence concepts are at the basis of western strategic thinking. See Michael J. Deane, "Soviet Perceptions of the Military Factor in the 'Correlation of World Forces'." Paper given at Naval Postgraduate School, Monterey, Calif., December 9, 1977.

15. See Lindberg, "Energy Policy and the Politics of Economic Development."

16. Ibid.; see also Charles F. Hermann, "Why New Foreign Challenges Might Not Be Met: Constraints on Detecting Problems and Setting Agendas" in Charles W. Kegley and Patrick J. McGowan (eds.), *Challenges to America: US Foreign Policy in the 1980s* (Beverly Hills, Calif.: Sage Publications, 1978).

17. See David Apter, *The Politics of Modernization* (Chicago: University of Chicago Press, 1965), pp. 422–64.

18. See Feit, "Political Groups under Severe Pressure"; and Etzioni, *The Active Society.*

19. See Arnold L. Horelick, "Soviet Policy Dilemmas in Asia," *Asian Survey,* 17 (June 1977), 499–512.
20. See Berliner, *The Innovative Decision in Soviet Industry.*
21. See Michael J. Deane, *Political Control of the Soviet Armed Forces* (New York: Crane, Russak & Co., 1977).
22. See David S. Landes (ed.), *Western Europe: The Trials of Partnership* (Lexington, Mass.: D. C. Heath, 1977).
23. See Zysman, "The French State in the International Economy."
24. See Bernard K. Gordon, "Japan, the United States, and Southeast Asia," *Foreign Affairs,* 56 (April 1978), 579–600; and Hideo Sato, "Japanese-American Relations," *Current History,* 75, (November 1978), 145–48.
25. See John Pinder and Pauline Pinder, "West European Economic Relations with the Soviet Union" in Richard Pipes (ed.), *Soviet Strategy in Europe* (New York: Crane Russak & Co., 1976), pp. 269–304; and Kreile, "West Germany"; Krasner, "US Commercial and Monetary Policy"; and Stephen Blank, "Britain: The Politics of Foreign Economic Policy, the Domestic Economy, and the Problem of Pluralistic Stagnation," *International Organization,* 31 (Autumn 1977), 673–722.
26. This observation refers primarily to the U.S.S.R. See references to Soviet military thought by Thomas W. Wolfe and John Erickson in Pipes (ed.), *Soviet Strategy in Europe,* pp. 129–68, 169–210.
27. See Robert O. Keohane, "International Organization and the Crisis of Interdependence," *International Organization,* 29 (Spring 1975), 357–66; and Robert L. Rothstein, "Inequality, Exploitation, and Justice in the International System," *International Studies Quarterly,* 21 (June 1977), 319–58.
28. For discussions of some of the problems of regulating transnational enterprises, see Paul A. Tharp, Jr., "Transnational Enterprises and International Regulation: A Survey of Various Approaches in International Organizations," *International Organization,* 30 (Winter 1976), 47–74; and Seymour J. Rubin, "The Transnational Corporation," *Proceedings of the Academy of Political Science,* 32 (1978), 120–27.
29. See C. Clyde Ferguson, Jr., "The Politics of the New International Economic Order," and Sidney Weintraub, "The Role of the United Nations in Economic Negotiations," both in *Proceedings of the Academy of Political Science,* 32 (1978), 142–58, 93–105.
30. For a critical review of the operation of the Lome Convention and a plea for more enlightened Western European policies, see Carol Cosgrove Twitchett, "Towards a new ACP-EC Convention," *The World Today,* 34 (December 1978), 472–83.

Index

Index